Transatlantic
Connections

Hans Norman & Harald Runblom

Transatlantic Connections

Nordic Migration
to the New World after 1800

Norwegian University Press

Norwegian University Press (Universitetsforlaget AS), 0608 Oslo 6
Distributed world-wide excluding Scandinavia by
Oxford University Press, Walton Street, Oxford OX2 6DP

London New York Toronto
Delhi Bombay Calcutta Madras Karachi
Kuala Lumpur Singapore Hong Kong Tokyo
Nairobi Dar es Salaam Cape Town
Melbourne Auckland

and associated companies in
Beirut Berlin Ibadan Mexico City Nicosia

© Hans Norman and Harald Runblom

Jacket design: Anne Guttormsen. Painting by Ben Blessum (1877–1954),
The Emigrant Museum, Hamar, Norway. Photo: Mittet

Published with a grant from Nordic Cultural Fund

ISBN 82-00-06988-5

British Library Cataloguing in Publication Data
Norman, Hans
Transatlantic connections: Nordic migration to the New World after 1800.
1. Scandinavia. Emigration to United States 1800–1987
I. Title II. Runblom, Harald
304.8'73'048.

Printed in Denmark
by P. J. Schmidt A/S, Vojens

Contents

PART I
THE EMIGRANTS AND THE COUNTRIES THEY LEFT
by Hans Norman

1. *Introduction* 3
2. *Migration Patterns in the Nordic Countries before Mass*
   Emigration 5
   Background 5
   External Movements 12
   Internal Movements and Seasonal Labor Migrations .. 17
3. *Nordic Emigration in a European and Global Perspective* . 24
4. *The Start of Nordic Mass Emigration: Underlying Causes* 35
   Population Development 35
   Transformation of Society 38
   From Mercantilist Constraint to Liberal Migration
   Laws 42
   Knowledge and Images of America before the Mass
   Emigration 44
   Greater Social Gaps – Growing Optimism 49
5. *Mass Emigration from the Nordic Countries* 52
   Initial Phase 52
   Motives for and Importance of Early Emigration 61
   Chronological and Regional Characteristics 63
   Distribution According to Countries 69
   Total Migration Pattern 73
      Emigration from Cities and Countryside 76
      Competing Migration Goals 79
   Demographic and Social Composition 84
6. *Regional Studies of Emigration from the Nordic Countries* 92
   Fredriksborg County (*amt*), Denmark 92
   Toholampi Parish, Finland 95
   Vopnafjördur Parish, Iceland 98

    Agder District, Norway 101
    The City of Stockholm, Sweden 103
7. *Re-migration* 107
8. *Economy, Society, and the Individual's Decision to Emigrate* 112
    The Atlantic Economy 113
    Transportation and Routes 114
    Commercial Organizations 116
    Attitudes towards Emigration – Legislation 121
    Some Fiery Spirits in the History of Emigration 126
        Cleng Peerson, Norway 126
        Mogens Abraham Sommer, Denmark 127
        Hans Mattson, Sweden 128
        Jón Ólafsson, Iceland 130
        Matti Kurikka, Finland 131
9. *Conclusion* 134

PART II
NORDIC IMMIGRANTS IN THE NEW WORLD
by Harald Runblom

10. *Introduction* 141
11. *Settlement Patterns, Internal Migration, and Demography
    in North America* 145
    Settlement Patterns 145
        Early Settlement Areas 146
        Canada 155
    Internal Migration 159
        Mobility on the Frontier 159
        Secondary Migration 162
    Cities 168
        Chicago and New York City 170
12. *Nordic Immigrants in Latin America* 175
    Scandinavia and Latin America 175
    Immigration Propaganda 176
    Group Migration 177
    Comparative Aspects 181
13. *Nordic Immigrants as Farmers* 183
    Adjustment to American Farming 184
    Attitudes towards Landowning 185
    Ethnic Mixture in Rural Areas 187
    Finnish-American Small Farmers 189

14. *Churches and Organizations* 191
  Churches 191
    Church Life in Scandinavia 193
    Transatlantic Religious Impulses 195
    Immigrant Churches 196
  Secular Associations 201
  Organizations in Search of a Past 206
15. *Nordic Immigrants and American Politics* 211
  Political Life in the Sending Countries 213
  Political Advancement 215
  The Homeland Legacy and American Politics 225
16. *Labor Union Acitvities of Nordic Immigrants* 228
  Early Immigrant Labor Activists 228
  Scandinavian Immigrants in Trade Unions 232
  Finnish-American Labor Radicalism 234
    Finns as Strikers 238
    Decline of Finnish-American Radicalism 240
    Migration to Soviet Karelia 241
17. *Immigrants and Languages* 243
  Language Maintenance in America 243
  Nordic Languages in America 244
  Demography and Language 245
  Inroads of English 247
  Competing Language Norms 250
18. *Immigrants and Literature* 253
  Immigrant Authors and Literary Systems 253
  Literary Careers on Two Continents 257
19. *The Nordic Experience in North America: Some Con-
  clusions* 266

APPENDICES

Research on Overseas Migration from the Nordic Countries:
A Bibliographical Essay. By Hans Norman & Harald Runblom 279
Statistics 288
List of Tables 298
List of Figures 299
List of Administrative Areas in the Nordic Countries 301
Bibliography 308
Index 327

Acknowledgements

The initiative to this book was taken by the Nordiska Kulturfonden (Nordic Cultural Fund), which first suggested that an English edition of the *Nordisk Emigrationsatlas* (1980) be published. Since we started, our ambitions have grown and the purpose of the present publication is to provide a survey of the transoceanic emigration from the five Nordic countries: the background history, the extent and course of the migration, the patterns of settlement in the new countries, and the immigrants' adaptation and social life overseas.

We wish to thank the Nordiska Kulturfonden for a generous grant. We are also grateful to the Letterstedtska föreningen, Stockholm, and the Nansenfondet, Oslo, for earlier financial contributions to create maps and elaborate statistics on which much of our analysis relies.

For critical reading of portions of the manuscript and worthwhile suggestions we thank Dag Blanck, Uppsala and Rock Island; Lars Furuland, Uppsala; Gísli Á. Gunnlaugsson, Reykjavik and Uppsala; Steffen Elmer Jørgensen, Copenhagen; Reino Kero, Turku; Helgi Skúli Kjartansson, Reykjavik; Thomas Nilsson, Uppsala; Andres A. Svalestuen, Oslo; and Erling Wande, Uppsala. Special recognition goes to Marie C. Nelson, who in all phases supported us and devoted much time and energy to the translation of the first half of this book, and to Richard Chapman, Minneapolis, who scrutinized the language of the second half.

Uppsala, Sweden
September 1987

Hans Norman   Harald Runblom

Part I

The Emigrants and the Countries They Left

by
HANS NORMAN

1. Introduction

The immense transatlantic emigration, which for the Nordic countries was primarily a nineteenth century phenomenon, is an unparalleled event in the history of humanity. Man has always migrated in various directions over both short and long distances, but this was the first and probably the last opportunity for Europeans to populate virgin continents on a large scale during a short period of time. The geographic discoveries around 1500, which in a few decades opened the way to previously unknown territories on earth, brought about a new situation. In the course of their increasingly expanding interest in exploitation, Europeans directed their attention not least to the continents on the other side of the Atlantic, the southern Europeans first to South America, the northern Europeans towards North America. Through an extensive system of trading companies which operated under the protection of governmental privileges, the countries in northwestern Europe, above all England, the Netherlands, and France, took the lead in the expansion in North America. When Europe became politically more stable during the nineteenth century after the upheavals of the Napoleonic Wars, interest grew in investing overseas. With the rise of a capitalistic world market system, capital, know-how, and people flowed with increasing rapidity into the transoceanic area and primarily to North America. The great emigration to America, which began in the countries of northwestern Europe, eventually gained great dimensions also from central, southern, and eastern Europe.

The mass emigration from Europe occurred after a sharp population increase and took place during a century of considerable demographic and social changes. Due to, among other things, medical advances and increased access to food, the death rate, especially the infant mortality rate, decreased from the later part of the eighteenth century. The birth rate continued on the same high level up to the second half of the nineteenth century, and the sharp rise in population which followed was accompanied by considerable problems.

3

Agricultural yields did increase through the cultivation of new land and more rational agricultural methods; but in many regions industrialization was slow and the surplus of labor resulted in growing social tensions. In many ways emigration served as a necessary safety valve for countries with too many people to feed.

Between 1821 and 1930 approximately fifty million people migrated from Europe to non-European areas. Thirty-three million of these went to the United States. In this gigantic population movement the Nordic countries accounted for nearly three million, of whom approximately one-fifth returned to their native countries.[1]

This great emigration was highly significant for the receiving countries, not only for their demographic and economic, but also for their political, social, and cultural development. That was likewise true for the lands which the emigrants left. Furthermore, emigration implied a great deal for individuals and eventually encompassed most social categories. A growing land-hungry proletariat could travel over the Atlantic and secure its own farms. Craftsmen and laborers without work in the home country were attracted by the opportunities in the expanding industrial areas. Young women sought employment with well-to-do families in the American cities. Labor with higher education in technical and other fields was also recruited in step with industrial and urban development. Through employment in mining, lumbering, and railway construction, many emigrants could earn and save enough capital to return and establish themselves in the home country. A current of resources began to flow in both directions. People, capital, and ideas now streamed back and forth over the Atlantic.

1. For a distinction between the two concepts, Nordic countries and Scandinavian countries, see p. 6.

2. Migration Patterns in the Nordic Countries before Mass Emigration

Background

Over the centuries the Nordic countries have shared much common history. Their various forms of migration must be viewed within the framework of an area with a high degree of ethnic and linguistic similarity[1] and their political borders have often been rather easy to pass. Because the borders on several occasions have been radically modified, it is not easy to present the long-range character of migration between the countries. What on one occasion have been moves within the same realm have on a later occasion become moves between two countries. It is therefore difficult to differentiate between labor migrations, internal migration, and migration out of the country, as these movements frequently overlapped. In the following analysis the political borders as they exist today will be used as the framework of reference. The location of the borders during previous centuries is first briefly clarified. For more than one hundred years (1389–1521) the Nordic countries were formally united under Danish leadership. In conjunction with Gustav Vasa's war of liberation, Sweden-Finland withdrew from this union. Norway and Iceland remained under the Danish crown, Norway until 1814, whereas Iceland was separated in practice in 1918, and formally in 1944. Until the middle of the seventeenth century the southern and a portion of the western parts of what is today Sweden (Skåne, Halland, Blekinge, and Bohuslän) belonged to Denmark-Norway. The Napoleonic Wars radically altered the political borders. As a result of the Russian attack on Finland and the peace concluded in Fredrikshamn in 1809, Finland, since the Middle Ages a part of the Swedish kingdom, became a Grand Duchy under the Russian Czar until 1917. Norway was detached from the Danish

---

1 The exception is Finland, where the population speaks primarily Finnish; however, a large Swedish-speaking population is found along the western and southern coasts and, above-all, in the southwestern part of the country.

5

realm by the Treaty of Kiel of 1814 and found itself under the Swedish monarch in a personal union which lasted until 1905. During the nineteenth century, however, both Norway and Finland had rather autonomous positions in their relationships with Sweden and Russia.

In this presentation a distinction is made between the expressions Scandinavia and the Nordic countries, even if these concepts are used synonymously in many other contexts. Scandinavia is here used to designate Denmark, Norway, and Sweden, while the term Nordic countries includes all five nations, that is, also Finland and Iceland. (See the maps in figure 1.)

High population mobility has existed in the Nordic countries for many centuries. Communications were facilitated by roadways, extensive lake and river systems, long coastlines, and waterways between the countries. The common method of contrasting the old, stable, and nearly unchanging agrarian society with the significantly more mobile industrial society has, to a great extent, proved to be false. Recent studies indicate that this older society was very mobile; agrarian laborers, both men and women, often changed jobs and moved, mostly short distances. Mobility also took the form of labor migration and moves to distant destinations both within and outside the borders of one's own country.

Figure 1. Changes of Political Borders in the Nordic Countries.

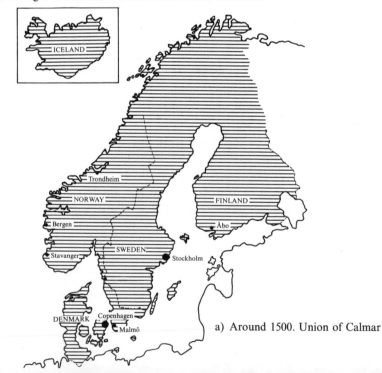

6   a) Around 1500. Union of Calmar

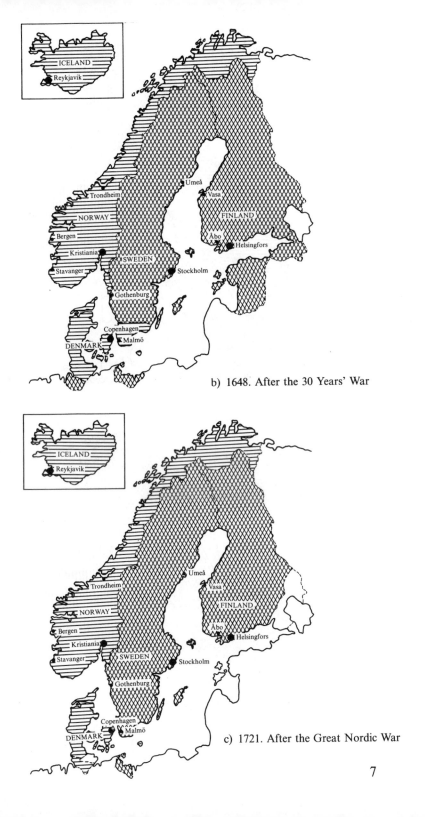

ICELAND
Reykjavik

Umeå
Vasa
Trondheim
NORWAY
FINLAND
Bergen
Åbo
Kristiania
Helsingfors
Stavanger
SWEDEN
Stockholm
Gothenburg
Copenhagen
Malmö
DENMARK

b) 1648. After the 30 Years' War

ICELAND
Reykjavik

Umeå
Vasa
Trondheim
FINLAND
NORWAY
Bergen
Åbo
Kristiania
Helsingfors
Stavanger
SWEDEN
Stockholm
Gothenburg
Copenhagen
Malmö
DENMARK

c) 1721. After the Great Nordic War

7

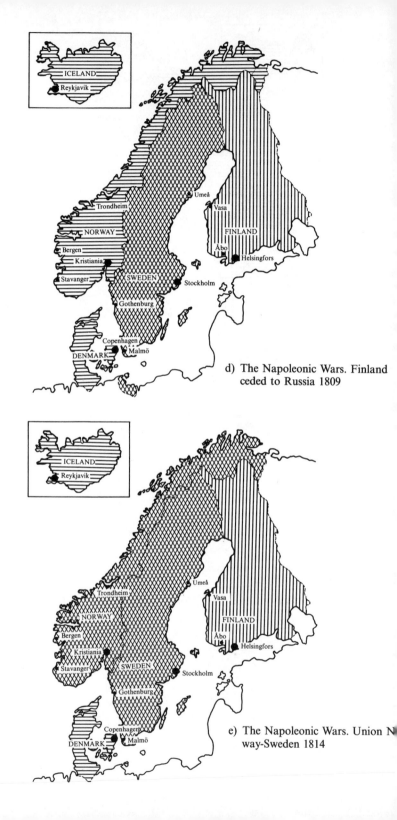

d) The Napoleonic Wars. Finland
ceded to Russia 1809

e) The Napoleonic Wars. Union N
way-Sweden 1814

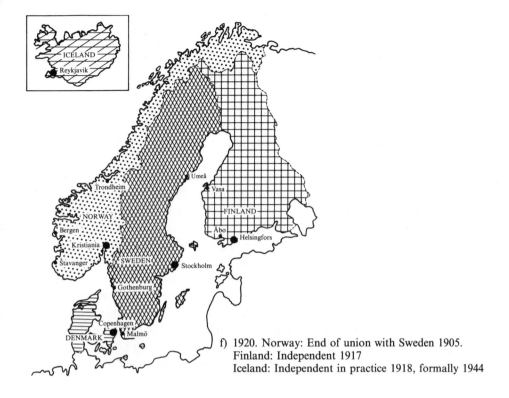

f) 1920. Norway: End of union with Sweden 1905.
   Finland: Independent 1917
   Iceland: Independent in practice 1918, formally 1944

The mobility rate has obviously varied according to political conditions and to fluctuations of the economic cycles. In the seventeenth century the Nordic countries, with their two political entities, Denmark-Norway-Iceland and Sweden-Finland, were characterized by lively domestic and foreign contacts. Moreover, the migration varied in intensity depending upon the social circumstances in each country. In Iceland, for example, an extremely large internal migration occurred during the eighteenth and nineteenth centuries because of the special conditions of land ownership that prevailed there.[2]

Starting at different points in time in the various Nordic countries from the nineteenth century onwards, there was a breakthrough in the transformation from a primarily feudal, agrarian society to a capitalistic and more industrialized one. A new era of uprooting began. It differed from earlier periods in that long-distance moves to economically expansive areas increased. So did also the seasonal

2 On migration in the older agrarian society, see S. Martinius 1967, S. Carlsson 1973, S. Lundqvist 1974, E. Österberg 1975, and L.-O. Larsson 1978. Concerning land ownership and social conditions in Iceland, see G. A. Gunnlaugsson 1986.

labor migrations, which for the individual often was the first step towards a definitive move to industrial and urban milieus. A consequence of this development was also an increased in-migration to the cities, at first modest, but eventually becoming quite substantial. Furthermore, the transformation of society meant that emigration to America gained momentum and reached a level that during half a century brought about very great changes in the migration picture in the Nordic countries.

In several respects migration serves as an indicator of social change. The demographic and social structures, the economic conditions, the job possibilities and the opportunities for making a living all contribute to the migration intensity of various areas. For example, if the population increase of a region is greater than its economic resources can provide for, increased social tensions generally result. Parts of the population are then inclined to move to other more favored areas to make their living. This increased migration thus reflects economic imbalance between areas. Certain factors force out the movers, while other factors attract them to certain destinations. The direction of the streams of migration therefore gives an indication of which areas are declining and which are expanding, while the social composition of the migration can provide information on the working and living conditions of various groups.

Migration in the Nordic countries took various forms. The *seasonal labor migrations* have a tradition dating back several hundred years. Groups of men and women – especially from districts with a large surplus of labor – went, for example, to the plains during harvests, to the fishing areas on the coasts, and to the larger cities. It is difficult to establish the labor migrations quantitatively, even after the keeping of parish registers became common from the second half of the eighteenth century onwards. These migrants were recorded in the parish registers only in exceptional cases, something which, on the other hand, was generally done with other types of moves where people definitely left their home parishes. During the nineteenth century with its large population increase, the labor migrations intensified to the cities and to expansive places of work such as railway construction sites, lumbering districts, sawmill industries, and newly cleared land. The criterion for labor migration is whether or not a moving certificate (*utflyttningsbetyg*) was requested and the migration was registered. By definition labor migration was thus intended not to lead to permanent settlement. Otherwise the length of the absence is usually used to determine whether or

10

not migration should be characterized as labor migration or as a regular move. Usually the line is drawn at one year. The domestic labor migrations and the short-term foreign migrations usually lasted only one season and were thus of shorter duration than one year. In certain cases the shorter journeys to America and to other far-distant destinations have also been regarded as labor migrations; such moves became more common in the later phases of the emigration period.[3]

Before the abolition of the guilds, a special form of labor migration took place; the *Wanderjahr of journeymen*. As apprentices, many had moved into the towns from the surrounding countryside. The training of journeymen was often complemented by the seeking of new places of employment in towns both within and outside the borders of their own country.[4]

Two categories of moves can be used to analyze population movement: moves which predominantly take place *within a social system,* for example, migration over short distances within the agrarian society; and moves which lead to fundamental *changes in the economic and social structure*, e.g., mostly migration over long distances and into the cities.[5] The majority of all migration during earlier centuries consisted of short-distance moves. These movements meant changing places of work within a limited region and, most often, within a social system. Agricultural workers of both sexes accounted for the greater part of these moves; according to tradition they usually sought a new place of work once a year. This type of migration seldom led to any net change in the composition of the population and has therefore been designated as *circular migration*. The longer migrations, which often were directed towards industrial areas, cities, or areas of colonization and thus implied a significant change in occupation and work milieu, have been described as *effective migration*. In the long run these moves meant a shift in the demographic and social composition of the population. The labor migrations, as mentioned earlier, may be difficult to distinguish from other types of moves. They often led to a more permanent move, as the labor migrants sometimes decided to regis-

3 On labor migrations, see especially H. Nelson 1963 and G. Rosander 1967. See also E. De Geer and H. Wester 1975, 13–16; A. Wirèn 1975, 17. Concerning the length of the stay in America of returning Swedish emigrants, see L.-G. Tedebrand 1972, 151–152.
4 Concerning craftsmen and journeymen, see E. Söderlund 1949.
5 I. Semmingsen 1971, 39–40.

ter themselves in the new locations as in-migrants. It is also difficult to distinguish between circular and effective migration, using only the distances as criteria. Because an important part of the short-distance moves involved migration from the surrounding areas into the cities, the distribution of the population between the country and the city was influenced, as well as the composition of the social structure in these areas.[6]

External Movements

Due to their geographical locations, Denmark and Norway have traditionally had their greatest external migration exchange with the areas surrounding the North Sea, while the corresponding movements for Sweden and Finland have affected the countries around the Baltic.

From the sixteenth century onwards a pattern of migration to and from the Nordic countries can be discerned which was partially determined by the location of the political centers of the kingdoms, Copenhagen and Stockholm, where the civil and military administration, as well as the economic centers, were situated. Administrators and military men in the midst of their careers, craftsmen, laborers, and soldiers were drawn towards these centers from the periphery and from outside the countries. At the same time there was a counterflow of administrators, mining specialists, traders, craftsmen, and other professionals from the capitals to the provinces.

The *movements to and from Norway* can serve as an illustration. Emigration from that country during the second half of the seventeenth century mainly followed two routes. One led to Copenhagen, which after 1536 was also Norway's capital. The other went towards the great sea powers, England and the Netherlands. While the latter route for the most part attracted seamen who voluntarily made their way there, the first consisted of men compelled to go, as many Norwegians were obligated to serve in the military at the naval base in Copenhagen.

The growth of centers for trade, banking, and shipping, such as Amsterdam and London, also had a significant power of attraction for the Nordic countries, and during the seventeenth century those

6 For a theoretical discussion of various types of migration, see S. Åkerman 1971, 101–102, 1976; C. Tilly 1978, 51–57. See E. Österberg 1975, 68–71 on agrarian society during the 1500's.

12

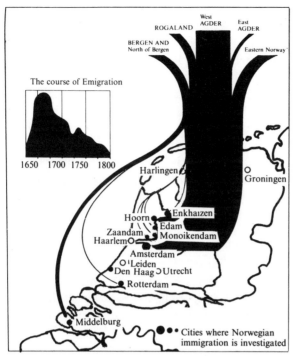

Figure 2. Emigration from Norway to the Netherlands in the Seventeenth and Eighteenth Centuries.
From the end of the sixteenth century many Norwegians found work in the cities in the Netherlands, most of them in Amsterdam. The majority came from West Agder and other places in the southern part of Norway, where farming could not feed the whole population.
Sources: K. O. Hodne 1976; K. Mykland 1979, map 87.

cities continuously had comparatively large populations of Nordic origin. Using the records of the published banns, Norwegian scholars have studied certain cities in the Netherlands to determine the place of birth of the population. It was found that Amsterdam and several other cities in the Netherlands contained a large number of Norwegians. During the period from 1626 to 1800, no fewer than 11,202 Norwegians had banns published in Amsterdam, most of whom were employed in the Dutch fleet. (See the map, figure 2.)[7]

Many immigrants came to Norway from countries around the North Sea, and those from the higher social strata often settled in the cities. Four main groups can be discerned. The administrators

7 K. Mykland 1977, 166–169; 1979 map 87; K. O. Hodne 1976.

13

came primarily from Denmark, and military officers were very often of German origin. German long remained the language of command in the Danish-Norwegian army. Furthermore, a large number of miners immigrated, many from Saxony in Germany. Finally, the numerous merchants and craftsmen of varied extraction should be mentioned. Characteristic is the fact that, of those who acquired burghership in Bergen (1621–30), 51 percent were born outside Norway. The immigration of administrators and burghers became socially significant, as they represented wealth, positions of power, and a European cultural orientation in the country.[8]

Emigration from the Swedish kingdom also occurred, mainly in a southerly direction. The government, which was eager to retain labor and soldiers in the country, found both in 1617 and 1620 not only an extensive emigration to Denmark, but also to the German states, Prussia, and Poland. That pertained especially to servants and laborers from Finland. Emigration to the continent was otherwise common from those Swedish provinces which at that time bordered upon Denmark (Småland and Västergötland); Copenhagen, Lübeck, and Danzig were frequent goals. A special type of emigration during the 1600's consisted of soldiers who fled the Swedish military contingents on the continent, as well as men who wished to avoid impending conscriptions.[9]

During the sixteenth century the Swedish government organized the recruitment of people from Finland. Some were encouraged to settle down as farmers; others were offered jobs in ironworks and mines. Of a total of 12,000 persons who came from Savolax, the majority settled primarily in the forested areas in central Sweden, especially in *Bergslagen* (the iron producing region in south central Sweden), i.e., the provinces of Närke, Värmland, Västmanland, and Dalarna. This migration even spread into Norway. The Savolax immigrants made their living by hunting, fishing, and, above all, slash and burn agriculture, which was practiced for approximately one hundred years. This forest-ravaging type of cultivation was forbidden by the middle of the seventeenth century, as the expanding ironworks needed all available wood for charcoal. The difficulties which the Finnish colonists had in cultivating their farms in the forest regions meant that many moved to the colony New Sweden on the Delaware River in America during its later phase. In spite

8· R. Fladby 1977, 118; K. Mykland 1977, 166–169.
9 L. O. Larsson 1972, 153–154.

14

of the great dispersion of Finnish settlements in Sweden and Nor-way, their language and, to a certain extent, even their material culture, survived in the so-called *finnmarkerna* (Finnish forest settle-ments) until the beginning of the twentieth century.

There was also a significant Finnish immigration to northern Sweden and Stockholm, which, as the capital of Finland (until 1809), exerted a constant force of attraction. A Finnish 'colony', consisting of more or less temporary residents, has continuously existed in the city. This group included many government officials born in Finland, but the proportion of laborers was particularly high among the Finns, where certain occupational groups, such as carpenters, were greatly over-represented. During long periods the shipyards in Stockholm, Karlskrona, and Kalmar recruited Finnish labor. Many Finnish men were also conscripted for the Swedish navy, especially during Sweden's Great Power period. Around 1800 the number of Finnish-speaking persons in Sweden proper was estimated to be at least 40,000. The Russian invasion of Finland, 1808–1809, led to another influx of Finns to Sweden. It was, how-ever, of a rather temporary nature, as many of the refugees later returned to Finland.[10]

From the seventeenth century certain categories were especially prominent among immigrants to Sweden, which as an expanding great power needed military, organizational, financial, and technical know-how, and became very cosmopolitan. The incorporation of the Baltic provinces (Estonia, Livonia, and Latvia) into the Swedish realm led to an immigration of officers and civil administrators from those regions and to frequent introductions of Baltic noble families into the Swedish House of Nobility (*Riddarhuset*).

Germans made up another important group of immigrants in Sweden. The German settlement in this country has roots in the Middle Ages when the most important categories were tradesmen and miners. During the Great Power Era many Germans were recruited into the army and the civil administration, and some Germans even reached positions as Councillors of the Realm (*riksråd*). Both cultural and business life had a German imprint, and the fact that five Swedish cities had German congregations bears witness to their great number.[11]

The political and economic expansion of Sweden during its Great

10 R. Broberg 1970, 91–95, 103–104; K. Ostberg 1978; T. J. Paloposki 1980, 27–43;
   E. De Geer 1980, 46.
11 S. Carlsson 1981, 9–31.

Power Era attracted not only immigrants from the other side of the Baltic. Significant numbers also came from Scotland and the Netherlands, especially Wallonia. Most important for the development of the Swedish iron industry were the Walloons. Under the leadership of the prominent merchant and financier Louis De Geer, they immigrated to Swedish areas, which through the commercial and technical skill of the Walloons were transformed into blooming centers for ironworks. The immigration was directed for the most part by De Geer himself, who hand-picked his workers. It took place during the period 1620 to 1660, first from the Wallonian regions of France (present-day southeastern Belgium) to the province of Östergötland, and later primarily from the area around Liège to Uppland.[12]

The most significant *immigration to Denmark* came from German areas. For centuries German craftsmen contributed to the development of Danish crafts and trade. Well-known are the so-called 'potato Germans', who were enticed to Denmark during the eighteenth century to colonize the heaths of Jutland. Many Dutch also came to Denmark and devoted themselves to trade, brewing, and market gardening.[13]

As long as the southern Swedish provinces Skåne, Halland, and Blekinge belonged to Denmark (until 1658) and as no larger body of water divided the countries, an extensive exchange of Danes and Swedes took place over the borders of the kingdoms. However, an even more intensive stream of emigration flowed later from Sweden to the neighboring countries in the south. During the 1850's emigration to Denmark and Germany from Kronoberg County (*Kronobergs län*) in southern Sweden was greater than to America. This emigration, however, was less conspicuous than emigration to America and did not imply the same drastic attention. Nor could the returnees from Denmark's cities or the manors of Holstein generally make a display of being especially rich. They usually remained within the lower social strata.[14]

Seen from the Danish side, southern Sweden comprised a source of cheap male and female labor. Many Swedish women found work in Denmark. For these young working women, their stay in the workers' barracks on the manors or in the sugar-beet growing areas on Lolland and Falster often led to social problems. The emigration

12 B. Douhan 1985, 22–27, 36–49.
13 Written communication from S. E. Jørgensen (1985).
14 L. O. Larsson 1978, 170–183.

16

from Sweden to Denmark culminated during the first half of the 1880's. Its decline a couple of decades later is a sign of the increased pace of industrialization in Sweden that provided opportunities for employment; the differences in income between the two countries had leveled out.[15]

In terms of net gains, *Norway* received most from the migration among the Nordic countries. During the years 1825 to 1865 that country had an immigration surplus in relation to the remainder of Scandinavia and Europe. The largest group of immigrants were Swedes, who sought employment in lumbering, agriculture, or construction work. Between Norway and Sweden the moves were naturally lively in the border areas, especially from the provinces of Värmland and Dalsland to the Christiania (Oslo) area. Further to the north moves of various kinds were common between Swedish areas and near-by Trondheim on Norway's Atlantic coast, which was a center of commerce for many Swedes.

A small but important group of migrants from Norway to Sweden and Finland consisted of the lumbermen who contributed to the development of the timber industry during the second half of the nineteenth century, which also attracted entrepreneurs from other countries. The political bonds between Norway and Sweden meant little for Norwegian-Swedish migration. Only in exceptional cases did public officials move between the two countries, but individual cases of marriage between members of the Swedish and Norwegian aristocracies are considered to have had a mitigating effect upon the political tension between the two halves of the union. The cultural contacts between Sweden and Norway were, on the other hand, few, and for the Norwegians, Stockholm never played the cultural role that Copenhagen had prior to the Norwegian union with Sweden in 1814.[16]

Internal Movements and Seasonal Labor Migrations

The major part of the migration during early centuries consisted of short-distance moves, primarily *in the countryside*. Furthermore, especially within certain areas, it was common to move seasonally to places with a strong demand for labor. (Compare, pp. 10–11.)

15 R. Willerslev 1982, 11–32, 96–124.
16 I. Semmingsen 1950, 145; S. Carlsson 1963–1964, 47–63.

The unmarried part of the rural population made up a very large portion of the short-distance movers. It was common for both young men and women, from about the age of 15 years until marriage, to be employed as servants and hired hands on local farms, but to some extent also in the cities. Even if there were jobs on their home farms, they usually sought work elsewhere. This form of employment was often regarded as training for young men and women to help them establish their own households and run their own farms. The migration rate was high, because it was customary to move once a year, usually in the fall. This pattern seems to have been similar all over the Nordic countries.

The situation in *Iceland* was exceptional with an extraordinarily high migration turnover. This was partly due to the small size of the Icelandic parishes, which caused the registered mobility across the parish borders to be high in comparison with the mobility in areas with larger parishes. The internal population movement was very high for other reasons as well. First, the servant class was very numerous, a reflection of the limited urbanization and the high marrying age. Secondly, the traditional and legal conditions of tenancy caused high mobility for the families in this category. The majority of the population did not possess land and thus was forced to seek employment or a tenancy from the few existing landowners. Among the landless there was also widespread poverty which the authorities attempted to limit by hindering marriage amongst the poor. The movement of the rural Icelandic population is similar to the 'frustration migration' of the Swedish wage-earning agricultural workers, the *statare*, in their search for decent working conditions.[17]

Although it was in the countryside that most of the population movement took place, significant migration *to and from the citites* also occurred in pre-industrial society. The urban movement was quantitatively less because only a small part of the population was urbanized. (See table 4, p. 39.)

The cities, furthermore, had another type of migration and a wider network of contacts than the countryside. An investigation of four Swedish cities (Nyköping, Norrköping, Västerås, and Arboga) during the seventeenth century shows that the migration goals were dispersed over much of the country, as well as in Finland, and Livonia and Köningsberg on the southern coast of the Baltic. It has

17 I. Eriksson and J. Rogers 1978, 229–236; G. A. Gunnlaugsson 1986, 12–16, 20–25.

also been shown that the migration was considerable to certain cities in Scandinavia at that time. They grew rapidly in spite of their high rate of mortality and their large birth deficit. Stockholm's population quadrupled during the years 1620 to 1670, increasing from about 10,000 to about 40,000, an exceptional growth phase in the city's history. Studies of Norwegian cities during the eighteenth century also show that the high death rates were compensated for by substantial in-migration. On the average every third new city resident was a migrant.[18]

Denmark was the most urbanized Nordic country during the pre-industrial era; Norway and Sweden were less urbanized than Denmark but more so than Finland and Iceland. At the beginning of the nineteenth century more than 20 percent of Denmark's population lived in cities, almost half of them in Copenhagen. Towards the middle of that century the proportion of the urban population grew; the provincial towns and especially the provincial administrative centers increased at the expense of Copenhagen.[19]

Sweden may be taken as an example of the insignificant urbanization in the Nordic countries. By the middle of the nineteenth century only one-tenth of the population lived in cities. In spite of considerable in-migration the urban proportion of the population did not increase noticeably. Possibilities there were limited due to, among other reasons, the guilds, which hampered competition, resulting in high out-migration. Furthermore, mortality in the cities was excessive. The situation changed during the second half of the nineteenth century. New legislation, which in several of the Nordic countries came during the middle of the century, brought about a freer economy that, coupled with growing industrialization, raised the proportion of the population living in the Nordic cities. By the year 1870 the Swedish urban population had thus grown to 13 percent, and by the year 1900 it had reached 22 percent.[20]

The *seasonal labor migrations* were, as mentioned above, not new phenomena, but they became more common during the nineteenth century. They were first and foremost the results of insufficient opportunities for employment in one place during certain parts of the year, while in other areas the possibility of getting work for one season at a time appeared. This meant an intensive use of labor, as

18 S. Lundkvist 1974, 224; L. O. Larsson 1972, 155; S. Dyrvik 1978, 220–221.
19 H. C. Johansen 1979, 56–57.
20 B. Öhngren 1977, 265, 270–271; H. Norman 1983 a, 91–92, 100–109. On legal changes concerning the guilds, see 38.

workers appeared where the need was greatest. As a rule these seasonal labor migrations went from the less developed to the economically stronger areas, and they were often important for people from small farms and for tenants, cottagers, and the so-called free laborers. It was primarily people from the forests and the highlands who sought the central areas to find work in sowing, planting, clearing, harvesting, and threshing, but also in mining and even in industrial endeavors. Much labor was drawn to the coastal regions when the fishing was good. In certain areas it was also common for the women to participate, as, for example, in the migration of people from the province of Dalarna to Stockholm, where they were often employed in construction work.[21]

Examples of labor migrations are found in many parts of the world. Since the 1500's there have been labor migrations from the Appennine highlands to the plains in southern Italy and Tuscany. In France they went from the marginal areas in Brittany and Normandy to the Seine and Loire Valleys. Labor migrations have long been common in Russia, where they increased after the abolition of serfdom in 1861. In other parts of Eastern Europe such movements were part of the everyday life of the farm households. Generally speaking, the directions of the labor migrations in the central parts of continental Europe during the last centuries have mainly been from the east towards the west and northwest, for example, from Poland and the eastern German areas towards the Rhineland and the coast of the North Sea. A labor migration could be an alternative to a definitive move; one still had close ties to relatives and to the home area, and in many cases the labor migrant had a family to support. Often, however, labor migration became the first step toward a definitive migration.[22]

During the nineteenth century one can distinguish five directions for the labor migrations *in Finland*. Construction work in Helsinki (Helsingfors), Turku (Åbo), and Viipuri (Viborg) attracted large numbers from different areas of Finland and often resulted in permanent settlement. Another stream went to the Stockholm area, while the fishing districts on the Norwegian and Russian coasts of the Arctic Ocean represented a third goal. From late winter until midsummer thousands of men went there for deep-sea fishing and

21 H. Nelson 1963, 27–29; G. Rosander 1967, 76–79.
22 R. B. A. Nilsson 1982, 17–20.

left women and children behind to take care of the farms. A fourth current of seasonal workers flowed from southeastern Finland to metropolitan St. Petersburg (Leningrad). Finally, during the second half of the nineteenth century, there was a significant seasonal movement to jobs in the forests, on log drives, and in the sawmills on the Swedish side of the Gulf of Bothnia.[23]

Iceland has a long tradition of labor migrations. In the winter the seasonal workers from settlements in both the northern and the southern parts of the island left for the coastal regions in the southwest to fish. During the summer the labor migrants went in the opposite direction to participate in harvesting. During the latter part of the nineteenth century the flow was from the more densely settled southwestern parts of the island along both the southern and northern coasts. Thus people went on longer fishing trips during the summer to the fishing grounds in the northeast.[24]

In Norway the most common seasonal workers during the 1800's were those who moved from the mountain areas to lower-lying mountain parishes or to the coastal plains and fishing districts both in the north and along the rest of the Norwegian coast. There the economy was differentiated and included harvesting, lumbering, ship-building, and fishing. Shipping, which was especially important in Norway, also offered a type of passage with work on the routes to Denmark, on the North Sea, and in coastal trade during the summer months. The large estates in Denmark, especially around Aalborg, were among the primary goals abroad for the Norwegian seasonal workers. Many from eastern Norway also made their way to larger places of employment on the Swedish side, particularly to the mines and to the forest industries.[25]

For centuries the domestic seasonal labor migrations *in Denmark* have gone from Jutland to the provincial trading towns and to Copenhagen as well as to grazing areas in other parts of the country. A common Danish pattern was also for workers from northern Jutland to travel to the large estates in northern Germany and to Holland. Quite a few Danes also traveled to Sweden. During the period prior to the First World War large numbers of Polish and Swedish seasonal workers made their way to Denmark, a pattern

---

23 G. Rosander 1967, 54–57; E. De Geer and H. Wester 1975; M. Engman. 1983, 131–145.
24 Written communication from Helgi Skúli Kjartansson (1985).
25 G. Rosander 1967, 57–60; H. Try 1979, 86–93.

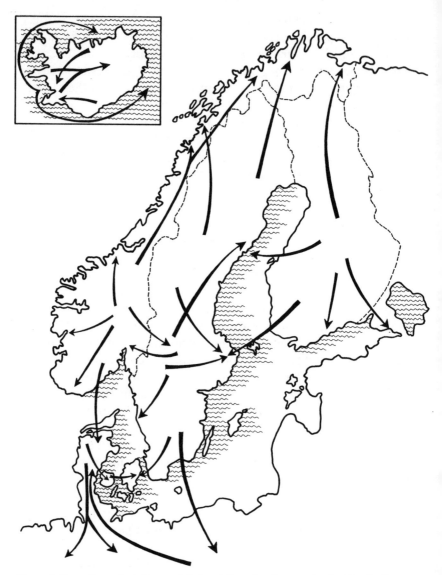

Figure 3. Some Important Seasonal Labor Migration Streams in the Nordic Countries.

which had a long tradition for men and women from southern Sweden.[26]

Areas *in Sweden* with numerous seasonal migrations during the eighteenth and especially the nineteenth centuries were Dalarna, Värmland, Dalsland, parts of Västergötland, Småland, and northern Skåne. The extensive partitioning of land coupled with relatively intensive population growth contributed to this pattern. A common destination for many of these labor migrations was the Mälar Valley with its large estates and cities, especially Stockholm. That is particularly true of the labor migration from Dalarna. In western Sweden many went to the Gothenburg area, while the labor migrations from the southern provinces were directed mainly towards Denmark and northern Germany, including both the wealthy agricultural areas and the cities of Copenhagen and Hamburg.

During the end of the eighteenth century, when the herring fishing on the west coast boomed, about 12,000 seasonal workers were employed in fishing, transporting, and preparing the catches. The majority came from Västergötland, Dalsland, and Värmland. Special foremen recruited work teams from individual parishes. When the herring fishery declined around 1810, the labor migrations from the western part of the country went instead to Norway, both to Østlandet and Christiania (Oslo) and to the Trondheim area.

After the middle of the nineteenth century a new attractive destination for seasonal labor migrations arose in Sweden, namely the lumber industry of Norrland. People from the entire country were attracted, but migrants from Värmland were especially common. The seasonal labor migrations from Norrland went in a northerly direction. Notable in this traffic were laborers from the western regions of the northernmost provinces, who found their way over the Norwegian border to Lofoten. Others, especially those who came from the Torne Valley, formed a parallel to the Finnish seasonal workers, and traveled to North Norway for fishing in the Arctic and work in the mines.[27] (Some of the main streams of seasonal migration in the Nordic countries are shown on the map, figure 3.)

26 H. C. Johansen 1979, 90–93; G. Rosander 1967, 60–61; R. Willerslev 1982.
27 H. Nelson 1963, 30–36; A. Norberg 1980, 9–38; M. Rolén 1979, 25–39; G. Rosander 1967, 91–145.

3. Nordic Emigration in a European and Global Perspective

Located at the periphery of Europe, the Nordic countries have been only marginally affected by the population movements on the European continent. During the centuries before the middle of the 1600's these migrations primarily went in an easterly direction. However, for the Nordic countries one can speak of movements both westward and eastward. The Danish and Norwegian Viking expeditions were mainly bound for areas in the west, while the Swedish ventures were mostly eastbound. From the thirteenth century onwards the political expansion of both Danes and Swedes was directed towards the eastern coast of the Baltic Sea. This expansion did not, however, result in colonization quantitatively comparable to that of the Germans, who during that century began to advance eastward and founded cities and made settlements (The German Order States).[1]

With the discovery of America and the rapid development of seafaring, interest in Europe became increasingly oriented towards transatlantic destinations. However, the transoceanic possessions were initially opened for immigration only to a limited extent. In accordance with Mercantilist thought the absolutist states did not permit unrestricted emigration to their colonies. Illustrative are the Spanish colonies in Latin America, to which immigration was strictly regulated by the mother country. In many cases the transoceanic colonies were initiated and administered by trading companies that were granted privileges for the enterprise there, but operated under the protection of the government in the homeland, which regulated migration.[2]

The Nordic countries participated only to a limited extent in the European scramble for colonies. From the end of the sixteenth

1 F. Braudel 1982, 84.
2 K. Hvidt 1971, 17; M. Mörner 1985, 6–10.

century *Denmark* had trading stations on the west coast of Africa (Danish Guinea), where trading companies received royal privileges and where the fortress Christianborg was established. In 1850 the colony was sold to England. Similarly Fort Dansborg was founded as a trading station in Tranquebar in the province of Madras, India. That colony existed from 1616 to 1845, when it was sold to the English. Finally, Denmark possessed some islands in the Virgin Island group in the West Indies: Saint Thomas (from 1666), Saint John (from 1684), and Saint Croix (from 1733). These islands were sold to the USA in 1917.[3]

The short-lived *Swedish* colonization attempts were also based upon protection by the state and the delegation of authority to trading companies in the hope of receiving a controllable income in return. In 1624 the Swedish Africa Company (*Svenska Afrikakompaniet*) received privileges for trade with Africa. On the Gold Coast the colony Cabo Corso was founded, which, however, fell into Dutch hands in the 1660's. During the years 1638 to 1655 the colony New Sweden existed on the Delaware River on the east coast of North America, south of present-day Philadelphia. The Swedish South Company (*Söderkompaniet*), partly founded with Dutch capital, induced the Swedish state to purchase land from the Indians there and received a monopoly on the colony's trade. Several smaller forts were established along the Delaware River, among them New Elfsborg and Fort Christina, the latter being the center for the colony. Sweden, however, in the midst of its period as a Great Power, was altogether too occupied with its efforts in the Baltic area to be able to send sufficient resources and people to support the colony, and the New Sweden Colony succumbed to Dutch pressure in 1655. The West Indian island of Saint Barthèlemy, which was purchased by Sweden from France in 1784 and held until 1878, was insignificant both commercially and in terms of immigration from Sweden.[4]

In contrast to England, France, the Netherlands, Spain, and

3 For information concerning the Danish colony in West Africa, see G. Norregaard 1953; in Tranquebar, see G. Olsen 1953; and in the Virgin Islands, see J. O. Bro-Jørgensen 1952.
4 For information on the Swedish Africa Company, see G. Novaky, 1985. Concerning New Sweden, see, among many other works, A. Johnson 1911. The New Sweden Company, as the South Company later was called, and the Swedish Delaware colony, especially under Governor Johan Risingh will be dealt with in S. Dahlgren's and H. Norman's annotated edition of the *Risingh Journal* (forthcoming 1988). Concerning Saint Barthèlemy, see J. Hildebrand 1951.

Portugal, the Nordic countries experienced little emigration before the great exodus to America in the nineteenth century. Although emigration from the European colonial powers was rather small during the seventeenth and eighteenth centuries, people in those countries were, to some extent, accustomed to moving to other parts of the globe as administrators and colonists.

Initially, the contacts between the European countries and the American continent were determined by their geographical location. The crossing of the Atlantic therefore took place primarily from the Iberian states, Spain and Portugal. Later the countries on the Atlantic coast in northern and western Europe increasingly experienced transoceanic emigration. That was especially true of the British Isles and, to a certain extent, France and the German states, even though the latter lacked colonies. On the North American continent the most visible result of these translocations, which occurred from the 1600's onwards, was the establishment of the English colonies along the Atlantic coast and the French colonies in Canada and the lower Mississippi River Valley. In the English and French colonies there were many who had fled from religious intolerance in their homelands.

Although emigration and settlement on the other side of the Atlantic had begun, the rigid emigration regulations and the low transportation capacity hampered emigration on a large scale during the next two centuries. It was only after the Napoleonic Wars that European emigration truly got under way.

The growing emigration must be seen in relation to the sharp increase in population which began during the later part of the eighteenth century. This increase was generally followed by a more liberal population policy and by the rise of a capitalistic world market system with its accompanying industrialization, which started at various points in time in different parts of the European continent. As shown in table 1, the population increase in Europe

Table 1. Total Population and Population Increase in Europe, Including European Russia, 1750–1950.

Year	Number of Inhabitants	Increase in %
1750	145 million	
1850	265 million	83
1900	400 million	51
1950	550 million	108

Source: C. Cipolla 1967, 91.

26

was greatest during the hundred years from 1850 to 1950 in spite of the drain which occurred in the form of extensive emigration.

Influenced by the population pressure and with economic capabilities and technical and military superiority, Europeans spread around the world. They populated America and Australia, and they controlled large parts of Africa and Asia. Of the 50 million Europeans who settled in non-European areas, the majority had North America as their destination, particularly the United States (33 million). Approximately seven million of the migrants settled in Asiatic Russia. The European dispersion on the transoceanic continents is shown by a compilation of European-born persons living outside Europe in 1930.[5]

	Number of Persons	Percent
In North America	14 million	70
In Latin America	5 million	25
In Australia and South Africa	1 million	5

In Europe as a whole, a significant emigration to the USA existed from the 1820's. On average, 15,100 persons per year arrived there during that decade. In the 1830's the figure rose to an average of 59,900 persons per year. In the 1840's a great wave went, largely due to developments in Ireland. Because of the catastrophic failure of the potato crops during that decade, a large proportion of the island's population chose to emigrate. The Irish emigration reduced Ireland's population from eight million in 1840 to four million persons in 1900. The proportions which the European emigration reached meant that during the 1840's an average of 171,300 emigrants left yearly. The flood of emigrants, however, increased even more during the coming decades. It culminated during the first two decades of the twentieth century, when the great masses of eastern and southern Europeans joined the crowds of emigrants. Thus during the five-year period 1905–10 no fewer than an average of 1,436,000 Europeans emigrated per year. The proportional size of the emigration from some countries can be compared in figure 4; initially there was a northern European dominance, especially from the German states, but later the scales weighed heavily on the side of the emigrants from southern and eastern Europe.[6]

5 C. Cipolla 1967, 91–93; A. Svalestuen 1971, 16.
6 K. Hvidt 1971, 18–19.

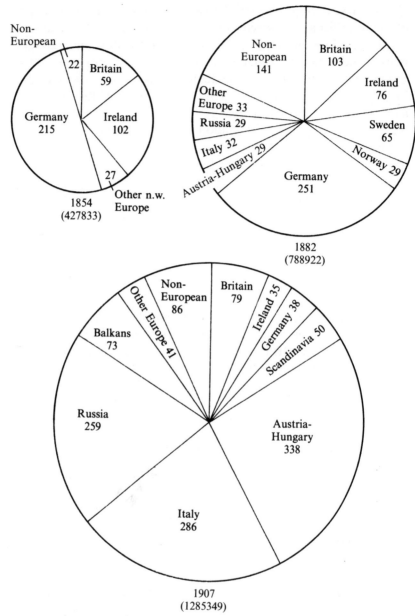

Figure 4. In-migration to the USA during the Peak Years of Emigration from Europe 1854, 1882, and 1907. Total Number of Emigrants in Thousands during the Respective Years.
Source: P. Taylor 1971, 63.

The *German areas*, like the *British Isles*, experienced a large emigration early on, which in some years between 1832 and 1892 surpassed an annual rate of 100,000. Emigration exceeded 200,000 persons per year in 1854, 1881, and 1882. In 1854 the German emigration made up over half of all Europeans going to America. The German emigrants came primarily from the areas in the west and south, fewer from Prussia with its manorial system. After 1892, on the other hand, the German emigration was remarkably low. Following its unification in 1871 Germany developed a very dynamic industry which could largely absorb the population increase. In this regard the situation differed from that in Great Britain, where the economy did not hinder emigration, which reached a high-water mark as late as the years prior to the First World War. On the whole the German areas, therefore, had a significantly smaller emigration, seen in absolute numbers, than did the British Isles. While thirty-five of every one hundred emigrants to America were English-speaking, only nine were German-speaking.[7]

France differed from the other nations of Europe by its strikingly small emigration. Because of its low birth rate, the country did not have the same great population increase which was common in so many other areas during the 1800's. Furthermore, the revolution had modified its agricultural and social organization. There was, for example, much fertile land available for new cultivation. France was thus an important country for immigration from its neighbors and from Poland. Excess population in France was absorbed by industry and by the cities, which grew rapidly during the second half of the nineteenth century. Many Frenchmen also moved to North Africa. Most America-directed emigration came from the peripheral, mountainous areas in the southeast and the southwest of the country.[8]

The eastern and southern European emigration began much later than that from western Europe and Scandinavia. In many areas of eastern Europe a large part of the emigrants consisted of ethnic minorities. Such was the case in *Russia*, which, for example, had a considerable emigration of Jews. In *Hungary* emigration was stronger from the peripheral regions in the north, southwestern, and southeastern areas of the country than from its central parts between the Danube and Tisza Rivers. The regional differences,

7 P. Taylor 1971, 43–47; K. Hvidt 1971, 23.
8 P. Taylor 1971, 47.

29

however, resulted less from ethnic reasons than from the long distances to places with good natural resources and to industrial centers.[9]

The *Polish* regions with much surplus labor had a varied emigration picture. Through a number of partitions Poland, until the First World War, was split into a Prussian, a Russian, and an Austrian section. A large part of the Polish labor supply annually went westward to industrial districts in Germany, where seasonal work was available. That was especially true of workers from the industrial regions in Silesia, as the wages there were significantly lower than in German industry. In time the Polish areas also had a significant American emigration, the greatest numbers having their origins in the Austrian and Russian parts of the country.[10]

Emigration from the Mediterranean areas also had a mixed pattern. From *Portugal* emigrants traveled mainly to Brazil, where the Portuguese had historical bonds, and people from *Spain*, similarly, to a very great extent traveled to Cuba and Argentina. The *Italian* emigration was especially complex. Up to 1900, people mainly moved to Latin America, especially Brazil, and a significant part consisted of seasonal laborers, the so-called *golondrinas* (swallows), who went to South America for the harvest seasons. Italian emigration to South America before the turn of the century outnumbered that to the USA. During the twentieth century, however, the USA became the foremost immigration goal, while Argentina took second place.[11]

By the middle of the nineteenth century, emigration from the Nordic countries was still insignificant. It was only from Norway that emigration to America took place on a larger scale during the 1850's. Schematically, one can say that England, Ireland, and Germany accounted for the first phase of emigration, as the outward flow became extensive from these areas as early as the 1840's. Norway, Denmark, and Sweden would constitute the second phase, while the eastern and southern Europeans consequently formed the third phase. During the 1850's most of the pioneer emigration from the Scandinavian countries took place (from Norway earlier than from the other countries), and during the 1860's they entered a

---

9 J. Puskas 1982, 56–63.
10 For an analysis of the economic and historical determinants of the migration from upper Silesia to Germany and the Polish emigration to America, see A. Brozek 1982, 1985, 34–38.
11 P. Taylor 1971, 60.

30

stage of massive emigration which culminated during the 1880's. Emigration from Iceland began abruptly during the 1870's, after which there followed a veritable flood during the 1880's and the early 1890's. Finland's emigration started on a very small scale in the 1860's, and did not reach great numbers until the initial decades of the twentieth century. (See the diagrams in figure 5.)

Comparing the emigration from the Nordic countries with that from Europe as a whole, several characteristics emerge that are particularly striking. Numerically, the emigrants from the Nordic countries comprise a very small part of the total European emigration. The entire population of these countries was small, only 5.25 million persons in 1850. By 1900 their population had increased to nearly eight million. From its beginnings up until the First World War, emigration from the Nordic countries made up only five percent of European emigration. Figure 6 provides a chronological comparison of the Nordic emigration with the totals for Europe. The Nordic emigration differs from that of Europe as a whole, which rose sharply to great heights during the years around the turn of the century, primarily due to the massive emigration from southern and eastern Europe.

Calculated, on the other hand, in relation to the population of the country of origin, the picture is entirely different. (See table 2.) During the decade with the most intensive emigration from the respective countries, an average of four of each thousand inhabitants emigrated annually from Denmark, nearly six per thousand from Finland, seven per thousand from Sweden, nine per thousand from Iceland, and almost ten of each thousand Norwegian inhabitants.

Ireland was hardest hit among the European countries with its more than four million transoceanic emigrants. In the 1860's and the 1880's fifteen persons out of each thousand inhabitants emigrated annually. What the table does not show, however, is that Ireland's highest rate of emigration occurred during the years 1846–1854. After Ireland, Norway was the European country from which emigration was proportionately most intensive. Calculated in absolute numbers during the period 1851–1930, the emigration from Norway totaled 0.8 million persons, from Denmark 0.4 million, from Sweden 1.2 million, and from Finland 0.4 million. The figure for Iceland, because of its small population, reached only 14,000.

The Finnish immigrants to the USA are usually included among the so-called 'new' immigrants, a term coined by the Dillingham Commission in 1911. The criteria used for defining the 'old' and

31

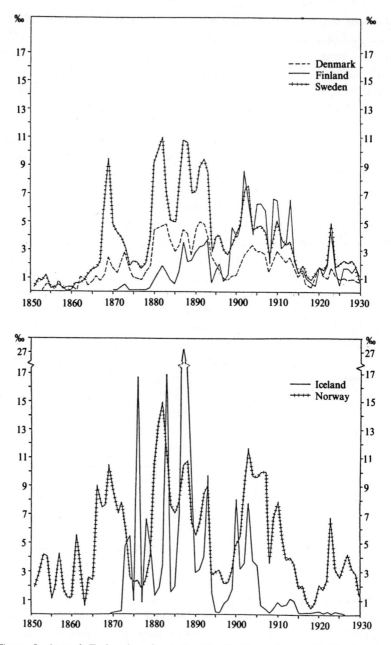

Figure 5. Annual Emigration from the Nordic Countries to North America, 1851–1930. Total Number of Emigrants per Thousand Inhabitants.
Sources: Official statistics of the respective countries; for Finland, also R. Kero 1974, 26; and for Iceland, written communication from Helgi Skúli Kjartansson (1980).

32

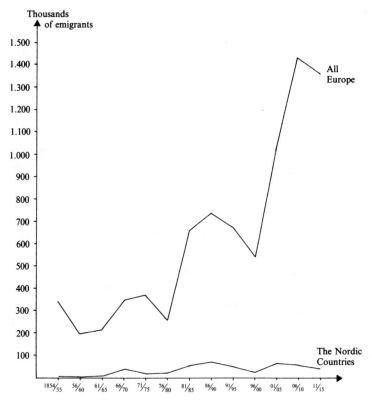

Figure 6. Total Transoceanic Emigration from Europe and from the Nordic Countries (Denmark, Finland, Iceland, Norway and Sweden). Mean Annuals per Five-Year Periods.
Sources: K. Hvidt 1971, 18; R. Kero 1974, 36; J. H. Kristinsson 1983, table 1.

Table 2. Transoceanic Emigration from the Nordic Countries and Some Other European Countries, 1851–1910. Mean Annual Emigration per Ten-year Periods. Promille of the Population.

	1851–60	1861–70	1871–80	1881–90	1891–1900	1901–10
Denmark	0.3	1.0	2.1	3.9	2.2	2.8
Finland			0.2	1.2	2.4	5.5
Norway	2.4	5.8	4.7	9.6	4.5	8.3
Sweden	0.4	2.3	2.3	7.0	4.2	4.2
Iceland			4.2	8.8	3.0	2.3
Ireland		14.7	10.2	14.9	10.1	11.1*
England		2.8	4.0	5.7	3.6	5.8
German Reich	2.6	1.7	1.5	2.9	1.0	0.5
France	0.3	0.2	0.2	0.3	0.2	0.1
Italy		1.0	3.2	4.9	10.8	

* 1901–08 only.
Sources: *Emigrationsutredningen,* bil. IV, tab. 26; Willcox 1931, tab. 9; Official statistics of the Nordic countries.

33

'new' immigrants were the point in time of immigration as well as their European origin. Western Europeans and Scandinavians, whose immigration began in the 1840's and 1850's and culminated during the last half of the century, were considered 'old' immigrants, while the southern and eastern Europeans, whose mass immigration started later, were included among 'new' immigrants.

A large part of the 'new' immigration was, according to the Dillingham Commission, of a temporary nature. Immigrants from eastern and southern Europe, furthermore, found their way primarily to industries and larger urban areas. Finnish scholars have rejected this division as altogether too rough. It is true that the main part of the Finnish emigration began later than in Scandinavia and western Europe, but in certain parts of the country, especially in northernmost Finland and in Ostrobothnia, a locally strong emigration had already begun during the 1860's. Nor did the Finnish immigrants primarily remain in industrial and urban milieus. Many of them were forced to first seek jobs in the mines and forests, for the most part in Michigan and Minnesota, but they showed ambitions as strong as those of the 'old' immigrants in obtaining their own farms. Nor have the Finnish emigrants been more likely to stay on a temporary basis in the USA than their counterparts among other groups of Nordic immigrants; the percentage of returning Finns is approximately the same. Thus there are few similarities between the Finns and the groups from the Mediterranean countries, such as Italy, where a system of 'commuting' between the homeland and the transatlantic labor market was actually developed.[12]

12 R. Kero 1974, 22–23, 1980, 63; K. Virtanen 1979, 219–227; Reports of the Immigration Commission (Presented by Mr. Dillingham). Vol. I, 23–25. 1911.

4. The Start of Nordic Mass Emigration: Underlying Causes

Emigration from Europe to North America began, as mentioned above, with lesser movements during the seventeenth century, and remained rather insignificant during the eighteenth. Not until after the Napoleonic Wars did it begin to get under way on a larger scale. It was, roughly speaking, from the middle of the 1800's that emigration from western and northern Europe gained momentum as a European mass phenomenon. Why did the large emigration flow start at that particular time? After all, America had been discovered by Europeans more than three centuries earlier. In this chapter the reasons for emigration will be analyzed using the conditions in the Nordic countries as a case study. Of course, it was not only the developments in Europe which gave rise to emigration; the impulses from America were also important. But it was the countries in Europe that people left. It is therefore of interest to establish what fundamental conditions dominated in those societies at that time and what may have motivated the emigration. The population development will be discussed and placed in relation to the radical social transformation which European societies underwent during the nineteenth century, factors which influenced opinion on the population policy in the individual countries. Other important aspects include the developing image of America in Europe and how information about the New World was received. It is notable that the social change, which was accompanied by great social tensions, also resulted in growing optimism and the willingness to seek new ventures.

Population Development

From the end of the eighteenth century until the beginning of the twentieth, most of the European countries experienced an unusually large population growth. The so-called demographic transition is often used to explain this phase of their development. The death rate, especially the infant mortality rate, began to decline sharply, while the birth rate maintained its high level. The result was an increase in population, which in certain countries became very significant. It was not until the birth rate also began to drop, which in most of the western and northern European countries occurred towards the end of the nineteenth century, that the situation gradually became more balanced again. Then the birth rate only slightly exceeded the death rate, but both remained on a significantly lower level than during the late eighteenth century. The demographic transition in the Nordic countries is illustrated in the diagram in figure 7.

The population increase in the Nordic countries followed the pattern of the rest of western Europe. England's and Scotland's population growth, however, stands out as particularly high and comparable with that in Finland: England's population doubled during the first half of the nineteenth century and Scotland's increased by three-fourths.

Finland experienced the sharpest population increase of the Nordic countries. In the second half of the eighteenth century the country's population rose markedly. Finland did not suffer the steep rise in the death rate which droughts and harvest failures caused in Sweden and Norway during the first years of the 1770's. Finland's population therefore doubled during the period from 1750 to 1800, and again from 1801 to 1850. The growth in Norway and Denmark was slower, but on approximately the same level in both countries, while Sweden had the smallest population increase of the countries in Scandinavia. In Iceland, one can speak of tendencies towards overpopulation in relation to economic resources during the whole of the nineteenth century, and the death rate often exceeded the birth rate. This country therefore had the lowest population increase of the Nordic countries. Finland's population increase during the second half of the 1800's was not as great as during the first half because of catastrophic harvest failures in the end of the 1860's, when the country suffered significantly more than its neighbors. Its death rate reached as much as 8 percent of the population in 1868.[1] (The information in table 3 should be compared with the development of the birth and death rates as seen in figure 7.)

1 E. Jutikkala and M. Kauppinen 1971, 283–285; L. Jörberg 1970, 383; M. Engman 1983, 227; H. Norman 1983 b, 9; G.A. Gunnlaugsson 1986, 15.

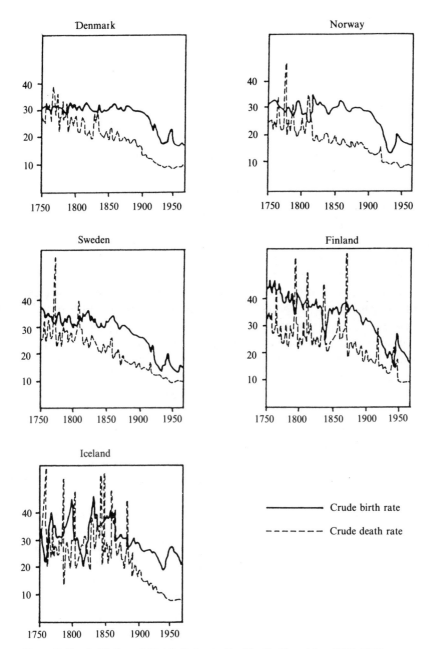

Figure 7. Crude Birth and Death Rates in the Nordic Countries, 1750–1950.
Source: S. Dyrvik 1979, 99.

Table 3. Population Growth in the Nordic Countries, 1801–1900. Percent, 50-year Periods.

	Denmark	Finland	Iceland	Norway	Sweden
1801–1850	53	97	25	59	48
1851–1900	69	62	33	60	47
1801–1900	159	219	66	154	119

Source: L. Jörberg 1970, 383, table 2.

Transformation of Society

The changes in population during the eighteenth and nineteenth centuries laid the foundation for social change and social problems. Initially it was most notable in the countryside, as urbanization had not developed particularly in the Nordic countries in comparison with many other European countries.

Denmark was the most urbanized of the Nordic countries: Twenty-three per cent of the population lived in cities in 1860. In Norway this proportion was 15 percent, in Sweden 11 percent, in Finland 6 percent, while in Iceland only 3 percent of the population lived in towns at that time. The cities grew slowly, because their economies had not yet developed sufficiently to absorb the in-migrant streams from their environs. The city residents who possessed the rights of burghers stubbornly defended the guild regulations which protected them from competition. Not until after the laws on economic freedom (abolition of the guild regulations) were introduced in Norway (1839 and 1842), Sweden (1846 and 1864), Denmark (1857), and Finland (successively in the 1860's and 1870's, the most important law being passed in 1879), did the new prerequisites for economic expansion and urbanization exist in these countries. Therefore the great in-migration to their cities began during the second half of the 1800's and was most intensive during the end of that century and the beginning of the next, when the industrialization process had gotten under way. This development occurred somewhat later in Finland and Iceland than in the other countries. Iceland granted the formal right to free trade in 1855, but the rights of the burghers had earlier been of little consequence in that country. From the turn of the century there was very rapid urbanization in Iceland. (See table 4.)[2]

2 L. Jörberg 1970, 385; S.A. Hansen 1972, 126; F. Hodne 1981, 221; G.A. Gunnlaugsson 1986, 13; written communication from Reino Kero and Helgi Skúli Kjartansson (1985).

Table 4. Urban Population in the Nordic Countries, 1850–1920. Percent of the Total Population.

Year	Denmark	Finland	Iceland	Norway	Sweden
1850	21	7	3	13	10
1860	23	6	3	15	11
1870	25	7	4	17	13
1880	28	8	5	20	15
1890	33	10	12	24	19
1900	38	13	21	28	22
1910	40	15	34	29	25
1920	43	16	44	30	29

Sources: The official statistics for the respective countries; Jörberg 1973, 385.

It was thus in the countryside that the increased population situation was most noticeable and influenced the changes which occurred there. In many areas agriculture underwent a restructuring towards more capitalistic forms. With a more favorable climate for profits, a more rational management of agriculture was introduced and attempts were made to consolidate the arable and pasture land of each farm into a single unit (the enclosure movement – *skiftesrörelsen*) and to utilize technical improvements and new tools and machinery. Another element in this development was the combination of all production units to form larger ones. Especially in the main farming districts, tenancies and leaseholds were annulled and property withdrawn to the major estates. Farmers and tenants on the lands that were withdrawn had to support themselves in some other way. In Sweden many of the countryside's landless became *statare* on the larger estates, something which initially seems to have provided a rather attractive source of income for young agricultural workers. In that way they obtained a place to live and sufficient income in cash and in kind, which, even if barely adequate, could support a family.[3]

The sharp population increase during the nineteenth century created a swelling of the landless classes within the rural population, and the social gap increased between the farm-owning class and the lower groups in the countryside. When the village common lands were divided among the land-owning farmers as part of the enclosure movement, the landless could no longer use these common lands for obtaining wood and for grazing. The proletarianization of the countryside became one of the most burning social issues. It was

3 M. Fridholm, M. Isacson, and L. Magnusson 1976, 13–21; I. Eriksson and J. Rogers 1978, 26–37.

true that the farmers with land of their own increased in number, a development which was common for the Nordic countries, but the landless groups simultaneously increased even more. Because the cultivated plots could only be divided to a certain limit and still be usable, many children of the land-owning group ended up in the landless category. The development in Norway illustrated in figure 8 was similar to the situation in Sweden.[4]

In Denmark the proportion of day-laborers and workers also increased. The country had a significant export of grain up until the 1880's, when there was a change to the sale of refined animal products. Because of this reorganization of agriculture for profitable export, the good opportunities for new investments, and the relatively early industrialization of the country, the problems appear to have been less serious for the landless class in Denmark than in the other Nordic countries.[5]

The size of the agricultural proletariat was larger in Finland than in the Scandinavian countries. The landless segment of the population greatly increased from 1800 and especially after the 1830's, resulting in growing social differences. The situation of the independent workers was strained because of compulsory employment (*tjänstetvång*), hindrances to migration, and an oversupply of labor. The late industrialization also contributed to the social problems in the country.[6]

The population also increased in Iceland during the nineteenth

1801

90,000 Farmowners and tenant farmers	39,000 Cottagers with land to cultivate	31,000 Day-laborers and others	41,000 Servants

1855

113,000 Farmowners and tenant farmers	65,000 Cottagers with land to cultivate	50,000 Cottagers without land to cultivate, Day-laborers and others	55,000 Servants

Figure 8. The Proletarianization of the Rural Population in Norway during the First Half of the Nineteenth Century. The Main Occupational Categories.
Source: F. Sejersted 1978, 121.

4 C. Winberg 1975, 46–63; F. Sejersted 1978, 121.
5 H.C. Johansen 1979, 27, 99–104; written communication from Steffen E. Jørgensen (1985).
6 M. Engman 1983, 227.

century, especially after 1820. Because industrialization and urbanization were insignificant factors before the turn of the century, the
growing population had to support itself nearly exclusively within
the framework of a traditional agrarian society. Thus the Icelanders
depended greatly on the raising of sheep and, in the coastal areas,
fishing. A slowdown in population growth occurred during the years
1855 to 1870 as a result of unfavorable climatic conditions, poorer
fishing catches, and an epidemic among the sheep. Although the
authorities had earlier kept an eye on the population growth and
attempted to regulate marriages among the poorer groups, the
situation became even more precarious. Iceland is one of few countries where marriage and family-building were forbidden for the
destitute. It was prohibited under all circumstances for those who
had received poor relief during the previous ten years – and had
not repaid it – to marry without the consent of the local government
in their home commune. Furthermore, the local authorities could
regulate the family-building of the poor elements in society by
invoking the legislation regarding cotters, lodgers, boarders, and
tenants. Despite deteriorating conditions for the poor groups, there
was an increase in the proportion of farms with owner occupancy,
from 17.4 percent of those who cultivated land in 1844–1846, to
37.5 percent in the year 1910. That did not, however, reflect a
radically improved situation in Iceland, but only different conditions
of ownership from those of the other Nordic countries. Earlier, the
ownership of land on the island had been concentrated in the
hands of the few, but during the nineteenth century the central
administration in Copenhagen and the Icelandic parliament (*Alþin-
gi*) encouraged an increase in owner occupancy by selling crown
and church properties and by issuing laws which gave tenants on
such properties first claim to buy them on reasonable terms.[7]

The population development during the nineteenth century meant
increased productivity in the Nordic countries. Higher output in
agriculture, together with decreased mortality, indicates a general
rise in the economy. But these factors do not explain how this
increased production was distributed. Those who owned farms
probably experienced increased well-being during the 1800's, but
large groups of the landless had a lower standard of living. The
restrictions on the cultivation of new land, the regulation of land

7 G.A. Gunnlaugsson 1985, 5–15; written communication from Gísli Á. Gunnlaugsson (1986).

ownership due to fear of excessive division of property, and industry's relative lack of importance led to social problems for the rural population. Generally, it is not correct to say that the Nordic countries were overpopulated. However, with the economic and social transformation in agriculture, the growing reserve of labor was simply no longer needed, and this large labor surplus could not yet find work in industry.[8]

During the first half of the nineteenth century the social problems increased in the Nordic countries. Problems of proletarianization and poverty were issues in the center of public debate. The higher classes were afraid that the lower classes – the 'dangerous' classes – would revolt and take power. One looked askance at the developments on the continent, especially after the events of the year of revolutions, 1848. Even if the fears were exaggerated, there were signs of social unrest in several areas of the Nordic countries. In Denmark the radical farmers' movement grew during the 1840's. The Thrane Movement in Norway, which demanded better popular education, the right to vote, and universal conscription, gained adherents during the 1850's among both urban workers and agricultural laborers, and caused bloody disturbances. The so-called March Disturbances in Stockholm in 1848 cost 30 lives due to suppression by the police and the army. In Finland the unresolved question of the tenants aggravated the tensions between the landed and the landless.[9]

From Mercantilist Constraint to Liberal Migration Laws

The new population situation with its social problems, which certain groups saw as threatening, contributed to the spread of a new population policy into many parts of Europe. Earlier, when the monarchies consolidated their national states during the sixteenth and the seventeenth centuries, there was interest in increasing the population of the countries. That entailed a restrictive position with attempts to supervise all types of migration and prevent people from leaving the country. A high mortality and the frequent mortality crises were serious threats to population growth. The Mercantilists

8 On the economic situation of the landless group in the countryside, see J. Söderberg 1978, 16–48; For a discussion of the question of overpopulation, see S. Tveite 1980, 43–51.
9 E. Jutikkala 1963, 460; F. Sejersted 1978, 419–426; B. Pettersson 1983, 16–88.

maintained that a large and growing population was an important resource and the basis for a strong and prosperous state, both from an economic and military point of view. During the seventeenth century many countries in Europe, among others Sweden, began keeping registers of the population under the direction of the church; the chief aim was to obtain a foundation for calculating the amount of labor and number of potential soldiers that existed within the country.[10]

The population was regarded as a natural resource and the subjects were seen as a source of income. Unauthorized emigration was therefore regarded as a crime against the country, which saw this as a deprivation of its labor. It was not uncommon, however, for governments to encourage useful, foreign population elements to immigrate. The migration of the Hugenots, Jews, and other groups constitutes examples of this. (See pp. 11–17 on the immigration to the Nordic countries.)

Facing the threats of overpopulation and consequent mass poverty, the earlier Mercantilist strivings were replaced by fears that the population would increase too much. Robert Malthus' hypothesis, which said that exponential growth of the population would outstrip the economic resources, gave support to this position. The fears were now of having too many mouths to feed and of the reactions of the poor masses. It was necessary to come to grips with the problems by means of a sensible population policy, social measures, regulations concerning vagrancy, and public information. The abandonment of Mercantilist population policy in the Nordic countries and in the rest of Europe was thus a consequence of the changes in population growth with its inherent social problems, and meant a breakthrough for a more liberal view of population policy in general.

The new liberal ideas paved the way for debates on individual freedom and conditions on other continents and in other countries, including those in America. Voices were thus raised for increased opportunities for emigration to other countries. A free exchange of labor, just as a free flow of capital and goods, was considered the best way of obtaining maximum exchange value from industry and other enterprises. In the spirit of the Enlightenment, arguments were also advanced for the liberty of the individual to freely determine his life and thus to move unhindered to the country in which he wished to live.

10 S.A. Nilsson 1982, 5–29. Starting in 1749, Sweden and Finland have the most complete population registers of the Nordic countries.

After the Napoleonic Wars the right to emigrate was established in many European countries. In most German states this occurred as early as 1820, but first around 1850 in Prussia, where military service was of great importance. In Great Britain a more liberal emigration policy was also introduced as a means of managing the population pressure and poverty, particularly in Ireland. In Denmark free emigration was accepted in principle from the 1830's, while in Norway there was, for the most part, full freedom to emigrate from 1854 with certain restrictions for those who were to be conscripted into the army. In Sweden the discussion in the Parliament (*Riksdag*) of 1840 meant a breakthrough for liberal ideas, and complete freedom to emigrate existed from the 1860's with the exception that those liable for military service were required to seek permission. According to acts passed in Finland in 1862 and 1888, those who obtained a passport were, in practice, free to emigrate. In Iceland full freedom to leave the country existed from the beginning of emigration as long as the individual had no unfulfilled obligations, such as debts or dependents for whom no provisions had been made.

The principles of free migration also became more accepted for internal migration. Sweden may be taken as an example. According to the Poor Law of 1847 an individual parish could no longer refuse in-migration to persons who might be considered prospective burdens. Thus the principle of a free and mobile labor market, which had been a constant liberal demand, was fully satisfied.[11]

Knowledge and Images of America before the Mass Emigration

In spite of the distance to the North American continent, it is clear that it was not an unknown land for most Europeans during the years before the middle of the nineteenth century. When the British colonies in North America gained their freedom during the end of the eighteenth century, the event was the focus of attention all over the world. A myth spread concerning America as the land of free-

11 Concerning Mercantilism and the debate on liberal population policy and legislation, see I. Semmingsen 1941, 170–178; K. Hvidt 1971, 30–40; A. Wirèn 1975, 30–31; A.-S. Kälvemark 1976, 94–106; B. Pettersson 1983, 61; K. Johannisson (forthcoming); written communcations from Reino Kero and Helgi Skúli Kjartansson (1985).

dom and opportunities. The conditions there, both those that bore witness to the country's merits and those which spoke of its drawbacks, were eagerly discussed in newspapers, pamphlets, and other writings. Letters from individual America-travelers were published in newspapers and read by a large public. Even though the destinations for emigration might be the neighboring countries as well as America or Australia, it was America which stood in the limelight.

A strong positive interest in America existed during the Age of Enlightenment, but during the Romantic Era this view was replaced with a strongly negative conception of the country, or as many people said, 'the traditionless USA'. As early as the 1820's, intellectuals in Europe began to show renewed interest in the growing republic on the other side of the Atlantic, and the public debate became very lively. In this way European liberalism inherited the positive picture of America from the Enlightenment.[12]

There were both static and dynamic strains in the discussions on conceptions of America. According to the static view America was a Canaan, an Eldorado, or a Utopia, and the advantages of agrarian America as well as her natural beauty were extolled. This view was based on the paradise myths where happy people exist in the natural state, and America was the garden of the world. These myths survived during the entire nineteenth century. The picture was strengthened by reports of cheap land in America, of the possibilities for an autonomous, self-sufficient agriculture, and of the freedom from employers and landlords. The notion was also common that America was industrializing rapidly and that Americans were practical, enterprising, and technically effective, and filled with the Yankee, go-ahead spirit. Much of that picture of America was the result of a commercial stereotype.

The other picture of America shifted depending upon the political situation in Europe and the current political ideas. The basic dividing line in opinions was between conservative ideas and the more radical views espoused by liberal forces. The conservatives maintained that the USA lacked naturally developed institutions and historical, ethnic, and religious homogeneity; a superficial materialism and egoism were said to dominate. The liberal proponents instead stressed the political and religious freedom and the democratic institutions and rights. Especially after the revolutionary

---

12 When nothing is stated to the contrary, the presentation of views on America is based upon N. Runeby 1969, 11–19, 453–463 and S. Skard 1976, 97–129.

events of 1848, the USA came to stand out as the land of social reforms, devoted to political and economic equality and sympathetic to the strivings of labor organizations.

While the discussions of America – its merits and disadvantages – took place within a small group of the intelligentsia and others involved in social debate, the more static, stereotyped picture of America that was supported by commercial interests probably became the view adopted by the broad masses.

The debate on America was lively in Norway after 1840. Much of it was conducted in the newspapers, often after the publication of America-letters sent home by earlier Norwegian emigrants. Even letters from the Swedish pioneer Gustaf Unonius were published in the Norwegian press. The editor of *Kristiansandposten*, Johan Reinert Reiersen, wrote intensively about emigration and saw a connection between its causes and the liberal demands for reforms. He received much support for his standpoint from other newspapers. He also published a book, *Vägvisaren (The Guide,* 1844), written after a trip to America, in which he praised the country. However, Reiersen met with firm opposition. One critic was the clergyman C.W.C. Dietridson, who had also traveled in the USA but had found that his countrymen lived under miserable conditions.

Many books with contributions for and against America were also published in Norway, starting as early as the end of the 1830's. The most famous was Ole Rynning's *Sandfaerdig Beretning om Amerika* (1839). Another example was Charles Dickens' *American Notes*, which was translated into Norwegian in 1843. The continued debate on America and the reasons for emigration were often linked to the political and social conditions in Norway. The liberal Henrik Wergeland maintained, for example, that it was the lack of freedom in the country, with its constraints on spiritual and economic life, that caused people to emigrate. In many contexts America was presented as a model which Norway ought to emulate.[13]

Many Swedes also traveled to America and stimulated the debate in the home country by publishing letters and printing books. The letters from the group of emigrants that followed Gustaf Unonius were of great importance when they were read in the homeland, as did his *Minnen från en sjuttonårig vistelse i Nordvestra Amerika (Memories from a Seventeen-year-long Sojourn in Northwestern America)*, published in 1862. Fredrika Bremer traveled in America

13 I. Semmingsen 1941, 84, 179–215.

from 1849 to 1851. She expressed her admiration for the country in the book *Hemmen i den nya verlden* I and II (*The Homes in the New World*) published in 1853 and 1854, in which she described in lyrical phrases the possibilities that the land offered: 'But that Minnesota is a wonderful land, and rightfully a land for the Nordic immigrants, rightfully a land for a new Scandinavia'. The Baptist Anders Wiberg who lived in the USA during the years 1852–1855 also merits attention. During his stay there he sent articles to the liberal *Aftonbladet* in which he lauded the country for its politics, its economy, and its religious conditions. For Wiberg, the USA and Sweden represented one single sphere of activity, but one in which the impulses came from America.[14]

In Finland newspaper articles on America and the discussion on the conditions in that country first appeared during the 1850's, which was later than in Norway, Denmark, and Sweden, but a couple of decades before the real onset of the emigration. Some intellectuals in Finland saw America as the ideal land of liberalism, a land of the future, where the social conditions were significantly better than in Europe. This attitude also gained support among the broad masses during the 1860's and 1870's.[15]

Another source of information on America for the general public was a number of *songs and broadsheets*. They were a form of 'mass media', which in popular terms told about the country on the other side of the Atlantic and expressed opinions on the conditions there. These songs undoubtedly greatly influenced people's conceptions of America, in spite of their gross generalizations. For instance, one song described the country as a land of thieves, and another as a pure paradise. The form of these songs is illustrated by one of the more well-known America ballads, *Amerika visan*, which was written in 1836 by the renowned Danish author Hans Christian Andersen.

The America Song

Brothers, oh so very far,
'Cross the salty sea
Rises up America,
Her golden shores to see.

14 N. Runeby 1969, 471. For information on Anders Wiberg, see K. Söderberg 1983, 212.
15 R. Kero 1974, 21–22.

Refrain:
Oh no! Can it be so true?
Is there so much joy for you?
A pity that America,
A pity that America
Lies way off so very far.

Trees which on the ground do stand
Sugar – oh, so sweet!
And everywhere about the land,
Girls are there to meet.
Refrain:

If you wish for one that's real,
Soon you will have four or more,
Meadows and the fields
Grow money by the score.
Refrain:

Ducks and chickens raining down,
Geese land on the table,
Forks are out 'n bird's done brown,
Eat now if you're able.
Refrain:

Oh the sun, it always shines,
Inside all the hearts,
Cellar's full of food and wines,
Songs in every part.
Refrain:

(Text by Hans Christian Andersen 1836. This English translation by Marie C. Nelson from Swedish and Danish versions of the text.)

Although the author gives a dazzling description of America, as overflowing with precious metals and the riches of the earth, he is also a bit ironic. For the general public, however, the text was perhaps understood as a description recounting all the fantastic and delightful things that existed in America. The song was very popular and widely sung, and one must assume that people commonly experienced it as a part of the general praise of America and con-curred with it. Most songs of this type were translated into Danish, Norwegian, and Swedish and widely dispersed throughout the Scan-dinavian countries. No such songs existed in Iceland. However, there was a lively newspaper and pamphlet debate in this country, as well as the play *Vesturfararnir* (*The Emigrants*) written by the national poet Matthias Jochomsson.[16]

All the publicity and discussion, as well as the other examples of information, reveal a well-rooted consciousness of America among many people before the great emigration began. In this way interest grew for the country in the west among the people in the prospective emigrant nations. When the time was right, the dam burst, and mass emigration began.

Greater Social Gaps – Growing Optimism

A number of contradictory aspects may be noted in the development of Nordic societies about the middle of the nineteenth century. As previously mentioned, the great population increase brought about a growing social stratification with a distressing growth of the land-less and the destitute groups. Some categories, craftsmen for exam-ple, experienced difficulties during the expansion of industrial capita-lism. Economic and social deterioration for some thus went hand in hand with progress and optimism for other groups.

Generally speaking, the nineteenth century was characterized by a strong economic and technical expansion, although interrupted by periods of recession. Declines in the business cycle were recorded during the 1830's, the end of the 1840's, in 1875, and in 1894. The mere existence of new countries on the other side of the oceans must have contributed to the general optimism during this time. In America and Australia enormous areas waited to be populated. The communications network was expanded, railroads were built, and the connections by sea were radically improved, especially by the introduction of steamships. In other words, both the space and the transportation opportunities existed to satisfy a considerable appetite for expansion.

The economic cycles were generally favorable, especially during

16 T. Thomsen 1980, 1–38; A Swedish text and music notes to the America Song in R.L. Wright 1965, and in H. Norman & H. Runblom 1980, 205–206; written communication from Helgi Skúli Kjartansson (1985). Numerous Norwegian songs are presented in I. Semmingsen 1950, 437–444.

the 1850's. The Swedish emigration scholar Gustav Sundbärg said that a new age was introduced in the history of the world's economy: 'With the 1850's the old poverty and lack of initiative are gone. The expressions of economic life become immense, world embracing.'[17]

The Crimean War also meant a boom for the world economy. Iron and wood, important export products for the Nordic countries, brought good prices. As demand became great for agricultural products, the cultivation of new land increased, and the turnover of rural property became livelier.

The economic upswing around 1850 was an important basis for the start of emigration in many parts of the Nordic countries. News of gold discoveries in California and Australia reached out over the world and contributed to increased expectations of economic success. It was necessary only to be sufficiently enterprising to reach that transoceanic goal. These were good times for shipping to America and Australia.

Some adventurers not only went to the California gold fields with all their hardships and risks, but shortly thereafter left for the gold fields of Australia to seek their fortunes. So did Peter and Anders Pettersson, sons of a farmer and iron producer from Bjurtjärn in the *bergslag* of Karlskoga, Sweden. They first departed for America as 'forty-niners'. When success was not sufficient in America, they went on to the gold digging area in Victoria, Australia, at about the same time that their brothers Erik and Jakob Pettersson founded the settlement Stockholm in Wisconsin.[18]

The first accounts of the California gold fields reached Norway during the late autumn of 1848. During the following year the Norwegian newspapers were full of tales about it and about the throngs it had attracted. In spite of this, the gold discoveries in California at first played a quantitatively small role in Nordic emigration, because the news arrived relatively late. Those in a position to go to California were a few adventurous persons and a number of seamen who jumped ship in San Francisco; emigrants during the years that followed went mainly to the Midwest to become farmers. As will be shown below, however, these first Nordic emigrants who traveled over in connection with the gold rush or shortly thereafter, that is, during the minor upswing in emigration which occurred in the beginning of the 1850's, were important for the continued

17 *Emigrationsutredningen Betänkande*, 1913, 142.
18 K. Nordqvist 1969; H. Norman 1978, 120–135; U. Beijbom 1983, 84.

development of emigration. They constituted a vanguard, spread knowledge of America, and provided information for continued emigration. Areas which had early pioneer emigrants as a rule also had a high rate of emigration during following years. That is especially true for many districts in Norway from which 18,000 emigrants had already gone to America before 1851. Pioneer emigrants thus served as catalysts in periods of pent-up hopes, when interest in America and the desire to try this land were high, as these dreams had been found for decades among the masses of the people.

California gold therefore had great importance for the continued emigration and the attitude towards America. In the USA the first half of the 1850's was prosperous, the so-called 'California gold inflation prosperity period'. The whole of the American continent gained a luster of gold. Ballads and tales were spread which told of wonderful things. More than ever before, America represented the land of hope and opportunity, and there was the common conviction that America was the land of the economic future. It was, not surprisingly, during the 1850's with its favorable business cycle, that the 'take-off' came for emigration from the Scandinavian countries.[19]

19 *Emigrationsutredningen, Betänkande* 1913, 139–142; J.A. Estay 1956, 20; H. Norman 1974, 79–82; I. Semmingsen 1941, 366–391.

5. Mass Emigration from the Nordic Countries

Initial Phase

Emigration must be seen as part of the total pattern of migration. The outward movement was quantitatively small compared to moves within local areas, labor migrations, and domestic movements over longer distances, particularly during the first phase. There was also a large quantitative difference between the so-called pioneer phase and the mass emigration that followed. Still, the early migration is of special importance, because in many cases it determined the future pattern of emigration.

The onset of emigration occurred at significantly different times in the various Nordic countries. Furthermore, there are obvious dissimilarities between Norway, which had the earliest, most extensive and long-lasting emigration, Denmark, which had something of a soft start and the least intensive emigration, and Finland, which was latest in entering a phase of extensive emigration. In Sweden emigration began relatively early and was of long duration, whereas in Iceland it started late, but ran a short and dramatic course.

As a rule a couple of decades elapsed from the first outward movement to the time when emigration can be said to have entered the phase of mass emigration. Roughly speaking, the 1830's and 1840's represent the initial phase for Norway, the 1840's and 1850's for Sweden, the 1850's and 1860's for Denmark, and the 1860's and 1870's for Finland. Finally, in Iceland emigration started abruptly during the middle of the 1870's. (See figure 5, p. 32.)

Because of these divergences in time, the basic conditions for the emigrants differed somewhat in the various countries; transportation and the information available changed notably over a few decades, as did opportunities for obtaining land and the state of the labor market in America. In these respects there was a considerable difference between departing during the 1830's or 1840's and the 1860's or 1870's. The first Norwegian and Swedish pioneers left nearly exclusively in order to obtain land, which, however, they had to purchase. According to the so-called Preemption Act of 1841 government lands in the USA were to be sold for a fixed price of $1.25 per acre. (An acre equals approximately 0.47 hectares). Previously this land had been sold at auctions. After the passage of the Homestead Act in 1862, land could be acquired without costs other than the registration fee. Thus each American citizen or immigrant who declared his intent to become an American citizen had the right to claim 160 acres (about 65 hectares) of land. Full rights of ownership were obtained when the land had been cultivated for five years. The offer of land under the Homestead Act could be used only once. Starting a farm required, however, equipment and animals. Generally it was necessary to invest about 1,000 dollars before a homestead farm could support a settler with a family. This was the reason why many emigrants first began to work at lumbering, in the mines, or in other industries before they procured farmland.[1]

Measured by Nordic standards, emigration *from Norway* had an exceptionally early start in 1825. This is an example of the general dispersion of the 'innovation' of emigration behavior, which came from the British Isles and northwestern Europe and spread eastward and southeastward to the rest of Europe. These first Norwegian emigrants came from the city of Stavanger in southwestern Norway, an area with historical links to England.

The majority of the fifty-two emigrants were Quakers, Haugians (adherents of the evangelical lay preacher, H. N. Hauge), or sympathetic with these religious groups, which were subjected to discrimination by the authorities. Important within this context was the fact that the Quaker congregation in Stavanger was founded by individuals who had been imprisoned in England during the Napoleonic Wars and who were in touch with leading English Quakers, the latter in turn having American contacts. There is also a possible link to some German emigrants who had been forced to seek harbor in Bergen in 1817. Preparations for a move to America had been made as early as 1821 by sending Cleng Peerson there to seek information; he would become a legendary spokesman and leader for further emigration (see page 126). He returned in 1824 with very positive experiences, a circumstance which should be seen as the triggering mechanism for the start of emigration the following

1 L. Ljungmark 1965, 78–83.

year. The emigrants who left at that time were not poor: they purchased the ship that transported them over the Atlantic, the renowned sloop *Restoration (Restauration)*, sometimes called Norway's *Mayflower*. The Kendall colony, which they founded in the state of New York, struggled with many difficulties and was therefore a rather short-lived phenomenon.

It was not until 1836 that emigration from Norway occurred yearly. One leader of the continued emigration from the Stavanger region was a Quaker emigrant from 1830, Knud Slogvig, who had returned to Norway in 1835. The importance of earlier emigration thus lay in the fact that contact was maintained with the home country. This was especially true of the well-known letter-writer Gjert Hovland, who emigrated in 1831. Together with Cleng Peerson, who had brought Norwegian emigrants westward to Fox River, Illinois, Hovland described the new land in fascinating letters, which were distributed in Norway and became significant factors in the further Norwegian settlement in the Midwest. They provided an impulse for the first group emigration from a Norwegian mountain community, Tinn in Telemark in 1837. The Tinn emigration became decisive for the distribution of the subsequent emigration. During the ten-year period from 1836 to 1845 not less than 45 percent of Norwegian emigration set off from Tinn or from Telemark as a whole. For many years the interior mountain communities in Norway belonged to those areas with the most intensive emigration in the country. (See the emigration map for 1865–69, figure 9a.) The continued history of Norwegian emigration abounds in pioneers who paved the way for emigration from their home districts. One such person was Stephen Olsen Kubakke, who left for America in 1846 and returned after two years. Like other travelers to America, he was met with enthusiasm in his home area and returned to America with a large group. He and his followers founded a settlement in Wisconsin and named it Valdres after their home community. Many emigrants later followed from the Norwegian to the American Valdres.[2]

Several parallels may be drawn between the first group emigration *from Sweden* and the early emigration from Norway. Both led to rather insignificant settlements, but they were of great importance as sources of information and stimulants for further emigration.

2 I. Semmingsen 1941, 9–90, 1983, 3–42; A. Svalestuen 1971, 29–30; A. Svalestuen 1972.

The Swede Gustaf Unonius departed for America in 1841 with a small group of people from Uppsala, mainly of middle-class origins. They were university students, officers, and merchants, often with failures behind them in Swedish society. A settlement with the name New Uppsala was founded on the shores of Pine Lake in eastern Wisconsin. The colonists saw America as an ideal land, but the colony did not survive long, as these romantic settlers were little accustomed to physical labor and lacked a sense of the realities of pioneer life.

Unonius studied to become a minister in the Espiscopal Church and became a controversial clergyman in Chicago, before he returned to Sweden in 1858 and assumed a post as a customs collector in Grisslehamn. The importance of his emigration experiment was that the colonists in Pine Lake were highly literate and willingly supplied their impressions by letters to the home country. Unonius sent home a series of letters, and his memoirs, *A Pioneer in Northwest America 1841–1858,* received a great deal of attention. One of the members of the colony, Lieutenant Polycarpus von Schneidau, kept in touch with his father by means of letters which were circulated and copied in his home community of Kisa in the province of Östergötland. They inspired the master-builder Peter Cassel to depart for America in 1845 at the head of a group of about thirty emigrants. This emigration appears to have been for political, religious, and economic reasons. The emigrants consisted of practical men, and the settlement of New Sweden, Iowa prospered, because the leader had carefully planned the entire enterprise. In the year 1852 about five hundred people lived there, including a hundred families. Cassel's letters with positive accounts of the colony were also printed in the Swedish press and contributed to an increased interest in America.[3]

Although religion was scarcely the major force behind the earlier Swedish emigration, religious motivation was more evident in the next group, led by the farmer-preacher Erik Jansson. This 'prophet' from Biskopskulla in the province of Uppland within a couple of years won a substantial following in Hälsingland and the surrounding provinces. The sect was rebellious in its repudiation of the state church, and its members were subjected to persecution, legal censure, and even imprisonment. In the year 1846, and for some years thereafter, most of the Janssonites emigrated under the leader-

3 L. Ljungmark 1965, 31–38; U. Beijbom 1971, 39–52.

ship of Erik Jansson and founded the famous colony of Bishop Hill on the Illinois prairie. Altogether about 1,500 persons joined this experiment, which was arbitrarily ruled by Jansson, and which applied communistic principles of ownership. However, the sect dissolved. When Erik Jansson was murdered, many moved from the colony, and in the beginning of the 1860's the system of communal ownership was disbanded.[4]

Because of its extreme character, the emigration of the Erik Janssonites has been viewed as a rather isolated phenomenon. Later research points in the opposite direction. Through all the publicity that it received in the press and even in debates in the Swedish *Riksdag*, it became important as a source of information on America for later emigrants. There is also a close relationship between this religious emigration and other group emigrations which were headed by clergymen in leading positions, for example, Lars Paul Esbjörn, who was in charge of a group emigration from the city of Gävle in 1849. It should also be mentioned that Erik Norelius emigrated in 1850 from Hälsingland, together with a large group of Hedbergians (followers of a Pietistic movement led by F.G. Hedberg). Esbjörn and Norelius both became outstanding leaders for the Swedish Augustana Lutheran Church in America and came to inspire further emigration and religious contacts with Sweden. Examples of other radical churchmen who emigrated were Anders Wiberg, mentioned above, and Gustaf Palmquist, who were both Baptists. It should also be noted that the members of the large Baptist emigration during the 1860's from Orsa in Dalarna to Isanti County, Minnesota had clear connections with Erik Jansson's separatist movement.[5]

During the beginning of the 1850's a large group emigration took place from Örebro län. The greater part of the emigrants came from a limited area, the *Bergslagen* district near Karlskoga, where no fewer than 256 persons took out certificates for emigration. Two successive groups crossed the Atlantic in the years 1853 and 1854 headed by Erik Pettersson and his brother Jacob. Earlier, Erik, together with two other brothers, had been attracted to America by California gold (see p. 50). He stayed, however, in the upper Mississippi Valley, where he was inspired to establish a settlement with the help of relatives and acquaintances. He wrote to his third

4 O. Isaksson and S. Hallgren 1969; In 1981 Bishop Hill was designated a National Historic Landmark in the USA.
5 K. Söderberg 1981, 200–217; R.C. Ostergren 1976.

brother, Jacob, in Sweden, telling him to prepare this exodus. It resulted in the founding of Stockholm in Pepin County in western Wisconsin. Among the emigrants were many well-situated iron-producing farmers (*bergsmän*), who before their departure sold their homes for large sums. This emigration illustrates how, during the first half of the 1850's, an era dominated by economic optimism, resources in the home country were disposed of and turned into good land in America.[6]

Denmark's early group emigration was not as extensive as that from Norway and Sweden, but otherwise the pattern was largely the same; that is, a few energetic pioneers led the way. There were many Danes caught up in the California gold rush, and there are also several examples of emigrated Danes who settled in various parts of America and from there stimulated more of their country-men to emigrate.

The early groups that emigrated from Denmark included the followers of the Pietistic minister C.L. Clausen from Langeland, who emigrated in 1843. He was minister of the Norwegian congre-gation in Muskego, Racine County, Wisconsin, and influenced Danes and Norwegians to come there. Through articles in his home newspaper in 1847–1848, he enticed many emigrants over to a settlement called New Denmark (*Nya Danmark*) in Brown County, Wisconsin. He also inspired Danes in 1853 to move to the settlement St. Ansgar in Mitchell County in northern Iowa, a fact that helped make that state the one most influenced by Danes in the USA. The innkeeper Christian Ludvig Christensen from Stokkemarke on the island of Lolland made a crossing to America in 1846 to investigate the opportunities for settlement there. The group which he inspired to travel with the rest of his family to Hartland and Pine Lake, Wisconsin, was small, but his sons and sons-in-law later brought over larger Danish emigrant groups to Wisconsin. Two persons very active in encouraging Danish emigration were the religious and political radical Mogens Sommer (see page 127) and the agrarian politician and preacher Rasmus Sørensen. Both served as itinerant speakers and distributors of information on America. Sørensen encouraged poor farmers to emigrate in protest against conditions in the home country. In 1848 he organized a large group of emi-grants that he intended to accompany to Wisconsin, where his sons were already living. However, as that time he was not able to finance

6 K. Nordqvist 1969; H. Norman 1974, 78, 232–236; H. Norman 1978, 120–135.

the journey for his large family—he was, furthermore, involved in the political movements of 1848—but his group left and settled in New Denmark. Most of them later moved to the Lake Winnebago area, and some of them were among the early Danish pioneers in Nebraska. Sørensen went to America himself in 1852, together with his family, and was important in initiating mass emigration from Denmark through all the information that he spread. After a visit to Denmark in 1861–1862 he personally led a large group of emigrants to the USA.[7]

The emigration of the Mormons more than anything else raised the volume of Danish emigration during the 1850's, and Mormon emigration propaganda became a significant catalyst. The Mormon movement had most of its followers among the poor, where groups such as cottagers, tenants, and craftsmen had ample reason to try the opportunities that emigration offered. The first Mormon emigrants left in 1852, and it is estimated that about 2,000 of the 4,000 Danish emigrants during the years 1850–1860 were adherents of that religious faith. Certainly the Mormons in Denmark met with much persecution, but the explanation for their large numbers there seems to be that the Danish authorities placed fewer hindrances in the way of their activities than the authorities in Norway and Sweden, who were strongly opposed to the movement. Moreover, the Mormons in Denmark found fertile soil in the many Danish Baptist congregations. Their emigration was stimulated by the fact that the Mormon teachings contained a direct exhortation to seek one's way to the promised land, Utah, which meant that the Mormons considered emigration an act of faith. They were also skillfully organized for winning proselytes and financing the trip over. Through the publicity they created about America, they acquired great importance for the continued emigration from Denmark. Next to England, Denmark was the European country which sent the most Mormon emigrants.[8]

The Mormon missionaries were also active *in Iceland* during the 1850's, resulting in the departure of about fifteen persons for America at the end of the 1850's, which is the sole example of early emigration from the island. In spite of unfavorable conditions in Iceland during the 1850's and 1860's, with epidemics among the sheep, deteriorating climate, and a decline in fishing catches, which

7 P.S. Vig 1908; K. Hvidt 1976, 71–78, 88, 285–286; E.H. Pedersen 1985, 55–70; written communication from Steffen E. Jørgensen (1985).
8 K. Hvidt 1976, 100–114; E. H. Pedersen 1985, 73–77.

ought to have created the desire for emigration, the Icelanders showed no signs of following the stream of emigrants to North America from Norway, Sweden, and Denmark. Information on America was very meagre, and there was no organized form of transport between Iceland and America. Not until 1870 did a modest emigration begin. During that year and the two following, four, twelve, and then twenty-four persons left who had the means and the opportunity to travel to Denmark or to Great Britain, from which they emigrated to the Midwest. Some news of America subsequently followed in the Icelandic newspapers, and, furthermore, a collection of translated America-letters was published.

When the first emigration agency in Iceland was established by the Allan Line (*Allanlinien*) in 1873, announcing that a ship would be sent to pick up emigrants, about one thousand persons expressed the intention to leave the country, a figure that equals no less than fourteen of each thousand inhabitants. About five hundred persons registered for North America with the Allan Line, while the rest applied for assisted passage to Brazil, which could be provided only for thirty-four persons. Therefore nearly all went to North America. Even though the shipping company did not presume to arrange regular direct lines, the number of Icelandic emigrants quickly rose to great heights. The Allan Line had direct traffic between Iceland and America only in 1874 and 1876. Other years they made a convenient arrangement whereby their passengers were sent via Scotland. The Icelandic emigrants who went via Denmark and Norway had to arrange the first part of their journeys privately. Already in 1876 the number of Icelandic emigrants reached seventeen per thousand of the population, a rate higher than in any other Nordic country. And, in the later part of the 1880's the emigration reached the record height of twenty-seven persons per thousand. (See figure 5.) In the beginning the Icelandic emigration went to Wisconsin in the USA, but later the Icelanders' interest was directed towards Canada. That country became the most popular destination. The most affordable boat trips went there, and the railway journeys were subsidized in Canada during the high tide of Icelandic emigration. During the 1880's the Icelandic emigration to Canada was twelve times as numerous as that to the USA. The Icelanders settled on a large scale in an area called New Iceland, near Winnipeg, Manitoba, and the major part of the Icelandic emigration was later concentrated in that part of the country. In spite of their comparatively small numbers, the Icelanders in Canada have preserved their ethnic unity and traditions to a greater degree than their Nordic neighbors, while at the same time adjusting to Canadian life.[9]

Prior to the 1860's there were not many emigrants *from Finland* to America. They consisted mainly of seamen who stayed in America, some of whom became gold seekers after leaving their boats in California harbors. A few of them returned home, while others wrote to the home country and told of the opportunities in America. Otherwise emigration from Finland received its first impulses primarily from two areas: from the mining districts on the Arctic coast of North Norway and from the sawmill districts of Sweden. Many of the pioneer Finnish emigrants had thus already been incorporated into an industrial capitalistic labor market.

The emigrants from northern Finland who left during the 1860's had received information about opportunities in America via the mining districts in northern Norway, where many Finns worked in the mines. A significant number of them emigrated from Kåfjord in 1864, when the mines offered little work. Moreover, agents from the Quincy Mining Company in Michigan spread information about the opportunities for jobs in the company's mines at a time when it was difficult to recruit workers in the USA, because so many American men were soldiers in the War Between the States. This resulted in laborers from Finland traveling across the Atlantic to work in the copper mines in northern Michigan. During the 1860's emigration had also started from the Torne Valley (*Tornedalen*). The impulses for emigration apparently came from Finns living in Finnmarken in Norway, and in 1866 sixteen persons left Ylitornio parish for America. Emigration also started early from Vaasa County in Ostrobothnia with some groups in the 1860's. Most emigrants came from Kokkola rural parish, which seven persons left in 1866, eleven in 1867, and fourteen in 1869. Contacts across the Gulf of Bothnia, particularly between the Swedish-speaking areas on both sides, had long been close, and they were intensified through the rapid expansion of the sawmill industry on the Swedish side. Many workers from Finland, especially from Vaasa County, sought work there, which helped to spread impulses for emigration to America over to the Finnish side. Eventually this area of Finland experienced a very intensive rate of emigration. (Compare figures 9a, 9b, and 9c.) The early emigration from Finland included the group from Uusimaa in the southwestern part of the country, a group that

9 H.S. Kjartansson 1977, 87–93; 1980, 53–71; H. Runblom 1977, 213–228.

consisted of fifty-three people who left for Alabama in 1869 under the leadership of Carl Sjödahl. This group emigration, however, did not produce vigorous continued emigration from the area.[10]

Motives for and Importance of Early Emigration

The information and debate on America created a general consciousness and curiosity among large groups of people about American society with its renowned economic opportunities and political and religious freedom, which made many eager to try the possibilities there. The circumstances which influenced people to migrate have often been discussed. There is general agreement that during the age of mass emigration the desire of individuals and their families to attain better economic conditions was paramount. There were also other motives for emigration, such as the wish to see the world, to try something new, to seek relatives who had left earlier, or to join prospective marriage partners. Sometimes it was simply the desire to travel and to satisfy a need for adventure. Lack of political and religious freedom has also been discussed as a reason for emigration.

On the European continent there are many examples of immigrants citing political motives, even if strong economic and social reasons also existed. In the Nordic countries only a few cases may be attributed to political conditions. Here the great emigration of Danes from Sönderjylland is usually included, as that area was annexed by imperialistic Prussia following the war in 1864. That extensive emigration, which the German authorities saw as alleviation of a troublesome element, seems, however, to have been mainly to Danish areas. The russification process pursued in Finland around the year 1900 also caused some people to emigrate, among them labor leaders. It appears, however, that the most significant influence upon emigration resulting from political discontent in the Nordic countries came from the radical press through its commentaries on existing evils.[11]

Studies of the connection between religious separatism and emigration in the Nordic countries also reveal that religious motives were for the most part of little importance during the era of mass

10 R. Kero 1974, 16–20, 160–161; H. Wester 1977; E. De Geer 1977, 37–63, especially the map. fig. 5; E. Niemi 1978, 60–61.
11 L. Ljungmark 1965, 59; K. Hvidt 1976, 145, 178–180; R. Kero 1980, 59; G. Moltman 1984, 296–297.

emigration.[12] However, there were clear examples of such a connection in continental emigration. One of these is the emigration of the Seceders from the Netherlands Reformed Church. The Seceders comprised no less than 35 percent of Dutch emigration in 1847, a peak emigration year for that country, while they made up only 1.4 percent of the total population. Some of the examples cited here from the Nordic countries during the pioneer period have also shown that religious motives did exist, as has recently been emphasized within emigration scholarship.[13]

A clear example of religious separatism as a cause of emigration is the emigration of the Quakers and the Haugians from Norway in 1825. Of the group emigrations from Sweden, the Erik Janssonites, furthermore, stand out as an unusually clear-cut case. That emigration also had a 'dispersion effect', influencing other moves from Sweden led by clergymen. In the early Danish emigration, in which the Mormons constituted a large element, there was, of course, a religious factor, although the motive in that case appears to have been somewhat different. Certainly the Mormons faced problems in their homeland, but part of the goal of conversion was to seek one's way to Zion, their paradise in Utah.

In other early group emigrations from the Nordic countries the economic and social motives appear to have been predominant. This was especially the case in the emigration from the Karlskoga iron-producing district (*bergslag*), where assets were sold at home in order to invest the capital in land in Wisconsin.

Although the religious factor was thus present as a cause of emigration in the early phase, it was hardly relevant when the Finnish and Icelandic emigration began. A general liberalization had penetrated Nordic society after the middle of the nineteenth century, as illustrated by the development in Sweden. A Conventicle Act (*konventikelplakat*) of 1726 prescribed strict penalties for all private religious meetings which could not be considered home devotions. These regulations, which were directed against the Pietistic movement, were revoked in 1858, but replaced by the Conventicle Rules (*konventikelbestämmelserna*). Accordingly, private

12 For a survey of the scholarly discussion on religious motives for emigration and an investigation of the relationship between the free churches and emigration, see S. Carlsson 1967, 118–131.
13 P. Stokvis 1983, 41, 47; K. Söderberg 1981, 125–226. After an investigation of the Bishop Hill emigration, Söderberg allots the religious factor greater importance in the history of the emigration to America than has previously been the case.

prayer meetings were permitted, but the church council had the right to take measures against preaching that was considered conducive to religious discord or scornful of the public religious services. The regulations were removed in 1868 after which formal religious persecution ceased to be a motive for emigration. If one views emigration in its entirety, religious restriction scarcely drove those not conforming to the state church to emigrate; rather the active nonconformist movement in America stimulated people to travel there.

In a broader perspective the economic factors were decisive. The early Finnish emigration from the mining areas of North Norway during the 1860's and the first emigration from economically hard-pressed Iceland during the 1870's have already demonstrated that. The first mass emigration from Scandinavia also came in conjunction with the years of famine at the end of the 1860's. These years not only meant shortages of foodstuffs, but also a general economic crisis which caused emigrants to make their way over the Atlantic *en masse*. One attraction was the Homestead Act of 1862, which gave many landless the opportunity to obtain free land.

The years of the crop failures in the Nordic countries, 1867 and 1868, illustrate the great significance of pioneer emigrants for continued migration. In the countries where emigration had started during the 1840's and the 1850's, there was, of course, already a tradition of emigration, and channels of communication were developed, so that emigration grew rapidly to great proportions. That was especially true for Norway and Sweden, but less so for Denmark, which did not experience any significant crop failures. In Finland, on the other hand, which suffered most during the famine years and where the death rate rose to a record high, no pioneer emigration of such importance had yet taken place which could highlight America as an alternative. Nor did Finland experience any significant emigration during the late 1860's.

Chronological and Regional Characteristics

Norwegian mass emigration started earlier than in the other Nordic countries. When the first Swedish group of emigrants under the leadership of Gustaf Unonius settled near Pine Lake in 1841, there were already more than ten Norwegian settlements in North America. Personal contacts with earlier emigrants and a tradition of migration to America thus existed in Norway at an earlier stage than in the rest of the Nordic countries. On the map showing emigration intensity from the Nordic countries 1865–69 (figure 9a), a distinct line can be seen between Norway and Sweden. On the Norwegian side the emigration rate was much higher. Denmark had few districts with extensive emigration, and in Iceland and Finland there was very little up to this point.[14]

The maps (figures 9a–c) show that emigration as a mass behavior phenomenon spread mainly from west to east. In Sweden this behavior was dispersed from the south to the northern parts of the country, in Finland from the west and northwest to the southeast, and in Iceland from the north to the east. While the wave of emigration spread over a steadily larger area, it continued to be intense in those parishes and provinces from which emigrants had previously come. Striking examples of this can be seen in central-southern and far northern Norway (for example, Telemark, Valdres, Hallingdal, Gudbrandsdal, Sogn, and Alta *fögderier*), northeastern Iceland (Norður-Þingeyjarsýsla and Norður-Múlasýsla), northern Jutland and the southern islands in Denmark (Hjørring, Praestø, and Maribo *amt*), the southern and southwestern parts of Sweden (the provinces of Småland, Halland, Öland, and Värmland), as well as in the province of Ostrobothnia in Finland.

A marked improvement in the economic situation in the Nordic countries during the early 1870's slowed down the previously high rate of emigration; Iceland, where emigration started suddenly in the middle of the decade, was the exception, because many prospective emigrants had not earlier been able to leave. The American economic recession that began in 1873 also held back emigration from all the Nordic countries for some years except in the case of Iceland, which registered an exodus due, among other things, to the volcanic eruption in 1875. (Compare diagrams, figure 5 and above, p. 59.)

A long economic recession in the Nordic countries in the 1880's, combined with brighter prospects in the USA, stimulated a new wave of emigration, mainly from the same areas as before. During this phase there was an increase in emigration from towns and industrial centers. Emigration gradually increased in Finland, primarily in the Swedish-speaking parts of the province of Ostrobothnia, but it also spread further inland. After a temporary decrease during the mid-1880's, emigration from the Nordic countries continued at a very high level until 1893. The network of contacts

14 I. Semmingsen 1977, 10–14. The maps, figures 9a, 9b, and 9c, are from the *Nordic Emigration Atlas* 1980, which contains maps of ten five-year periods from 1865 to 1914. Of these, three have been included here, 1865–69, 1885–89, and 1900–04.

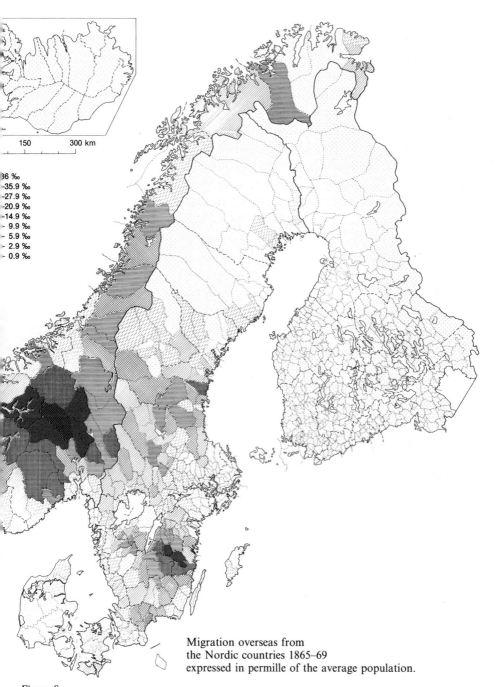

36 ‰
-35.9 ‰
-27.9 ‰
-20.9 ‰
-14.9 ‰
- 9.9 ‰
- 5.9 ‰
- 2.9 ‰
- 0.9 ‰

150   300 km

Migration overseas from
the Nordic countries 1865–69
expressed in permille of the average population.

Figure 9a.
Source: *Nordic Emigration Atlas* (*Nordisk Emigrationsatlas*), eds. H. Norman & H.
Runblom 1980.

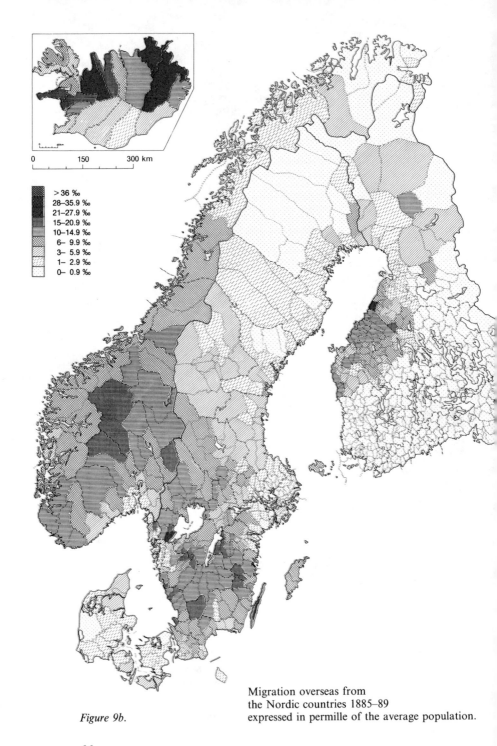

░	> 36 ‰
	28–35.9 ‰
	21–27.9 ‰
	15–20.9 ‰
	10–14.9 ‰
	6– 9.9 ‰
	3– 5.9 ‰
	1– 2.9 ‰
	0– 0.9 ‰

Figure 9b.

Migration overseas from
the Nordic countries 1885–89
expressed in permille of the average population.

66

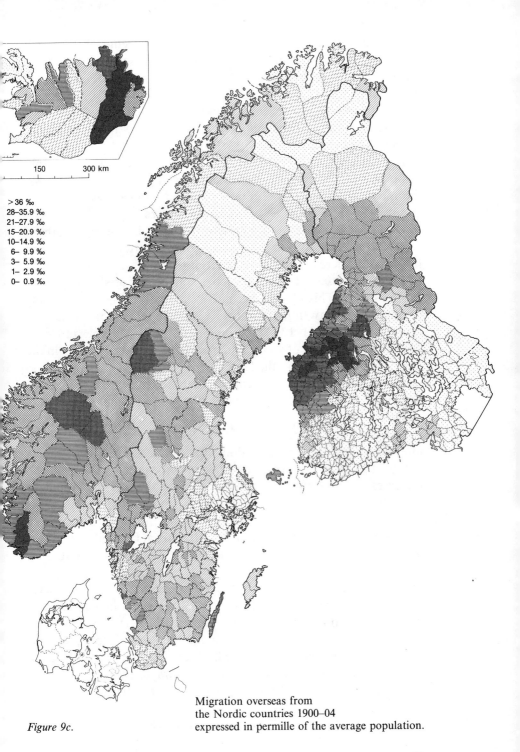

> 36 ‰
28–35.9 ‰
21–27.9 ‰
15–20.9 ‰
10–14.9 ‰
6– 9.9 ‰
3– 5.9 ‰
1– 2.9 ‰
0– 0.9 ‰

150   300 km

Figure 9c.

Migration overseas from
the Nordic countries 1900–04
expressed in permille of the average population.

across the Atlantic had become denser, and knowledge of the North American labor market increased among prospective emigrants through letters, newspaper articles, and shipping agents' brochures. Almost half of the emigrants in the 1880's traveled on pre-paid tickets. In Iceland, however, pre-paid tickets were almost unknown because they were considered illegal, and relatives in America sent money instead.[15]

The regional distribution of emigration remained remarkably stable. As can be seen from the map showing the period 1885–89, the most notable change from the period 1865–69 was a higher intensity in most parts of the Nordic countries, especially northern Iceland, the northern and southern parts of Denmark, southern Norrland in Sweden and from Finnish Österbotten and the Åland Islands. An increased emigration from the south coast of Norway can also be observed because of the conversion of shipping from sail to steam. This change became even more pronounced in the beginning of the twentieth century. (Compare section on emigration from Agder, pp. 101–103.)The combination of hard times in North America, 'The Panic of 1893', and increasing industrialization in the Nordic countries during the later 1890's was reflected in emigration statistics. The strong flow of emigrants was checked. Re-emigration increased sharply, and in Sweden in 1894 it was almost as large as emigration that year.

The improved economic climate in North America in the beginning of the 1900's once again stimulated emigration. The emigration pattern of the Nordic countries, shown on the map for 1900–04, indicates a strong flow from Sörlandet and the interior mountain districts of Norway, and from traditional migration areas such as eastern Iceland and western Sweden. From northern Sweden the stream increased steadily, while emigration from Finland culminated in this period. (Denmark remains blank due to the lack of statistical data.)

After the turn of the century there was a change in the character of emigration. Many emigrants intended to work in America for only a few years before returning home with their savings. In addition, the flow of emigrants to Canada increased. Improved communications, especially the rapid, safer, and more comfortable transatlantic crossing, had by now made migration easier in both directions. There was, however, a growing reaction against emi-

15 Written communication from Helgi Skúli Kjartansson (1985).

gration expressed primarily within government circles, by military authorities, and by employers. Measures to check emigration were introduced, and national associations were formed in several Nordic countries to oppose emigration. (Compare pp. 121–26.)

During the years prior to World War I the flow of emigrants gradually decreased and ceased almost completely during the war. Thereafter until the Great Depression the rate was generally low, but with some exceptions, such as the sharp rise in 1923, caused by a recession in the iron industry, during which many persons left the iron-producing districts. The gap in industrial development between northern Europe and the USA increasingly narrowed, making emigration a less attractive alternative. After the war attempts were made in the U.S. to limit immigration, leading to the establishment of national quotas in 1921 and 1924.

The Quota Act of 1921 limited the yearly number of emigrants from a specific country to 3 percent of the number from that country who lived in the USA in 1910. In 1924 the quota was reduced to 2 percent and based upon the 1890 census. After 1929 the quota was reduced further.

It has been maintained that the quota laws were not significant, because emigration as a mass phenomenon already was in its final phase. Actual emigration from Sweden during the fiscal year (July 1–June 30), which was used by the American immigration authorities, has been investigated and compared with the annual quotas permitted. This study shows that during the 1920's the quotas were used maximally with the exception of 1921–1922 and 1930–1931. Over a couple of years the number of immigrants reached 100 per cent of the number allowed. For the remainder of the ten-year period the quotas were filled to within a few percent of the total, which may be explained by the fact that the shipping companies needed a safety margin for the indirect immigration of Swedes via Canada. If the quota was exceeded, the shipping companies were required to transport the rejected immigrant to his port of departure and, in addition, pay a fine of 200 dollars for each person in excess of the maximum.[16]

Distribution According to Countries

The vast majority, approximately 95 percent, of transoceanic emigrants from the Nordic countries went to the USA. For Sweden

16 M. Höjfors Hong 1986, 108–110.

this proportion was somewhat higher, while for Denmark it was significantly lower, as emigration from that country was dispersed more to Canada, South America, and Australia. In the beginning the USA was the dominant goal of Finnish emigration, but after the Quota Acts were introduced, the majority went to Canada and Australia. Norwegian emigration was largely directed to the USA and Canada, while Iceland had quite another pattern, with the bulk of its emigration going to Canada. (See table 5.)

For Finland and Iceland the statistics are not quite clear concerning the distribution between the USA and Canada. The proportion of Finnish emigrants in Canada increased towards the end of the emigration period, and the information in table 5 has been estimated on the basis of the available statistics.

Of the Norwegian emigrants in 1910 and 1920, approximately 4,000 lived in Australia and New Zealand, while about 2,000 settled in South Africa and nearly as many in South and Central America. Furthermore, the increased Finnish emigration to Australia meant that during the period 1924–30 no less than 3 percent of all Finnish emigration went to that continent. Before World War I there were also about 1,500 Finnish emigrants in South Africa.[17]

In 1867 *Canada* received dominion status within the British Commonwealth. A plan was devised for the settlement of the Canadian West, and the government started to actively promote immigration. Initially, however, these plans had no significant effects in the Nordic countries.

The first Nordic emigrants who arrived in Canada in substantial

Table 5. Overseas Emigration from the Nordic Countries According to Destination, 1871–1925, Finland 1901–1923. Distribution in percent.

Destination	Denmark	Finland	Iceland	Norway	Sweden
United States	87.9	93.0	15.0	95.6	97.6
Canada	5.4	6.2	84.8	3.8	1.2
Latin America	3.8	0.3	0.2	–	0.6
Australia	2.2	0.1	–	0.4	–
Africa	0.5	} 0.4	–	0.2	0.6
Asia	0.2		–	–	–
	100.0	100.0	100.0	100.0	100.0

Sources: A. Jensen 1931, 299, table 107; O. Koivukangas 1974, 58–59; R. Kero (1985); H.S. Kjartansson (1985).

17 I. Semmingsen 1950, 292; O. Koivukangas 1974, 59; written communication from Reino Kero (1985).

numbers were the Icelanders during the latter part of the 1870's. Immigration from the other Nordic countries to Canada became more intense during the 1890's, when a significant part of this migration occurred via the USA. While the Danish, Norwegian, and Swedish immigration was spread over the provinces of Saskatchewan, Alberta, and British Columbia, the Finnish immigrants were concentrated in Ontario, and the Icelanders in Manitoba. (Compare the maps in figure 24.)

Finns, Norwegians, and Swedes often took jobs as railway workers and construction workers in Canada. In British Columbia they worked in the forests and mines. Many worked for short periods and then returned to their homelands with their savings. During the twentieth century the Nordic, and especially the Norwegian and Swedish, emigration to Canada frequently took the form of temporary labor migration.[18]

There were some isolated episodes of emigration from the Nordic countries to Latin America, especially to Brazil and Argentina, with Denmark having the largest proportion of emigrants to that part of the world. Significant emigration also took place from the Nordic countries to Australia from the 1850's onwards, although it appears small according to the officially reported statistics.

The emigration to *Brazil and Argentina* reached its peak during the 1890's. This was not least related to the rapid expansion in the export of Brazilian agricultural products and the intensive cultivation of coffee, together with the repeal of slavery in 1888. In the Nordic countries, emigrant agents received support from the Brazilian authorities in distributing propaganda. From time to time free travel or generous contibutions to travel expenses were offered, which attracted emigrants with large families who otherwise would not have had the means to emigrate. This explains why the emigration to South America was characterized by a larger proportion of families than the emigration to North America in the same period.

From Denmark 14,065 emigrants to South America were registered between the years 1869–1924, 70 to 80 percent of whom landed in Argentina. Concentrated Danish settlements were located in the provinces of Buenos Aires and Mendoza.

Until 1906 Finnish emigrants to Latin America were few and scattered. At the beginning of the century plans were made in

18 H. Runblom 1977, 213–228.

Finland for a Finnish colony in southern Argentina, and in 1906 a group of intellectuals established 'Colonia Finlandesa' in the province of Misiones in Argentina. This Finnish emigration can be seen as a statement of discontent with the Russian regime in Finland and its policy of russification.

The first Swedish emigration to Latin America went mainly to Brazil and was distributed between three different periods: during the year of famine 1868–69, during the winter of 1890–91, and from 1909–11. An important element in the emigration of 1890–91 from Sundsvall and Stockholm was discontent among various labor groups. The emigration from Kiruna in northern Sweden 1909–11 had a clear connection with the nationwide general strike in 1909. From Iceland only thirty to fòrty emigrants went to South America, where they settled in Brazil.

A characteristic in Nordic emigration to Latin America was that the migrants came from only a few areas and from cities. In many cases these people had recently moved into the cities from the countryside before they left their home countries. Copenhagen was the place of residence for half of the Danish emigrants, whereas the Swedes bound for Brazil came primarily from three cities: Stockholm, Sundsvall, and Kiruna. Most Finnish emigrants in 1906 were from Helsinki, Turku, Vaasa, and Kokkola.

In Brazil and Argentina the majority of the Nordic immigrants found themselves in miserable circumstances. Their situation was characterized by material want and cultural dissolution, and the death rate was very high. Many considered themselves to have been deceived by Brazilian propaganda. The evacuation and transportation home of hundreds of Swedes in 1912 by the Swedish government can be seen as an indication of the difficulties faced by Nordic emigrants in Latin America.[19]

Emigration from the Nordic countries to *Australia* has been significantly greater than the official statistics reveal. Least documented are the movements which took place during the first period of emigration, when many arrived having first been in America or made their way to Australia without having registered as emigrants. Rumors of Australian gold in 1851 enticed many Nordic emigrants to give up their search in California and to seek their fortunes in Australia. In addition a small group came directly from the Nordic

19 K. Stenbeck 1973; H. Runblom 1976, 301–310; K. Hvidt 1971, 399–407; written communication from Reino Kero and Helgi Skúli Kjartansson (1985).

countries. Approximately 5,000 Nordic emigrants are estimated to have arrived during the 1850's and 1860's, with the gold fields of Victoria as their prime destination. Jumping ship was a common way of getting to Australia, to the great irritation of the shippers. During the ten-year period from 1882 to 1891, for example, no fewer than 1,421 Swedish seamen, most of whom were members of the crews of British ships, deserted in this way.

Some emigrants returned to their native countries, while others participated in the 'from mines to soil' movement and found their livelihood in agriculture. A great wave of Nordic emigration occurred from 1870 to 1914, periodically stimulated by 'assisted passage' from the Australian authorities. As earlier, the male dominance was great. The largest element of family emigration was among the Danes and the Finns. Until 1940 the Danes were the largest Nordic group, while the Swedes made up the second largest. Since the Second World War Australia has been a common transoceanic destination of Nordic emigration, rising sharply in certain years. In this movement the Finns predominated even over the Danes. (See diagram, figure 10.)[20]

Total Migration Pattern

Nordic transoceanic migration must be seen as part of the total migration pattern, which also includes domestic moves over short and long distances, labor migrations, migration between neighboring Nordic countries and western Europe, and moves between the city and the country. Emigration went hand in hand with other long-distance migration as well as the migration to the cities. They were aspects of the same phenomenon, that is, a rupture with the older agricultural society. According to migration traditions in the different areas, emigration could be a great proportion of the total out-migration, while in others it constituted only an insignificant part. In Finnish Ostrobothnia, for example, which was the area with the highest emigration intensity in Finland, external migration during several decades constituted half of the total moves from that county. Similarly, in the fjord and mountain regions of Norway, where emigration was especially large, it constituted about two-thirds of the surplus out-migration. In Denmark, on the other hand, with its lower rate of emigration, the outflow to overseas areas was

20 O. Koivukangas 1974, 1975, 182–194; U. Beijbom 1983, 263–269.

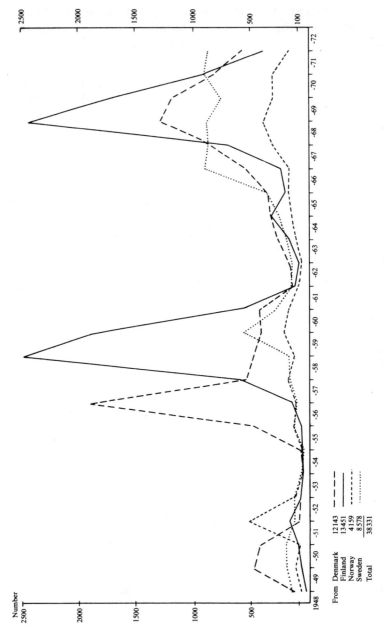

Figure 10. Emigrants to Australia from Denmark, Finland, Norway and Sweden, 1949–1971.
Sources: *Consolidated Statistics*, No. 5, Canberra 1971, table 22. *Australian Immigration*, Vol. 3, No. 25, September 1972, table 12. The figure is from O. Koivukangas 1975, 19.

a substantially smaller proportion of the total migration. Periodically the country's emigration reached only a total equal to that of the net in-migration to the city of Copenhagen.[21]

The major characteristics of the earlier migration pattern within the Nordic countries (see chapter 2) remained the same, even after the coming of mass emigration after the mid-1800's. Local short-distance moves in the countryside had approximately the same extent and the same directions as earlier. Similarly, a large part of the labor migrations followed traditional paths. What did change, however, was the intensity, as increased industrial activity with larger places of employment attracted more labor. Extensive railroad construction was going on in many areas, much labor gravitated to the ship-building industry, particularly in Norway, and large groups of migrant laborers were drawn to the expanding lumber and sawmill industry along the Swedish coast of Norrland. Generally speaking, a considerable flow of population also made its way north within Norway and Sweden, and westward in Denmark (the cultivation of the Jutland heaths) in pace with new settlement in these areas. In Norway this movement largely occurred along the coast. The northernmost part of Scandinavia (*Nordkalotten*) was at that time also the object of a significant labor migration and in-migration. The traditional Arctic fishing season in the spring attracted many people, as did the Norwegian mining industry in Kåfjord and in other parts of Norwegian Finnmark, where a large part of the labor force was Finnish-speaking. In the year 1875 the Finnish-born population in this northern part of Norway consisted of 2,700 persons. In-migration to this area declined, however, when the employment situation in the mining industry worsened. Some of the in-migrants turned to agriculture and fishing in north Norway, but, as previously mentioned, many set out for the mining fields of Michigan.[22]

Regarding intra-Nordic migration, one can discern a pattern in which the migration surpluses went southwest and west. One reason was that Denmark and Norway were industrialized before Sweden, which, in turn, was affected by industrialization earlier and more thoroughly than Finland. An extensive movement occurred between the southern Swedish areas and Denmark and Germany, with migration surpluses for the latter two countries. Likewise, the net

21 I. Semmingsen 1950, 220–221; K. Hvidt 1971, 495; H. Wester 1977, 76.
22 E. Niemi 1978, 59–60; H. Try 1979, 65–66; written communication from Steffen E. Jørgensen (1985).

migration between Sweden and Norway was to the advantage of Norway, while the migration surplus from Finland favored Sweden. Especially during the 1860's and the 1870's, in-migration from some of the western Swedish provinces to Norway was high due to the attraction of the sawmills, factories, and construction work there, mainly in the Christiania (Oslo) area. In 1865 there were 15,000 Swedish-born residents in Norway, and by 1870 their numbers had increased to 31,000.[23]

From the middle of the nineteenth century there was a substantial increase in the population of the cities. The transformation of an agrarian society to an industrial and urban one, and the flow of the rural population into the cities, constituted the greatest social and demographic changes during this time. The growth of the cities depended, above all, upon the growing in-migration from the countryside. This in-migration had been high earlier, as seen in relation to the total number of inhabitants in the cities. In most cases, however, the cities had not increased their resident population significantly, since guild regulations forced most in-migrants to return to the country and mortality was especially high in the cities. A decrease in the death rate, coupled with the introduction of laws granting economic freedom, which enabled a greater number of in-migrants to stay, earn a living, build families, and reproduce in the cities, led to a continuing growth of the urban population. In absolute numbers the in-migration, furthermore, increased rapidly during the latter part of the the nineteenth century and the beginning of the twentieth century. The burgeoning urbanization in the Nordic countries can be seen in table 4, page 39.

Emigration from Cities and Countryside

Emigration is commonly looked upon as a rural phenomenon, where people from the countryside sought a new existence in America or some other transoceanic country. This picture is largely correct. In the Nordic countries the major part of the emigrants came from the countryside, because most of the people lived in rural areas at that time. That can also be seen on the map (figure 11), which shows the rural and urban distribution of the emigrants during the peak decade of each respective country. The map also gives an idea of the distribution of the total number of migrants in the various

23 H. Try 1979, 65–66.

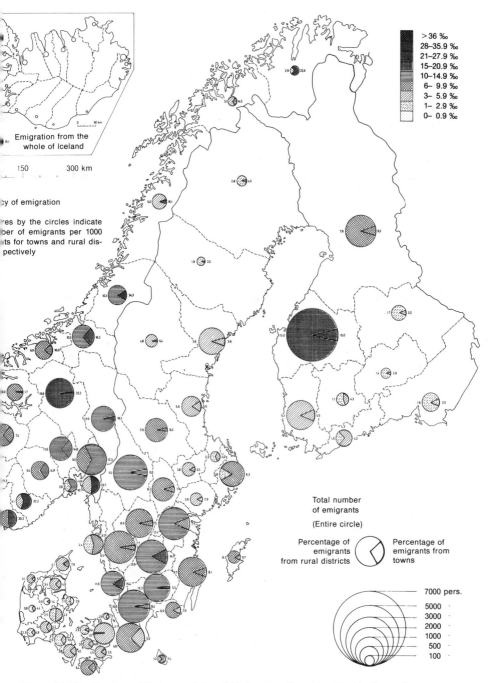

Legend (upper left inset):

> 36 ‰
28–35.9 ‰
21–27.9 ‰
15–20.9 ‰
10–14.9 ‰
6– 9.9 ‰
3– 5.9 ‰
1– 2.9 ‰
0– 0.9 ‰

Emigration from the
whole of Iceland

150   300 km

cy of emigration

res by the circles indicate
ber of emigrants per 1000
ts for towns and rural dis-
pectively

Total number
of emigrants

(Entire circle)

Percentage of
emigrants
from rural districts

Percentage of
emigrants from
towns

7000 pers.

5000
3000
2000
1000
500
100

Figure 11. Distribution of Urban and Rural Emigration from the Nordic Countries during Peak Decades. For Denmark, Iceland, Norway and Sweden, 1880–1889; for Finland, 1900–1909.

Source: *Nordic Emigration Atlas* (*Nordisk Emigrationsatlas*), eds. H. Norman & H. Runblom 1980.

areas; the great volume from Vaasa County in western Finland should be especially noted.

If emigration on the other hand is seen in relation to the size of the population in the countryside and in the cities, the picture is different. Generally speaking, the cities had the most intensive emigration in relation to the size of their populations. The rates of emigration from the cities were proportionately higher than from the countryside during the peak decades in all countries except Sweden. (See table 6.) When calculated on the basis of the period of mass emigration as a whole, Sweden also had a relatively greater rate of urban emigration. Because Denmark was urbanized earlier than the other countries, the cities' proportion of the total emigration is especially large (41 percent). Part of the high rate of urban emigration can also be attributed to the fact that large rural parishes belonged to the provincial Danish market centers. In Denmark some of the rural emigrants thus were registered as urban emigrants, because they were recorded as leaving the city where their passports were issued.[24]

It is important to understand the interplay between the country and the city, which was also revealed in migration behavior. As a rule the cities were centers of trade and crafts for their environs, as well as of administration and education. The people in the surrounding countryside made regular visits to town in connection with fairs, market days, and a number of other errands. Servant girls, laborers, and people of various occupations moved in for employment in the households and businesses of the city dwellers; many apprentices

Table 6. Emigration to North America from Denmark, Iceland, Norway, and Sweden 1880–89 and from Finland, 1900–09. The Average Yearly Emigration (N) and the Emigration per Thousand Inhabitants (‰) from the Cities and the Rural Areas together with the Cities' Portion of the Total Emigration to North America (%).

	Cities		Rural areas		Cities' portion of the total emigration
	N	‰	N	‰	%
Denmark	2,589	4.6	3,789	2.7	41
Finland	2,026	5.8	13,078	4.4	13
Iceland	78	13.1	494	7.2	14
Norway	6,032	17.1	13,529	8.4	31
Sweden	5,258	6.9	29,849	7.1	15

Source: *Nordic Emigration Atlas, Texts and Commentaries, (Nordisk Emigrationsatlas. Texter och kommentarer)*, eds. H. Norman & H. Runblom 1980, 23.

24 Written communication from Steffen E. Jørgensen (1985).

and journeymen were attracted to crafts. These highly mobile groups stayed a while, returned, or moved on to some other city. One can say that an organic bond existed between the city and the country. Thus, too great a distinction should not be made between the urban and rural areas as far as emigration is concerned. Chance many times determined whether the emigrant happened to be registered in one place or the other when leaving the country. That is also illustrated by the fact that, of the persons who emigrated from the cities and were themselves in-migrants, the majority came from areas where the emigration was intensive.

The debate concerning rural versus urban emigration is based upon an unclear premise, since such a large part of those who emigrated from the cities were in fact people from the countryside who had recently moved into the city and who emigrated after a short time there. Emigration by stages has been the topic of a lively scholarly debate. One question in this context is, of course, how long one should have lived in the city to be considered a city dweller. In some Swedish studies those who lived in the city five years or more have been included. Nearly half of those who emigrated from Stockholm and Halmstad were in-migrants who had lived there less than five years. A similar pattern has been found in Denmark. In Norway more than half of those who left the country via Bergen had earlier moved into the city from the countryside. In Christiania (Oslo) the same was true of more than two-thirds during the years 1870–1900.

Emigration by stages applied particularly to women, who as a rule had a higher rate of migration to the cities than men, because of the demand there for household employees. In total numbers women also had higher emigration rates from the cities than men; during the years 1881–1910, 114 women left Sweden for each 100 men. While men usually departed for America directly from rural areas, women who made the same move more often did so after a sojourn in a city milieu in their native country.[25]

Competing Migration Goals

The extent of emigration varied a great deal from one region to the other, as the maps of the transoceanic emigration from the Nordic

25 I. Semmingsen 1950, 233–236; F. Nilsson 1970, 61–87; K. Hvidt 1971, 105–123; H. Norman 1974, 71–73, 144; B. Kronborg and T. Nilsson 1975, 139–140.

countries show. Local variation becomes even more evident when emigration is studied on the parish level.

In many areas emigration remained high during the entire period of emigration, while others had low levels throughout. That pattern was to a great extent determined by the competing migration goals, which differed in character from area to area. Emigration was usually limited in the environs of larger expanding cities. The so-called urban influence field of these cities meant that movers were attracted there. It was natural for migrants to direct their attention to places with industrial, commercial, and other central functions, with which contacts had been long since developed. That inward movement is most notable in the proximity of the capital cities, and emigration was consequently low around Copenhagen, Christiania (Oslo), Stockholm, Helsinki, and St. Petersburg (Leningrad). This was not the case in peripheral areas far from the urbanized and industrialized centers. If for some reason these areas had an early and vigorous emigration, contacts and knowledge about conditions in America grew and determined the direction of their migrations. Here an emigrant tradition was maintained, so that America became a natural alternative as a destination.[26]

The migration traditions of an area, whether directed towards destinations in the home country, a neighboring country, or America, were thus of the greatest importance for the potential migrants' choice between rival migration goals. This can be illustrated by the most frequent migration destinations for two Swedish parishes, Gräsmark in Värmland County and Revsund in Jämtland County. Both counties border on Norway and are consequently situated a long way from Stockholm and other large cities. In Värmland the population growth was large, and the opportunities for making a living limited, which meant that people often sought work outside the county. In certain communities, as in Gräsmark, a strong tradition of labor migrations or of moving northward to the growing lumber and sawmill industry in Norrland had been established. Migration from this parish during the 1860's and the 1870's to locations outside of the county had four major destinations. Most frequently they went to Norrland's lumbering and sawmill industry (43 percent), but a large part also sought their way across the Atlantic to North America (28 percent). It is also clear that Gräsmark's location in western Sweden meant that movements were

26 E. De Geer 1977, 89–115; H. Norman 1976, 153–164.

more common over the border to Norway and the Christiania area (6 percent) than to the Lake Mälaren Valley and Stockholm (3 percent). In Revsund the population grew rapidly, especially from the 1870's onwards, mostly due to the surplus of in-migrants. A number of sawmills were established there, and Jämtland's forests provided the raw materials for the burgeoning sawmill industry in the Sundsvall area on the coast. During this period of economic prosperity in the forest and timber industry, a significant part of the labor moved to the area from Värmland, from which both the traditions within lumbering and the migration traditions were transferred to Jämtland. When the demand for labor declined after the 1880's, one result was a significant out-migration, which to a great extent consisted of workers, farmers and tenants. Within that context it is striking that the out-migration from Revsund during the 1890's to destinations outside of Jämtland County coincides to such a great extent with corresponding moves from Gräsmark a few decades earlier. Figure 12 shows that the patterns are very similar. Norrland's lumber industry exerted a very strong attraction (about 40 percent), while a significant emigration to America comprised the second most important alternative (20 percent). Norway did not play as important a role as a migration goal for Revsund as it did for Gräsmark. Finally, the figures were about the same for migration to the capital city, Stockholm, and to surrounding counties in the Mälar Valley from these two peripheral parishes. Only 3 to 4 percent went to destinations there.[27]

From the southeastern parts of Finland an example of an entirely different picture of migration can be found in which the dependency upon St. Petersburg, capital of czarist Russia, was very great. The city's position within the hierarchy of metropolises was strengthened significantly during the nineteenth century and, by northern European standards, it became a very dominant urban center. It attracted trade and in-migration from expanding environs, including not only southeastern and southern Finland, but also the areas along the western coast of Finland. During the first part of the nineteenth century southern Finland could be divided into a 'Stockholm Finland' and a 'St. Petersburg Finland', as far as urban influence was concerned. By the middle of the nineteenth century, however, the Russian capital's area of influence and dominance had expanded sharply at the expense of Stockholm. In addition, Finnish cities,

27 A. Norberg 1980, 38–46; M. Rolén 1979, 210–217.

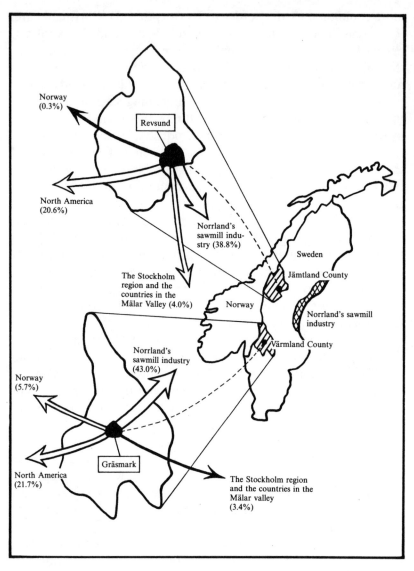

Figure 12. Major Directions of the Migration from Gräsmark Parish (Värmland County) 1860–1879 and from Revsund Parish (Jämtland County) 1890–1894 to Destinations outside the Counties.
Sources: A. Norberg 1980, 41–46; M. Rolén 1979, 210–217.

such as Viipuri, Helsinki, and Turku, were overshadowed by St. Petersburg. By about 1890 the development had gone so far that there were as many Finns in St. Petersburg as in Turku and Helsinki. Stage migration often occurred by which the Finnish cities first attracted from their own field of influence migrants who later left for St. Petersburg. The process is outlined in the diagram in figure 13, which shows St. Petersburg's field of influence overshadowing the cities in southern and southeastern Finland. During the 1890's, however, this trend was broken. At that time the Grand Duchy's own capital, Helsinki, gained importance and grew rapidly.[28]

During the second part of the nineteenth century a shift also occurred in the dominance of the competing migration destination goals in Finland, which can be noted in the flow of migration in the western part of the country. The Finnish pattern of migration thus illustrates periods of constancy as well as periods of change. That change can be seen clearly in Vaasa County, located along the country's west coast. As the Swedish sawmill industry on the other side of the Gulf of Bothnia expanded, the population in Vaasa County increased its migration to the Swedish side to seek work there instead of in St. Petersburg. This change came in the early 1870's, while the next came during the 1880's. At that time interest in America grew, not least through the contacts that existed with the Swedish side. When the sawmill industry's rise had culminated

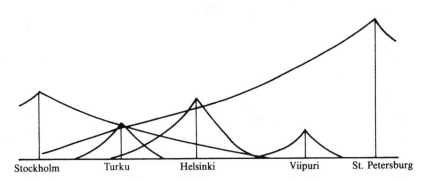

Figure 13. The Influence-fields on Migrants of Some Cities in Southern Finland during the Middle of the Nineteenth Century. Schematic Outline.
Sources: E. De Geer 1977, 94–95; M. Engman 1983, 258–265.

28 M. Engman 1983, 258–265, 388–393.

and a low in the business cycle came in the beginning of the 1890's, emigration to America increased sharply from Vaasa County. The development is illustrated in the diagram in figure 14, where the migration to St. Petersburg, the migration to Sweden, and the migration to America supercede one another in repeated waves.[29]

Demographic and Social Composition

All demographic strata and all social classes were represented among the millions of emigrants who journeyed to the transoceanic areas. Some categories, however, were more common than others, and certain age groups were more apt to migrate. The conditions which led to emigration also varied in both the sending and receiving countries during the long emigration epoch, circumstances which contributed to the changing trends in the demographic and social composition of the emigrants.

During the *very first period* before the beginning of group emigration, it seems to have been mostly private individuals who left. Typically, men comprised the majority, and only few emigrants had

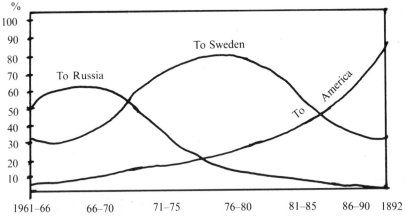

Figure 14. Migration to Russia, Sweden and America (transoceanic countries) from Vaasa County, Finland, 1861–1892. A Schematic Diagram of the Total Migration to Destinations outside Finland.
Source: E. De Geer & H. Wester 1975, 51.

29 E. De Geer and H. Wester 1975, 35–51; L.-G. Tedebrand 1972, 175–181.

their origins in the agrarian population. Many were merchants and craftsmen, and some officers and diplomats. Often they left, not with the intention of emigrating, but rather for specific jobs. The Norwegian emigration, however, started with family groups from the very beginning.

The emigration which took place during the 1840's and the 1850's was characterized by a high representation of entire families and households. They often moved in unified groups and in the company of other families. In Sweden, for example, during the years 1841–50, more than two-thirds of the emigration consisted of families. Later this pattern was broken, especially *when emigration had gained the character of mass migration* and more and more people had relatives and acquaintances in America. In the 1890's family emigration had declined to one-third. The emigrants were now mostly young adults, primarily unmarried men and women under 25 years of age. This general tendency for the composition of emigration to shift from families to individuals appears to have been largely the same for Norway, Sweden, and Denmark.[30]

In Finland emigration of families increased until the 1890's, when mass emigration began in that country. This indicates a somewhat consistent pattern, where the shift from family emigration to individual emigration depended on how old or new the emigration phenomenon was in each country. It implies that the early phase of each country's emigration had a strong element of family emigration. The emigration from Iceland, however, had a different pattern with a large proportion of families during the entire emigration period.[31]

Sources do not always allow distinctions to be made between family or individual emigration. In many cases a married man emigrated first, followed after several years by his wife and children. In other cases the man might return and take his family with him back to America. Sometimes the husband and some of the children traveled first and the rest of the family later. A closer study of persons registered as individual emigrants also shows that many of them were relatives and traveled on the same boat or rejoined one another in America.

The development from family emigration to individual emi-

---

30 For Sweden, see N.W. Olsson 1967; A. Friman 1974, 18–35; S. Carlsson 1976, 130–132. For Norway, I. Semmingsen 1941; A. Svalestuen 1971, 44. For Denmark, K. Hvidt 1971, 192–199.
31 A. Svalestuen 1971, 44–45; R. Kero 1974, 119–130; J.H. Kristinsson 1983, tables 2–7.

gration, as revealed in the migration statistics, thus fails to provide a complete picture of the role of the family in the emigration process. Emigration often occurred within the family framework at different times and from different places, especially during the later part of the emigration period. Many young emigrants with departure certificates from cities traveled westward and there joined emigrating family members who had left the countryside directly. When this 'gradual family emigration' is taken into consideration, the bonds of family and kin stand out as important throughout the entire emigration era.[32]

The following example of a family from Karlskoga parish in Bergslagen, Sweden, who emigrated around 1880, illustrates how the emigration process could develop. (See table 7.)

After the death of Peter Peterson, the eldest son, Karl, took over the farm. Of the other brothers and sisters who reached adult age, all emigrated to America, as did their mother. First to leave was the fourth son Olof Viktor, who went via Gothenburg to America in the spring of 1879 at the age of 21. His younger sister Maria Ulrika, only 12 years old, followed him. Their destination was Oskaloosa, Iowa. In April the following year the fifth son, Anders Conrad, 19 years old, left for the same place, and in May the married daughter Emma Lovisa, together with her husband and their three small children, also emigrated to Oskaloosa. In spring 1881 the second oldest son Erik Johan was the next on the list to go to America, after a seasonal labor migration to Söderhamn in the sawmill area along the coast of the Gulf of Bothnia. In the fall of the same year, finally, the widow Maria Jacobsdotter went across the ocean together with two remaining children, the daughter Amanda Karolina and the son Per Gustaf, who earlier had migrated to Björskog, Västmanland County, for railroad work. In addition three of Karl's four children emigrated to America at a later date.

In the new country most of the family kept together. They settled in a coal-mining area in the vicinity of Oscaloosa, Iowa. The exceptions were Erik Johan, who became a farmer in Minnesota and Per Gustaf, who was described by his relatives as a 'drifter', and did not marry or settle down.

As a rule, men have had a higher rate of emigration than women in the Nordic countries. Certain differences in the pattern can be found, however. In Finland male emigrants predominated much

32 H. Norman and H. Runblom 1985, 45.

Table 7. Birth Dates and Emigration Patterns of the Family of Peter Peterson, Brickegården, Karlskoga Parish, Örebro County, Sweden.

Name	Date of birth Yr Mo Da	Date of death Yr Mo Da	Migration in Sweden	Special remarks	Emigration to America Date Age Destination
Peter Peterson part owner of a smelting house, blast-furnace master	1817 09 10	1869 12 31			
Maria Jacobsdotter wife	1824 05 30			took over the farm	1881 08 24 57 Oscaloosa, Iowa
s. Karl	1844 11 17				
s. Erik Johan	1846 10 02		to Söderhamn 1880	seasonal labor certificate	1881 05 20 35 Round Lake, Minnesota
d. Maria Ulla	1849 06 27	1853 09 29			
s. Per Gustaf	1852 05 30		to Björskog 1847	railway worker	1881 09 09 29 Never settled down
d. Emma Lovisa*)	1855 06 08			emigr. with family (below)	1880 05 07 25 Oscaloosa, Iowa
s. Olof Viktor	1858 07 29		to Gothenburg 1879		1879 04 25 21 Oscaloosa, Iowa
s. Anders Conrad	1861 03 30				1880 04 11 19 Oscaloosa, Iowa
d. Amanda Karolina	1863 09 20				1881 08 24 18 Oscaloosa, Iowa
d. Maria Ulrika	1867 04 26				1879 04 18 12 Oscaloosa, Iowa
August Emil Sjögren crofter	1839 04 23				1880 05 07 41 Oscaloosa, Iowa
Emma Lovisa*) Pettersdotter, wife	1855 06 08				1880 05 07 25 Oscaloosa, Iowa
d. Emma Augusta	1873 09 28				1880 05 07 7 Oscaloosa, Iowa
s. Karl August	1877 03 28				1880 05 07 3 Oscaloosa, Iowa
d. Elin Lovisa	1880 02 16				1880 05 07 0 Oscaloosa, Iowa

Sources: Church records, Karlskoga parish. Written communication from Kjell Nordqvist, Karlskoga Regional Archive (1986).

more than in the other countries. In Sweden the difference between the sexes was smallest, and during the middle of the 1890's there were in fact more female than male emigrants. Iceland deviates notably from the other countries. In the entire body of emigrants, women slightly exceeded men (7,230 women as opposed to 7,038 men). That the female element among the emigrants was so comparatively great in Iceland, appears to have had a connection with the desire of the authorities to encourage emigration in order to avoid high expense for the care of the poor. (See p. 41.) From the start of emigration up to the 1890's the general trend was otherwise towards an increasing proportion of women in Denmark and Sweden, and, above all, in Finland, where women initially made up only 20 percent of the emigrants. In Norway, however, the development was the opposite. Contrary to the pattern in most other Nordic countries, the proportion of male emigrants increased in Norway in relation to the female. This Norwegian pattern is also confirmed in a study of Ullensaker parish, situated in the Oslo region, northeast of the capital. The emigration from this area became more male-dominated during the later part of the emigration period.[33] (See the diagram in figure 15.)

It was perhaps natural that female emigrants were fewer than male during the very first emigration period, a time when emigration was a hazardous, physically daring enterprise. When emigration was more comprehensive and transportation better, other factors influenced the sex composition.

Men and women were not equally sensitive to fluctuations in the American economy. Male emigrants often worked within branches that quickly responded to variations in the business cycles, such as building, railway work, and other construction work. Women, on the other hand, had employment which was more independent of economic variations. Many sought household work, that is, became housemaids, in the large American cities. Therefore, the proportion of men among the emigrants grew with the upswings in the economy and decreased during the recessions, while the women did not respond in the same way. Contributing to the difference in the sex composition was also the fact that women many times followed their husbands to America several years after their men had emigrated. One explanation for the high percentage of men among the early emigrants from Finland may be that they largely came from

33 A. Svalestuen 1971, 40–41; E. Koren 1976; J.H. Kristinsson 1983, table 7.

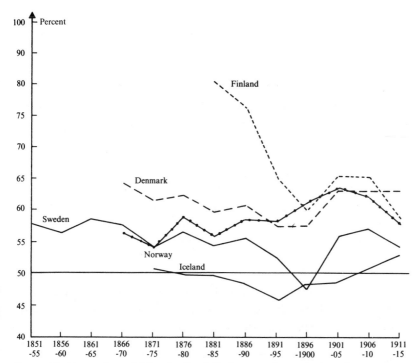

Figure 15. Proportion of Men in Total Emigration from the Nordic Countries. Percent.
Sources: A. Svalestuen 1971, 40; J.H. Kristinsson 1983, table 2–7.

the countryside, while the emigrants from Denmark, Norway, and Sweden to a greater extent came from the cities. This fact must have influenced the sex proportions among the emigrants as a whole, as it was the women who outweighed the men among the urban emigrants. While two-thirds of the Finnish emigrants were men, men made up only half of the emigrants from the Finnish cities.[34]

A significantly greater number of emigrants during the emigration epoch came from the agricultural sphere than from other parts of the economy. If the numbers are viewed in relation to the distribution of the population among various branches of the economy, the picture, however, becomes a different one. In analogy to the situation whereby the cities had a larger proportion of emigrants in relation to their population than the rural areas, a number of local studies have shown that those with non-agricultural livelihoods also had a higher

34 K. Virtanen 1979, 222.

89

rate of emigration than those with agricultural ones. A clear tendency also emerges over time; the number of emigrants from industry, trade, and communications increased as the emigration period progressed. This development is only natural considering the increased industrialization and urbanization in the Nordic countries. Developments in America also played an important role. For the emigrants arriving during the early part of the emigration epoch, there was still an abundance of unoccupied land in the Midwest, where most of the Nordic emigrants made their way in order to acquire land. Those who arrived later did not have the same opportunities and therefore came to America in order to get jobs. Often they were relatives of earlier emigrants who had already managed to acquire farms. But more and more of the later emigrants sought a living in other areas, above all in the growing industrial sector.[35]

Naturally enough, emigration was dominated by the groups who were not bound by the possession of property, a business, or a family in their homelands. Employees with relatively secure means of subsistence have also had proportionately little tendency to emigrate. As the largest number of emigrants originated in the rural sector, the largest part of the emigrants consisted of sons and daughters of farmers and tenants, as well as farm laborers and servant girls. In many cases these comprised a common category, as it was usual in the Nordic countries for youths from both well-situated and landless homes to take employment as farm hands and servant girls. Most people in this large category were unmarried, and their prospects within the agrarian society were dim; it was difficult to divide the farms further, and there was a limit to how many new areas could be cultivated. If there were many brothers and sisters on a farm or a leasehold, one, or at the most two, could have access to a part to cultivate. The others had to choose between trying to find work within industry or moving to a city. However, industrialization and urbanization had not developed rapidly enough to absorb all of them, and in areas where the emigration tradition was strong, many chose to emigrate instead. One category of the agrarian lower class with a low rate of emigration was the Swedish *statare*. They were nearly always married, and the greatest part of their wages was paid in kind from the farms where they worked. Several factors thus contributed to making the *statare* little inclined to emigrate. They had a certain security in this employment, even if the work

35 A. Svalestuen 1971, 48–49; R. Kero 1974, 81–90; S. Carlsson 1976, 132.

was burdensome and poorly paid, and it was hard for them to obtain enough cash for an American ticket.[36]

One occupational category significant in numbers among the emigrants was the young women who took positions as housemaids in the American cities. The development of society in the Nordic countries meant that daughters, both of farmers and of the growing rural proletariat, increasingly moved to the cities, where they supported themselves as servants among the upwardly mobile middle class. Their working and living conditions were often hard. Many of them took the opportunity to emigrate and to seek work in American urban families, where they, generally speaking, had a better work situation and better social status. This contributed to the higher proportion of women than men among the urban emigrants mentioned above.[37]

Towards the end of the emigration period larger groups of well-educated persons were included among the emigrants from the cities and industrial areas. Personal contacts in industry and business between America and the Nordic countries had then developed and became increasingly close, which led to an exchange of skilled labor in both directions. One particularly significant group was the engineers, who played an important role in the expanding industry.[38]

---

36 S. Carlsson 1976, 140–148.
37 Concerning the emigration of women, see A.-S. Kälvemark 1983, 140–174. For the situation of the female emigrants in Chicago, see U. Beijbom 1971, 119–127.
38 H. Norman 1974, 67, 269.

6. Regional Studies of Emigration from the Nordic Countries

This chapter presents a case study from each of the Nordic countries in order to illustrate various aspects of emigration and some characteristic features of the emigration pattern in each country. These studies differ from one another both in extent and character, from short articles to doctoral dissertations. The study from Denmark by Nils Peter Stilling deals with a central problem: the comparatively low emigration intensity and its relationship to the degree of urbanization as well as the restructuring of agricultural production. The Finnish investigation, conducted by Reino Kero, Auvo Kostiainen, Eero Kuparinen, and Esa Vaino, deals with largely agricultural areas and clarifies the overall movement within a region and the traditions of mobility that existed both before the period of great emigration and after it had become a mass movement. The Icelandic study which is recounted here was carried out by Junius H. Kristinsson. The conditions of deprivation under which the population lived, mainly due to the island's harsh nature, are brought to light. Furthermore, it appears that the intensive emigration to America had a demographic composition differing from that of the other Nordic countries. From Norway an investigation by Sverre Ordahl is presented which explores the implications of the conversion of shipping from sail to steam for the extent of emigration from southern Norway. For Sweden some results from Fred Nilsson's dissertation on the emigration from Stockholm will be summarized; the complex pattern of movement in a large city with its differentiated economy and structure is thus illustrated.

Frederiksborg County (*amt*), Denmark[1]

Frederiksborg County covers the northern part of the island of Själland. At the end of the nineteenth century this area was one

1 N.P. Stilling 1978.

of the most densely populated in Denmark. Land ownership was characterized by manors and large farms cultivated by their owners. Industry, chiefly the iron industry, shipbuilding, brick works, textile mills, and gunpowder factories, was concentrated in the largest city in the county, Helsingör. In other parts of the county there were also industries with large numbers of workers. The southwestern part, Hornsherred, isolated from the rest of the county by the Roskilde fjord, differed in its economic structure and was distinguished by large manors and a great number of cottagers.

The course of the emigration from Frederiksborg County is quite representative of the entire Danish emigration. It was high around 1870, but declined sharply during the years that followed, reaching new heights in the 1880's and 1890's. In general, emigrants during the early period were recruited from the agrarian milieu, but as industry expanded and the restructuring of agriculture got underway, the proportion of industrial workers and artisans increased. On the whole, the majority of emigrants were from the countryside, even if urban emigration was greater in relation to the number of city inhabitants. (Compare urban and rural patterns in figure 16.)

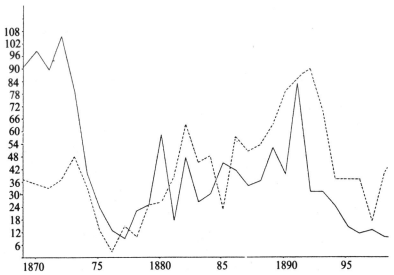

Figure 16. Emigration from Frederiksborg *Amt* 1869–1899 by Occupational and Social Groups. Number of Emigrants.
---- urban occupational and social groups, industry and handicraft
—— rural occupational and social groups, farming
Source: N.P. Stilling 1978, 116.

93

There was a strong male dominance; among adults, men outnumbered women by approximately two to one, but this dominance weakened towards the end of the period as family emigration decreased in importance. The proportion of young, unmarried women increased especially, many of them planning to marry in America, where their husbands-to-be had gone in advance.

Family emigration later slowed down. Three phases can be discerned with regard to the composition and character of the Frederiksborg emigration. Until the decline during the 1870's, it was largely families or groups that emigrated. During this first phase women traveled with their husbands and children. This emigration was primarily rural, although there was a certain element of urban artisans. Phase two occurred in the 1880's, when emigration included large groups of unestablished artisans, farm laborers, and female servants. Groups with lower social standing were drawn into the emigration stream. Phase three began in the 1890's and consisted mainly of individual emigration from all social categories. There was a large element of industrial workers and single women, especially from urban milieus. Artisans also comprised an increased proportion, since many found it difficult to compete as industrialization spread. On the whole, industrial workers did not have a high rate of emigration, as industry had the capacity to retain its labor. During the entire period the largest categories of emigrants were tenants 9 percent, servants 25 percent, artisans 19 percent, laborers 10 percent, and single women 10 percent.

Emigration intensity varied considerably between areas within Frederiksborg County and was highest in locations far away from market towns. Old traditions of mobility were decisive when people chose their form of migration. In Denmark the village inn traditionally served as a source of information in the region. Inns provided gathering places where the rural folk could gain knowledge of the world outside, and the innkeepers were often well-informed and influential persons. There are even Danish examples of innkeepers who emigrated and took their customers with them to America.

The population in Denmark grew rapidly during the nineteenth century. Within the Nordic countries only Finland's population increased more. (See pp. 35–37.) The question remains: why did Denmark have such a relatively low rate of emigration? To answer this question, references are often routinely made to the relatively high degree of urbanization and industrialization within the country.

To study this issue more closely, the development within the agrarian sector must be analyzed. Contrary to the situation in the other Nordic countries, where the areas with the best land often had little emigration, in Denmark the most fertile areas had the highest rate of emigration. This is related to the fact that the largest manors and the strongest centralization of land were found there. The above-mentioned Hornsherred provides a good example. In that area a farmhand had little hope of obtaining land of his own, since the price of land was high. Furthermore, the manors employed largely foreign labor who accepted lower wages than the domestic labor, which, in turn, regarded America as a migration alternative. The intensity of emigration must also be viewed in relation to the restructuring of agriculture. In areas where the land was less productive, there was a greater tendency to convert production from grain to animal products, which increased the demand for labor and reduced the rate of emigration.

Of course, the growth of the industrial centers and towns has been important in retaining a lower rate of emigration in Denmark. In most countries emigration has been low within the field of influence of the cities, where it was easy for the rural population in the vicinity to seek work. The proximity of the city also gave the population in surrounding areas the opportunity to sell their agricultural products there. Thus agricultural conditions have greatly influenced the size of the Danish emigration.

Toholampi Parish, Finland[2]

Toholampi parish is located in Vaasa County in the province of Ostrobothnia, Finland. At the end of the nineteenth century this very strongly agrarian parish had nearly 3,000 inhabitants. Tar production provided a supplementary source of income in this area. The farms in Toholampi were rather small, and the element of freeholders large, more than 55 percent, a figure above the average for Vaasa County. The second largest group consisted of hired servants, who made up about one quarter of the work-force. The tenant farmers comprised about one-tenth, as did the cottagers.

During parts of the nineteenth century the population increase in Toholampi was quite large, as it was in Vaasa County and in Finland as a whole. There was a drop in population growth in the 1850's and 1860's, and an especially notable setback occurred towards the

2 R. Kero 1976.

end of that period, when the Finnish rural population was very hard hit as a result of harvest failures. During the second half of the 1860's Toholampi's population decreased by 227 persons, and during the harshest year, 1868, only 51 children were born in the parish, while 252 died. When there was a large surplus of births over deaths during the 1880's, the population still stagnated because of high emigration rates.

A steady increase in the number of moves in Toholampi occurred during the years of investigation, from 720 during 1870–74 to 1,648 during 1885–89. From the second half of the nineteenth century long-distance moves also became more common than earlier, and in number they outweighed the moves to and from the parishes bordering on Toholampi. Moves to the cities also increased, especially to the closest one, Kokkola (Gamla Karleby). Viipuri (Viborg) was a very common goal for longer distance moves due to its proximity to the expanding St. Petersburg.

Toholampi's total population movement is presented in figure 17, which includes the mobility within the parish. As can be seen, intra-parish mobility made up a large portion (35–47 percent). Two social groups are notable: hired hands and female servants, who changed their places of employment and had the highest mobility in relation to their total number, and women who moved because of marriage. The latter contributed to the female domination in short-distance moves. During the years 1870 to 1879 women made 151 more moves than men within the commune, and of these moves 143 were because of marriage.

Migration goals and distances follow a clear pattern. Movements within the parish or to the neighboring parishes were strongly dominated by females (60–65 percent). Long-distance moves to other parts of Finland were rather evenly divided between the sexes. Emigration to America was strongly dominated by men. When this emigration increased during the 1880's, it replaced the moves to and from the bordering parishes and to places in other parts of Finland, for example, Viipuri. It is notable, though, that the moves within the commune at the same time increased.

During the 1880's Toholampi had the highest emigration rate of all the parishes in Österbotten. Freeholders, including their sons and daughters, comprised more than half of all emigrants. Proportionally, agricultural laborers and female servants had the highest rate of emigration, and this despite the difficulty for landless workers to buy a ticket to America. Although the proportion of children

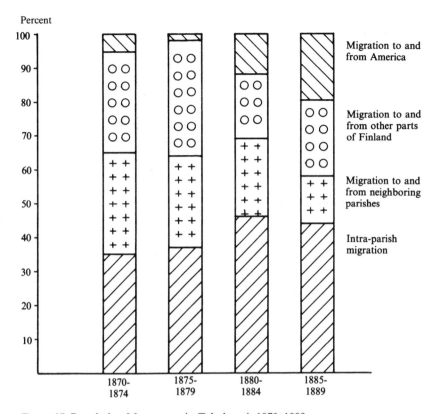

Percent

Figure 17. Population Movements in Toholampi, 1870–1889.
Source: R. Kero 1976, 18, table 3.

was not great, a surprisingly large number of married couples emigrated, and many rather newly married couples made the crossing.
Emigrants from Toholampi had different destinations in America
than most Finnish emigrants. While the majority of the Finns went
to the northern parts of Michigan, Wisconsin, and Minnesota, the
most important destination for the Toholampi emigrants was a
particular place in the eastern USA, Fitchburg, Massachusetts.

The study of Toholampi illustrates the total pattern of movement
in one locality. That picture was, on the whole, in accordance
with that for Finland as a whole. The pattern of Toholampi's

97

long-distance moves, where the St. Petersburg region (Viipuri) was important during the first phase and where America became the overwhelming alternative during the second phase, is reminiscent of the common pattern for Vaasa County, although moves to Sweden do not appear to have been as frequent for people in landlocked Toholampi. (Compare pp. 81–84.)

Vopnafjördur Parish, Iceland[3]

Vopnafjördur is a parish located in the northeastern part of Iceland. Farming, especially sheep-breeding, was the dominant livelihood there. After 1880 fishing became an increasingly important supplement for many farmers along the coast.

Vopnafjördur's population increased sharply during parts of the nineteenth century. From 1820 to 1840 it grew from 400 to 1,000 persons, that is, an increase of 150 percent. The corresponding figure for Iceland as a whole was 40 percent. The parish's large population growth depended both upon a surplus of births and a high rate of in-migration. The 1860's were a turning point, and the following decades were characterized by large fluctuations in population growth. Vopnafjördur had long been an area mainly of in-migration, but after 1870 out-migration dominated, largely because of substantial emigration. (See figure 18.) Both birth and death rates were higher than those for Iceland as a whole.

After 1873 emigration from Vopnafjördur gained momentum, as it did in other areas of Iceland. During the twenty years that followed, until 1893, no fewer than 756 emigrants were registered, a very high figure in relation to the population of the parish. As can be seen in the diagram, the extent of emigration varied sharply from year to year. It was most intensive in 1876, 1878–1879, 1887–1888, and 1893.

The Icelandic emigration has been influenced by the country's natural resources and the harsh climatic conditions. Furthermore, volcanic activity has played a dramatic role. For example, 191 persons moved into Vopnafjördur in 1875, while only 25 moved out. Most of these in-migrants were persons who had moved from homes that were destroyed in the catastrophic volcanic eruption of Dyngjyfjöll in the neighboring district. The following year, 1876, a total of 154 persons moved out of Vopnafjördur, 88 of these were

3 J. Kristinsson 1973.

Number

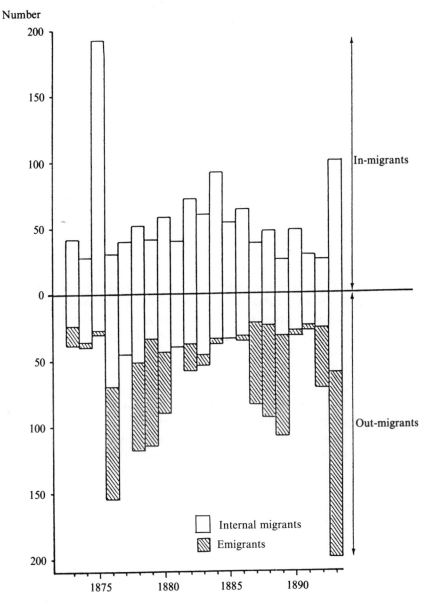

Figure 18. Migration in Vopnafjördur, 1873–1893.
Source: J. Kristinsson 1973, figure III-7, 29.

emigrants, and of these emigrants 35 had moved to Vopnafjördur after the catastrophe. In all, no fewer than 62 of those who were left homeless in the wake of the volcanic eruption emigrated from Vopnafjördur to America during the years 1876–1880, and thus triggered emigration from that part of Iceland.

Emigration from Vopnafjördur may be considered representative of emigration from the country as a whole, which differed from the prevalent pattern of Nordic emigration. The differences include age and sex distribution, as well as social composition.

The number of women who emigrated from Iceland as a whole was greater than the number of men. Such was also the case in Vopnafjördur. During the years 1873–1893, 52 percent of those leaving were women. In Nordic emigration the age group 15–30 years is commonly overrepresented in proportion to the composition of the total population and makes up as much as 50 to 60 percent of the emigrants. Among those leaving Vopnafjördur they comprised only 31 percent. On the other hand, a comparatively larger proportion of the emigrants were 31 to 35 years old, and there was also a greater number of children than is usual. Furthermore, a surprisingly large proportion was between 51 and 60. The reason is that no less than 70 percent of the emigration from Vopnafjördur may be characterized as family emigration, which largely consisted of three generations. The fact that the older generation followed provides part of the explanation for the dominance of women, because women as a rule live longer than men.

Conditions in Iceland were harsh: its natural resources were not easily utilized, and small changes in climate and other conditions made survival difficult for the growing poor population. The Icelandic authorities therefore looked favorably upon the emigration of those who could not support themselves. They even encouraged such emigration, as it was considered more economical to pay once for a ticket to America than to continually pay support. The Icelanders who had earlier emigrated to Canada reacted against this policy, and a letter was written to the authorities in Iceland which stated that if the Icelanders' good reputation was to be maintained in the receiving country, no more poor could be accepted.[4]

The study of the emigration from Vopnafjödur illustrates many of the characteristics of Iceland's emigration. The bitter reality within which the Icelandic people lived caused the composition of

4 G. Gunnlaugsson 1978, 75–150.

emigration to differ from that of the other Nordic countries. It consisted not only of predominantly young men and women; it was to a great extent the emigration of three generations, and it was partially stimulated by the authorities.

Agder District, Norway[5]

East Agder County and West Agder County lie in the southernmost part of Norway. The economy was dominated by shipping and shipbuilding. The economic fluctuations in those branches have played a decisive role in determining the extent of emigration from that part of the country. Norway's relatively high rate of emigration as early as the 1850's certainly affected Agder, but, for a thirty-year period there was remarkably little emigration. It was not until the 1880's that Agder was drawn into the intensive mass emigration. From the 1890's until World War I this district sent more people overseas in proportion to its population than any other county in Norway. The chronology of emigration was also different from the rest of Norway, as figure 19 shows. Why did its emigration develop in this way? The answer lies in the restructuring of shipping.

The thirty years from 1850 to 1880 were a golden era for sailing vessels and meant economic expansion in the cities and towns along the southern coast of Norway. Many ships were built in the districts where the shipowners lived, and the shipping companies often had shipyards both for repairs and for the construction of new vessels. For example, in the Grimstad toll district, a little area comprising three parishes with a total of 8,000 inhabitants, no less than 1,000 persons were employed within that part of the economy. It is therefore not surprising that the emigration rate was low during times of economic prosperity. These conditions changed, however, when mechanically-powered steel vessels replaced sailing ships during the 1880's. The former were more costly to construct and too expensive for small, widely dispersed shipyards in the coastal communities, and consequently many people lost their jobs.

Because the Norwegian sailing fleet had grown rapidly during the years after 1850, it had been easy for laborers to find work within the region. It was also common in these areas for youths to go to sea in their teens before they were ready to enter working life ashore.

5 S. Ordahl 1983.

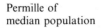

Permille of
median population

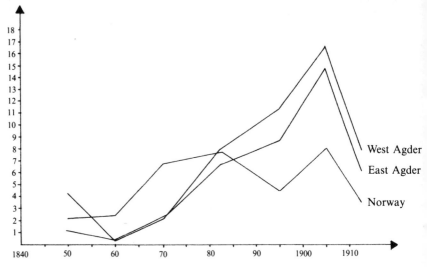

Figure 19. Emigration from East Agder, West Agder and All of Norway, 1850–1915.
Source: S. Ordahl 1983, 314.

Most men in their 20's had this experience. In Spind near Farsund
nine out of ten 19-year-olds had been to sea.

When the restructuring of economic life took place, the situation
on the labor market became more strained. The industry was concentrated in fewer and fewer localities. Certain places, such as
Flekkefjord and Kristiansand, grew, while others declined. The
transition was accompanied by a soaring emigration rate. During
the years 1860–1875 only about 350 persons annually left Agder for
America. This figure rose to 1,150 during the years 1876–1890 and
during the 1890's it reached as many as 1,625. During the period
when it achieved its maximum, that is, the first years of the twentieth
century, an average of 2,525 persons emigrated yearly. In 1906,
when the emigration peaked, nearly 3,400 persons (2.1 percent of
the population) left the district.

The small towns in East Agder were the hardest hit by the
crisis in shipping, and some places thus lost a great part of their
population. In Grimstad, which was most severely affected, the
population decreased from 3,000 to 2,400 persons. No less than a
fourth of the population, 700 persons, left the town during a ten-
year period. From Arendal, with 11,000 inhabitants, 2,000 persons

emigrated. Agriculture could at least temporarily support those who had lost their jobs, which explains why the rural areas reached their highest rate of emigration first after the turn of the century. Even for the people within that sector it became clear that they would have to leave the country for America, if they were to maintain their standard of living. Many male emigrants from Agder were attracted to shipping in America, as illustrated by the common expression that one should move away from Agder 'to sail on the Great Lakes'. As was the case in the other Nordic countries, many women from Agder were employed as housemaids in American cities.

The large quantity of emigrants led to many returnees. Many crossed the Atlantic several times, which was made possible since the Agder emigration was late and communications well-developed. Often emigration created a situation where brothers and sisters were divided by the Atlantic. In certain families, most of the children went to America; in other families, none. The way in which families could be split in America and in the home country is illustrated by the following example: in 1910 the couple Severin and Tea settled on the farm called Saevik in Spind, Norway. He was born in Herad and she in Saevik, both areas with considerable emigration. Both had been in America and were married there before they settled in Saevik. Severin was born in 1882 and was the second child of twelve, eleven of whom reached maturity. Tea was born in 1884, the youngest of six. Of this total of seventeen brothers and sisters only three did not go to America. One died in his teens; the two remaining, both girls, left their home tract and settled in eastern Norway. Agder was thus a district where the population was accustomed to extensive geographic mobility.

The City of Stockholm, Sweden[6]

The emigration from the Swedish capital was considerable. During the years from 1851 to 1910 about 65,000 people moved to foreign countries, and the city's emigration has over the years been intense. The course of the emigration from Stockholm was similar to that of the country as a whole although it culminated in 1891; the corresponding high point for Swedish emigration came in 1882. Emigration peaks in the cities generally occurred later than in the

6 F. Nilsson 1970.

countryside. In 1891 more than 3,600 emigrants left Stockholm. About 2,500 of these were destined for North America, more than 500 for Brazil, and approximately 600 for other countries. That year Stockholm had an emigration intensity of fifteen persons per thousand in contrast to a national average of eight per thousand. There has always been a higher rate of emigration from Stockholm to countries outside of North America than from Sweden as a whole. These moves were almost without exception to the European countries, except for the years 1890–1891 when the emigration to Brazil was especially large.

Emigration from Stockholm varied in several respects, depending upon the socio-economic structure of the different parts of the city. Residents of working-class parishes most often emigrated to America, while people from areas with middle- and upper-class populations were relatively more likely to emigrate to the European countries. Much of the latter emigration, however, did not result in permanent settlement. The surplus of women in Stockholm affected the distribution of emigration between the sexes. The largest female emigration came from the upper middle-class parishes, where female servants were most frequently found. The latter can be seen in the compilation below of the number of emigrated women calculated per hundred men within Stockholm's wards.

Centrally located wards with a large upper middle-class element		Peripherally located wards with industrial and working elements	
ward 2	147/100	ward 4	78/100
3	120/100	6	82/100
7	128/100	8	71/100
9	135/100	12	81/100
		14	78/100
		16	69/100
		17	80/100

There were several reasons behind the emigration of those involved in household work. About 90 percent of that category were in-migrants to the city. Positions for female servants in America enticed servant girls in Stockholm. Letters, emigrant brochures, and oral information from earlier emigrants and returnees created a very attractive picture of American working conditions. On average a housemaid in America earned seven crowns a week, and a cook might receive up to ten crowns, the normal wage for a whole month's labor in Stockholm. Servants in America were usually guaranteed certain free days and could dispose of their own time after work was completed (usually 6:00 p.m.). It was also possible to resign with one week's notice. In Sweden, according to the terms of the *tjänstehjonstadga* (a law which regulated the conditions for servants and employees), they had a less favorable situation. The great tendency of servant girls to emigrate was thus related to their lower wages, harsher working conditions, and the social degredation of their work.

Certain groups were overrepresented among the Stockholm emigrants in comparison with their proportion in the total population: for example, people in industry and crafts, household work, and unspecified work. Occupations with especially high rates of emigration were metal workers, construction workers, shoemakers, tailors, seamstresses, and housemaids. Remarkably low frequency of emigration was found among civil service employees, such as railway, postal, and telegraph personnel. Laborers were clearly overrepresented in relation to their share of the population as a whole. As a rule clerks and businessmen did not frequently emigrate, with the exception of certain years of extensive migration, when small businessmen, shopkeepers, and skilled laborers emigrated in large numbers.

It is apparent that the social unrest caused by unemployment increased the emigration rate, for example, from 1886 to 1888 and from 1891 to 1892. The unemployed had their own organization which became very active in inducing the authorities to improve the situation. In 1891–1892 about 2,000 persons were members of the Association for the Unemployed (*De arbetslösas förening*). Many socialist petitions and resolutions were issued but did not result in sufficient aid from the authorities. There was no distribution of emergency help or free food. Protest meetings and street demonstrations met with police action and arrests, which contributed a heightened working-class consciousness. A total of 6,700 persons emigrated from Stockholm 1891–1892.

Another factor contributing to high emigration rates was the boarding system which was widespread at that time and which undermined normal family relations. The background was the dearth of inexpensive residences suitable for the purses of unskilled laborers.

In spite of the often harsh conditions for workers in the city and the great interest in emigration, the newspapers had a surprisingly negative attitude to America. This is true of three newspapers known to be sympathetic to the laborers: the social democratic newspaper, *Socialdemokraten*, and the liberal newspapers, *Dagens Nyheter* and *Fäderneslandet*. They were largely negative towards conditions in America. Difficulties in obtaining work were pointed out, as well as low wages, and both successful and unsuccessful strikes were mentioned. In the year 1891 unemployment, decreases in wages, and the violent labor conflicts in the USA dominated newspaper reporting. The information from the press which can be assumed to have reached the strata of society most likely to emigrate thus drew a remarkably negative picture of the possibilities of obtaining a well-paying job in the USA. The newspapers consequently were not 'pull' factors during these years of very high emigration from Stockholm.

It has been assumed that the social democratic labor movement maintained an almost antagonistic position on the question of emigration, although this did not prove to be the case in Stockholm. Occupations with a stronger labor organization and socialist views sent more people to America than others; included here are metal workers, construction workers, tailors, and shoemakers. In several cases union leaders were encouraged by trade unions, which even organized emigration, as was the case with the emigration to Brazil in 1891 and 1892. The by-laws of some unions also stressed the responsibility of helping comrades to emigrate. This help generally took the form of voluntary collections among union members. The Social Democrats were eager supporters of obligatory instruction in the English language in the schools, which was necessary for workers who planned to emigrate. Several prominent labor leaders of the early Swedish trade union movement also ended up in the United States, often because they were blacklisted by employers. The labor union movement's harsh criticism of social conditions in the USA, with its supposedly large class differences and mighty capitalistic interests, had to yield to the reality that workers preferred eating their fill in America to starving in their home country. The more or less forced departure of labor leaders from Sweden seems to have contributed to a sense of solidarity between Swedish workers on both sides of the Atlantic.

7. Re-migration

Of the total who emigrated from each of the Nordic countries, the same proportion, approximately one-fifth, returned. There are several other similarities in the re-migration pattern in Sweden, Finland, Norway, and Denmark. Because of the quality of the source materials, this phenomenon is easiest to study for Finns and Swedes. Thus far, no study of the re-migration to Iceland has yet been conducted.

During emigration's earliest phase, re-migration was insignificant. The nature of the pioneer emigration, which consisted of cohesive groups and whole families, normally meant a definitive break with the Old World. Before the 1880's, for example, less than five percent returned to Sweden. The first peak in re-migration occurred after the great wave of emigration during the beginning of the 1880's and in connection with the depression in America in the middle of the decade. Thereafter a steady increase followed which culminated in Sweden in 1894 and in Norway in 1908. The proportion of returnees to Sweden during the 1890's as a whole was as high as 23.5 percent. Although the Finnish emigration started late, the return of emigrants to that country followed the pattern of the other Nordic countries, something which must be explained by the economic fluctuations on the American labor market and the improved communications.

Re-migration generally increased after years of high emigration. For the majority of returnees the stay in America was a matter of a few years. Periods with high rates of emigration were therefore usually followed by high rates of re-migration. It became extremely high when crises occurred in the American economy, for example, the 'Panic of 1893' and the 'Panic of 1907', with peak years for Swedish re-migration in 1894 and for Norwegian in 1908.[1] (Compare patterns in figure 20.)

1 I. Semmingsen 1950, 430; L.-G. Tedebrand 1976, 209–213; K. Virtanen 1979, 223; written communication from Helgi Skúli Kjartansson (1985).

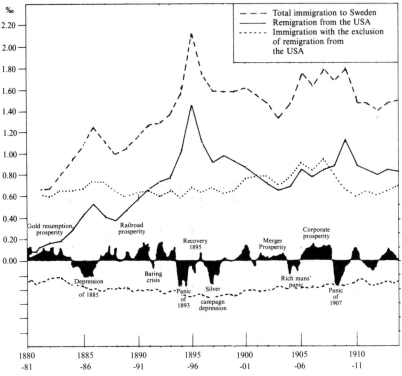

Figure 20. Immigration to Sweden per Thousand of the Median Swedish Population, 1875–1913, and Trade and Business Cycles of the USA.
Sources: L.-G. Tedebrand 1976, 210; J.A. Estey 1956, 20.

Generally speaking, the later during the emigration period people crossed the Atlantic, the greater was the probability that they would return. All who re-migrated, however, did not remain in the home country. Many made the journey several times. For example, about ten percent of Finnish emigrants traveled to America more than twice.

There is a clear connection between the tendency of those who returned and stayed in their home countries and their prospects of making a living there. As a rule those who acquired farms and leaseholds in the home country stayed, while their children often emigrated. Although the decisions of re-migrants were often a product of their economic opportunities, these decisions were certainly, and perhaps most frequently, determined by purely personal considerations. Many emigrants had only intended to stay a few years in America in order to try out the labor market there and to return with their savings. Among the Norwegian returnees most thus came

108

back after achieving economic success and social advancement in America. Other re-migrants did not like American working life and society from the beginning and therefore wished to return as soon as possible. In remarkably many cases the reason for returning has been attributed to homesickness. For many, however, the return did not always mean a rendezvous with the picture of home that they remembered. During the time in America friends of their youth had moved and much else had changed.[2]

The majority of those who returned were of working age. Most were relatively young people who had not been in America long enough to take root and forget conditions in the old country. In Norway over 80 percent of the returnees were under forty when they re-migrated, and investigations from Sweden and Finland have shown that two-thirds were between twenty-one and forty years of age. The decision to stay or not seems to have been made within a few years. But when emigrants, after having first worked in mines, industries, or the woods, made their way to agricultural areas in America to acquire a farm, the thought of returning was often definitively abandoned. One-third of the Norwegian re-migrants made their decision after two to four years in America; over half of the Finns came back within five years after their emigration, as did more than 70 percent of the Swedes. Only six percent of those who returned to Sweden had stayed longer than ten years in America. The older the emigrants were when they left, the greater was the chance that they would return. The younger were better able to adjust. On the other hand, the very old who went to join their children in America stayed on as a rule. Re-migration frequency also varied depending on which continent the emigrants were destined for. Swedes and Danes bound for Latin America and Australia had higher re-emigration rates than those to North America. Over half of the Finnish emigrants to Australia returned, while the re-migration rate of Finnish emigrants in Latin America was even higher.[3]

Re-migration from America was, to a great extent, a male phenomenon. This pattern has also been observed among Italian and Greek returnees. Of the Swedish emigrants who came back during the 1880's, three-fourths were men, and during the 1920's men still made up two-thirds of them. The types of jobs that emigrants had

2 I. Semmingsen 1950, 461; K. Virtanen 1979, 225–226.
3 I. Semmingsen 1950, 461; K. Hvidt 1971, 324–330; L.-G. Tedebrand 1976; K. Virtanen 1979, 225–226.

were probably decisive for this pattern, since women were oriented towards areas of work that were less sensitive to economic fluctuations than those of men. Differences in working milieu may also have been significant in another way. While the first jobs which the males had often were in such branches as mining, lumbering, etc., with large work teams of the same nationality, women learned the language and the country's customs through their work in American households and in service occupations. That adjustment probably made them less likely to return than men. An important part of the female migration also consisted of wives whose husbands had emigrated. Their inclination to return ought therefore to have been rather minimal.[4]

The later one gets into the emigration period, the larger the number of emigrants who intended to travel over to 'try their luck' on the American labor market for a short time to save money. Instead of moving from agriculture to industry in the home country, where the chances of being employed were somewhat uncertain, one could hope for better conditions in America. This behavior can be traced in the exceptionally high re-migration tendency of men who had reached thirty-five to forty years of age and who emigrated to America during highs in the economic cycles. The returnees of this category often used their earnings to purchase farms or other businesses in the home country.

In the Swedish parish of Långasjö in Småland many of the farms were bought with dollars of returning emigrants. Of the re-migrants from Canada more than 60 percent bought land in the parish. An investigation of returnees to Långasjö from 1865 to 1955 includes their major occupations in Sweden before they emigrated, in America, and finally, after their return. The results are shown in the following summary in absolute numbers.[5]

	Before emigration	In America	After returning
Work in the forests	–	15	2
Railway work	4	81	1
Carpentry	6	12	14
Mining and smelting	–	22	–

4 L.-G. Tedebrand 1976, 223; K. Virtanen 1979, 224.
5 L. Ljungmark 1965, 176; *En Smålandssocken emigrerar*, 814. Cf. H. Runblom 1977, 220–225.

Workshops and factories	–	6	1
More than one occupation (agriculture, lumbering, railway, and mining)	–	20	–
Agriculture	145	14	114
Other occupations	13	–	18
Retired persons, sick persons, minors, unknown	15	11	33

Emigrants from the Nordic countries largely emanated from the agricultural sector, while in America they often worked within industry or the urban occupations. This is illustrated in an investigation of Norwegian re-migrants. The largest part (40 percent) found employment in industry and in the mines in America, while only ten percent worked in agriculture. After re-migration the situation was reversed; only eleven percent were engaged in the industrial and urban sectors, while 40 percent became farmers. The former emigrants were often energetic: the men practiced new forms of industrial and agricultural management, and the women tried new methods and routines in the household. The re-migrants, however, were less important for the economy in the Nordic countries than in southern Europe, where emigration and re-migration became a more pronounced part of a transatlantic labor market and where the economy, as in Italy, blossomed from the lively traffic between the home country and the western hemisphere. Most re-migrants from the Nordic countries moved back to the rural milieu from which they had originated. Slightly more than one-tenth of the Finnish travelers to America came from the cities. Still fewer returned to the cities, which can be explained by the fact that many of them before emigration moved to urban milieus, but after the stay in America preferred to move directly back to the countryside. A local study in Västernorrland County, Sweden points in the same direction; as much as 80 percent of the returnees settled down in the parish from which they had departed. Re-migration thus shows a very conservative strain.[6]

6 I. Semmingsen 1950, 460–470; L.-G. Tedebrand 1976, 216–227; K. Virtanen 1979, 221, 226.

8. Economy, Society, and the Individual's Decision to Emigrate

One of the classic issues thoroughly discussed in European scholarship is what motivated the departure of the emigrants. There is, of course, no general explanation, since the decisions of millions of people were involved. Moreover, when an attempt is made to explain why a person emigrated, it is often difficult to distinguish a single reason.

In the discussion of why people left, one should differentiate between the reasons given by individuals, which were often colored by personal situations and emotions, and the larger societal forces which steered the streams of emigration. The motives should be analyzed in the light of both short-term migration fluctuations and the changes in migration over a longer time-span. Fluctuations in the emigration curve in the short term generally depended upon such factors as the swings in the economic cycle, the level of employment, and the level of wages, while the causes for the long-term changes in migration trends depended more upon circumstances such as population development and changes in society.

Scholars have tried to isolate the economic factors behind the variations in migration, mainly the differences in employment opportunities and wages. If such arguments are to be pursued, they assume that the migrants possessed total rationality and complete information on the available alternatives. Furthermore, no hindrances to movement should exist. Since situations of that type are unusual, one must assume that a number of both rational and irrational reasons contributed to the emigration decisions of individuals.[1]

One should also take into consideration how people react to different types of information and how it reaches them, that is, how

1 For an econometric investigation of the variations in Norwegian emigration in relation to economic fluctuations, see T. Moe 1970.

men and women influence one another. In this regard it has been shown that 'face-to-face' communication is very important for acceptance of information. News is assimilated at various points in time and in different contexts, depending upon the location and economic and social situations. According to the so-called two-step hypothesis, information first reaches opinion-builders who then communicate information and attitudes to the people upon whom they exert influence. The inclination to accept news depends on the influence network. In general, one is likely to be influenced by one's peers and, to a certain extent, by persons of higher social status. It also takes a while before information penetrates to a person, is accepted, and results in a decision to change one's situation.[2]

That process of converting information to action – in this case, emigration – is influenced both by economic and demographic developments in the wider perspective, as well as by hindrances to migration and the different types of information that the individual happens to come into contact with. This information is, in turn, dependent upon which opinion-builders appear on the scene and upon the migration tradition that dominates the particular areas.

The Atlantic Economy

Contemporary observers had already noted that the course of European emigration was strongly coupled with the cyclical pattern of economic development, both in America and in the home country. In the discussion during the 1920's of the driving forces behind emigration, the expressions 'push' and 'pull' were used. The first includes the circumstances in the home country which contributed to the desire to leave it, and the latter, the conditions in the receiving country which attracted the emigrants.[3]

In a study of push and pull factors, the English economist Harry Jerome found that the fluctuations in the emigration curves coincided most with the economic conditions in America and concluded therefore that the pull was stronger than the push.[4]

When the American sociologist Dorothy Swaine Thomas applied

---

2 H. Wester 1977, 11–22 contains a description and analysis of the various models and theories concerning the dispersion of information and the spread of innovations.
3 B. Odén 1971 contains an analysis of the economic theories used by emigration scholars.
4 H. Jerome 1926, 205–208.

Jerome's theory in an analysis of Swedish conditions, she reached two main conclusions. The situation in the sending country with its population increase and its slow industrialization created a latent emigration push. On the other hand, it was the American economic cycles which caused the great variations in the emigration curves.[5]

This research was continued by the English economic historian Brinley Thomas, who based an explanatory model on the changes in what he called the Atlantic economy. He saw a relationship between, on the one hand, the greater British investments in, for example, steel production and construction in North America and England, and, on the other hand, the movement of the population. When investments in America were on a high level, construction activities in England were low. Expectations of high interest rates in America attracted not only capital to America, but also people. The streams of emigration thus followed the streams of investment, so that when the flow of capital decreased, emigration did likewise. When this whole process had begun, its effects spread to the rest of western Europe.[6]

During the emigration epoch the Nordic countries were drawn more and more into the Atlantic economy, and the USA and western Europe during the nineteenth century were increasingly woven together into something of a common market for capital and labor.[7]

The pull factors mainfested themselves on several levels: first, through personal contacts in the forms of emigrant letters or visits from returned emigrants who informed and enticed people; secondly, through the offers of the transatlantic shipping companies, who outbid one another with increasingly comfortable possibilities for crossing; and finally, the propaganda from the American states and from the land companies, railways, and industries, who wanted to recruit immigrants from Europe. In many cases all of these comprised a cooperating network of impulses.

Transportation and Routes

The increase in the capacity of transportation and the massive supply of information was of enormous importance for the size of emigration. Without this 'emigration business' the outward movement would probably not have attained such proportions as it did.

5 D.S. Thomas 1941, 165–175, 318–326.
6 B. Thomas 1954, 96–122.
7 F. Hodne 1981, 417–420.

Initially sailing vessels were used, and those who wished to make the crossing had to come to an agreement with a shipping company on passage to a suitable harbor. As many ships had a heavy, but less bulky cargo to America (for example, iron) than they had on the return, it was advantageous to complement the freight with emigrants on the westward journey. Soon, however, the emigrant traffic across the Atlantic developed into a large industry, and the gradual shift from sailing vessels to steamships, which began in the 1860's, brought about an important change with both safer and more rapid passages. The improvements are evidenced by the following facts. In 1872 the average crossing from Liverpool to New York by sailing vessel took 44 days, but with a steamship the trip was made in less than 14 days. The number who died during the passage decreased from 1 per 184 passengers on sailing ships to 1 per 2,195 passengers on the steamers. The conversion from sail to steam occurred very rapidly, which is illustrated by the development in Norway. Until 1865 most of the Norwegian emigrants were carried on sailing ships. In 1866, when British shipping companies entered the market in Norway, the proportion was still 90 percent. In less than ten years the situation changed completely. The last sailing ship loaded with emigrants departed from Norway in 1874.[8]

Until the 1830's Rotterdam and the other Dutch cities were Europe's most frequented ports of departure, because such a large part of the emigrants came from the German areas and thus used river traffic to reach the coast. Le Havre, France, was also an important port for embarkation. Many Norwegian emigrants took that route before 1850. The increasing emigrant traffic was, however, successively drawn north towards Hamburg and Bremen, which competed intensely for the greatest part of the northern European emigrant traffic. It was, however, Liverpool that came to dominate as the port of embarkation for the emigrants from northern Europe during the phase of mass emigration. Most emigrants from the Nordic countries used the route via England, especially those who came from Sweden and Finland. From Denmark and Norway many emigrants went directly from domestic ports to America. The Danes also utilized the German shipping companies more than other emigrants from the Nordic countries. The greater part of the Norwegians landed at Quebec, Canada, in the years 1850 to 1873. It was a golden age for the Norwegian shipping companies that transported

8 G. Moltman 1985, 3; L. Pettersen 1985, 1–4.

emigrants over the Atlantic and returned from Quebec with timber. The most common ports of departure for the emigrants in the Nordic countries were Christiania (Oslo), Bergen, and Trondheim in Norway; Copenhagen, Denmark; Gothenburg, Sweden; and in Finland, Vaasa and later Hanko. The larger part of the Nordic emigrants who traveled via England went first with North Sea shipping companies to Hull. From there they traveled by train across England and continued from Liverpool with the larger Atlantic ships over to America. (See the map in figure 21.)

Atlantic shipping companies were eventually established in the Nordic countries. During the years 1871 to 1876 a Norwegian-American line was active. It became a serious competitor of the Allan Line, which had dominated Norwegian emigrant traffic during the first years of the "steamship age". In Denmark the Thingvalla Line was established in 1879. Its ships departed directly for America from harbors in the Nordic countries, and it was used also by the Norwegian emigrants. Its successor, the Scandinavian-American Line, later held the leading position in emigrant traffic from Norway. It was not until 1910 that a new Norwegian-American Line was established. Its first ship crossed the Atlantic in 1913. Until 1894 Finnish emigrant traffic usually went via Sweden and across the North Sea for continuation from Liverpool. Later the Finland Steamship Company gained a monopoly on the emigrant traffic from Finland, and about 90 percent used that company to cross the North Sea. The first direct Swedish steamship connections with America came in 1915 with the establishment of the Swedish-American Line. As mentioned above, most Icelanders went via Scotland.[9]

Commercial Organizations

The emigration business built up a large cohesive network of cooperating units, which could be found all the way from the areas of settlement in the west to the emigration districts in the home countries.

On the American side there was great interest in maintaining immigration. During the years following the War Between the States, several states in the Upper Mississippi Valley were in a hectic stage of settlement and, therefore, organized immigrant promotion,

9 I. Semmingsen 1950, 129; L. Ljungmark 1965, 105; K. Hvidt 1971, 353–384; R. Kero 1974, 131–159; H. W. Nordvik 1985, 1–2; L. Pettersen 1985, 1–4.

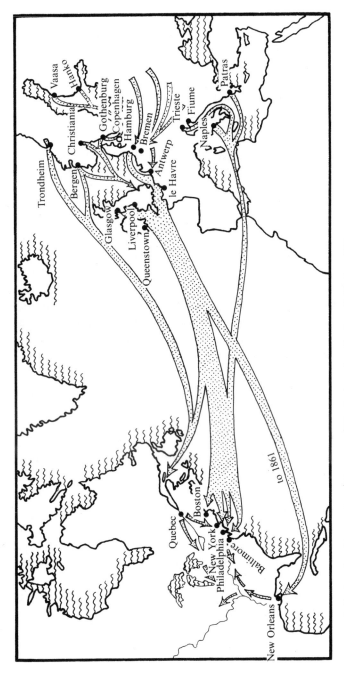

Figure 21. Emigration Routes from Europe to North America. Source: P. Taylor, 136.

117

as the frontier had reached there. Various groups had a common interest in encouraging immigration: the land-selling companies, industries and mines, and the railroads. To a great extent the railways based their expansion upon the land grant system. They had received government land to sell along the projected railway lines and sought immigrants both as labor to complete the construction work and as settlers to provide the basis for traffic. In addition there were the earlier emigrants who as a rule were interested in having newcomers in their settlements. Initially it meant both purchasers for their products and many times also cheap labor. In America ethnic groups, whether purposely or not, came to be an important driving force in immigration.[10]

The commercial interests for immigration on the American side worked closely with shipping companies that dealt with emigrant transport, an example of Brinley Thomas's so-called Altantic economy. The ticket prices from Europe often included both the sea passage and the continued railway journey to various destinations in the new country, where the shipping companies and the railways tried to win market shares with the help of various discount systems.

The British shipping companies with their dominant position cooperated in the Liverpool circle. It included the Allan, Cunard, Dominion, Inman, Guion, Nation, and State Lines. The competition was hard, especially with the *Hamburg-Amerikanische Paketfahrt AG* in Hamburg and the *Nordwestdeutsche Lloyd* in Bremen. For example, as a convenience for its passengers, in 1906 the Hamburg shipping company initiated the construction of an entire little city adjacent to the harbor with elaborate housing facilities, where no less than 5,000 persons could be housed simultaneously. This complex was unique in Europe.[11]

By the middle of the 1880's more than twenty shipping companies regularly crossed the North Atlantic in the emigrant traffic. Cooperation was in their interest in order to avoid depressed ticket prices. Through a series of agreements, called conferences, common prices were set and principles were arrived at concerning how the activities of agents should be organized in the sending countries. The first Liverpool conference lasted from 1868 to 1874 and the next between 1875 and 1884. Some of the shipping companies wished to withdraw and new ones to join, and thus it was necessary to renew these

10 A comprehensive study of the organized promotion of Scandinavian immigration has been published in L. Ljungmark 1971.
11 B. Brattne and S. Åkerman 1976, 179; B. Gelberg 1973, 25–28.

agreements on a number of subsequent occasions during the emigration period. An illustration of the market situation is given by the conference held in Liverpool in 1884. A total of sixteen shipping companies participated, twelve of which were British, three German, and one Danish, *Thingvallalinjen*.[12]

For contact in the European harbors the shipping companies used permanently employed agents who recruited passengers for their vessels and who worked primarily on a commission basis. Their offices were located in the most important ports of departure. In Copenhagen, for example, the Liverpool group was represented during the 1880's by six to eight agents, the Hamburg-Bremen shipping companies by two, and the *Thingvallalinjen* by one or two agents.

These emigrant agents generally operated on three levels to get passengers. They were responsible for advertising and brochures, they pursued a differentiated price policy, and they operated through nationwide networks of affiliated sub-agents. Furthermore, they often utilized so-called 'Yankees', earlier emigrants who had returned home and were paid to recruit new emigrants willing to join them on their return journey. It is difficult to get a clear picture of the extent of the 'Yankee' system, since they were not registered. They constituted a form of agent activity which was not sanctioned by the authorities in the Nordic countries, in contrast to the affiliated agents, who were subject to government regulations and were supervised by the main agents. The increased activities of the authorized agents is illustrated by the following summary of conditions in Copenhagen.[13]

1868	6 main agents	126 affiliated agents outside the Danish capital.
1878	12 main agents	571 affiliated agents outside the Danish capital.
1886	15 main agents	1,053 affiliated agents outside the Danish capital.

The local agents played essential roles in the information network. They were usually persons who had good contacts in their local districts and thus could spread news of the opportunities for emi-

12 B. Brattne 1973, 124.
13 K. Hvidt 1971, 426. A comprehensive study of the transportation and information activities is found in chapter III in Hvidt's book, 337–480.

gration and of the prevailing situation in America. They were often local merchants, inn or tavern keepers, elementary school teachers, or employees of the post office or railway. They were chosen because they held certain key positions in their areas and from a social point of view could be expected to have a good basis for conveying information to a wider circle. With their knowledge of people they were able to efficiently circulate to potential emigrants the shipping companies' alluring brochures, which were often colorfully illustrated. In all the Nordic countries, the sub-agents and their promotion efforts were concentrated in areas with strong emigrant traditions. They were surprisingly numerous during the culmination of mass emigration, as the summary of the number associated with Copenhagen illustrates. In Sweden the Guion Line alone in 1882 had 220 affiliated agents throughout the country. In the 1880's the National Line had 350 affiliated agents in Norway, the Allan Line 400, and the Thingvalla Line at least 600.[14]

As emigrant recruiters, the 'Yankees' may have been more useful than the officially registered affiliated agents. With their personal experiences in America they were more capable of persuading people than local affiliate agents who had not themselves been in America. Furthermore, the 'Yankees' returned most often to a circle of relatives and earlier acquaintances, whom they could impress with their American style. The 'Yankee' system was used systematically by the railway and Atlantic shipping companies, which usually offered free passage round trip if a certain number of new emigrants returned with the Yankee.

Both contemporaries of the emigration and later scholars have emphasized the importance of the advertising and propaganda of the shipping companies and their agents in driving the emigration rates to their heights. A number of later studies have shown, however, that the transportation apparatus, with its investment in the expansion of tonnage and its regular advertising in the press, had little influence upon the oscillating intensity of the emigration rates. On the contrary, both the increase in freight capacity and the amount of advertising were steered by the size of the emigration. With rising emigration rates, investments were made in the expansion of the transport fleet, and advertising was intensified in an attempt to fill the overcapacity in periods of decline. Nor did the

14 I. Semmingsen 1950, 129; K. Hvidt 1971, 426; B. Brattne 1973, 157; R. Kero 1974, 146.

price policy determine the size of the emigrant flood. Rather the shipping companies and cartels were forced to adjust their prices to existing demand. In times of intensive emigration they could maintain high prices, while in the slow periods they lowered prices, but with marginal results. Thus, when emigration was intensive during the first years of the 1880's, the ticket price from Gothenburg to New York was 105 crowns, 74 of which were for the ocean fare. With decreased emigration in the middle of the 1880's the price sank to a low of 70 crowns, and 47 crowns were for the ocean fare. When emigration increased again during the latter half of the 1880's, the price rose to the level of the beginning of the decade. The curves showing the intensity of the emigration thus had their own course, regardless of the commercial exertions, the American and European economic cycles being decisive for the propensity of the individual to emigrate.[15]

It remains clear, however, that the enormous effort to offer safe and fast ship connections and to provide information on the opportunities for Atlantic passage and prospects in America must have contributed to the size of the emigration as a whole. It meant that the opportunity to emigrate was made readily available to the broad masses. Furthermore, all sources which provided information on the current economic situation in America contributed to the fluctuations in the emigration curves. Private letters from America have perhaps been especially important for the presumptive emigrants as gauges of the real situation in America, because they came from relatives, most of whom had direct contact with the labor market. Similarly the returnees, whether they were commercially interested 'Yankees' or not, strengthened the pull effect through their experience and insight into the conditions on the other side of the Atlantic.[16]

Attitudes towards Emigration – Legislation

The reaction to emigration in the sending countries can be divided into several distinct phases. In the beginning a laissez-faire attitude dominated, where little attention was paid to the mass movement

---

15 B. Brattne 1973, 122–154; H. Norman 1974, 92–100; B. Brattne and S. Åkerman 1976, 199–200.
16 K. Hvidt 1971, 487, 1978, 202–203. An emigration research group at the University of Copenhagen is devoting attention especially to the significance of emigrant letters for the extent of emigration. Written communication from Steffen E. Jørgensen (1985).

that had begun. After a few decades legislation was enacted to protect emigrants against exploitation by agents and steamship companies. Towards the end of the century attempts were made in some countries to stop the emigration of young men eligible for military service due to the increased demand for defense by conscripted armies. Finally, around the turn of the century and thereafter, it was argued that emigration was detrimental to the home country and that one must support the retention of people of working age; measures were also taken and associations formed to stem the emigration.

The generally noninterventionist attitude during the greater part of the emigration period was in line with liberalism's concept of the individual's right to settle wherever he wished. The hindrances for emigration were therefore few. Especially during the beginning of the mass emigration epoch, emigration was often officially viewed as a phenomenon which could help to solve some of the population problems in the sending countries. One can refer to cases in Denmark, Iceland, Norway, and Sweden where authorities assisted emigration by giving economic support not only to the poor, but also to other groups considered burdensome for society. That was, however, far more common in other countries, such as England and Switzerland, where it seems to have been systematized. Otherwise, a general impression is that migration, which included so many people, was accorded a relatively small place as a problem in the public debate. It was therefore an exception when in 1882 Sweden's King Oscar II gave the provincial governors (*landshövdingarna*) the task of studying the reasons for the increasing emigration in each of the counties. This action did not lead to any government measure, but resulted in more understanding of the motives for emigration among people in various areas and officials at different levels.[17]

In the Nordic countries many sympathized with emigrants' hopes of attaining better economic positions by moving to America. In conservative circles, though, the emigrants were often depicted as disloyal to their native country, when they did not remain and try to find a source of livelihood at home. By way of comparison, in the Netherlands and other colonial powers patriotic groups encouraged the emigrants to travel to their colonies rather than to America. In Finland the authorities had a very negative attitude toward emigration during the 1870's. Emigration propaganda was viewed

17 A.-S. Kälvemark 1972, 46–56.

with uneasiness, and newspapers with articles on emigration were confiscated. Throughout the Nordic countries, on the other hand, radicals used emigration as proof of the poor conditions in their own countries.[18]

With the increasing emigration volume, growing transportation business, and flourishing activities of agents, a need arose for the state to protect the rights of the emigrants. During the nineteenth century all European countries passed laws to defend the emigrants against the commercial interests of shipping companies and agents. England led the way with the passage of regulations in 1803 which were supplemented several times during the first half of the nineteenth century. During the 1850's several of the German states followed suit. The 1860's saw the passage of such laws in the Nordic countries: Norway in 1863, Sweden in 1864, and Denmark in 1868. Furthermore, these regulations were later complemented in the Nordic countries. Common for such legislation was the emphasis placed upon the conditions of transportation, such as space on the ships, the quality of the food, and the emigrants' economic security. The form and content of the emigrant contracts were also regulated, so that the responsibility of the emigrant agents was carefully specified. In addition to personal information on the emigrants, Swedish regulations required contracts including information on the place of departure and destination, the day of departure, the name of the vessel, and data about the arrangements for the journey in the receiving country. Furthermore, the possible waiting times prior to and during the journey were to be noted, as well as the support provided for the emigrant until he reached his place of destination. Similarly, the terms of the agents' responsibility for the belongings of the emigrant were to be stated. Contracts could not include any agreement for the payment of travel costs after the end of the journey. This regulation was designed to prevent emigrants from being enticed to travel under apparently easy conditions and later required to fulfill unspecified economic obligations after their arrival. Emigrant regulations also commonly attempted to bind the agents with financial guarantees. A Danish law of 1868 required the agent who entered the business to deposit 10,000 crowns as security for the fulfillment of his obligations to the emigrants.[19]

An indifferent attitude towards emigration characterized Swedish

18 I. Semmingsen 1950, 405–423; R. Kero 1974, 133; A.-S. Kälvemark 1976, 100–102, 106–112; E.H. Pedersen 1985, 263–264; P. Stokvig 1983, 46–47.
19 K. Hvidt 1971, 40–46, 412, 417; B. Brattne 1973, 110–112.

society during the greater part of the nineteenth century, and there was nearly complete freedom to emigrate. One exception was limitations on the emigration of those liable for conscription. The political climate in Europe grew harsher with increased nationalism, growing economic competition, and rivalries during the decades prior to the First World War. Tensions also grew between Sweden and Norway during the years around the turn of the century before the dissolution of the Union in 1905. Swedish officials were irritated because many men liable for conscription emigrated without permission via the Norwegian ports and Copenhagen, and the Swedish authorities expressed to the neighboring countries their wish that this traffic be limited. As military defense became more and more based upon general conscription and the training period for the conscripts was lengthened, the authorities became increasingly concerned about the emigration of men of conscriptable age. The situation in Sweden serves to illustrate the obligations of men eligible for military service. The length of this service was 30 days after 1857, 42 days after 1885, 90 days after 1892, and from 1901 onwards 240 days. Men were liable for military service between twenty-one and twenty-six years of age. In 1892 that period was extended to the age of thirty-two. In both Sweden and Norway men who were of the age liable for military service had to apply for permission to emigrate, though it was usually granted. However, the authorities became more restrictive towards the end of the century, as reflected statistically in the reduction in the number of emigrants of conscriptable age in comparison with those in the slightly older and younger age groups. In Finland men were conscripted at the age of 21, when they had to draw lots to determine whether they had to enter the military service for three years or the reserves with a training period of 90 days. In the beginning of the twentieth century most Finnish men did not report to the conscription centers, because the Finns considered conscription unconstitutional. In fact, there was a conscription boycott. In Denmark conscripts had to ask for permission to emigrate, but there were few real hindrances for them. Only active service or a war situation could stop young men from emigrating. In Iceland there were no forms of military duty for young men.[20]

The obligation to do military service has often been presented as

20 A.-S. Kälvemark 1976, 102–105, 164–175, has conducted a thorough study of the effects on emigration of the regulation of those liable for military service; I. Semmingsen 1950, 432–434; L. Ljungmark 1965, 60–63; Written communications from Steffen E. Jørgensen, Reino Kero, and Helgi Skúli Kjartansson (1985).

a cause of emigration. It is, however, difficult to determine how common a cause it was, as the intensity of emigration varied sharply from year to year for other reasons. In Finland, only a small number are supposed to have fled from military service. It was clear, however, that the young men who decided to emigrate often preferred to do so before they attained the age when they were liable for conscription.[21]

In certain circles there was a fundamental change in attitudes towards emigration during the first years of the twentieth century. With increased industrialization and urbanization, anxiety grew among the agrarian employers about a lack of labor, and among national defence advocates, who felt that emigration threatened to undermine the army's manpower.

Many conservatives and nationalists saw emigration as a negative factor for the country. In Sweden this sentiment manifested itself in the foundation of the National Society against Emigration (*Nationalföreningen mot emigrationen*) in 1907 and its affiliated Movement for the Ownership of One's Home (*Egnahemsrörelsen*), whose program aimed at persuading young people to obtain smaller rural homes in the country rather than emigrating. The same spirit brought about the patriotic Society for the Limitation of Emigration (*Selskapet til Emigrationens Indskraenkning*) in Norway in 1908. In Finland some highly educated Swedish-speaking persons in the county of Ostrobothnia founded an 'emigration society' in 1908 to restrain heavy emigration among the Finland-Swedish population of the area. It was active for only a couple of years and was of little importance.[22]

Official investigations aimed at checking emigration were also initiated. In Sweden a Royal Investigating Commission on Emigration (*Emigrationsutredningen*) under the leadership of Gustav Sundbärg was at work during the years 1908–13 and produced a twenty-one volume report; in 1912 Norway appointed a departmental committee to investigate how new emigration laws should be formulated. Denmark had no official commission to analyze the size and causes of overseas migration. However, the law passed in 1899 which facilitated the parceling of certain types of landed property with financial guarantees for smallholders was implicitly meant to help stop the flight from the rural areas and thereby limit emigration.

21 A.-S. Kälvemark 1976, 164–175.
22 A.-S. Kälvemark 1976, 106–110; L. Ljungmark 1965, 163–170; written communication from Reino Kero (1985).

In Finland emigration statistics had been collected since the end of the nineteenth century, and in 1918 an official emigration committee was appointed which delivered its report in 1924. Nothing comparable occurred in Iceland.

In spite of investigations and discussions in the parliaments, no formal obstacles to emigration were ever introduced in the Nordic countries with the exception of those previously mentioned concerning men liable for military service. The questions soon became irrelevant, as emigration decreased drastically with the onslaught of the First World War. Emigration then dwindled with the American quota legislation in the 1920's and the growing industrialization in the sending countries.[23]

Some Fiery Spirits in the History of Emigration

Many people had special significance in influencing their country-men to emigrate. Some are known because they have been presented by scholars, while others are more or less forgotten. All attempts at being exhaustive in such a presentation are meaningless. Here one example has been selected from each of the Nordic countries. These men differed in many respects from one another: in their personalities, their motivations, and their methods. They were also active in different phases of emigration, and the results of their involvement can scarcely be compared. Their stories do, however, reflect how emigration was stimulated and how the interplay between the interests in the receiving country and the sending countries was expressed.

Cleng Peerson, Norway

The Norwegian *Cleng Peerson* was born in 1783 in Tysvaer. He was looked upon as a restless soul and a controversial person by his contemporaries. Undoubtedly he was of great significance as the inspirer of and guide for Norwegian emigration during its first years. Peerson had traveled widely and had a circle of acquaintances who listened to his descriptions. In 1821 he traveled to America on behalf of a group of Quakers in the city of Stavanger and the surrounding Rogaland in order to investigate conditions for prospective emi-

23 I. Semmingsen 1950, 434–435; L. Ljungmark 1965, 163–170; A.-S. Kälvemark 1976, 110–113; written communication from Steffen E. Jørgensen, Reino Kero, and Helgi Skúli Kjartansson (1985).

grants. Upon his return he gave lively accounts of the opportunities in America, which became the direct reason for the emigration of the so-called 'sloop people' in 1825. (See pp. 53–54.) Peerson did not leave Norway with that group. He had already departed in 1824 and prepared a settlement in the northwestern part of the state of New York. For that purpose he had received help through contacts with Quakers there. Land located in Kendall Township in Orleans County could be bought for five dollars per acre. Difficulties arose, however, for the Norwegian settlers in this area, since Peerson was more of a wanderer than a land-clearing settler and farmer. By some he has been regarded as a reckless and asocial adventurer who never did a decent day's work, living at the expense of honest and diligent people. Others saw him as a romantic and eccentric pathfinder with no regard for his own person, a generous nature who did not spare himself, whether he became involved in a new religious belief or a new settlement project, but only sought new possibilities for his countrymen in America. After a few years he went west and discovered better opportunities for settlement. In 1835 many of his countrymen followed him to an area near Fox River in La Salle County, Illinois, about one hundred kilometers southwest of Chicago. Here good government land was purchased for $1.25 per acre, and through the initiative of Cleng Peerson a foundation was laid for the coming great Norwegian settlement in the Midwest. Peerson did not stay there either, but continued first to Missouri and from there to Texas, where he remained until his death in 1865. He called himself the father of Norwegian emigration, and on his gravestone the words 'Cleng Peerson, the first Norwegian emigrant in America', are inscribed. A fictionalized trilogy of his life has been written by Alfred Hauge.[24]

Mogens Abraham Sommer, Denmark

The Dane *Mogens Abraham Sommer* is best characterized as an idealistic, itinerant emigrant agent with a stamp of both political and religious fanaticism. He was born of Jewish parents in Haderslev, Denmark, where he taught for a short time in the Cathedral School in 1853. He had a restless nature and wandered around the country on foot as an evangelist. He was often prosecuted and was thrown

24 I. Semmingsen 1941, 19–36; A. Hauge 1961.

into jail several times, which further increased his radicalism and sense of martyrdom.

Sommer was rather one-sided in his judgement of society and of militarism, but had a penetrating understanding of serious contemporary social problems. In 1861 he sold all his possessions and traveled to America where he spent twelve weeks distributing edifying treatises to soldiers drafted in the War Between the States. Thereafter he sailed back to his native country, and in the middle of the 1860's he took up emigration as one of his fields of interest along with being a distributor of books, a preacher, a homeopathic doctor, and a photographer. He was alternately in America and Denmark, and as a skilled speaker he tried to promote his emigration ideas among those returning from the Danish war with Prussia and among persons without a foothold in society. On the whole he tried to make great numbers of poor working people aware of their miserable circumstances and interest them in emigration. For that purpose he published the journal *The Emigrant* (*Emigranten*) and established an emigration agency in 1864, first in Hyskentraede, later in Nyhavn in Copenhagen. His hundreds of meetings in Copenhagen and in the countryside, the sale of his works *The Emigrant, The Little American* (*Den lille amerikaner*), and *Guide for Emigrants* (*Vejledning for udvandrere*), along with his distribution of radical edifying writings, increased the American fever in many of his countrymen. By the time he died, poor and forgotten in Aalborg in 1901, he had traveled across the Atlantic approximately twenty times, most often with large groups of emigrants. There is no doubt that this idealist and eccentric did much to stimulate the emigration of thousands of Danes to America. A biography entitled *The Agitator Mogens Abraham Sommer* (*Urovaekkeren Mogens Abraham Sommer*) has been written by Emil Larsen.[25]

Hans Mattson, Sweden

The Swede *Hans Mattson* was born in 1832 in Önnestad in Skåne from which he emigrated in 1851. Via Boston, New York, and Moline, Illinois he came to Minnesota, where, with his innate leadership ability, he led a small group of Swedes who sought land. They found a place suitable for settlement on the prairie west of Red

25 K. Hvidt 1971, 271–273; E.H. Pedersen 1985, 113; E. Larsen 1963.

Wing, Godhue County, where Vasa was founded, which was initially called Mattson's Settlement. In a letter published in the Swedish-American newspaper *The Homeland* (*Hemlandet*) Mattson described the colony. His articles reached Swedes on both sides of the Atlantic and led to a continual immigration to the settlement. To Vasa came, among others, the aforementioned Erik Norelius, who for many years served as pastor of its Lutheran congregation. When Mattson moved to Red Wing in 1856 in order to conduct his business, two hundred Swedes already lived in Vasa. His time was then taken up by law, local politics, and real estate transactions in the 'paper cities', which grew up during the economic boom of the 1850's. He also acquired a large farm in Kitson County, Minnesota. When the War Between the States broke out, Mattson sent out a call and recruited a Scandinavian company, which he led as captain. When the war was over, he had advanced to colonel in the Union Army. An active man, he assumed a number of responsibilities, including Secretary of the Minnesota State Board of Immigration, which was founded on his initiative and whose leading figure he became. Its activities were very much directed towards emigration propaganda and protection of the immigrants. Brochures were printed in Norwegian and Swedish, and furthermore, he wrote articles in the leading Scandinavian newspapers in the USA with factual information on Minnesota and its advantages for immigrants. In 1871 Mattson took over the post of land agent for the Lake Superior and Mississippi Railways. He realized that the best recruiters of emigrants were the early settlers, and through personal visits in the settlements he encouraged them to write positive letters home, a task made easier by his distribution of stamps. For recruitment purposes the railway company exerted great efforts to make the first days easier for the new arrivals. Representatives met them when they arrived, and they received assistance both with temporary living quarters and in selecting land. Mattson visited Sweden several times. After one recruiting trip he returned with about 450 persons to Minnesota, and his activities resulted in a large number of Swedish settlements in that state. Mattson was scarcely an idealist as far as the emigration of his countrymen was concerned, but rather a skillful administrator with business talent. In addition Mattson also served as the director of a bank, of land grant companies, and of an insurance company, and for two years served as U.S. Consul General in Calcutta. When he died in 1893, he was editor and owner of the newspaper *The North* in Minneapolis. His memoirs, *Minnen,* were published in Sweden in 1890 and in English, *Reminiscenses: The Story of an Emigrant*, in 1891.[26]

Jón Ólafsson, Iceland

The sojourn of the Icelander *Jón Ólafsson* in America illustrates in a nutshell an important stage in the history of Icelandic emigration. At the age of 23 he arrived in America in 1873, the same year that the first large group of emigrants left Iceland. He went to America because he had been fined for critical newspaper articles written in opposition to the Danish administration and its highest representative in Iceland. The Icelanders who already had left for North America had mainly been destined for Milwaukee and nearby places in Wisconsin. From the beginning they settled together in order to avoid mingling with other nationalities. Nor did they wish the Norwegian Lutheran Synod to gain too great an influence among them. The Icelanders' therefore wanted an area at their disposal where under favorable conditions they could retain their language and national identity and tend to their own affairs. Attempts had been made to create such enclaves in the unsettled regions of Wisconsin, Iowa, and Nebraska in the USA and in Ontario, Canada, but all had failed. When Ólafsson came to America he worked conscientiously for the fulfillment of this goal and for an Icelandic immigrant association. Through an American friend, Marston Niles, who was deeply interested in the Icelanders' cause, he learned that Alaska could become a suitable area for Icelandic settlement. That idea won many adherents among Icelanders in America. Alaska, purchased from Russia in 1867, was still an unexplored area. The first immigrants who arrived there came mainly from Canada and Scandinavia. With the aid of Niles, Ólafsson was able to interest the U.S. government in supporting an expedition to Alaska led by him. Through Niles' contacts he was employed by the U.S. Navy, and the naval vessel *Portsmouth* in San Francisco Bay was placed at his disposal. Together with his two fellow emigrants, Olafur Olafsson and Páll Björnsson, he received free railway transport to the west coast, whereupon he sailed to Alaska at the end of August 1874. In the beginning of November Ólafsson returned after completing his mission. As a result of his

26 L. Ljungmark 1965, 42–43, 97–103, 197; L. Ljungmark 1971, 267–268; H. Mattson 1890, 1891.

reconnaissance, which was facilitated by the captain and the crew of the vessel, he decided that Kodiak, a large island off Alaska's south coast, was suitable for settlement. Several areas on the island were well adapted for the type of farming to which the Icelanders were accustomed. The Sitka region was especially well-suited for livestock raising and fishing. Ólafsson submitted a detailed report to President Grant, which was favorably received in several American newspapers. Public opinion supported a project allowing the Icelanders to settle a country generally considered too cold and isolated. The Icelanders, however, were not successful in getting their proposal passed in the American Congress, probably because the requests made for free transportation from Iceland and the USA to Alaska for the prospective settlers were too great. Ólafsson returned to his home country with the intention of soon traveling to America again. He worked eagerly for the idea of an Alaskan colony among his countrymen but eventually had to give up. At the same time the Canadian government exhibited interest in Icelandic immigration by providing advantageous terms of transportation and offering land in Manitoba, where New Iceland was founded. The reduction of his fines made it possible for Ólafsson to stay in Iceland, and he received help in paying the remainder. His short-lived Alaskan adventure comprised a colorful episode in the Icelanders' striving for a collective settlement and provides a background for their ethnically and culturally homogeneous settlement in America. A biography by Hjörtur Palsson has been published (1975) entitled *Alaskaför Jón Ólafsson 1874,* which focuses on Ólafsson's Alaskan expedition.[27]

Matti Kurikka, Finland

The Finn *Matti Kurikka* (1863–1915) was a utopian socialist and labor leader. He studied at the University of Helsinki, published a few books, visited Denmark and Germany, and advanced to the position of editor of Finland's leading labor newspaper, *The Worker* (*Työmies*). He was strongly nationalistic, and therefore ran into trouble with the Russian authorities in Finland. He also repudiated the Marxist phalange of the Finnish labor movement, because he held the opinion that class struggle fostered hatred and bitterness. Kurikka left his leadership role in his home country and in the

27 H. Palsson 1975, 183–191.

spring of 1899 traveled to Australia with free passage offered by the Queensland government. His goal, shared by other Finnish radicals, was to found a settlement based upon cooperative farming, a society in which he could believe. The adversities were insurmountable in this project, with infertile soil and a lack of understanding from those around him. In addition many of the colony's members were dissatisfied, critical of Kurikka, and left the group. He then received a letter from Finns in the Vancouver area who wanted help in building a better society. At that time socialist ideas had gained a foothold among the Finnish miners near Nanaimo, British Columbia, who hoped to live in harmony with one another in a communal home apart from the capitalistic world. Kurrika welcomed the opportunity and left Australia, accompanied by some of the Finns. A colony was established on Malcolm Island, soon renamed *Soitula* (the Finnish word for place of harmony). The site was carefully chosen in the sound between the mainland and the large Vancouver Island, about 300 kilometers north of Vancouver with a good location for shipping and, supposedly, for agriculture. Kurikka became president of a corporation with the nationalistic name, The People of Kalevala Colonization Company.[28] Enthusiasm was great, and local newspapers hailed the initiative. Kurikka devoted much energy to the enterprise, a school was started, and a newspaper, *Time* (*Aiko*), was published. He conducted a lecture tour in America and in his home country to recruit more of his fellow countrymen, and he maintained that Finnish girls had the opportunity of obtaining good jobs in America as housemaids. Women were badly needed for the colony, which had a large male surplus. After some years about one hundred persons had settled there, and the colony appeared to flourish.

However, Kurikka's creation, built upon his theosophic socialism and unrealistic economic investments, proved vulnerable. A disastrous fire in 1903, in which eleven of the colony's members perished, became the turning point. The agricultural conditions were poor, and it was difficult to find pasturage for the livestock. Furthermore, the colony was too remote from the markets. The only profitable parts of the enterprise were fishing and lumbering. Kurikka was a gifted leader who was deeply religious and possessed a sharp intellect. Through his personal charisma and passionate speeches he could exhort his comrades to the greatest sacrifices. He had, how-

28 Kalevala is a Finnish folk epos that is a symbol of Finnish nationalism.

ever, a number of weaknesses, such as impatience and restlessness, and he lacked the gift of turning ideas into reality. Furthermore, he was often at odds with those around him. In addition his philosophy of marriage caused problems; he advocated free relations between the sexes, something which he practiced with the wife of a colleague. The situation became untenable. Kurikka left and the colony was dissolved in February of 1905. He continued his restless activities and soon founded a new colony named The Smiths of Sampo (*Sampon Takojat*) together with a number of followers from Soitula. Even here the name of the settlement referred to the national epos Kalevala. Wiser from the earlier experience, the colony was located closer to markets, about 40 kilometers east of Vancouver. Kurikka enthusiastically started a new lecture tour, but did not return. Instead he left for Finland, where, however, he found it difficult to adjust to the ideology of the Finnish labor movement. He became engaged to a 19-year-old piano teacher, but left her and their expected child. He soon went back to America with another woman, his second wife, who, however, soon returned to Finland. When Kurikka wanted to rejoin his former group in British Columbia, he was not welcome. Instead he became actively involved in the cause of the Finnish emigrants in Brooklyn, New York, emphasized their need for homeland-oriented organizations, and helped them found The Knights of Kalevala. The idealist, utopian radical, and charismatic leader Matti Kurikka ended his days as a chicken farmer in Penkere, Connecticut in 1915. His colonization efforts were short episodes, but the spirit of radicalism and the cooperative forms of enterprise have remained alive among the Finnish immigrants in America.[29]

29 O. Koivukangas 1974, 131–142; Kurikka's biography entitled *Matti Kurikka: Finnish-Canadian Intellectual* in J.D. Wilson 1981, 131–153.

9. Conclusion

The transatlantic emigration from the Nordic countries, starting in the middle of the nineteenth century, did not imply radical changes in people's tendency to move. It was rather the choice of destination that was different: America.

In traditional agrarian society people had been very mobile, although most moved short distances, primarily within the same social system. The moves between rural and urban areas and those over longer distances affected the demographic and social composition of the population. Long-distance moves were often between the Nordic countries or to and from neighboring countries on the continent. In the cities a high mortality rate made continual inmigration from the countryside necessary to maintain the population level. A sharp increase occurred in the number of inhabitants of certain cities, such as the capitals, of which seventeenth century Stockholm is a good example. This century stands out as one of extreme mobility, marked by several periods of war between the two realms in the Nordic area, Denmark-Norway-Iceland and Sweden-Finland. Due to small, short-lived colonial ventures, there were also certain transoceanic contacts and moves. Hundreds of people went to New Sweden on the Delaware River. However, this settlement lacked significance for the massive emigration which followed two centuries later.

Seasonal labor migrations constituted a special form of population movement with old traditions in the Nordic countries and most parts of Europe. Labor flowed from areas with a surplus – often forested or mountainous regions – to areas with a need for labor, such as central or coastal regions and cities. People were also attracted to locations for new settlements and to fishing villages in the northern parts of the Nordic countries. The northernmost regions of Norway, Sweden, and Finland were largely populated in this way.

The nineteenth century was an era of radical economic, demographic, and social change in much of Europe. The growing market orientation transformed the Nordic countries from a pronounced agrarian society, little influenced by market forces, to one characterized by ever-increasing agrarian and industrial capitalism. Significant demographic changes took place parallel with this development. From the end of the eighteenth century declining death rates combined with continued high birth rates caused a rapid increase in population. This rise led to the rapid growth of landless groups in the countryside and to a labor surplus.

Industrialization and urbanization in the Nordic countries started later than in England and the other countries of northwestern Europe. Development was earliest in Denmark. In 1850, 21 percent of Denmark's population lived in urban areas. The corresponding figures for Norway, Sweden, Finland, and Iceland were 13 percent, 10 percent, 7 percent and 3 percent, respectively. In Norway and Sweden there was some industrialization during the 1860's which expanded in the 1870's, both in the newer lumber and sawmill sectors and in the traditional mining and metal industries. The real industrial breakthrough did not come until the turn of the century, as did the intense movement into the cities. In Finland and Iceland industrialization and urbanization occurred still later.

The economic and demographic development led to a widening gap between the landless and the propertied, and the 'social problem' became a burning question. Certain groups felt threatened by the lower classes, which resulted in a totally new population policy. The earlier Mercantilist view held that a country should retain as many of its people as possible, because a large population was a prerequisite for a prosperous state. This idea gave way to an increasingly liberal policy with emphasis on individual freedom and the freedom to settle in the country of one's choice. From about 1860 the Mercantilist migration laws were entirely repealed, resulting in a situation where emigration restrictions were virtually lacking. Formal restrictions existed only for those liable for military service, but even this category could usually emigrate after permission was granted.

The public debate often centered upon the advantages and disadvantages of American society. In newspapers, books, and other writings from the 1820's onwards experiences and views about conditions in the USA were discussed. For the general public America stood out more and more as the promised land in matters of politics, religion, and economics.

135

In the 1840's and the 1850's, the early phase of emigration, America was attractive to those groups in the emigrant countries who considered themselves discriminated against because of religion or who found themselves in difficulties due to their political orientation or to changes in the political climate. However, it was the difficulties faced by the growing landless element in the countryside that primarily caused increasingly larger groups to emigrate to a country which offered rich, inexpensive land and industrial jobs.

The economic development of the middle of the nineteenth century brought progress and grounds for optimism. The improved transportation system at sea and on land and the building of railways resulted in a significant increase in freedom of movement. Distances on the globe felt smaller, and the virgin continents seemed to be waiting to be populated. When gold was discovered in Australia and America and the news of the gold rushes – in particular to California – spread, America stood out even more as the land of hope and promise. Only a few left for America at that time, but they were important, as they became the vanguard that spread specific knowledge about the country and the opportunities there. During the 1840's the emigration from the British Isles, especially Ireland, and from Germany had already gained significance. It was, however, during the 1850's with its favorable business cycles and the Crimean War boom that the 'take-off' came for emigration from the Scandinavian countries.

The pioneer groups that made the move over the Atlantic during the 1840's and 1850's were of overriding significance for future emigration. As a rule early emigration from an area resulted in continued strong outflow from that area. The pattern is especially clear within certain districts: Småland and Bergslagen, Sweden, and, to an even greater extent, Norway's south-central mountain regions, which very early had an extensive emigration. In Denmark, Sweden, and, above all, Norway, the first mass emigration peak came in conjunction with the years of famine and the hard times towards the end of the 1860's. In these countries emigration culminated during the 1880's and the 1890's, but high rates of emigration continued until the turn of the century. The emigration from Iceland did not begin until the middle of the 1870's, but was very intensive from its start and reached large numbers in relation to the total population during the 1880's and the beginning of the 1890's. Finland's emigration began on a small scale during the 1860's and did not peak until the first decade of the twentieth century, that is, later than in the other Nordic countries. Thus the Finnish migration in certain respects is often regarded as part of the 'new' immigration to the USA, while the chronology of the emigration from the other Nordic countries coincides with the 'old' immigration.

The largest part of the Nordic emigrants were bound for North America; only a small percentage went to other transoceanic areas, primarily Latin America and Australia. Approximately 5 percent of the emigrants went to Canada, but only one percent of those from Sweden. In that regard Iceland deviated from the usual pattern, as 85 percent of the Icelanders had Canada as a goal.

The emigration from the Nordic countries comprised only 5 percent of the total European emigration. However, calculated in terms of the population of these countries, it was large. Only Ireland had a higher rate of emigration than Norway, while Sweden experienced the third highest rate per capita in Europe. Between 1821 and 1930 a total of nearly three million persons migrated to the transoceanic areas from the Nordic countries, which in 1850 had a population of 5.25 million persons, and at the turn of the century nearly eight million. Gradually the number of re-migrants grew, and towards the end of the emigration period, when improved transportation made the crossing to America comfortable, emigration increasingly became movements on the transatlantic labor market. In all approximately one-fifth of the emigrants from the Nordic countries returned.

The increased opportunities for long-distance migration during the second half of the nineteenth century modified the migration pattern and intensified all types of migration. Labor migrations increased with the growing industrialization both within the countries, for example, to railway construction sites, and to other countries. Moves were made northward to fishing and mining areas along the Arctic coast; southward to the large agricultural districts in Denmark and northern Germany; to Norway, especially the economically expanding Christiania (Oslo) area; and to the sawmill industries along the Swedish coast of the Gulf of Bothnia, often the goal for labor from the Finnish side of the gulf. From southern and southeastern Finland there was an extensive migration of both permanent and temporary settlers to the St. Petersburg area. Finally, a vast number of inhabitants of the countryside were attracted to the cities after the economic expansion had gotten under way in the urban areas.

Through emigration the Nordic countries were drawn into the

Atlantic economy. In an era of economic liberalism and growing, largely unregulated capitalism, America, with its large areas of virgin territory and vast natural resources, exerted a strong power of attraction on the surplus labor in Europe. On American soil there were many interest groups who sought to stimulate emigration: land companies, railways, industrial leaders, and even countrymen who had emigrated earlier and willingly saw to it that new immigrants came and brought the settlements cheap labor and an increased circle of customers. Several states played an active role in the immigration propaganda, as illustrated by the activities of the Swede Hans Mattson. There was close cooperation between American capitalistic interests and large Atlantic shipping companies, whose transport capacity expanded enormously. The shipping companies employed general agents in the major European ports of embarkation, and a network of representatives was created and dispersed in the emigration regions. In the 1880's the National Line had 350 affiliated agents in Norway, the Allan Line 400, and the Thingvalla Line 600. With their experiences of conditions in America, 'Yankees', that is, emigrants who temporarily returned and were employed by the shipping companies, were probably the most successful in the 'great hunt for emigrants'. Furthermore, the numerous letters from America recounted for relatives and acquaintances the opportunities for employment and the free land available under the terms of the Homestead Act. Often pre-paid tickets were also included. During the 1880's nearly half of the emigrants from the Nordic countries traveled on such tickets. All these commercial forces influenced younger people in the Nordic countries and Europe as a whole, holding them in their grasp, which resulted in the flow of millions of emigrants to the 'promised land' on the other side of the ocean.

Part II
Nordic Immigrants in the New World

by
HARALD RUNBLOM

10. Introduction

In the first part of this book the migration process has been viewed mainly from the perspective of the sending countries, although the connection between places of emigration in the Nordic countries and places of immigration in America has been mentioned in passing. We will now change the perspective and concentrate on the view from the western side of the Atlantic. One of our main concerns is to investigate to what extent links and interconnections between Europe and America persisted. When looking at settlement, organizational life, language, and other cultural expressions of the immigrants in their new countries, we will try to determine how much of the immigrants' behavior derived from the homeland on the one hand, as against the impact of the new surroundings of immigrant life on the other.

In asking these questions one should remember the shifting interpretative frameworks that have shaped historiography during the twentieth century. The study of mass emigration from Europe and mass immigration to America were for long periods mostly separate undertakings. In this view the crossing of the ocean marked a *hiatus* between distinct worlds. An explicit interpretation of American immigration history along this line is Oscar Handlin's now classic *The Uprooted*. Handlin described the story of immigrants who 'lived in a crisis because they were uprooted. In transplantation, while the old roots were sundered, before the new were established, the immigrants existed in an extreme situation. The shock, and the effects of the shock, persisted for many years; and their influence reached down to generations which themselves never paid the cost of crossing'.[1] According to Handlin's interpretation the daily life of the immigrants was a struggle to shake off memories and traditions from the Old World. Handlin resisted seeing the immigrants' alternative strategies for survival: to mix Old and New World cultures, to

1 O. Handlin 1951. Quotation from the introduction.

separate out and preserve the useful from the old cultures, and to integrate old habits in the new surroundings.

The aforesaid should not be read as if historians before Handlin were unwilling to acknowledge the importance of the immigrants' background to their way of behavior overseas. Theodore Blegen and George Stephenson, two Minnesota scholars who made Scandinavian immigration history a respected field in U.S. academia, combined insights into immigrants' cultural background with their labor and life in America and wrote inter-hemispheric histories about Norwegian and Swedish transversees.

To return to Handlin's *The Uprooted*, this work brought to fruition a historiographic tradition that based its interpretations on the melting-pot ideology. Since 1951, when *The Uprooted* appeared, much has happened that has led to a deeper understanding of transatlantic migrations. European scholars have entered the field with strong commitments to counterbalance biased interpretations from the receiving countries. American historians have redefined immigrants into ethnics, and U.S. and Canadian scholars have consistently penetrated the transplantation of European elements into U.S. and Canadian surroundings.[2] Bridges have been built between the earlier separated worlds of migration researchers in America and Europe and this has affected the interpretations of immigrant life.[3] Many of the results from two decades of research along new paths were synthesized in John Bodnar's *The Transplanted*, published in 1985. In sharp contrast to Handlin he described the immigrants' experience as one heavily based on maintained links to the Old World.[4]

What has been said is also true for the history-writing about migration overseas from the Nordic countries. Finnish and American researchers have combined perspectives to explain Finnish immigrant settlement, culture, organizational life, and union activities in the U.S. and Canada.[5] Swedish researchers have integrated demographic studies of migrants on two continents.[6] Already in 1976 Robert C. Ostergren used the metaphor of transplantation when labeling the relationship between lifestyles in one parish in

2 E.g., R.J. Vecoli 1964 and 1972; W.D. Kamphoefner 1982; R.F. Harney 1984.
3 A fruit of transatlantic cooperation is e.g. Dirk Hoerder 1986b.
4 J. Bodnar 1985.
5 A manifestation of this cooperation are the two volumes edited by M. Karni 1981 after a conference organized by the Multicultural History Society of Ontario.
6 U. Beijbom 1971; H. Norman 1974.

mid-Sweden and another in southeastern Minnesota, two areas that were connected by an axis of migration that lasted for decades.[7] The design of Ostergren's geographical study followed one of the current tendencies in social history research at the time: to observe a restricted number of individuals and to follow them over an extended period of time. Another American scholar adapted much of his technique to illuminate many facets of cultural transfer among a group of Norwegian immigrants.[8]

The transatlantic migration will best be studied as a process over generations. The mass movement from Scandinavia to America which started in the 1840's almost came to an end during the years before the Great Depression. But even though the integration of the Scandinavian populations in America has been relatively rapid, past migration remains an important factor in forming cultural and commercial relations between the sending and receiving countries.

Celebrations of past population movements have become a prolonged effect of migration itself, for example, when Norwegians in Norway and the United States in 1975 celebrated the 150th anniversary of the arrival of the first mass contingent from the Stavanger area on the Atlantic coast of southern Norway.

Hence there is no doubt that the intense population exchange between the United States and the Nordic countries has led to economic, cultural, and social contacts between the two areas in a wide variety of spheres that would have less likely taken place had there been no mass movement over the ocean directed to the New World. To take another example, the Swedish colonization of land along the Delaware River during the seventeenth century has led to ever-increasing outbursts of commemorative manifestations. In 1888 Swedes in America emblazoned the year 1638, when the first contingent of Swedes had arrived in America. In 1938, the 300th anniversary of Swedish settlement occasioned a meeting between Swedish royal lustre and American presidential dignity in Wilmington, Delaware. At the time of writing, preparations are being made for the 350th anniversary of the foundation of the New Sweden Colony along the Delaware River.

The examples given are a few among hundreds which show that past migrations live on in the imagination: They are used to strengthen the feeling of group cohesiveness among the immigrants and their descendents alike.

7 R.C. Ostergren 1976.
8 J. Gjerde 1985.

Both laymen and scholars have made forecasts of future immigrant behavior and launched many interpretations of the respective groups' inclinations to assimilate and to fall in with the social and cultural behavior of the host societies. Theodore Roosevelt, for one, expressed his belief in the young nation's capacity to form one body of the country's population, saying in 1900 that within two or three generations most descendents of non-English immigrants would be 'absolutely indistinguishable from other Americans and share their feelings exactly'.[9]

It is obvious that Roosevelt was wrong. Even Dutch and Scandinavians, who according to many variables have assimilated quickly in terms of social behavior and who display the lowest mother tongue retention of all non-English-speaking immigrant groups in North America, are still distinguishable.

In the following we will look at various aspects of Nordic immigrant life overseas: settlement, internal migration, social life, as well as political and cultural activities. The task here is to throw light on five immigrant groups and to ask how long and in what respects they preserved their homeland culture and to what extent they adapted to life in their new countries.

9 Cited from L.L. Gerson, 1964, 19.

11. Settlement Patterns, Internal Migration, and Demography in North America

Settlement Patterns

During the nineteenth and twentieth centuries the Nordic immigrants displayed a variety in their settlement patterns in North America. The diversity depended, in part, on shifting times of arrival in the new countries. Looking at Nordic immigration from a spatial perspective, one of the fundamental questions is why Norwegians and Finns showed a stronger concentration to few areas (the Norwegians in Minnesota and Wisconsin, the Finns in Michigan, Minnesota, and Ontario), while Swedes and especially Danes followed a pattern of more even distribution over several regions. In the end one has to answer the question whether the Danish tendency to quick assimilation (in terms of high rate of intermarriage, low language retention, weak press and low organizational profiles) was an effect of wide geographical distribution or if the low degree of ethnic cohesiveness, to the extent that this statement is correct, led to wide geographical spread in the New World and only a small number of tight Danish communities in the New World.

There is a general correlation between the latitude of the emigrants' location in the homeland and the latitude of settlement area in North America. The more to the north they lived in the Nordic countries, the more to the north their location tended to be in America. This is demonstrated when one lists the core immigration areas of the Nordic national groups:

Iceland   Manitoba, Saskatchewan
Finland   Northern Michigan, Northern Minnesota, Ontario
Norway   Upper Midwest, the Canadian prairies
Sweden   Midwest and the Canadian prairies
Denmark   Wisconsin, Iowa, Nebraska, Kansas, California

Part of the explanation for this pattern is to be found in the nature of emigration behavior in Scandinavia which spread from south to north (and at the same time from west to east). In other words, Denmark and southern Sweden became involved in the emigration process earlier than northern Sweden and Finland. At the same time a northerly tendency characterized the frontier process in America. Since colonization occurred earlier in the lower Midwest, where immigrants from southern Norway settled, than in the upper Midwest, immigrants from 'northern' Scandinavia discovered more land available to the north when they arrived. The distribution of Nordic immigrants in 1910 is displayed in table 8.

Early Settlement Areas

Illinois has been labeled the cradle of Swedish America, an appellation that is correct, since the first settlements with significant numbers of Swedish immigrants were founded in this state. Illinois has continued to be a stronghold in Swedish America, and this is due not only to the role of Chicago, which became the American city with the largest number of Swedes. Bishop Hill in the western part of the state has come to symbolize the early phase of Swedish mass migration, and today the town is a historic site of importance and is being preserved under special regulation. Another place of early Swedish immigration is Galesburg where the first Swedish newspaper in America was published; and the city also served as the base for land companies which bought land farther west and

Table 8. Concentration of Nordic Minorities in the United States in 1910. Distribution by States with at Least 5 Percent of Foreign-Born Persons.

	Swedes	Norwegians	Danes	Finns
Minnesota	18.4	26.0	8.8	20.5
Illinois	17.2	8.2	9.5	
Iowa		5.4	9.9	
Wisconsin		14.1	9.0	
North Dakota		11.4		
South Dakota		5.2		
Michigan				24.0
Nebraska			7.5	
New York	8.1	6.2	6.9	6.8
Massachusetts	5.9			8.2
Washington		6.9		6.7
California			7.8	

Source: U.S. Population Census 1910, here after A. Svalestuen 1971, 53.

146

sold it to colonizing Swedish immigrants. Illinois also came to house the headquarters of the largest Swedish synod in America, Augustana, founded as a joint Norwegian and Swedish undertaking in 1860 in Chicago. It soon moved to Paxton and later to Rock Island, where Augustana College is situated. One could add that Chicago has been the strongest center in America for Swedish organizations, most of which have had as their prime goal to preserve Swedish traditions in the New World. In this respect Illinois competes with Minnesota, which has also housed a larger Swedish population than any other state and, as time went by, has become the heartland of Swedish America.

Wisconsin has played a role for Norwegians much like Illinois has for Swedes, while the Danish state *par préférence* has been Iowa. The explanatory factors seem to be the same in all three cases: early settling and the creation of church and educational institutions.

Some of the earliest settlements with Norwegian immigrants were founded in Wisconsin. Three counties in the southern part of the state, Jefferson, Rock, and Dane, developed into a tight Norwegian area and served as a base for further colonization in the west and the northwest. It is no coincidence that Norwegian Area Studies in the U.S. has its strongest base at the University of Wisconsin, Madison, located in this early-established and cohesive Norwegian area. When Ingrid Semmingsen published the second part of her main *oeuvre* on Norwegian immigration in 1950, she reported that La Crosse and Eau Claire, Wisconsin, remained among the most Norwegian cities in the United States.[1]

Early Danish immigrants settled in Illinois, Wisconsin, and Iowa, but it took a long time for Danes to form large and compact settlements in the Midwest. This was because emigration did not consist of many strong groups from distinctive places in Denmark and also because there were fewer Danish migrants than Norwegian and Swedish. Iowa, however, developed as a Danish core state. Iowa became the prime goal of Danish immigrants, when mass emigration from Denmark gained momentum in the 1870's. The state has since been the stronghold of Danish culture in the United States. In 1900 Iowa had a larger Danish population than any other state in the union. Of importance was the work of the Danish pastor C. L. Clausen, who early made Iowa a stronghold for Danish religious life in America. Danish agricultural innovations too be-

1 I. Semmingsen 1950, 245.

came important in Iowa, which housed one of the first Danish cooperative dairies.[2]

The first Icelandic immigrants in North America arrived as followers of Danish Mormons who travelled through Iowa. Later small groups of emigrants found their way to Wisconsin, Minnesota and the Dakota territory, but in the mid-1870's the main destination shifted to Manitoba. Climatic conditions in Iceland caused the exodus, but their new location, the New Iceland colony on the western shore of Lake Winnipeg, left them with a smallpox epidemic and harsh conditions. The Icelanders, unaccustomed to grain farming and lumbering (and even trees), experienced many hardships. The difficulties led to a splintering of the group and the out-migration of New Icelanders to Winnipeg, where, as time went by, the largest urban Icelandic community outside Iceland developed. Winnipeg became and has remained the center of Icelandic culture overseas.

The mining districts on Keweenaw Peninsula in upper Michigan and the Mesabi Range in northern Minnesota are intimately related to Finnish immigration. The inflow of Finns to Michigan's copper country started on a small scale in 1864–65, when some twenty Finns arrived by way of Northern Norway. They were lured by agents of the Mining Immigrant Association, which organized overseas recruitment campaigns when the mining companies were short of labor during the Civil War.

The 1864–65 Finnish immigration acted as a magnet to entice other Finns. Some families settled in the mining areas, particularly so in places in Michigan where Laestadians, followers of a religious sect from northern Sweden and Finland, moved in. Other Finnish settlements were heavily male-dominated; men comprised 81 percent of the mobile Finnish community on the Mesabi Range in 1895, a figure that speaks for itself.[3]

The Northern Great Lakes Region became a core area of Finnish settlement in the United States around the turn of the century, and Finns made up the largest foreign-born group in this region in 1900. In some counties in upper Michigan they even constituted the majority of all foreign-born.[4]

The mining districts had a multi-ethnic population. In twelve towns and villages on the Mesabi Range immigrants from the Aus-

2 T.P. Christensen 1952; E.H. Pedersen 1985.
3 M. Kaups 1975, 72.
4 A.R. Alanen, 1982.

tro-Hungarian empire, Canadians, Finns, Italians, Norwegians and Swedes made up all together 89 percent of the non-native-born population. There were also small numbers of Englishmen, Irish, and Russians.[5]

The agrarian milieus in northwestern Finland where immigrants originated contrasted sharply with the mining industrial area where they ended up. The mining industry left its imprint on the physical and social landscape. Work in deep and dangerous shafts took its toll in the form of lives. New arrivals normally found housing in company-owned units. Companies to a certain extent set the rules of social life, and Finns lived and worked largely segregated from other ethnic groups. When they could afford it, Finns tended to leave smaller mining units and move to larger mining towns where they could live more on their own terms.

The strong cohesion among Finns in the mining districts led to so-called Finn Towns, where they dominated a section of the city and formed communities with stores, cooperatives, saloons, and halls. This concentration permitted the Finns to stick to many Old World traditions. Hancock, Michigan, populated early by mining Finns, developed as a vital Finnish city and headquartered two important Finnish institutions, the Suomi Synod and the Suomi College.

The geography of settlement and mass immigration during the first phase underlines what has been discussed above about factors of tradition. The early immigrant groups' settlement choice in many cases determined the destinations of later arrivals. Several early settlements also became important foci for further immigration and some became important symbols for the transmission of people and culture from the Old World to the New.

Traditions arose around many, but not all, early places of settlement. Indeed, some early-chosen gathering grounds were deserted because lands were infertile or because they were off the main roads and could not entice newcomers. Oleana, Pennsylvania, where Ole Bull tried to found a quasi-utopian Norwegian colony in the early 1850's soon dissolved because of bad location, inhospitable natural conditions, and clumsy management.[6] The Kendall Settlement, northwest of Rochester in upstate New York, where some Sloopers found a refuge, had the character of a transit place for Norwegians

5 M. Kaups 1975, 75.
6 C.C. Qualey 1938, 12, 187.

on their way west and never developed as a real settlement.[7] Another example is Pine Lake (New Upsala), Wisconsin, where 'the father of Swedish mass emigration', Gustaf Unonius, founded a settlement in 1841. The middle- and upper-class settlers, whom Unonius had led to this swampy and unhealthy location, soon abandoned the place. They were unable to cope with practical matters and lacked the ambition to go on as agriculturalists in an environment that demanded hardship and deprivation.[8]

The Bishop Hill Experiment. Other places did not develop the way they deserved because of ineffective leadership and mismanagement. Like most utopian colonies in the United States the Swedish colony at Bishop Hill got into trouble after a few years. The Erik Jansson colony in western Illinois, founded in the late 1840's, was one in a series of communist experiments that sprang into existence in various places in the United States during the years around 1850. The driving force behind the emigration of Erik Jansson and his thousand followers was religious persecution in Sweden.[9] The colony rested on certain principles, community property (including landed as well as personal estate), strong discipline in work and family life, and above all strict and severe unity in religious matters in which the leader, Erik Jansson, played the role of prophet. The place chosen for settlement was most suitable for agriculture, and thanks to discipline and economic foresight the colony soon prospered. Houses, estate offices, and various types of buildings, including a hotel, were quickly built according to a town plan which in itself reflects the rigorous discipline and resolute leadership during the colony's early years.

But the Bishop Hill colony bore from the beginning the germ of its own foundering. Upon its arrival in New York, the group's confidence in its leader diminished when God did not endow Erik Jansson and all his followers with the ability to speak English as the leader had earlier promised in his sermons. The first drop-outs left at the port of disembarkation, and one after another members left the group. After some years unity could not be secured, and Erik Jansson's charismatic gift was not enough to keep the colony together. When Erik Jansson was murdered, his successors involved themselves in far-reaching speculation with the common assets of

7 C.C. Qualey 1938, 17.
8 H. Nelson 1943, 132.
9 Above, p. 55.

the colony, and their mistakes led to an economic collapse in the early 1850's.[10]

The factor behind the colony's success in the early years, the communal holding of property, was also the root of failure. Prosperity led to rivalry and litigation and the community dissolved during the 1850's. The activity at Bishop Hill declined when many former members moved to neighboring places in Illinois.

Land Policy. One decisive factor for the development of settlement location during the first decades of mass migration was the availability of free land. A set of American laws regulated the availability of cheap land to immigrants: the Preemption Act of 1841, the Homestead Act of 1862, the Enlarged Homestead Act of 1912, and the Stockraising Act of 1916. The last two aimed at securing large enough farms in the dry plains and the Cordillera area. Together these acts constituted the basic legal instruments by which many Scandinavians gained access to inexpensive land. The market, however, diversified and prices shifted. Escalating land speculation, in which small private owners, large land magnates, and private colonization companies all played a part, gradually led to increased prices, a factor of importance for secondary migrations, not least from the Midwest to the Canadian prairies.

Railway companies enticed settlers with offers of land which the federal government originally made available on the condition that the railroads should develop these land grants. The Scandinavian immigration to Minnesota was partly a result of very conscious efforts to sell this state in Norway and Sweden. The promoting agency involved former immigrants who via letters and visits to the home countries influenced their fellow countrymen; in addition, an arsenal of maps, brochures, and other promotional appeals led Scandinavians to Minnesota.[11]

Since the Nordic immigrants were interested primarily in agricultural settlement, they headed towards the frontier, which from the 1840's to the 1860's gradually moved from the longitude of Chicago westwards through the so-called Homestead Triangle. The gradual progression of Norwegians along the frontier in Wisconsin and Minnesota is illustrated in figure 22.

The geographical stronghold of Nordic immigration has always been the Midwest which, however, gradually lost some of its exclu-

10 K. Forsberg 1958.
11 L. Ljungmark 1971.

Figure 23. Immigrants from the Nordic Countries in the United States, 1910. Distribution by States.
Source: U.S. Population Census 1910.

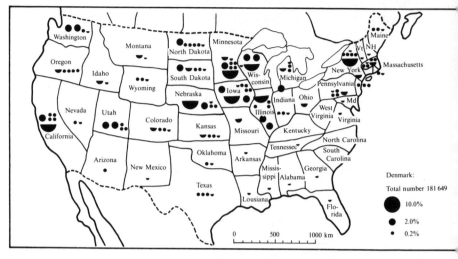

Immigrants
born in Denmark

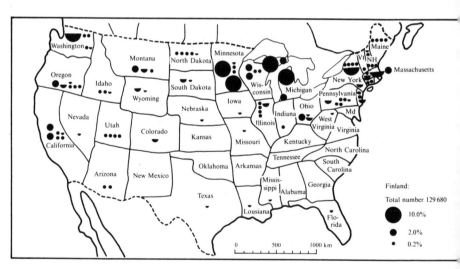

Immigrants
born in Finland

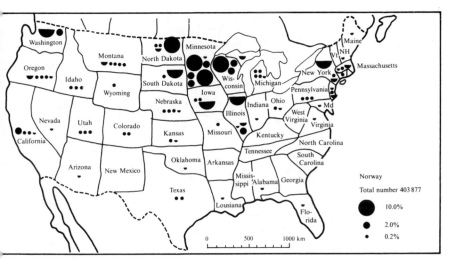

Immigrants
born in Norway

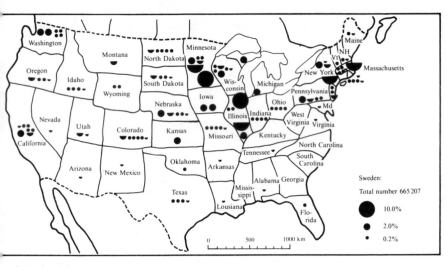

Immigrants
born in Sweden

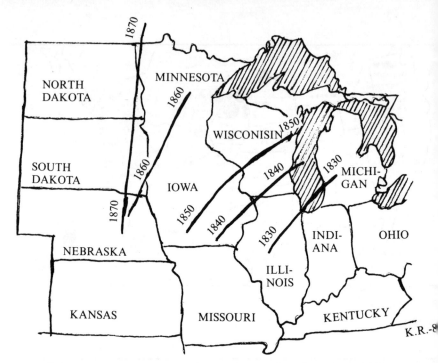

Figure 22. The Spread of Norwegian Settlements in Wisconsin and Minnesota, 1830–1880. After E. Haugen 1953, I, 26.

siveness as a migration target. In 1880 the Midwest housed, for example, 76 percent of the Swedish-born population in the U.S., but this figure dropped to 64 percent in 1900 and even further in 1920. This decline occurred while shares increased in the West and the East. The explanation for these figures is at least twofold: First, land became less accessible in the Midwest; second, the social composition of the immigration from Scandinavia shifted from overwhelmingly rural to more and more urban.

With the arrival of cadres with increasingly urban and semi-urban backgrounds in the 1800's, the classical migration targets lost some of their attraction. At the same time an out-migration from the rural areas of the Middle West to urban areas and to areas farther west and to Canada took place. Second generation rural immigrants who had difficulty finding land in their home states took the lead in this movement, but first generation settlers also responded to the exhortation to go west.

The distribution of Nordic immigrants in American regions is given on the maps in figure 23, which disclose some important differences between the various Nordic groups.

Canada

The movement of Nordic immigrants to Canada falls in line with the main patterns of Canadian immigration in general. The influx of people in the modern history of Canada can be divided into four phases. The first ended at the turn of the century, in 1901. The second phase started in 1901 and lasted until the outbreak of the First World War. As a result of strong immigration propaganda, directed by Sir Clifford Sifton, Minister of the Interior, the Canadian west was settled. The First World War interrupted the strongest influx ever to the country. A new era commenced with the 1920's but ended with the Great Depression. Due to its small population relative to its resources the country has been one of the world's largest recipients of immigrants during the period after the Second World War. Even during this fourth period immigration from the Nordic countries has been considerable.

With the exception of Icelanders, Canada served until the last decade of the nineteenth century mainly as a transit country for Scandinavians *en route* to the U.S. The city of Quebec became a port of disembarkation from the early days of Scandinavian mass immigration, but settlement in Canada was no vital alternative. There were exceptions among Norwegians and Swedes. Swedes populated Kenora, Ontario, early in its history, and did the same in Waterville, Quebec. Norwegians formed an early settlement in Gaspé, Quebec. The move to this place was a result of purposeful efforts by Canadian authorities to attract Norwegians on their way to the Midwest.[12]

When the prairie provinces opened for settlement in the 1890's, Swedes and Norwegians, and some second generation Swedish and Norwegian Americans, moved from the Midwest, first from Minnesota, to take land in Manitoba, Saskatchewan and Alberta.[13] This movement north across the U.S.–Canadian border accelerated after the turn of the century and led to Swedish and Norwegian settlement in these provinces.[14]

Later on immigrants arrived directly from the Nordic countries.

12 Th. Blegen 1940, 373–387.
13 H. Runblom 1977.
14 K.O. Bjork 1974; H. Palmer 1972.

155

This has led to a pattern of geographical distribution of the Nordic peoples in Canada where Icelanders are found mainly in Manitoba and Saskatchewan, Finns in Ontario, and Swedes and Norwegians mainly in the prairie provinces and British Columbia. (See maps, figure 24.) The weaker Danish element reflected the general low level of Danish emigration, especially during the first three decades of the twentieth century. On the other hand a substantial Danish emigration to Canada took place after 1945.

For the Nordic immigrants of the 1920's Canada offered a strong alternative to the U.S. In Canada land was still available, while this was not true in the U.S. The Canadian propaganda during the 1920's still aimed at immigrants willing to start farming, especially at the northern frontier in the prairie provinces. The Canadian recruitment campaign continued in Northern Europe during the 1920's, but the result did not meet expectations. Scandinavian settlers tended to go to the cities, while eastern and southern Europeans had a stronger inclination to start as farmers. The Finns welcomed the possibility to come to Canada, especially since the immigration quotas to the U.S. were considerably lower for the Finns than for the other Nordic groups. Hence the Finnish immigration to Canada from 1924 numbered around 5,000 every year until the Depression impeded the flow and in 1931 the Canadian government implemented a restrictive immigration policy.[15]

Despite very active measures taken by the Canadian government to entice Finns to the fertile soil of the prairie provinces and to settle as farmers, the Finns preferred to stay in the eastern part of the country, mainly Ontario, where Toronto, Sudbury, and Thunder Bay have large Finnish populations.

The Finnish immigrants finally ended up in other districts and occupations. Why did Finns, whose land hunger has so often been witnessed, avoid farming in Canada? One may speculate in this matter. Lack of capital and a very unbalanced sex ratio played some role. Another factor, whose importance is hard to determine, would be tradition: Finns accustomed to woods and a variegated landscape avoided the flatlands with endless prairies. Where Finns did take land in Canada they diversified labor, alternating as farmers, fishermen, miners, and woodsmen.[16]

The radical tendencies of Finns in Canada made authorities pon-

15 V. Lindström-Best 1981; O. Saarinen 1981.
16 V. Lindström-Best 1981; E. Laine 1981.

Figure 24. Nordic Population in Canada 1931. Number of Persons Born in Respective Nordic Country, Distribution by Provinces.
Source: *Seventh Census of Canada*, 1931, Volume II, *Population by Areas*. Ottawa 1933, pp. 709–713.

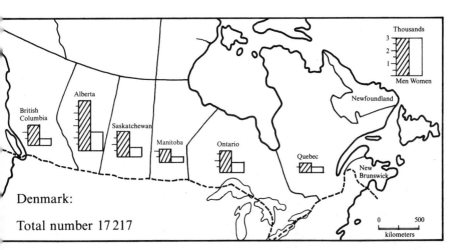

Denmark:

Total number 17 217

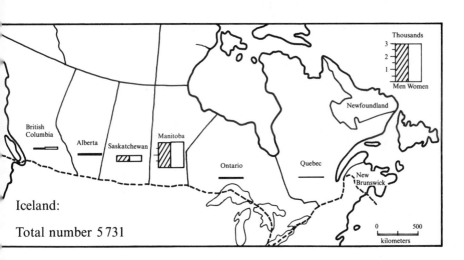

Iceland:

Total number 5 731

157

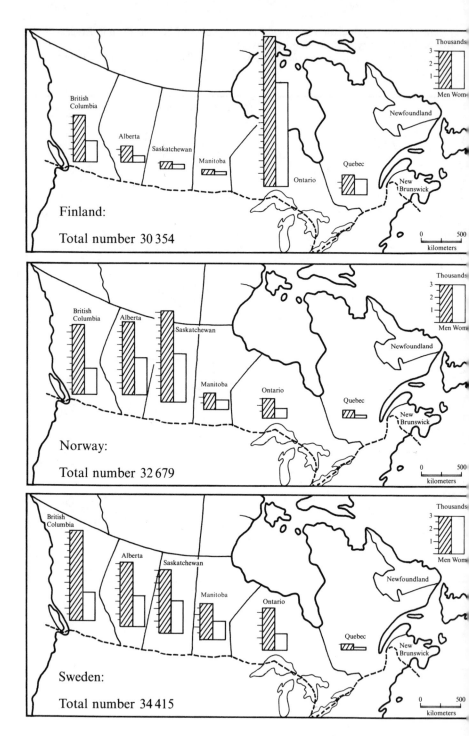

Finland:

Total number 30 354

Norway:

Total number 32 679

Sweden:

Total number 34 415

158

der whether immigration recruitment from Finland should continue. Some officials, proposing that Finnish inclination to socialism made them undesirable, attempted to curb Finnish immigration. This evidently had no real effect. On the contrary, when Finland had lost part of its territory after the Winter War, Ontario's Premier Hepburn worked out a plan to entice 100,000 Karelians to settle in Canada, a plan which never materialized.[17]

Internal Migration

The main direction in the settlement of the American continent was from east to west, and the frontier movement which started in the seventeenth century gradually moved from the Atlantic seaboard to the Pacific. (See figure 25.) The speed of this process was accelerated during the nineteenth century, and the secondary migrations of Nordic immigrants must be viewed in this context.

As to Nordic immigrants, three main directions can be distinguished and examined here:

a. The westward movement;
b. Migration to cities and industrial areas; and
c. The northerly movement to the Canadian west.

The tendency towards the south, so prevalent during the period after World War II, had barely begun when the mass emigration period ended in 1930. The main tendency was rather northwards, a movement in which especially the black population participated during the first decades of the twentieth century.

Mobility on the Frontier

Geographical mobility continued to be considerable even when land on the frontier was scarce. Land speculation led to land-leasing and an increased share of tenants, many of whom hoped to become landowners themselves. For example, in Nebraska one can distinguish a group of farmers who bought land in order to sell it quickly, make a profit, and move again.[18] Also in Trempeleau, Wisconsin, with a large Norwegian population, individual land speculators were active.[19] There was a high rate of population turnover among settlers in Illinois and Iowa in the 1850's.[20]

17 V. Lindström-Best 1981, 10.
18 M. Curti 1959, 65.
19 M. Curti 1959, 66.
20 E.H. Pedersen, 1985, 87.

1810

1850

1870

Figure 25. The Frontier
Movement in the United
States, 1810–1890.
Source: L. Ljungmark 1965,
19–20.

1890

160

Merle Curti found, in his study on Trempeleau County, Wisconsin, that population turnover was high during the initial settling period and the following decades.[21] Married persons were, hardly surprisingly, less prone to migrate than unmarried. American studies generally support the observation that people over 40 become less mobile. The ethnic composition of rural communities also seems to have had an impact on mobility. Swedish immigrants in Pepin and Burnett Counties in Wisconsin, fairly compact ethnic settlements of Swedish character, had a high degree of persistence, which led Hans Norman to the tentative conclusion that tight ethnic settlement promoted stability.[22]

There are varying interpretations of the social processes that constituted frontier life. Referring to observations of life in North Dakota in the 1880's and 1890's, John C. Hudson has launched the notion of the frontiersman as employed in mulitple jobs. The way of life in this northern plain state, settled near the closing of the frontier, had little of the character of a melting pot. There was a high degree of mobility, and much of this was seasonal migration. The division of labor was marked. To supplement their regular income farmers worked as carpenters and teamsters or took jobs with the railroad companies which laid tracks through the Dakotas during the 1880's and 1890's. This was most common during the early years of settlement before these new landowners had established their economy.[23]

To a large extent, first and second generation immigrants with a background in the Midwest populated the North Dakota frontier. Many Swedes had been working in lumber camps in northern Minnesota, while Norwegians came from overpopulated areas in the southwestern corner of the state and from adjacent areas in northern Minnesota. Seasonal migration brought many recent Scandinavian settlers back to their old areas of activity, not least in Minnesota, and hence helped to spread the interest in the Dakota frontier.[24]

Normally the frontier seems to have been a place of migrational turbulence. The immigrants did not arrive and settle all at the same time in one place and not once and for all. In their search to find good land and a place to settle the new arrivals made movements within the frontier areas. Frontier volatility is illustrated in a study

21 M. Curti 1959, 65–69.
22 For a discussion see H. Norman 1976, 267–269.
23 J.C. Hudson 1976.
24 J.C. Hudson 1976, 242–265.

of the migration to the prairie land in South Dakota. Settlers who during the years 1868 to 1873 arrived in the Vermillion area in Clay County were mostly Scandinavians. Some immigrants moved directly to Clay County, evidently those who already knew of the area upon departure from Scandinavia. Local provenance in Sweden was important in forming settlement behavior. Those from Dalarna in Sweden had a tendency to go directly to Vermillion while those from other Swedish provinces tended to make intermediary stops, mainly in Iowa and Illinois. It is evident that certain settlements east of Clay County served as staging places for migrants going west.[25]

The frontier movement can be described as a drifting westwards but can also be seen as a consolidation of already settled locales. The attraction of new settlers to an area already partially claimed could take place in different ways, and early settlers were in a position to manipulate the rest of the settlement process. The interesting question here is whether any ethnic differences can explain the behavior of Norwegians, Danes, and Swedes in this respect.

In the Vermillion Valley land acquisition took place between the years 1868 and 1873. The largest groups among the settlers were Danes, Norwegians and Swedes, but only Norwegians and Swedes formed settlements with consistent forms. The Norwegians chose to settle west of the river, the Swedes east of the river, while the Danes spread and formed communities in various locations across the county.[26]

If the Vermillion case is typical, Danes had a lower inclination to stick together than their Scandinavian brothers and sisters. One may, however, look for specific factors that shaped the make-up of this community. A large share of the Swedes who settled in Vermillion hailed from a couple of districts in Dalarna, and this common local background can be considered a cohesive force in maintaining settlement. Corresponding data about the Norwegians and Danes is not available.

Secondary Migration

The patterns of internal migration in America shifted over time. For the purpose of illustration five individual cases will be presented

25 R.C. Ostergren 1980, 80–84.
26 R.C. Ostergren 1980, 76.

here, which reflect this changing pattern. All five originated in Långasjö, a parish in the province of Kronoberg in southern Sweden.

Långasjö began sending migrants to America during the pioneer years of Swedish emigration around 1850, and through the whole mass emigration period this parish had high emigration rates, and its migration history exemplifies the so-called stock effect. The area was agricultural, but farms were generally small, and it is probably correct to describe the social situation at the middle of the nineteenth century as overpopulated. Långasjö has become well-known through two of its sons, Wilhelm Moberg, who wrote the emigrant trilogy, and Amandus Johnson, who emigrated at the age of three in 1880. Johnson became professor in Scandinavian languages at the University of Pennsylvania in 1913 and devoted much time to the study of early Swedish history in America. His books on Swedish-American history are monumental.[27]

The five 'case study' emigrants (whose routes of migration are described in figure 26) emigrated in 1853, 1892, 1910, 1911, and 1911, respectively. Although three of the five emigrated during a short period of time (1910–1911) they nonetheless represent different immigrant types. The *first* migrant, Carl Abrahamson, who emigrated in 1853, is typical of the first decade of mass emigration. A landowner in Sweden, he left in hope of developing a larger farm in America. He went directly to his destination in Franconia, Minnesota, where he spent the rest of his life. The *second* migrant, Simon Petrus Johansson, left Sweden in 1892 having no landed wealth in his home parish; he moved about on a smaller scale, working in railway construction in southern Sweden before he left for America. He lived a mobile life in America, made little social advancement, and after working in various jobs moved to the Pacific coast, finally settling as a small landholder. The *third* migrant, Karl Edvin Karlsson, who emigrated in 1911, is typical of many Långasjö emigrants. He lived in America for a long time, accumulating funds in order to return to the home parish to find a life comrade and a piece of land or a business. Like many Långasjö emigrants of this category, Karlsson spent an ambulant life in western America on both sides of the U.S.-Canadian border.

Our *fourth* example, Johan Albert Eliasson, who arrived in America in 1911, represents many Scandinavian emigrants around the

27 A. Widén 1970.

163

turn of the century in the sense that he went directly to the Pacific coast. The *fifth* migrant, Alma Linnéa Augustdotter, typifies a group who, when they could afford it, chose to spend their age of retirement in the sun belt, preferably on the Atlantic or the Pacific coast. Alma Linnéa first lived in Chicago before, in her last stage of migration, she moved to Miami.

With the exception of the first migrant, all made further steps of migration in America after their first settlement, and this was probably normal for a majority of immigrants from the Nordic countries. Among those who first went to the Middle West, secondary movements in the westward direction often followed and illustrate the gradual movement of the Scandinavian immigrant groups towards the Pacific.

Second-stage migrations often took place within certain networks, in which common background in the Old World was important. This is discernible in material collected by Carl-Erik Måwe, who traced American descendents of emigrants from Östmark parish in Värmland, Sweden, a wooded province close to the Norwegian border which experienced rapid population growth during the nineteenth century and an accelerated parcelling out of land into many hands. The emigration intensity of Östmark easily exceeded the average for Sweden and Värmland.

The case of the Östmark immigrants illustrates some basic migration patterns. Like many Nordic emigration parishes Östmark had some main destinations in America. During one early period Minnesota received the greatest number, two counties taking the lion's share of the Östmark migrants, namely the adjacent Wright and Meeker Counties. In Wright County the towns of Buffalo and the more rural Stockholm were important targets. These places had the character of gathering places and transit areas for further moves.

Östmark migrants as a whole joined the westward movement, and even in their second and third steps the cohesive tendency remained strong. Along the Pacific some cities located close to the Canadian border became new gathering places, primarily Troy in Idaho, and Spokane and Seattle in Washington. The further spread, to Alaska and California, which was mainly a second generation phenomenon, seems, however, to have meant a dissolution of the bonds from the homeland. But[28] in Troy, Spokane, and Seattle the feeling of common local background in Östmark was so strong that

28 C.E. Måwe 1971.

1. *Carl Abrahamsson*, born 1820, emigrated 1853, died 1914.

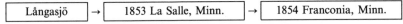

Note. Abrahamsson was born in Långasjö, where he in 1850 inherited the farmstead of his parents-in-law. He emigrated with his family, and the stop-over in La Salle was enforced since they arrived so late in the year 1852 in the United States. Abrahamsson was the first known America emigrant from Långasjö. He stayed in Franconia until his death in 1914, where he by and by acquired a property of 300 acres. (Source: *En Smålandssocken emigrerar*, 1967, 63–69).

2. *Simon Petrus Johansson*, born 1851, emigrated 1892, died 1907.

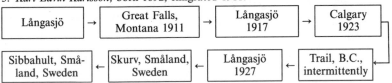

Note. Before emigration in 1892 Johansson worked as navvy on the line Kalmar-Emmaboda and for the Gefle-Dala Railway Co. As newly-arrived immigrant he worked as farmhand; in Minneapolis he was carpenter at construction works. In Alberta, finally, he became a petty freeholder 'with cow, horse and fowls'. (Source: *En Smålandssocken emigrerar*, 1967, 139).

3. *Karl Edvin Karlsson*, born 1892, emigrated 1911.

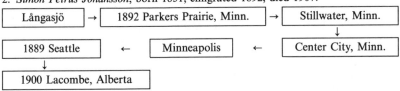

Note: Karlsson was the son of a farmer. He joined an earlier emigrated brother in Montana in 1911. After at least one visit to Långasjö, he finally re-emigrated and married, whereafter he died in Sweden.

4. *Johan Albert Eliasson*, born 1892, emigrated 1911, died 1961.

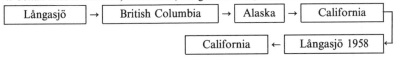

Note. Eliasson was the son of a petty-farmer; in Canada he worked in the forests, possibly also in the mines. In California he was a farm worker. (Source: *En Smålandssocken emigrerar*, 1967, 428–429).

5. *Alma Linnéa Augustdotter*, born 1892, emigrated 1910.

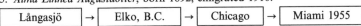

Note. Augustdotter was one of six children to a farmer. Four of the six emigrated to America. In America she worked as a maid before she married. Her husband was a doctor. (Source: *En Smålandssocken emigrerar*, 1967, 419).

Figure 26. Five Typical Cases of Migration among Långasjö Emigrants in America.

the local 'colony' could entice new arrivals directly from the home parish in Sweden.

The high frequency of second-stage migration in America was not necessarily socially disruptive, even if the quest for land and economic opportunities sent individuals and small groups far away from families and kin. Turlock, California, was a gathering-place for groups of Swedish Covenants who came from various places in the United States. Founded in 1902–1903, this colony enticed migrants from several places, but not directly from Sweden.[29]

In his study of Balestrand migrants from Sogn *fylke* in Norway, to refer to another migratory group, Jon Gjerde unveiled a string of settlements from eastern Wisconsin to the Dakotas based on bonds of kinship, cultural affinity and common theological orientation.[30] Gjerde even states that migration tended to increase the importance of the nuclear family, since the rising cost of labor led to a situation in which the family became the optimal unit of production.[31]

There was a tendency among both Norwegians and Swedes to go further west to join fellow countrymen who had already made second stage migrations. Preferably one moved to settlements where one could join people with the same local background. The Balestrand emigrants illustrate this phenomenon (figure 28).

Recessions in the American economy resulted in increasing re-emigration. Men were more sensitive to deteriorating conditions on the labor market than women, and the male re-emigration curve

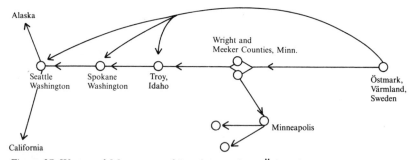

Figure 27. Westward Movement of Immigrants from Östmark Parish, Sweden. Source: Based upon information in C.-E. Måwe 1971.

29 Ph. Fjellström 1970.
30 J. Gjerde 1985, 160.
31 J. Gjerde 1985, 138.

followed more closely the ups and downs of the business cycles than did the female. Those who went back had only been a short period in America.[32] Consequently, one could ask to what extent internal migration of immigrants correlated with recessions in business. One may surmise that immigrants who had been in the new country four or five years, which seems to be a critical time span after which the probability of returning to the home country drastically decreased, must have looked for alternative migration targets in the new country. The data on Nordic immigrants are scarce in this respect, but we know at least that the 1893 recession stimulated interest in the Pacific Northwest among Norwegians in the Midwest.[33] Despite its devastating effects on the immigrants' economic and social situation, the Great Depression did not lead to any mass movement back to Scandinavia, but there is evidence of some 'de-urbanization' during the years after 1929 in which Scandinavians also participated.

The fact has often been repeated, and indeed correctly, that

Figure 28. Settlements in the Upper Middle West Populated by Immigrants from Balestrand, Norway.
Source: J. Gjerde 1985, 144.

32 L.-G. Tedebrand 1972, 251–255.
33 K.O. Bjork 1972, 81.

Norwegians in America were more rural in their settlement pattern than any other immigrant group. On the other hand, there has been a tendency to overlook the strong urbanization of Norwegian (and Swedish) immigration. Much has been written about rural life in Minnesota and Wisconsin but few have paid attention to the large communities of Norwegian immigrants in New York, Chicago, and Seattle. The tendency to dwell in cities was strong compared to the situation in the sending countries, even if Nordic immigrants were less urban than most, or perhaps all, other immigrant groups.[34]

Cities

Some middle-sized cities in America received much of their distinctiveness from their Scandinavian populations. A handful of them have been centers for specialized industries. One is Jamestown, New York, sixty miles southwest of Buffalo, where the native-born Americans comprised the largest portion of the population around 1850 when Swedish immigrants began arriving in larger numbers. Availability of land and forest and a pleasant climate enticed the first Swedish contingent to the area, but they arrived without much capital. The Swedish element continually grew. In 1930 there were 7,738 Swedish-born and 9,046 second-generation Swedes out of Jamestown's total population of 45,000, rendering the city a distinct Swedish flavor. The next largest immigrant community was Italian. The Italians started to arrive around the turn of the century when the Swedish population had achieved a leading position in the economic, political and social life of the city. Swedish Hill in the southern part of the city revealed a concentration of Swedish residents, but the Swedes were found all over the city.

Jamestown is in a sense typical of a score of medium-sized cities having strong Scandinavian populations which made their imprint on various spheres of activity. In time Swedish furniture and mechanical industries dominated the city's economy and Swedes constituted a large part of the economic leadership and the labor force on the shop floors. Another city of this kind is Worcester, Massachusetts, which boasted considerable Swedish and Finnish populations of which a large number worked in the iron and ceramic industries.[35] Still other examples are Rockford, also dominated by

34 E.P. Hutchinson 1956, 26–27.
35 H. Nelson 1973, 107–111; A. Myhrman 1972; R. Rosenzweig 1983.

inland. Emigration from Finland was of a rural character, mainly because a large part of the population lived in the countryside. Moreover, the landless segment of the population increased during the 19th century, forming a group that was inclined to move to America. Slash and burn was common in this heavily forested country. This painting by Eero Järnefelt from 1893, with the title *Sved* ("Burning the Forest Clearing"), shows a strong social tendency in its presentation of agricultural proletarians from Savolax in eastern Finland. Photo: Museokuva, Helsinki.

Iceland. The climate and soil in Iceland were such as to limit the possibilities fo agriculture. During the 19th century the poor population made its living almost exclus ively from stock-raising and fishing along the coasts. The authorities tried to limit th growth of the poorer groups by regulating marriages. When emigration from Icelan gained momentum, it soon reached an intensity higher than that from the other Nordi countries. Oil painting with a motive from Thingvellir, by Thórarinn Thorlaksson 1900. (Listasafn, Reykjavik). Photo: Department of Art History, University of Uppsala

Denmark. This painting, "The Signalman", gives a good illustration of the Danish landscape with its prosperous agriculture. During the second half of the nineteenth century Denmark was more industrialized and urbanized than the other Nordic countries, and the modernization of agriculture provided new job opportunities in the countryside. This was also an important factor behind the country's low emigration rate. Oil painting by L. A. Ring, 1884. Photo: Nationalmuseum, Stockholm.

Norway. The central mountain region of Norway was deeply affected by emigration In these vast areas people lived along the valleys. Space for agriculture was greatl limited, and the population often struggled under harsh conditions. An importan prerequisite for survival was the pasture on the mountain sides. This oil painting is calle "Peasant Burial" (*En bondebegravelse*), with a motive from the County of Telemark, b Erik Werenskiold, 1885. Photo: The National Gallery, Oslo.

weden. In relation to their population, cities in the Nordic countries had a higher
migration rate than the countryside. Stockholm is an example of this, and the Swedish
apital experienced higher emigration than the other parts of the country. From the
arger cities with their differentiated population structure, a proportionally large part
f the emigrants went to European countries, even though the numbers who left for
merica were still larger. This canvas, "Pulling Down the Old Orphanage in Stockholm"
Rivningen av det gamla barnhuset i Stockholm), was painted by Anshelm Schultzberg
a 1886. Parallels have been seen between this motive and August Strindberg's poem
The Esplanade System" (Esplanadsystemet) 1983: "Here shall be torn down to give
ght and air." ("Här rivs för att få ljus och luft"). Photo: Nationalmuseum, Stockholm.

America. This canvas from 1886–1887, called "A Reindeer Scene in Lapland", painted by the Swedish American Olof Grafström, illustrates the divided identity of an immigrant. He portrays a view from the northern part of his home country showing a group of Lapps (*Sami*) in their daily life with a herd of reindeer and a multitude of objects typical of their way of life. The landscape is, however, more typical of the western United States, and the cliffs do not resemble those of Lapland in character. Whatever his intention, the painting represents an intriguing link between the aesthetics of the Old World and the artistic tastes of the American West. Photo: Augustana College Collection.

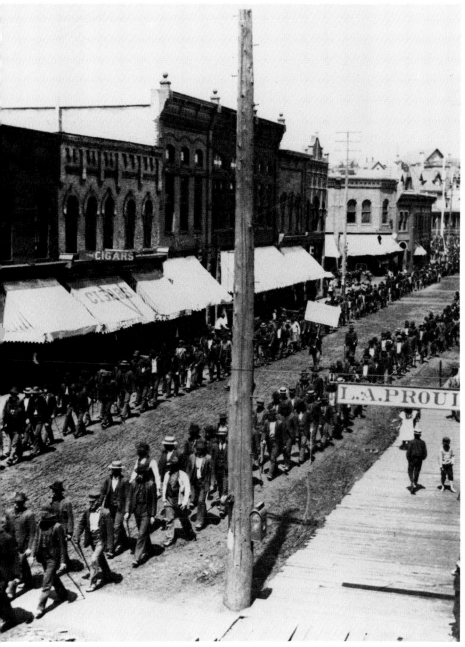

nnish Copper Strike Parade. Finnish immigrants played an active role as strikers in e mining districts in northern Minnesota and northern Michigan around 1910. From nnish Photo Collection, Minnesota Historical Society, St. Paul.

"Papa is Striking for Us." Parading Children. From Finnish Photo Collection, Minneso ta Historical Society, St. Paul.

Interior of a Workers Hall, Hibbing, Minnesota. Finnish immigrants built halls, whic housed many cultural activities. From Edith Koivisto Papers, Minnesota Historic: Society, St. Paul.

a large Swedish labor force and enterprises, as well as Moline in Illinois. Decorah, Iowa, developed as a center for Norwegians in a largely agricultural area. The city took a leading role in the shaping of Norwegian culture in the New World partly through Luther College and the influential and widely spread *Decorah-Posten;* the literary society *Symra* still functions as a bridge between Norwegians in the homeland and America.[36]

Some cities housed large populations of more than one Nordic immigrant group. Chicago became at an early stage a center for Swedes and Norwegians, and to some extent also Danes, but this city never held any large Finnish population. Minneapolis and St. Paul have since the 1860's had a large Scandinavian population, but these cities' share of Swedes has normally exceeded the share of Norwegians, although Norwegians were more numerous in the state of Minnesota as a whole.

Though being the foremost port of disembarkation for Scandinavian transversees, New York City did not until the 1870's become an important center for Finns, Norwegians, and Swedes. This reflects the importance of the Midwest for early Scandinavian immigration. For example, not until the 1870's did Swedes start to settle down in New England in any considerable numbers. According to the 1870 U.S. Population Census there were only 1,558 Swedish-born inhabitants in New York City, and cities like Providence, Rhode Island, and Worcester, Massachusetts, which later developed a strong Swedish element, only numbered a handful of Swedes that year.

Minneapolis and St. Paul became something of a Scandinavian metropolis during the last decades of the 19th century. The American muckraker and literary city investigator Lincoln Steffens in 1903 called Minneapolis the second largest Scandinavian city in the world. In those days this would better have fit Chicago, judging by statistics alone, because Chicago had a larger mixed Norwegian, Swedish and Danish population. On the other hand Minneapolis (together with St. Paul) was the city where the Scandinavian impact was most powerful, something Steffens described in his own way; according to him Minneapolis was composed of 'a Yankee with a round Puritan head, an open prairie heart, and a great, big Scandinavian body'.[37]

36 Th. Blegen 1940, 165, 521; O. Lovoll 1983, 125–126.
37 L. Steffens, *The Shame of the Cities* (New York, 1904), 64.

Chicago and New York City

The life of ethnic neighborhoods can be described as an evolutionary process: growth, culmination, deterioration, elimination. Studies of Chicago have systematically shown how this description is applicable for almost all ethnic neighborhoods in the city. Following deterioration and elimination, which can be more or less definite, is succession: One group comes in and takes over the area from an earlier group that moves away.

Germans, Norwegians, Swedes and Irish were the first immigrant groups to come to Chicago, but the Norwegians were much smaller in number and did not leave their mark so distinctly as the other three groups. All four groups chose areas where they dominated the neighborhoods: Norwegians in The Sands (east of La Salle Street), Irish in Kilgubbin (between Kenzie and Eric Streets, west of State Street), the Germans in Dutch Settlement (around Chicago Avenue), and the Swedes in Swede Town (north of Chicago River). The Irish and Swedish settlements were geographically almost identical. Seen over a long time span the dispersion from the above-mentioned location has been more complete for Swedes and Irish than for most other ethnic groups in Chicago. One reason for this may be that these groups came early (at least compared to Italians, Russians, Poles, and Blacks), could pave their own way and grow as ethnic groups when the city prospered most. Compared to the Irish and the Swedes, the Italians have shown lower geographic mobility as a group. It took a very long time for them to move out of Ward 2, where a majority of them lived at the turn of the century.[38]

Three phases are discernible in the mobility of Chicago's Swedish population. The early Swedes settled in a compact area, first known as Swede Town, later as Old Swede Town. The first groups to settle there were some of the transient travelers to the Bishop Hill colony. Some of the early settlers were squatters without legal right to the property they occupied. The early churches, e.g. St. Ansgarius Church, stores, and newspapers, strengthened the area's Swedish character.

The more numerous Irish had a tendency to penetrate the area in a way which threatened the Swedes. Quite early Swedes tended to move north toward Chicago Avenue and Old Swede Town became more and more a 'transient' area for new arrivals until, after

38 U. Beijbom 1971, 1973.

170

the turn of the century, the Swedes abandoned it and the South Italians and Sicilians turned it into 'Little Italy'.

The story of Norwegians in New York City has some parallels and some differences compared to the Swedish movements within greater Chicago. One resemblance is the territorial movement from one original location to other parts of the city. One striking difference is the timing of dissolution and dispersal. Another is the relative cohesiveness of the Norwegian neighborhoods as compared to a more gradual dissolution of the Swedish neighborhoods of Chicago.

The earliest Norwegian colony in New York was formed on lower Manhattan in the 1850's and it was strongly linked to the city's role as a maritime center. Most of those who settled in New York during the early decades of Norwegian mass immigration were seamen who jumped ship. The majority of Norwegians who came to North America during the era of sailing vessels arrived in Quebec and not by way of New York. But Norwegian shipping in the North Atlantic trade was brisk and many cargo freighters also called at U.S. eastern ports, especially New York, and ship-jumping created a great problem for the Norwegian shipping trade.[39] Those who settled in New

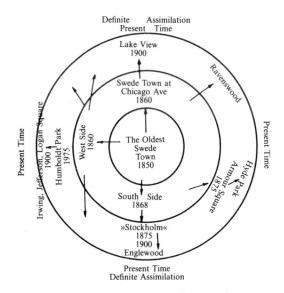

Figure 29. From Downtown to Suburbs. Swedish Population Movements in the Chicago Metropolitan Area.
Source: U. Beijbom 1973, 207.

39 I. Semmingsen 1950, 278–280.

York hailed largely from parts of southern Norway and from places that earned their livelihood from fishing, shipping, ship-building and other sea-related trades. Hence there were strong craft links between the sending area and the recipient eastern harbor. The Norwegians in New York worked as longshoremen, sailors, and dock-builders, and they preferred other jobs in businesses connected with shipping. 'There was always a strong whiff of the briny sea over the Norwegian colony in those early days'.[40]

One scholar, Christen T. Jonassen, has described the transformation of the Norwegian colony in New York City in terms of micro- and macro-ecology. The strong dependence on maritime-related occupations lasted until the 1940's, and as a consequence the colony changed its location with the shifting conditions and geographical movements of the metropolitan city's sea trades. As Brooklyn gradually took over Manhattan's role in this respect the Norwegian neighborhoods moved over East River. Around 1870 a new Norwegian community took shape in Old South Brooklyn. It prospered during the last decades of the 19th century and then declined when great numbers of Southern Europeans, mainly Italians, moved in. As the city grew, the Norwegian center moved south in Brooklyn and finally also moved away from the sea front. One location, Sunset Park, went through the same process as Old South Brooklyn from a Norwegian point of view, but in this case Puerto Ricans played the role of newcomers who took over the residential area.[41]

One can discern four distinct moves by the Norwegian group and five distinct locations (Lower Manhattan, Green Point, Park Slope, Sunset Park, Bay Ridge, cf. figure 30) before it dispersed and largely lost its character as a well-defined ethnic neighborhood when many Norwegians and Norwegian descendants moved to the suburban areas. It may be evidence of strong Norwegian cohesiveness that the Norwegian center in Brooklyn, despite the heavy out-migration from the area, has survived as an ethnic entrepôt into the 1980's. This perhaps means that ethnic traditions among Norwegians are stronger than those of other 'old' immigrant groups.

Brooklyn witnessed strong ethnic competition, and one question is whether Norwegian ethnic expression in New York City has stemmed from the challenge of other ethnic groups, especially Jews and Italians. Numerically the Norwegians were but a minority in

40 A.N. Ryg 1941, here cited from C.T. Jonassen 1985, 80. On Norwegian immigrant sailors and shippers see also above, pp. 101–103.
41 C.T. Jonassen 1985.

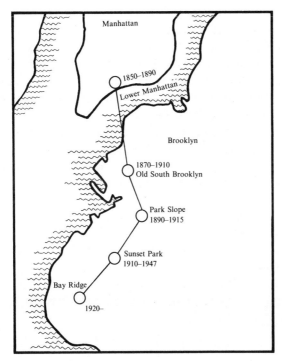

Figure 30. The Gradual Movement of the Main Norwegian Neighborhood in New York City.
Source: After C. T. Jonassen 1985, 87.

the areas where they resided, and their population small compared to the other ethnic groups. In 1910 there were 25,013 Norwegian-born residents in New York City, which also meant that the Norwegian share of the city's population was much smaller than the Swedish.

The movement of the Norwegian neighborhood in New York reflects a general pattern in the ethnic geography of large American cities: the shifting character over time, the movement of ethnic groups from one section of the city to another, the succession of younger immigrant groups when the area deteriorated, and the gradual dissolution of the ethnic neighborhood. Chicago, New York, and Toronto have over and over again experienced these patterns. What is most striking in the case of the Norwegian neigborhood in New York is its longevity, which probably has something to do with the unceasing flow of Norwegians into the city. The ethnic Norwegian community has always had a small stock of new

173

arrivals to draw upon. Somewhat of the same phenomenon can be observed among Swedes in Chicago in the 1980's. Andersonville in northwestern Chicago, with North Park College as one of its cultural resources, still maintains the character of a Swedish neighborhood. Blacks and recent immigrants have moved in and taken over part of this area, but Swedish organizations, clubs and shops have tended to remain in the neighborhood.

Of the Norwegians in New York one may ask what their relations have been with the rest of the Norwegian community in the United States which has been so strongly concentrated in the Midwest. New York gradually became the largest Norwegian concentration outside Norway. In 1930 the city had 63,000 Norwegians, sixty percent of whom were born in Norway.[42] There were strong links between Norway and New York: intense sea traffic, continous migration, and frequent visits by famous Norwegians. As a consequence, relations with compatriots in the rest of the U.S. were relatively weak. For example, the *bygdelag* movement which, was strong in the Middle West and the West, 1900–1930, never developed branches in New York.

42. O. Lovoll 1983, 172.

12. Nordic Immigrants in Latin America

Scandinavia and Latin America

Of the total overseas migration from the Nordic countries the number who finally landed in Latin America is marginal. In contrast to many countries in southern Europe, a strong migration tradition to the areas south of the Rio Grande never developed in northern Europe. For centuries South America had, however, attracted individuals and small groups from Scandinavia: adventurers, sailors, businessmen, explorers, and some social outcasts. The independence movements in South America at the beginning of the nineteenth century heightened Scandinavian curiosity in the area and raised the expectations of businessmen. Diplomatic relations were slowly but gradually extended between Scandinavia and the new countries. Shipping, not least on Norwegian keels, led to contact between the areas, and one may surmise that this trade contributed many who jumped ship. For Australia and New Zealand, systematic studies of different sources (naturalization lists, reports of aliens, marriage registers) have been conducted in which thousands of Scandinavian sailors have been identified who were stranded and for various other reasons went ashore to start a new life on dry land.[1] A scrutiny of Latin American sources would probably yield a similar result.

In most respects the migration to Latin America had its own distinctive features if compared to the migration that was directed from the same countries to North America. It differed in volume, geographic origin, social composition, sex distribution, and rate of re-migration. Looking first at the quantitative aspect of the Scandinavian presence in Latin America, one must point to the unreliability of the figures in the statistics both from the sending and the receiving countries. During the period between 1850 and 1940 half of all Nordic immigrants came from Denmark (around

---

1 U. Beijbom 1983; O. Koivukangas 1974; O. Koivukangas 1986, 21–30.

17,000), a third from Sweden (approximately 10,000), while Norway (between 3,000 and 5,000) and Finland (around 2,000) had lower figures.[2]

The importance of Latin America for Scandinavian migration grew from the nineteenth century to the twentieth, a shift linked to the continent's development of international industry and trade. Much of the Swedish migration to the ABC countries (Argentina, Brazil, Chile) and Mexico has taken place in the wake of the establishment of Swedish daughter companies and trading firms.[3] Another example of 'elite' migration is the continuous flow of Nordic engineers who found jobs on that continent. Between the years 1910 and 1940 two hundred left Norway; they had many forerunners prior to World War I, the majority of whom stayed in the overseas countries and were 'hispanized'. Many were pushed from Norway in this brain drain, since, especially during slumps, the Norwegian economy could not swallow the output of the new engineers from the technical schools.[4]

Immigration Propaganda

In Brazilian history the 1880's and 1890's witnessed a strong influx of migrants from Europe, a fact which can be linked to very specific changes in production. It coincided with a boom in the cultivation of coffee, when new areas were put into use. This change, in turn, came when slavery was abolished, a process that lasted over several decades, although the final decision to abolish slavery was taken in 1888. As production moved to new areas and as the demand for free labor expanded, immigration became the solution.

Brazilian propaganda drives in Europe sought to attract the necessary labor. The Brazilian government opened recruitment offices in Europe, and their activities in Scandinavia were directed from a huge office in Hamburg. One agent named Reeh, connected with the firm R.O. Lopedanz in Hamburg, succeeded in sending 800 Danish emigrants to Brazil between the years 1886–1887.[5] Several sub-agents were active in Malmö in southern Sweden, and from this city deceptive descriptions about Brazilian conditions were spread. In his reports to Copenhagen the Danish counsel in Sao

2 G. Stang 1976, 304.
3 Cf. H. Runblom 1971.
4 G. Stang 1976, 320–330.
5 B. Essinger 1979, 90.

Paolo vigorously contradicted misleading information in the Brazilian propaganda, and this may help explain the low Danish emigration to the country during the peak years in Brazilian immigration.[6]

From around 1870 Argentina also increasingly attracted European immigrants and settlers, partly due to a breakthrough in the intercontinental trade in meat and cereals. As a major grain supplier Argentina played a similar role for the European market as did the U.S. Midwest. The transport revolution led to lower freight prices and an easier access to the European market. There was, however, a clear difference between the structures of Argentinean and Midwestern agriculture. In Argentina the *latifundia* structure gave no room for homesteading as in the United States and Canada. The Argentinean propaganda in Scandinavia, unlike the Brazilian propaganda, did not encourage 'nationally pure' settlements.

In South America the Scandinavians settled almost exclusively in the temperate regions, as did most Europeans during the mass migration period. Southern Brazil and Argentina were the main targets. The culmination occurred during the years around 1890, and an important factor was the propaganda described above. Individuals and smaller groups had gone earlier, and in the Danish case, they drew others during the peak period. In other words, this was a case of chain migration.

Group Migrations

The first Nordic group emigration to Latin America is in a sense typical, resulting from poor navigation and lack of money. A group of 106 travelers left Trondhjem in 1850 with the intention of finding gold in California. Their frigate *Sophie* ended up in Rio de Janeiro and was not in a condition to continue. The group accepted an offer to establish an agricultural colony in the province of Santa Catharina. The colony soon dissolved when its members, almost all men, dispersed in various directions, some of them back to Norway.[7] This story was repeated when a Swedish group bound for Australia capsized near the same spot in 1871.[8]

Scandinavians bound for South America went largely in groups, and they intended to build colonies. A Dane, Hans Christensen

6 B. Essinger 1979, 90.
7 G. Stang 1976, 298–299.
8 A. Paulin 1951, 569–571.

Fugl, founded the oldest in Tandil south of the Argentinean capital; his background was significant for his later role as colonist. Fugl left a teaching career in his home town Stege on the island of Møn in 1844. He was followed by a doctor and his wife, started to farm and developed a *charca*, became successful and went back to Denmark, returning to Argentina with more followers. Møn and Lolland were, until the 1870's, the areas in Denmark from which the colony drew its immigrants, but later on Tandil and its sister colonies in the region attracted immigrants from other parts of Denmark. Wheat and dairy farming were the main economic activities, and the colonies became centers for the transmission of agricultural techniques in these fields. Tandil became a Danish cultural stronghold in Argentina.

The Danish migration to Brazil was more limited and more often consisted of individuals. Those who arrived during the 1880's frequently found work on the coffee plantations in the state of Sao Paolo. It is hard to relate Danish emigration to South America to certain events in the countries of departure and arrival, conforming with the general character of the Danish mass migration movement: The curve is smooth with low peaks. The bulk of the Swedish migration to South America, in contrast, was very strongly related to dramatic events. It consisted of three main contingents:

1. 1868 emigration to Brazil, in the main departing from the Stockholm area;
2. 1890–1891 emigration, mainly to Brazil, numbering some 2,000 emigrants, 500 from the Sundsvall area and 700 from Stockholm;
3. 1909–1911 emigration to Brazil, mainly from the mining town of Kiruna in Lapland.

The 1868–1869 emigration can be linked to bad economic conditions during the setbacks in Swedish agriculture at that time, which resulted in a peak in the early Swedish mass emigration. A driving force behind the Brazil-directed move was the Swedish publicist Johan Damm, who was also an emigration agent.

The culmination in 1890 and 1891 coincides with a general peak in European migration to Brazil; in the Swedish case one can clearly see the work of agents in Malmö who concentrated their campaigns on certain cities and towns. One large group emanated from the sawmill areas around the city of Sundsvall, where distressed workers took part in so-called Brazil meetings, where as one voice they expressed their embitterment towards their employers and Swedish society and their strong belief that Brazil was liberty's place of origin.[9]

The upswing in Swedish emigration to Brazil during the years 1909–1911 originated much like that from Sundsvall twenty years earlier. As a mining town Kiruna was hit hard by the Great Strike (*storstrejken*) of 1909. Local newspapers provided important information concerning migration alternatives. The two dailies, the conservative *Norrbottenskuriren* and the socialistic *Norrskensflamman*, contained during the three years 1909–1911 as many as 1,744 advertisments for shipping companies and emigration agents, although only a minor part concerned Brazil. The resultant fever caused several families to leave for Brazil, especially since the agents made special offers to impecunious people who could not afford passage on the North Atlantic route. This led to a different social and demographic composition compared with the contingents that generally left Sweden for North America at the same time. While the latter had a large strain of individual migrants during the 1880's, the groups destined for South America consisted mainly of families, some with many children.

Since the Brazilian federal and state authorities drew a large number of Swedish immigrants to Brazil, these migrants were assigned places of settlement in the country. A settlement with the 1868 migrants in Dona Francisca in the state of Catharina soon dispersed due to dissatisfaction among the colonists over the limited possibilities of acquiring land and obtaining gainful work. The 1890–1891 passages experienced a similar situation. Brazilian authorities directed them to distant places in the State of Rio Grande do Sul, where they were isolated from one another. The living conditions were harsh, and many immigrants succumbed to disease, hunger, and poverty. 'The settlers' severe living conditions often lead to drunkenness and apathy', concluded one observer; superstition and primitive behavior became widespread in their living habits and customs.[10]

The 1909–1911 emigrants faced circumstances nearly as grim, unveiling the inflated promises of the agency propaganda. The groups of 1890–91 and 1909–1911 moved farther and crossed the border to Argentina. Thereby a type of secondary settlement of

9 K. Stenbeck 1973.
10 S.A. Flodell 1974, 36–45.

Swedish character grew up in the old Jesuit province Misiones. The settlement became so concentrated that a basis for ethnic solidarity was established. In the mid-thirties 927 Swedes were reported in the area around Oberá. There are signs that the Swedes there retained Swedish longer than in comparable places in the U.S., probably an effect of their isolation and limited contacts with the outer world. Like many immigrant churches in the area, the Swedish congregation became a conservative element advocating cultural solidarity with the mother country. This is one of history's many ironies, since the immigrants who in Argentina praised the old country had left Sweden disenchanted with the mother country, many even feeling contempt.

The rather scant migration to Latin America has played a significant role in the popular imagination. In one of his autobiographical novels, the Swedish Nobel laureate in literature Eyvind Johnson has related what impact the Laplanders' journey to Brazil (1909–1911) made on his mind.[11] One who returned from this journey, Gerda Pehrson, has published books of fiction where she recapitulates the tragic stories of less blessed chevaliers of fortune. *The Flood Took* is the expressive title of one of her novels.[12]

Turning to the Finns, it is even more striking than in the Swedish case how conditions at home stimulated emigration. Specific figures for emigration from Finland to Latin America are not given in Finnish statistics until 1924, and therefore discussions about numbers are based on relatively fragile information up to this year. Finnish emigration to South America is almost wholly a twentieth century phenomenon. One large group emigrated in 1906. The 1920's was a peak period, spurred by the introduction of quotas in the U.S., which admitted few Finns. Like the Danes and the Swedes, the Finns moved mainly to Argentina and Brazil, but settlements were also founded in Cuba, the Dominican Republic, and Paraguay.

The earliest Finnish settlers built their new homes in Misiones. The 1906 contingent consisted initially of about 150 people, mostly men and almost all Swedish-speaking, a factor that stimulated contacts with Swedish settlers in the same area. The ambitions of these Finns coincided with the plans of the Argentinean authorities.

11 Eyvind Johnson, *Se dig inte om*. Stockholm: Bonniers, 1936.
12 Gerda Pehrson, *Floden tog*. Stockholm: LT, 1965.

Comparative Aspects

There are striking differences among the emigrations to Latin America from the Nordic countries. The earliest group migration emanated from Denmark, was directed to Argentina, and resulted in a colony with a continual inflow of Danes and the preservation of Danish culture. Relatively few Danes were lured by Brazilian propaganda during the latter part of the nineteenth century, probably because Denmark had better channels of information and Danes made their own interpretations of the situation in Brazil. On the other hand, the majority of the Swedish emigrants went to Brazil, and all group migrations resulted directly from Brazilian efforts to entice labor to the country.

There was no connection between the various Brazil-directed group emigrations from Sweden. In comparison, the Danish flow of emigrants to Argentina stemmed from a stock effect. Once a bridgehead was erected in Tandil, this location became a center and magnet for Danes who later wanted to seek their fortunes in South America. This difference also led to contrasting cultural situations. Because of the continous inflow of new people, the Tandil settlement received new impulses from the mother country, giving it fresh infusions of Danish culture. The Swedes, on the other hand, were caught in a vicious circle. Once they had arrived in Brazil they were unable to remain cohesive, partly because the Brazilian authorities sent them off in different directions, and partly because they had to disband in search of some means of support.

The group emigrations from Denmark, Finland, and Sweden consisted of different social and occupational categories. Even if many Danes who emigrated to Argentina during the nineteenth century were unskilled agricultural laborers or semiskilled urbanized workers, the Danish contingents, as a group, brought technical skill and entrepreneurship to Latin America. The agricultural knowledge they brought from Denmark found a market in the developing Argentinean agriculture. The Danes found positions in their new country, while the Swedes lacked specific competence upon their arrival. It is ironic that less urbanized Sweden sent unskilled workers from the cities and industrial areas to agricultural work in Brazilian forests and fields. Nor was the Finnish group better equipped for agricultural work with its many intellectuals seeking a refuge and a possibility to realize political dreams in a subtropical milieu. Hence their utopian adventures were predestined to failure.

181

The role of leadership is also illuminated by the Nordic experiences in Latin America. The initiative for the migrations from Sweden came from the receiving country, Brazil, and middlemen in Sweden organized the travel. They gathered people from wherever they could, and with the exception of the Sundsvall contingent of 1890–1891, the groups were not united before departure and had no common goal when they arrived in the new land. One could add that the Sundsvall group was more united in its opposition to the existing social order in Sweden than in its ambition to build a new existence beyond the ocean. In the Swedish case no strong individuals took the lead. In contrast, the Danish colony in Tandil and its adjacent sister settlements had their way paved by a forerunner, Hans Christensen Fugl, who became a uniting force among his fellow countrymen, and when he left strong personalities took on his mantle.

13. Nordic Immigrants as Farmers

In the Old World perspective the Scandinavian immigrants in North America have been connected more closely with the rural than with the urban milieu. Three outstanding series of novels have contributed to this picture. Per Hansa and Beret and their companions in Ole Rølvaag's *Giants in the Earth* (1929, published first in Norwegian 1924–1925) settled on the frontier in North Dakota. Karl Oskar and Kristina in Vilhelm Moberg's emigrant trilogy (the first volume of which was printed in Swedish in 1949) cleared the backwoods at Chisago Lake a couple of years before Minnesota gained statehood.[1] In one of the Swedish author Sven Delblanc's bestselling novels published in 1984, another couple, Maria and Fredrik, started as farmers in Manitoba a couple of years before the Great Depression. In reality, though, the overwhelming majority of Scandinavians in those years made their way to urban areas.[2]

Against the backdrop of fiction's eloquent but biased historical picture one may ask what, in actuality, Nordic immigrants who cultivated the soil experienced. The Danes, Norwegians, and Swedes who arrived in North America during the early decades of mass immigration had a greater tendency to seek agricultural areas and occupations than other immigrant groups. As farmers the immigrants gradually adapted to the new environment. It was important for the new arrivals to get a quick return in order to acquire cash for tools, seed, animals, and building material. This led the farmer to grow grains that could be sold easily on the market. The first years were critical, and the immigrant who had taken up a homestead was pressed to till his lot within a stipulated time span. No systematic study of failures among early Nordic homesteaders has been made, but there are drastic examples of individuals who had to leave because they did not manage to cultivate their claims.

1 V. Moberg 1949, 1952, 1956, 1959.
2 S. Delblanc, *Kanaans land.* Stockholm: Bonniers, 1984.

Adjustment to American Farming

There is some scholarly disagreement about how immigrants a-dapted as farmers in their new milieu. One study of immigrant farming in several Kansas counties has shown a certain diversification of production along ethnic lines: Swedes had more cattle and cultivated more types of crops than Mennonite and Canadian farmers.[3] One Danish historian presupposes (without pointing at real evidence) that Danes were more capable farmers upon arrival in America because of their experience in Denmark during periods of strong agricultural development. He also concludes that Danish farmers were less specialized than others on the American prairies.[4] This evidence can be juxtaposed against a very thorough study of farming in Chisago and Isanti Counties in Minnesota, 1870–1900. That study showed that Swedish farmers cultivated the same crops as native farmers, but that the Swedes did not have as large acreages nor as many horses as their American-born neighbors. Most observations led to the conclusion that practices inherited from the homeland played a negligible role. On the other hand, the fact that Swedes kept more sheep may go back to Swedish local traditions, while their higher and more intense use of the land and higher production per acre was a function of relative land shortage.[5] Generally the American farmers had a lead in farm size that Swedes could equal only in time.

A crop almost unknown to Scandinavian agriculture was tobacco. The Norwegian settlers in Wisconsin started to cultivate this product early on; it remains a staple product and a symbol of Norwegian agriculture in this state.[6]

Nordic immigrants came from areas with shifting agricultural practises and traditions. Sixty percent of the Danes who left rural areas for America during the years 1868–1900 were farmhands, and they left an agricultural economy in rapid transformation. The share of peasant proprietors increased despite the decrease of total employment in agriculture. Cattle breeding expanded at the expense of grain production, a shift closely related to Denmark's vulnerable position as an exporter of agricultural products. This restructuring gave rise to the production of ham, bacon, butter, and eggs and

3 D.A. MacQuillan 1978.
4 E.H. Pedersen 1985, 155.
5 E. Hamberg 1976.
6 P.A. Munch 1954, 104.

was necessary to maintain Denmark's shares of the market abroad when cheap American and Russian grain inundated Europe. One feature of the transformation was the founding of packing-plants and the expansion of dairy production and the dairy business. In typical Danish fashion strong producers' cooperatives developed.

An important question is whether Danish rural migrants who left a milieu in such swift transformation brought new technology to America and if they contributed to the spread of innovations. The Danish economic historian E.H. Pedersen has made observations that can provide part of the answer. Early Danish farmers had no profile, being too isolated and too few.[7] Danish farmers in Minnesota quickly shifted their production in the nineteenth century when their output on exhausted soils diminished, and they switched from grain to animal production according to the Danish model.[8]

Undoubtedly, experiences from the Danish dairy business were brought to Minnesota, and the first cooperative dairy in the state was founded in the Danish settlement Clarks Grove. Many of the 630 cooperatives in Minnesota before 1918 are said to have been modeled on the one in Clarks Grove.[9] Contacts among Danish settlements in the U.S. also led to the spread of cooperative ideas.[10]

Attitudes towards Landowning

One important factor is the attitude towards land. Many immigrants came from overpopulated areas, where a far-reaching partition of farmsteads and land shortage led to reclamation of marginal lands which produced meagre yields. The endless prairies must have been an overwhelming sight for the farmer's son when compared to the unfertile soils of upper Värmland or the hilly lands of Hardanger. Hence land hunger characterized Nordic immigrants. In his history of Finnish-Americans William Hoglund reiterates the notion that Finns had a built-in longing for the land and a farm.[11]

Scandinavian-American literature abounds in stories about the pioneering farmer's quest for land and his drive to enlarge his landholding and improve the buildings. The fiction also mirrors the

---

7 E.H. Pedersen 1982, 53.
8 E.H. Pedersen 1982, 59.
9 A. Regan 1981, 281. Pedersen warns against exaggerating their Danish characteristics.
10 G.R. Nielsen 1981, 151.
11 W. Hoglund 1960.

clash between Old World and New World values: should the oldest son take over the farm and should the relatives have the option to buy land in the manner of the homeland when the family wanted to sell out? Rølvaag's Beret does not hesitate: 'Peder is not to have the right to sell the farm outside the Holm family as long as there is any of them willing to buy'.[12]

What Rølvaag touched on in the novel has been systematically studied by the geographer Robert C. Ostergren who scrutinized land transfer patterns on the Minnesota frontier within families with different ethnic background. He stresses two different attitudes towards land use. It could be viewed either as an economic asset and an object of speculation or as the 'giver of life', a symbol of familial accomplishment and identity in the community.[13] After examining the inheritance patterns Ostergren discerned shifting strategies. In Isanti County settlers from Rättvik, Sweden, planned the transfer of land to the next generation. By passing landed wealth to their heirs step by step they secured a continuation of familial traditions. American farmers did not practice this transfer of land prior to death, and non-Rättvik Swedes followed practices somewhere between the Rättvik and the American 'model'.[14]

Ostergren's observations constitute another modification of Frederick Jackson Turner's thesis, showing that the frontier did not cast all settlers in one mold. They also highlight the role of ethnicity on the frontier. In Isanti the Rättvik people acted with collective goals in mind. The American farmers showed an individualistic attitude: Everybody should be the architect of his own life, which also was the parents' attitude towards their children. One can speculate about the values of the Rättvik people from Dalarna, Sweden, a province with very special relations between man and land. Land partition was far-reaching, and an extremely large part of the population consisted of landowners. Many, however, had only narrow parcels or long but inaccessible strips of wooded land. Since the Swedish enclosure movement (*skiftesrörelsen*) proceeded slowly in the Dalarna province and has continued so even to this day, collective cultivation and harvesting have been necessary. There is reason to believe that, in the case of the Dalecarlian people, local attitudes

12 O. Rølvaag, *Their Father's God*, 1931, 253, here cited from D.B. Skårdal 1974, 207. Skårdal 1974, 205–211, has a chapter on 'love of land'.
13 R.C. Ostergren 1986.
14 R.C. Ostergren 1981 and 1986.

toward land as a concern of family and kin were transferred to America.

Ethnic Mixture in Rural Areas

The Isanti case also actualizes relations between ethnic groups and subgroups in surroundings where many categories of people were residing. In many settlements one group, especially one that arrived at an early stage when land was initially claimed, purchased land from others and consolidated its position. The Rättvik people formed a dominant group in some townships in Isanti and acted in this manner. There was, indeed, no uniform pattern on the frontier but rather a variety of different economic and social developments. Studying Norwegian settlements in Wisconsin, sociologist Peter A. Munch distinguished two different types of growth, one *intensive* and one *extensive*. The *intensive* led to an increased colonization of the settlement. In this type the Norwegians deterred other foreigners from settling. This led to a decrease in numbers of other ethnic elements within the restricted area of settlement and could also lead to reduced social contacts with other groups and the outer world. The second type, *extensive growth*, led to expansion into neighboring areas and to more open contact with other ethnic groups that were admitted to the core areas.[15] Looking at the long-term trends in Wisconsin, Minnesota, and the Dakotas one may hypothesize that the intensive type of growth was most frequent among the Norwegians, who kept their rural character (and outlook), while other groups, for example Swedes, had a much stronger inclination to urbanize.

It is difficult to isolate the factors behind this process, in which economic factors intermingled with institutional and cultural factors, but we have the opportunity to examine the microcosmic world of frontier settlements and further ponder the role of ethnicity. Kandiyohi County in central Minnesota was a rural area probably typical of many regions in the state. Groups of different national backgrounds settled the county. Swedes settled early and families from Gagnef and Mockfjärd in Dalarna, who started to emigrate during the famine years at the end of the 1860's, arrived in significant numbers. Among the early settlers were also found Yankees, emanating from New England, and Irish, who did not arrive directly

15 P.A. Munch 1954.

187

from Europe but had farmed their way through Canada. Norwegians also pioneered in Kandiyohi. (See figure 31.)

In many respects the ethnic groups displayed little uniformity in their behavior. During the forty years following 1870, the Old Americans and the Irish tended to leave the area, as did the Norwegians, who did not have any regionally based settlement there. One important Swedish subgroup from Hälsingland even began to disperse while the Gagnef group functioned as a magnet for others from the same area of Sweden. Swedes from Småland and Skåne first increased in number and then remained. The geographer John Rice, who has compiled this data, points out a strong correlation between ethnic cohesion, persistence, and economic success.[16]

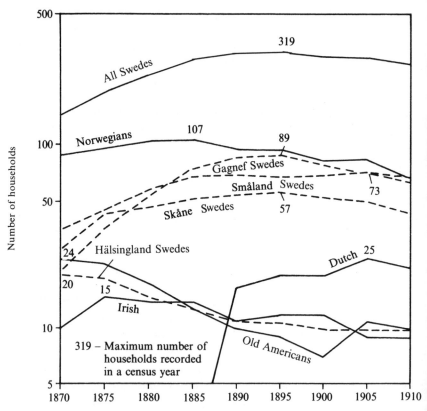

Figure 31. The Size of Culture Groups in Six Townships in Kandiyohi County, Minnesota, 1870–1910. Number of Households at Five-Year Intervals. Source: J. Rice 1977, 161.

16 J. Rice 1977.

188

Finnish-American Small Farmers

Mass emigration from Finland started too late to allow many Finns to settle as farmers or farm workers upon their arrival in America. When the Finnish exodus gained momentum around the turn of the century there was a shortage of land in the United States. Finns for various reasons did not settle on the Canadian prairies. Nonetheless 15,000 Finnish-born 'farm operators' were reported in the 1920 U.S. census. Behind this figure was a shift from mining and urban occupations to agriculture among first generation Finnish immigrants. The question presents itself: Was this tendency to leave industrial work an example, after all, of Frederick Jackson Turner's safety valve theory?

An attempt to explain the tendency to abandon mining for marginal farming has pointed to the Finns' position in the mining industry. Being among the 'new immigrants', Finns were at a disadvantage compared to earlier arrivals, and advancement along the social ladder was difficult, because a sort of hierarchy had evolved among the ethnic groups with each group having its own 'niche'. For the newly arrived Finns this led to relative subordination in the mining fields and may have contributed to a desire to leave this trade.

Swedish-speaking Finns also participated in this urban-rural movement and ended up as farmers, especially in areas with many Swedes, primarily Michigan and Minnesota, but also in the state of Washington. Land fever reached its peak among Finnish immigrants at the close of the First World War.[17]

When Finns left industry and mining for agriculture, they acquired land mainly in two areas. The first lay in denuded forest areas, stump lands, in the upper Midwest (Michigan, Minnesota, Wisconsin) and, since no longer useful to timber companies, came relatively cheap.[18] Swedish-speaking Finns mixed with the Finnish-speaking group in this farming enterprise. In the second area, in New York and New England, Finns resettled land which native farmers had abandoned when they entered other occupations or, in some instances, when children had not taken over the farmsteads. Finns who settled on abandoned farms in New York during the 1910's and 1920's arrived with little capital and therefore selected low-priced units in hilly areas which they bought on credit.

17 W. Hoglund 1964.
18 A. Myhrman 1972, 35.

The Finnish experience described here has no parallel among other Nordic emigrants, and it is difficult to point out exactly what social forces led Finns to subsistence farming after a period of working at other occupations in America. Their rural retreat was a one-generation interlude; the second generation moved away from this small-farm world. The small isolated farm that required hard work for low returns hardly met the expectation of America that these people had on the eve of emigration. Lacking data on the group's social background, one can only suppose that the majority emanated from the rural proletariat in Finland. The Finnish countryside cried for a solution to the problem of the burgeoning rural proletariat when these groups left Finland during the 1890's and the first decade of the twentieth century. Seen against their background in the homeland, their lives nonetheless ended in social advancement.

14. Churches and Organizations

The inclination to organize seems to be catholic among immigrants in modern societies, and the historiography of European immigrant life in America overflows with notions about the respective group's urge to develop a rich associational life.[1] As far as is known, comparative studies on these phenomena do not exist, and it is therefore problematic to single out what form and content of organizations were related to the homeland heritage as against those which reflected impulses from within the receiving countries.

In the Scandinavian case this is so much more of an onerous task since the homelands underwent dramatic changes during the mass emigration period, including the development of a rich flora of so-called popular movements: free churches, temperance orders, labor unions, cooperatives, etc. One of their prime criteria was opposition to the state.[2]

Churches

In one respect, though, it is obvious that homeland patterns shaped the overseas configuration, namely within the religious sphere. The establishment of Nordic churches in America mirrored religious trends and ecclesiastical formation in the respective home countries.

The development of church life and religious mentality of Nordic immigrants in America must be viewed in several contexts: first, the opposition to the established state churches in Scandinavia and the spiritual counter-movements that led to the rise of free churches in the nineteenth century; second, the international exchange of ideas and the traffic of preachers and evangelists between America and Scandinavia, a traffic which had religious repercussions in both worlds; and third, the right of free establishment of churches and the existence of religious pluralism in the United States.

1 E.g., J. Puskas 1982.
2 S. Lundkvist 1977; J.A. Seip 1981; H. Try 1985; V. Wåhlin 1979.

Nordic church life in America inherited and accentuated doctrinal tensions from the mother countries. Religious strife pressed heavily upon Norwegian social life in America, and Norwegian communities were split for half a century over the question of the means of grace and other complicated doctrinal matters. Even families were tormented by the factionalism within Norwegian American Lutheranism as is reflected in literary accounts: 'The ties of old friendship broke. Neighbor did not speak to neighbor. The daughter who was married to a member of the other party became a stranger in her father's house. Man and wife turned into dog and cat. Brothers and sisters were sundered from one another'.[3] The strong influence of the German-based Missouri Synod became a controversial factor among Norwegian American church leaders; one dimension of the debate concerned whether established American traditions should supercede traditions from the homeland.

The Danish Church in America had a built-in split originating in Denmark, which in 1894 led to a division of the Danish Church in America into two separate units, one Grundtvigian and one Inner Mission.[4] Within Swedish America the influential Lutheran Synod, Augustana, dominated the religious life: Heated theological discussions took place but they never seriously threatened to cause schismatic movements. At the same time, the free churches had more believers among Swedish Americans than among the other Nordic immigrant groups. In Finnish American society the strongest demarcation divided believers in the church's message from ardent sympathizers of Marx's and Lenin's political philosophies.[5]

Since Nordic churches in America were from the beginning transplants from the home countries one must begin in Scandinavia. As has already been pointed out, religious oppression was only a marginal cause of Scandinavian mass migration, but in all countries many resented curtailed religious freedom, an attitude which affected the atmosphere of many emigrant groups during the initial phase of mass emigration to around 1860.

Religious dissenters took the lead in the early group migration; from Norway, Quakers in the 1820's; and from Sweden, the Erik Janssonists in the 1840's. Mormons and Baptists were pioneers in the Danish emigration in the 1850's. All these movements reflected

3 J.A. Erikson, 'Større end det største', *Ved arnen*, Vol. 65, nr. 32 (Febr. 14, 1939), here quoted from D.B. Skårdal 1974, 181.
4 E.H. Pedersen 1985, 213–229.
5 D.J. Ollila 1977.

the limited elbowroom for those who did not endorse the official creed of the established churches. In this sense emigration provided an outlet for individuals and groups who found the ecclesiastical tutelage of the state objectionable. Founding a new religious order; building congregations; forming new communions of the faithful; these marked the quintessence of migration for many of the early emigrants. No wonder then that early emigration led to the establishment of a variety of denominations in the new country with its unlimited religious freedom. The total number of new religious organizations was high considering that all, except Mormons and Quakers, were of Protestant character. The Scandinavians therefore contributed to the already complex organization of American Lutheranism.[6]

One could, to simplify matters, describe Scandinavian immigrant church life during the second part of the nineteenth century as a period when synods and congregations sought identity. The early decades of the twentieth century signalled a period of maturity, while the period since has been marked rather by erosion of ethnic identity and, in most cases, dissolution and merger with American religious bodies. This transformation mirrors the process of mass immigration as a whole and can be separated into three quite distinct phases: profiling, acculturation, and assimilation.

The transformation of Nordic immigrant churches also reflects the vehement social and economic changes that occurred in the North Atlantic world. The arrival of Scandinavian immigrants during the peak decades beginning in the 1880's contained a growing share of 'secularized' people who showed little interest in doctrinal disputes within the synods. These masses had been born into the state churches in Scandinavia, and many were indifferent enough in religious matters to shun congregational affiliation in the new country.

Church Life in Scandinavia

The immigrant churches reflected not only the religious atmosphere in the sending countries but also the more general political and social conditions there: To fully comprehend the character of the immigrant churches one must pay attention to the features of ecclesiastical life in the homelands and to the churches' roles in the society

6 Cf. S.E. Ahlstrom 1972, 220–221; G. Westin 402–414; K.A. Olsson 1982.

as a whole. In all Nordic countries the state churches were established during the 1500's in the wake of the Protestant Reformation. As such the Swedish State Church became the most thoroughly organized and in Sweden the links between the state and the church were stronger than in the other Nordic countries. This difference is due to the role the church played during the strong nationalistic period under Gustavus Vasa and during the country's territorial and political expansionism in seventeenth-century Europe.

The Reformation was more important to the process of nation-building in Sweden than in Denmark, and during the 1600's the Swedish Church developed as a means to control the common people, not only in confessional matters. Responding to Sweden's aspirations for hegemony on the European battlefields, ministers acted more or less as recruiters of potential soldiers for the country's military campaigns. The development of a meticulous registration of individuals at the parish level, which emigrating church leaders brought to America in the 1800's, successfully undergirded the state's ambition to organize through and through. Using yearly catechetical meetings, household by household, ministers of the Swedish Church supervised the people's piety and chastity. No deviation from the strict orthodox evangelical faith was accepted. Some of these authoritarian traits surfaced overseas in Augustana's church order in the early immigrant period, when those who departed from the 'true Evangelical faith' and its strict moral code were castigated.

Many a centralizing tendency in present-day Sweden can also be traced back to this consolidation of the nation state during the seventeenth century and, as already touched upon, the same history left its mark in Swedish America. In sum, the thesis here is that the Augustana Synod, although it deviated in many respects from its Swedish model, inherited organizational stability and strength from Swedish Church traditions.

In Denmark the church was not as intimately connected with national ambitions; consequently, its sway over members was not as rigorous. Denmark historically stands out as a somewhat more tolerant society, and the country's authorities were at an earlier date than in Sweden more indulgent with adherents of alien creeds, such as Catholics and Jews. In Norway it took a rather long time for the Reformation to penetrate the country, partly because of the distance to the capital, Copenhagen, and on account of resistance to the Danish authorities.

Transatlantic Religious Impulses

For the free churches that sprang up in Sweden around the middle of the century, American impulses and American experiences were important, and the group migrations of Baptists, Methodists, and Covenants can best be understood against the interchange of ideas between the two countries. This also included Mormonism and Adventism, two American sects which recruited believers and established churches in Scandinavia. This dynamic involved emigration, re-emigration, and repeated emigration of pastors, missionaries, and ardent believers. An early example is *Olof Hedström*, a tailor from southern Småland, who emigrated in 1825. In New York he moved into a middle-class milieu where he became a Methodist and a preacher. During a four year visit to Sweden he preached about his religious experiences, then returned to America, and later became the founder of Swedish Methodism in the Midwest, where he recruited some proselytes from the Bishop Hill colony.[7]

Another Methodist, *Vilhelm Henschen*, worked on both continents and diffused impulses in both directions. Born in 1842, Henschen had a Pietistic background and received a solid education at Uppsala before emigrating in 1870. In America he was an active writer, became Methodist, held the post of director of the Methodist seminary in Evanston, Illinois, but returned to Sweden, where he taught at the Methodist school for preachers in Uppsala. This commuter between the Old World and the New returned again to the United States where he was active as publicist and evangelist.

Swedish Baptists have been America-oriented, but early Swedish-American Baptist leaders also had careers that straddled two hemispheres and spread influences in two directions. *Fredrik O. Nilsson*, born in 1809, and sometimes named the father of Swedish Baptists, received a powerful awakening in New York through a Methodist pastor in 1834, had fresh religious experiences in Sweden, especially through George Scott, was baptized and became a Baptist in 1848. Exiled from Sweden in 1850, he came to America in 1853 after a stay in Denmark. In America he worked among Swedish immigrants. In 1860 Nilsson returned to Sweden. After an active period as Baptist leader in Sweden, he re-emigrated to America in 1868 but was side-stepped by younger leaders. Still another example is *Gustaf*

---

7 W. Mulder 1957; I. Lindén 1971. Some of the facts on migrating church leaders are taken from E.H. Thörnberg 1938.

Palmqvist (born in 1812), also from Småland. He came early under Pietistic influences, moved to America in 1851, where he became leader of the first Swedish Baptist congregation in Rock Island, Illinois. In the late 1850's Palmqvist returned to Sweden where he worked as publisher, preacher, and teacher at the Baptist seminary in Stockholm.

This list of religious leaders who were influential in both Sweden and America also included pastors and preachers who were attached to the Swedish State Church. Not all had positive experiences. Gustaf Unonius, when recapitulating his life, concluded that he had made two mistakes: the first when he left Sweden for America, and the second when he left America to return to Sweden.[8] He tried to start an Episcopal branch in Swedish America but failed. The church leader Lars Esbjörn, one of the founders of the Augustana Church, also returned to Sweden where he served as a pastor. To summarize, Swedish religious influences operated most strongly among those who were active in the free church movement.

Immigrant Churches

Although circumstances in America, above all pressure towards Americanization, were in many respects present from the beginning in the church life of Nordic immigrants, the organization of Nordic churches in America mirrored religious trends and ecclesiastical formation in the respective countries of origin. The historiography of Swedish-American church life abounds with descriptions of the history of various parishes, churches and synods. These need not be repeated here. It would be rather more useful to construct a comparative description of the encounter between Nordic traditions and circumstances and American conditions, and to point at some factors that gradually pushed Nordic immigrant churches away from their ancestral organizations in the Old World. With the exception of Scandinavian Mormons, most of whom were converted around 1850 and recruited for the promised land of Utah, few immigrants upon arrival went immediately to churches not connected to the homeland.

One strong element in Scandinavian-American church life is the tendency to organize along national lines. The immigrants wanted

8 Gustaf Unonius, *Minnen från en sjuttonårig vistelse i Nordvestra Amerika*. 2 vols. Uppsala, 1862.

to hear God's word in their own language, and only in cases of a weak population base did congregation-building occur over the language borders. The founding of joint Norwegian-Swedish and Norwegian-Danish congregations were therefore more like experiments which ended unsuccessfully. Norwegians, for example, joined Swedes in the St. Ansgarius Congregation, founded by the Swede Gustaf Unonius in Chicago in 1849, but they soon left to gather and organize on their own.[9] Also, during the 1840's and 1850's Norwegian churches attracted Danish immigrants who were few in number. A Dane, Claus Lauritzen Clausen, whom the Norwegian Church sent to restore order among the religiously divided Norwegian immigrants, contributed to this cooperative mood. Early on Norwegian synods accepted Danish congregations, though the latter lacked much of the missionary zeal they had experienced in the home country. Even among Swedish-speaking Finns there was a strong tendency to form distinct religious bodies. Thus, in the industrial city of Worcester, Massachusetts, there were separate Swedish, Finland-Swedish, and Finnish congregations of the same confessional, Evangelical Lutheran, brand.[10] This separation along national and language lines is compatible with the churches' role as carriers of ethnicity. The history of the Swedish immigrant churches in America can be written in terms of a struggle for identity, both religiously and *vis-à-vis* the mother country. Most church leaders who emigrated during the 1840's and 1850's opposed the state character of the Swedish Church.[11]

Swedish Immigrant Churches. Five large Swedish churches were established in America: the Augustana, the Methodist, the so-called Free, the Baptist, and the Mission Covenant. The early Lutheran congregations and the Augustana Synod, founded in 1860, were offshoots of the Swedish State Church, but in their early stage they reflected much of the oppositional neo-evangelical movement that was active within the Swedish Church in the mid-1800's. Some of this movement's early leaders who emigrated to America, such as Lars Paul Esbjörn and Tuve Nilsson Hasselquist, had, while in Sweden, criticized the State Church and viewed emigration as a means to free themselves of the bonds of the Swedish Church. In Sweden they were named *läsarepräster* (literally 'reading preachers').

One of the main issues at stake for these founding fathers of the

9 U. Beijbom 1971, 231–236.
10 A. Myhrman 1972.
11 G. Stephenson 1932.

197

Swedish denomination was whether to subscribe to the principle of a congregation of believers or of all nationals. While many early Augustana leaders in Sweden had opposed the idea of *folkkyrka* (folk church), they, in forming a Swedish Church overseas, returned to and supported the principle of a church for nationals. Competition with Baptists and Methodists, disappointment with the Evangelical Lutheran Synod of Northern Illinois, which the Swedes had joined in 1851, and the expectations of many immigrants, led them to take this stand.[12]

Hence, the Scandinavian Lutheran Augustana Synod, founded on cooperation between Swedes and Norwegians, built on the principle of a people's church. The church leaders approved of a 'free' church in America but the Synod nonetheless adopted much of the character of the Swedish State Church. After a short period of liberalism, the Augustana Synod thus turned conservative. It baptized children, confirmed them, and received as members those who stated an avowal. Its pastors upheld strong church discipline, kept a watchful eye on its members' church-going and banned secular tendencies, such as drinking, card playing, dancing, and theater, and they also opposed freemasonry.[13]

Vis-à-vis Sweden and the Swedish Church the Augustana Synod developed a 'double standard'. It saw itself as inheritor of Swedish Church traditions but at the same time it was anxious to demonstrate its independence of the homeland church. For example, Augustana did not accept the Episcopal character of the Swedish Church.[14]

After initially discounting the Swedish Church as a model and an accommodation to American influences during the 1850's, the Swedish Church leaders in America felt the need to revise their attitude to the homeland church. There were two main reasons. One was strictly financial: the Synod needed support to uphold the religious standard among the poor immigrants. The other reason was shortage of ministers. The two factors were interrelated: It was difficult to recruit pastors from Sweden willing to work under meagre conditions on the frontier, and it was a heavy financial burden to train ministers in America.

The Augustana Synod approached the Swedish Church to get financial help and moral support; less, though, for spiritual guid-

12 H. Söderström, 1973.
13 B. Walan 1963.
14 G. Stephenson 1932.

198

ance. The break with the Northern Illinois Synod confirms this tendency, for soon after the founding of the Augustana Synod in 1860 a legate was sent to the Swedish archbishop Reuterdahl, who was asked to raise money for the Swedes' church in exile, a petition which was denied.[15]

Gradually official relations developed between the Augustana Synod and the Swedish State Church. The Swedish Bishop von Schéele's visit to America in 1901 made great strides, and the culmination came with the Swedish archbishop Nathan Söderblom's grand tour of Swedish America in 1923. Söderblom, much of whose work as a church leader had a strong ecumenical character, came in close contact with the leading figures of the Augustana Synod.[16] Söderblom's visit to the United States more than anything else marked the Swedish Church's official recognition of the country's overseas population and of Augustana's role as the church of the overseas Swedes.

At the end of the nineteenth century the stress on the Swedish heritage became more pronounced in the ideology of Augustana. It made itself felt in the curricula of the Synod's main educational institution, Augustana College. Not only church leaders but also several pastors in the field were concerned with how to strengthen Swedishness in America, the preservation of Swedish culture, and the future of the Swedish language. In many respects the Augustana Church had its golden age during the first two decades of the twentieth century. After this period Americanization tendencies became more and more pronounced: the gradual loss of the language, the cessation of new arrivals from Sweden, the loss of members, the need to cooperate with other denominations, all of which led eventually to the merger with the Danish and Finnish synods, resulting in the Lutheran Church of America in 1962.

The Swedish Methodists, early on, established strong traditions in the Midwest. The earliest congregation was founded in 1846. On the question of sanctification (*helgelse*) the group separated from American Methodists, and the Swedes were allowed to form a congress of their own within the United Methodist Church. The congress had a strong identification with the Swedish language, but suffered heavily when Swedish immigration come to a halt in the 1920's. Much of its identity, more so than for Augustana, was bound

15 G. Stephenson 1932.
16 Nathan Söderblom, *Från Uppsala till Rock Island. En predikofärd till Nya Världen*. Uppsala 1924.

199

to the Swedish language. After a period of hardship, the promise of support from the American Methodists led to total incorporation in 1943.

The Evangelical Covenant Church, established in the U.S. in 1885, was an outgrowth of Swedish religious revivalism. Gradual Americanization started during World War I. The history of Swedish Methodism in America has several parallels with Swedish Baptists: It was founded early, maintaining strong reliance on Swedish language and Swedish spiritual traditions, and also Americanized rapidly from the 1940's. Among Swedish free churches in America the Evangelical Covenant Church expressed the strongest identification with Swedish Pietistic ideals.[17]

Norwegian Immigrant Churches. The history of Norwegian churches in America can be described roughly in three phases:

1. Organization-building based on the variation and richness of religious movements within Norway (1840–1900);
2. Tendency to form a united Norwegian church body in America (1900–1917); and
3. Gradual Americanization and loss of Norwegian identity (from 1917).

As in the Swedish case, opponents of the state church system actively established congregations among Norwegian immigrants around the middle of the century. An early alliance with the Missouri Synod led Norwegian ministers to defend slavery as well as to subscribe to dogmatism. Their firm stand in these respects drove them into confrontation with the Church in Norway and its followers in the immigrant churches. For recruitment purposes, these cleavages entailed risk, since the Norwegian immigrants lived in an environment where many American sectarian churches zealously proselytized.

The main division in Norwegian-American church life, however, separated pastors in the Missouri Synod from those in its main competitor, the Augustana Synod, founded in 1860 as a Swedish-Norwegian church. Nevertheless, reaction to this nationalistic church resulted in the creation of the Conference of the Norwegian Danish Evangelical Lutheran Church of America which had a low church character but cared about old Norwegian church customs

17 K.A. Olsson 1962; D. Weaver 1985.

and rituals. It had a good recruiting ground among immigrants arriving in the 1870's and 1880's who were influenced by new democratic ideas infiltrating Norwegian politics then as well as by new waves of revivalism.[18]

It would take too long to mention other schismatic causes that emerged during the 1880's, when the movement to unite brought Norwegians together step by step. The Norwegian conflict over theological matters distressed the local communities and challenged the loyalty of small groups. Among some groups this also resulted in social exclusiveness and alienation from the larger American society.

There were, however, centripetal forces operating. Immigrants arriving around the turn of the century expressed more indifference towards religious matters, mainly because they were more urbanized and secularized. Nationalism in Norway and the Norwegian struggle for independence from the union with Sweden also had an impact on Norwegian-American church life. Furthermore the social aspirations of Norwegian immigrants brought new orientations that made many theological disputes seem futile.

Unity in religious and church matters concerned the laity far more than the priests. The Norwegian Lutheran Church in America, the result of final mergers in 1917, made the Norwegian Lutherans strong in number and organization on the 400th anniversary of Luther's protest in Wittenberg. This manifestation of unity happened during the year of the strongest drive for loyalty in the United States, 1917. Even so, the climax of Norwegian church life coincided with the Church's movement towards Americanization and the subsequent loss of its Norwegian identity, a process which concluded in the 1960's.

Secular Associations

With the present state of knowledge it is impossible to provide an overview of the wild flora of secular organizations that Nordic immigrants founded in America.[19] Within a few years after their arrival, settlers formed congregations and built churches in the rural settlements. The social functions held by churches should not be

18 O.S. Lovoll 1983, 99–116.
19 The best treatment of organizational life among Swedish immigrants is U. Beijbom 1986.

overlooked; within the churches' sphere were choirs, women's groups, Sunday schools, youth clubs etc.

In many communities, and especially the cities, a polarization developed between church-organized people and those who belonged to secular organizations.[20] In larger cities the immigrant churches had difficulty in enticing the many young unmarried men and women who arrived during the high tide of immigration and who had experienced opposition to the established church and secularization in the homelands. Loneliness and isolation were factors that made young people join clubs, guilds, temperance orders and sports associations of an ethnic brand.

In many early Swedish associations upper-class immigrants assumed leadership, and association life mirrored the social structure of the immigrant populations. Early Swedish associations also displayed sex segregation, such as the Swedish Brothers (*Svenska Bröderna*), the leading organization among Minneapolis Swedes, founded in 1876. Normally club life was reserved for men, but in some cases there were parallel women's auxiliaries. But women also founded associations of their own, for example the Swedish Women's Society (*Svenska Fruntimmersföreningen*) in Chicago in 1867.

One type of society combined several objectives, providing both leisure activities and minimal social protection for its members. These groups often functioned as sickness and aid societies. Many workers' associations had this combination.

The founding of the Sons of Norway (*Sønner av Norge*) in 1895 marked the beginning of a new phase in ethnic organization-building among Nordic immigrants. First, this organization reached out nationwide. In 1914 it had 12,000 lodges (*losjer*) from the East to the West Coast. Second, it was a secular organization which opposed Norwegian churches and the Norwegian priesthood in America. Third, although it originally had a rural base, it soon spread to cities and quickly acquired an urban character. Fourth, socially it could be labeled a grass-roots movement, and it had its membership base among laborers. From its inception Sons of Norway had the appearance of a mutual aid society, but this function receded increasingly while social and nationalistic functions became more and more salient. Among its goals Sons of Norway sought to promote the use of the Norwegian language by its members. In

20 U. Beijbom 1971.

1897 a sister organization was founded with the name Daughters of Norway (*Døtre av Norge*).[21]

Among Scandinavian organizations in America, the Norwegian *bygdelags* (home valley organizations) have held an exclusive position. A *bygdelag* is an association of members who have their roots in the same *bygd* in Norway. A *bygd* is normally a region which consists of a valley or a couple of adjacent valleys. Only an intimate knowledge of Norwegian topography will make the *bygdelag* phenomenon wholly understandable. From time immemorial high mountains have been barriers between Norwegian regions and this has meant isolation which, in turn, has led to social and cultural unity within the regions. To this day, the unison within the Norwegian *bygd*s is stronger than that within equivalent geographical entities in the other Nordic countries, possibly with the exception of Iceland, a country which in social terms could be characterized as a large Norwegian *bygd*. On the other hand it would be misleading to say that the Norwegian *bygd* regionalism is equivalent to political particularism. The stress has been on cultural aspects, and the Norwegian *bygd*s are not large enough to constitute strong political entities.

However, the sense of community created in the Norwegian *bygd*s was brought over to America and manifested in several ways. As stated above, immigrants from the same *bygd* tended to settle close to each other.

The first *bygdelag* to organize in America was *Valdres Samband*. Its first meeting (*stevne*) convened in Minnehaha Park, Minneapolis in 1899. The participants shared a common emigration background in Valdres, a valley in south central Norway with a high emigration. During the first two decades of the country Norwegian immigrants formed numerous *bygdelags*, foremost in Minnesota and Wisconsin, and normally their members gathered for meetings every, or every second, year. Odd Lovoll, historian of the Norwegian *bygdelag* movement, has counted 129 *bygdelags* in America. A majority of these were active for only a short period, but two score remained active until after the Second World War. The golden age of the *bygdelags* spanned the years from the turn of the century until the early 1930's.

The individual *lag* sought to show its own profile and to demonstrate and articulate the characteristics of its own *bygd*. Hence they

21 O.S. Lovoll 1983.

shifted their objectives. Some aimed to document the culture of the respective valley in Norway and to extoll the history of the region. Others chose to focus on music and other artistic expressions originating in the home region. Thus the Harding fiddle won popularity in America through the propaganda of *bygdelag* people with roots in Hardanger. There was also a sort of competition between *lags*, mostly of a friendly character but not without boastfulness.[22]

What explains the strength of the Norwegian *bygdelag* movement in America? In the first place, associations based on regions in the home country are not isolated phenomenona but can be found in many immigrant groups. For many Italian immigrants, for example, feelings of attachment and loyalty towards the province were stronger than within the republic. Many Sicilians and Calabrians brought to America a disappointment with the unification of the peninsula because they thought it had strengthened the North at the expense of the South. This chagrin did not, however, prevent them from participating in the Italian-American commemorations of Christopher Columbus and similar Italian celebrations.[23]

The *bygdelags* sprang up during a period of ethnic mobilization among Norwegian immigrants, the background of which must be set against the political and cultural situation in Norway at the time. Norway's opposition towards Sweden and the country's discontent with the political union had many sympathizers in America. That Norwegian *lags* were most frequently linked with the regions rather than with the national culture may sound paradoxical, considering the strong national movement in Norway and the marked interest of Norwegian-Americans in undoing the Swedish-Norwegian union. When the political bonds were severed in September 1905, Norwegian immigrants in America greeted the event with enthusiasm and experienced an enhanced identification with the home country as a result.

The political dissolution also led to intensified contacts between Norwegians on both sides of the Atlantic Ocean. But there was little incompatibility between national and regional loyalties. Rather the *bygdelag* movement absorbed the new wave of Norwegian-American nationalism, and it nourished no political undertones of separatism.

In Norway the regional and local cultures received increased

22 O.S. Lovoll 1975.
23 J.W. Briggs 1978, 125–126.

recognition in the latter part of the nineteenth century. And in Scandinavia as a whole the new nationalism was linked to an interest in folk culture. The study of folklore became in vogue, and the interest in popular culture comprised mapping and investigation of provincial and local cultures. An interest in local culture became the hallmark of the nationalist impulse which spread across Scandinavia during the latter part of the nineteenth century. Among learned people and opinion leaders a new feeling for the *bygd* arose and, along with it, renewed local identity.

This interest for local culture was also obvious in Sweden, where local history associations (*hembygdsförening*) and regional associations with the same object (*hembygdsförbund*) were founded. Some hoped to write the history of a parish, a city, or a region, and to inventory and secure local and provincial artifacts and monuments. This was not, however, done in opposition to the national culture but was rather supported and organized on a national level. In Norway, again, the movement for shaping a new language *(nynorsk)* added recognition to local culture, because this language had its foundation in dialects and local variants.

Immigrants brought the interest in regional cultures with them to America and, apart from that, improved communications transmitted similar impulses. The Norwegian *bygdelags* in America had a counterpart, although much weaker, in the Swedish-American home region associations (*hembygdsföreningar*) which were founded later, most in the 1920's and 1930's. In contrast to the Norwegian *bygdelags*, which had a strong agrarian base, the Swedish associations were urban phenomena, established in cities with large Swedish populations, such as Chicago, Minneapolis, and Rockford. Associations on the west coast, for example in Vancouver and Seattle, began at an even later date. The members of a home region association had common roots in a certain Swedish province (*landskap*), for example, Värmland, Dalarna, or Öland. At the beginning of the 1980's a dozen of them were still active. They give an opportunity for social intercourse and to praise the home region in literary and musical forms.

Also, among Finland-Swedes, one could find the same type of home region associations, but in reality they appealed to Swedish-speaking immigrants from the whole of Finland. A good example is the Närpes festivals (*Närpesfesterna*), which started in Worcester, Massachusetts, and had branches in other eastern cities.[24]

One reason why the Swedish home region associations had a

more urban character in America, as compared to the Norwegian *bygdelags*, is that Swedes to a higher extent lived in cities and metropolitan areas. But what was the prime motivation for Swedes who joined guilds, societies, and clubs that focused on a particular Swedish province or region? Was it love for the home area in the old country, for the larger province, or for the home parish or home town? Wilhelm Berger, prolific Swedish-American author and journalist, offered one answer. Considering the Swedish immigrant's relation to his old country, he wrote: 'There is much talk about the longing for home of the Swedish American, but he does not long for Sweden, he longs for his home region (*hembygden*). The many home province associations (*landskapsföreningar*) which during the last years have been formed among Swedes in America, evince that it is the home region that the Swedish Americans have at heart, not the country as a whole. When a Swedish American returns to Sweden and settles there, he normally choses to do so in the old home parish, even if any other area would provide him with better opportunities'.[25]

It is also tempting to see the Swedish-American home province associations corresponding with the same phenomenon in Sweden proper, where expressions of love for the home area or one's fore-fathers also signalled urban man's longing to return to nature. If this is correct, the *Östgöta Gille* on Chicago's North Side and its sister organization on the South Side bear witness not only of nostalgia for the birches and runestones of Östergötland but also a general yearning after meadows and forests amidst compact housing and factory chimneys in the American city jungle.

Organizations in Search of a Past

To conquer history is important for almost every ethnic and religious minority. Not least essential is to prove that the story of one's group goes far back in time. For this objective the recapitulation of the early settlement is a serious matter, and the group's legitimacy is strengthened if one can show evidence that one's fellow countrymen had been in the area of immigration at an early date.

This also holds true for the Nordic immigrants in America. In their history-writing they have insistently kept track of the early

24 A. Myhrman 1972, 93.
25 V. Berger 1916, *Svensk-amerikanska meditationer.* Rock Island, Ill., 1916.

feats of Norse presence in the New World, and celebration of historic events have been vital elements in the life of immigrant organizations. For example, when Swedes in Providence and other places in Rhode Island published their own story in a magnificent book in 1915 much of the space was devoted to the Viking landings on the northern strip of the eastern seaboard.[26]

Four events in history stand out as especially useful reference points for celebration: Leif Eriksson's arrival at the American shore; the Delaware years in Swedish history, a period which has been exploited by persons of both Swedish and Finnish descent; the participation of Scandinavians in the War of Independence; and finally, the contributions of Nordic immigrants during the Civil War.

Leif Eriksson has been used as a symbol by Icelanders, Norwegians, and Swedes, and he has been held forward, for example, in heated controversies with Italian immigrants who exploited Columbus for the same purpose. This antagonism reached a climax on the 400th anniversary of Columbus's arrival in the New World. After the ecstatic Columbus celebrations in 1892, Johan Enander, sometimes named the ideologist of early Swedish-Americanism, wrote a pamphlet entitled 'The Norsemen in America or the Discovery of America: Historical Disputation in Connection with the Columbus Celebrations in Chicago 1892–1893'. In this booklet he stressed the much earlier and hence more significant arrival of Leif Eriksson.[27] Two decades earlier the Norwegian immigrant Rasmus B. Anderson had published 'America Not Discovered by Columbus' which tried to prove that Norsemen were the earliest colonizers on American soil.[28]

The Viking legacy became the vogue in America in the 1890's. The combination of the early Scandinavian discoveries in America and the many heroic aspects of seafaring Vikings seemed especially useful during a decade when the American frontier movement came to a close and the horizons of a people with a manifest destiny were extended overseas to Hawaii and the Philippines. During this period also old immigrant groups felt competition from the new immigrants from Eastern and Southern Europe. In this atmosphere of increasing

26 J.S. Österberg, *Svenskarna i Rhode Island.* Worcester, Mass., 1915.
27 J. Enander, *Nordmännen i Amerika eller Amerikas upptäckt. Historisk afhandling med anledning av Columbifestligheterna i Chicago 1892–93.* Rock Island, Ill., 1893.
28 R.B. Anderson, 1974.

207

inter-ethnic rivalry Nordic immigrants brought their heroic trans-oceanic ancestors to the fore.[29]

Swedish immigrants used the Vinland voyages as a means to legitimize their own group experience up to the 1910's, but other historic achievements gradually became more important. References to the Swedish engineer John Ericson's great technical inventions played the same role. John Ericson's ship design helped the Northern States win the important sea battle at Hampton Roads in 1862: this has always been a trump card in the hands of the Swedes in America. The John Ericson Monument near Lincoln Memorial in Washington, D.C., bears witness to Swedish-Americans' keenness to make America remember Swedish contributions to the nation's progress. To this day the John Ericson statue in Battery Park on lower Manhattan is a place where New York Swedes gather to remember a man whom many consider the greatest of all Swedish-Americans.

The Norwegians cultivated the image of Leif Eriksson and have continued to do so. The immigrant group with the truest claim to Leif Eriksson are, however, the Icelanders, since Leif was born in Iceland and emigrated to Greenland, Iceland's 'colony', whence he voyaged further west and touched American soil. Norwegians seem, however, to be the most intense about using him as a symbol. Several are the statues erected in his honor.[30] The first one in America was unveiled in Boston in 1887, and others have been raised in Chicago, Duluth, and Seattle. As late as 1949 a magnificent statue was placed outside the Capitol in St. Paul. An interesting combination of two phenomena in a single celebration began in 1964. Since that year, October 9, the day the Norwegian 'sloopers' arrived on the American shore in 1825, is observed as Leif Eriksson Day after a proclamation by the President.[31]

The history of the homeland proper was also important in the immigrants' search for a heroic past. In searching for suitable events in Norwegian history, Norwegian-Americans, for obvious reasons, had to return to more distant pasts than Swedish-Americans. Beside the Viking Age, the Era of Greatness (*stormaktstiden*) 1617–1718, was a cherished period for Swedes in America. When searching for the core of Swedish national character they proudly pointed at Charles XII, but in the eyes of Swedish immigrants nobody com-

29 Cf. D. Blanck 1986.
30 'Leif Erikson-fester i Amerika', article in *Nordmans-Forbundet* 1924, 423–426.
31 A.W. Andersen 1975, 47–48.

pared with Gustavus Adolphus II. He combined the elements of strength and unselfish sacrifice for the right religious creed. Therefore it is no coincidence that one of the largest Swedish colleges in America carries his name.

The search for a past also led to the founding of associations which aimed primarily to preserve the memory of the ethnic group, to trace and print records, and to document important aspects of the group's history. For the early Icelandic organizations preservation of the links to the past was essential, as was also true of the Icelandic National League, founded in the United States in 1919.[32] Early Swedish attempts to form historical societies go back to 1888, the year marking the 250th anniversary of the arrival of the first Swedes in Delaware. Fifteen thousand people attended a meeting in Minneapolis and received the blessing from the Augustana Synod's grand old father, Tuve Nilsson Hasselquist, and listened to Swedish-America's foremost historiographer, Johan Enander. This celebration led to the yearly celebration of the 'Day of Our Forefathers' (*Våra förfäders dag*). One Swedish historical association formed in 1889 was not long-lasting. A more successful attempt occurred in 1905 with the establishment of *Svenska Historiska Sällskapet* (Swedish Historical Society), also with Enander as *primus motor*, and led to collections of material and publication of documents. With the entrance of university historians such as George M. Stephenson in the 1920's, the society obtained more of a professional character. Publications were made in English, and scholarly standards were introduced, something which made itself felt in the way history itself was viewed.[33]

There were other parallel initiatives. The 150th anniversary in 1926 of the Declaration of Independence was an occasion for some immigrant groups to manifest their solidarity with the New Nation. For more than a decade Swedes had prepared for this occasion by collecting money for a John Ericson Memorial in Washington. It was inaugurated in the presence of the Swedish crown prince, Gustaf Adolf, and President Calvin Coolidge. In his speech the latter appealed to the sensible minds of the Swedish-Americans and stressed that a John Ericson could only spring up as an incarnation of the superior qualities of a people. The same year, 1926, saw an institutionalization of the feelings that permeated those Swedish-

32 V. Bjornson 1980, 477.
33 U. Beijbom 1977, 23–30.

209

Americans who welcomed Coolidge's message. The American Sons and Daughters of Sweden was founded, an organization which wanted to combine good American citizenship and patriotism with the best of Swedish culture, love of music, respect for law, and conviction in religion.[34] Also, it was decided in those days to erect a building in Philadelphia to house a Swedish museum, later to be named the John Morton Building.

Calvin Coolidge, who hailed the Swedes, one year earlier visited the Minnesota State Fairgrounds to participate in the Centennial commemorating the arrival in America of the first Norwegian immigrants in 1825.[35] He delivered a message in praise of the Norwegian people in America. The centennial was also chosen as the time to found the Norwegian-American Historical Association, an act prepared for decades but for various reasons not realized earlier.[36]

The life-expectancy of most immigrant historical societies is short, and the Norwegian-American Historical Association therefore stands out as somewhat of an exception, partly explained by the strong professionalism that from the beginning imbued it.[37] In the postwar years there have been national historical associations for all Nordic immigrant groups, but a general problem has been to reach beyond historians with professional interests and small groups of enthusiasts.

34 E.G. Westman and E.G. Johnson, *The Swedish Element in America* (1931), vol. II, 446–447.
35 C.C. Qualey and J.A. Gjerde 1981, 241.
36 O. Lovoll and K.O. Bjork 1975.
37 J.J. Appel 1960, 385.

15. Nordic Immigrants and American Politics

Several observers have highlighted the specific characteristics of Minnesota politics. The *Almanac of American Politics*, a useful reference guide to the current political scene in the United States, poses in its 1980 edition the question as to why Minnesota has become so liberal. In addition to iron ore and wheat this state produced political talent, and it is emphasized that no state of comparable size has produced so many front-rank political personages (Humphrey, McCarthy, Freeman, Blackmun and Mondale) during recent years. One may only add that none of the state's several presidential candidates has reached the nation's highest political office. The Almanac also reminds its readers of the talented governor Floyd Olson who was leader of the Farmer Labor Party but died an early death. The authors of the Almanac, however, do not give any explicit explanation for Minnesota's liberal character but hint that the Scandinavian legacy left a distinctive mark upon the state.

Since Minnesota, demographically, is the Scandinavian state *par préférence* in the United States, and since one of the themes of this book is the role of cultural heritage, there is reason to ask to what extent the Nordic peoples have brought cultural and political experiences to Minnesota and to other areas with heavy Scandinavian populations. This perhaps somewhat ethnocentric question, if asked by a Scandinavian, implies methodological problems hardly touched upon in the historical literature, and leads in turn to the question of historiography as far as the issue of Scandinavians in American politics is concerned. To start on a negative note, one can take a point of departure in a 1982 American doctoral dissertation in political science by Patsy Hegstad. She characterizes research on Scandinavians in American politics as being in an 'embryonic state', and she classifies the existing literature in three categories: traditional impressionistic literature, traditional scholarly studies, and modern scholarly studies. There is no reason to fully agree with Hegstad's characterization, but her classification will be used here to show that political studies focusing on the Nordic populations have produced a variety of investigations and results using varying methodological   approaches.[1]

Early literature was distingished by ethnic introspection but none-theless with sweeping generalizations concerning the group's be-havior based on minimal comparisons with other ethnic categories. In this literature (which had a strongly nonscientific function) state-ments were often made about far-reaching assimilation and the willingness of the immigrants to become full-fledged Americans. This work aimed at extolling one's own nationality's superior virtues and unquestionable loyalty to the new homeland.

A good exponent of this genre is John Wargelin's *The Ameri-canization of the Finns*, published by the Finnish Lutheran Book Concern in 1924. Wargelin, who wrote about an ethnic group har-rowed by deep schisms not only in the homeland but also in the new fatherland, repudiated many popular suspicions and supposed disloyalties of the Finnish-Americans. Wargelin tried to de-empha-size the role and influence of Finnish socialism in America, which he traced back to the political oppression that Finland had suffered 'under the hands of Russian autocrats'.[2] Arguing for future contri-butions by Finns in America, he referred to the situation in Finland. The Finns had fought for religious and political freedom for centu-ries, and as a result Finland had become a republic with one of the most democratic forms of government found anywhere. In America Finns were, according to Wargelin, very anxious to become natural-ized. The sensational press had painted a negative portrait of the Finns during the famous Copper Strike of 1913. Because of their recent arrival in America it was natural to place Finns among the rank and file in politics. However, they had advanced to important positions in many cities, and the first woman mayor in the United States was Finnish.[3]

The second historiographic phase, which Hegstad labels 'early scholarly literature', included the pioneering generation of academic writers such as Blegen and Stephenson, but they scarcely penetrated the immigrants' activities in the purely political sphere.

1 P. Hegstad 1982, citation from page 1.
2 J. Wargelin 1924, 175.
3 J. Wargelin 1924, 166, 176, 179.

The third historiographic phase began with renewed interest in the study of immigration that came during the 1960's. Political aspects of Scandinavian life in America were illuminated by fresh approaches, including the use of quantitative data and statistical methods. Many research tasks still remain, but the study of Scandinavian-American political history has at least left the 'embryonic' stage. One must regret, though, that with the exception of the Finns, no comprehensive study exists on Nordic immigrants in the American labor movement.[4]

It is tempting to combine the political behavior of Nordic immigrants on the American political scene with the social order and the political traditions in the home countries. For example, is it a mere coincidence that the first woman mayor of an American city came from Finland, the first country in Europe to grant women the franchise? Or, was the early Norwegian influence in Minnesota and Wisconsin politics a reflection of the political mobilization at a relatively early stage in Norwegian society? These questions will here be linked with the general problem of the extent to which immigrants as individuals and collectives relied upon political and labor union experience in the Old World.

Political Life in the Sending Countries

Several authors associate the political success of Norwegians in the Midwest with the political milieu in Norway during the latter half of the nineteenth century.[5] Among the Scandinavian countries 'modern' politics had an early breakthrough in Norway. Political parties with popular bases, more than mere ad-hoc groupings, appeared in the parliament in Norway earlier than in the other Nordic countries. Organizations of the wider electorate emerged in Norway around 1870, while political parties with a popular base were not established in Sweden until the last decade of the nineteenth century. The principles of parliamentarism were fully accepted in Norway in 1884 and resulted from the growing opposition towards the Swedish king and discontent with the Swedish-Norwegian union. In Sweden, on the other hand, parliamentarism was fully acknowl-

---

4 So far the best introductions to this field are H. Bengston 1955 and D. Hoerder 1980, who has edited a volume of reprints. Taken together they provide a starting-point.
5 Most notably J. Wefald 1971, see below.

edged in 1917 (although there were gradual steps towards this new set of principles); in Denmark this change occurred in 1920.

Other reforms in the political system were also introduced in Norway earlier than in the neighboring countries. Universal suffrage for men was introduced there in 1898, while in Sweden men were granted this right in 1909 and women in 1921. In Denmark the development was unstable; full suffrage for men was introduced in 1849 but revoked in 1866. In Finland strong forces brought about fundamental political reforms in 1906 when the Russian czar and his government were paralysed by Japan's victory and frustrated by strikes and revolutionary tendencies in St. Petersburg and other cities; in one stroke a one-chamber parliament and a system based on universal franchise for men and women replaced the obsolete Finnish diet of four estates in 1906.

These political reforms reflected the different pace of political mobilization in the Nordic countries, which in turn stemmed from the shifting content of political conflicts. The social forces were indeed very different: the dominant political group in Denmark had its social basis in the wealthy landed proprietors, while yeomen farmers were an important factor in the Swedish parliament, especially after the Parliamentary Reform of 1866 when the old estate *Riksdag* was replaced by a two-chamber parliament.

Because of historical factors and the country's natural features Norway had only a small class of people whose position was based on landed wealth. Thus, the country lacked the conservative political force so strong in Denmark and Sweden. The leading political force in Norwegian politics from the middle of the nineteenth century was liberal, while conservatives played equivalent roles in Denmark and Sweden. On the other hand, the labor movement got an earlier start in Denmark due to earlier industrialization and proximity to Germany, whence many impulses to organize labor emanated. Finnish labor radicalism had other roots and influences and developed later. The country's foremost social problem at the end of the nineteenth century was the growing rural proletariat, which also made itself felt in the cities, especially Helsinki. Proximity to St. Petersburg and other industrial centers in western Russia promoted revolutionary impulses. When assessing possible Scandinavian impulses in American politics one should also consider the early advent of communal self-government in Denmark, Norway and Sweden.

Three Nordic peoples felt the preponderance of superordinate powers from which they wanted to be freed: Norwegians to a man sought to throw off the bonds with Sweden and to dissolve the union that they, to quote Bjørnstjerne Bjørnson's words, 'hated and were infected by'. In Finland opposition to Russian czardom increased during the decades around the turn of the century, and the russification campaigns undertaken in all peripheral areas in the Russian empire evoked strong resentment at all social levels in Finland. Nor were the Icelanders satisfied with the home-rule-like arrangement introduced in 1874; they wanted full independence from Denmark.

The unsolved national problems of Scandinavia comprised a political heritage that many Nordic immigrants carried to America. Although this experience did not constitute an active political consciousness at the time of departure from Europe, the native political heritage was a reservoir to fall back upon. As was the case with many East Europeans, full consciousness of the political situation in the home countries did not awaken until after a period in America.

Political Advancement

There is little reason to presume any considerable involvement of Scandinavian immigrants in American party politics until some time after the beginning of mass migration, since it took time for newcomers to learn the language, to make a minimal adaption to the milieu, and to become acquainted with the way political matters operated. The 1850's saw the entrance of Norwegians and Swedes into the political arena, although in the beginning they primarily played the role of spectators. Swedish- and Norwegian-language newspapers reflect the stand-by character of their participation, but some editors did not hesitate to formulate points of view on important matters. The Swedish *Hemlandet* (founded in Galesburg, Illinois, in 1855), after its move to Chicago in 1859, declared itself Republican.[6]

Two topics of national interest caused an almost unanimous political reaction among Scandinavians, the Know-Nothing movement and slavery. Probably because of their small numbers, Norwegians and Swedes, located mainly in rural areas with a strong Lutheran stamp, were not swayed by Know-Nothingism. Scandinavians resented its general anti-foreign crusade, although they might

6 U. Beijbom 1971, 316.

have harbored harsh feelings towards Germans and especially Irish, the two groups under heaviest fire from the Know-Nothing movement.[7] Norwegian editors accused the Republican Party of Know-Nothing tendencies and criticized political bills making it more difficult for immigrants to achieve political rights.[8]

The issue of slavery caused Norwegians and Swedes to choose between the two dominant national parties. The leading Norwegian newspaper *Emigranten* and its editor Knud Fleischner took an early stand against the Kansas-Nebraska Act of 1854. The newspaper foresaw the collapse of this 'rotten institution of slavery', declared itself Republican, and supported the Republican candiate John C. Frémont in 1856.[9] Some Norwegian Lutheran theologians affiliated with the conservative Missouri Synod expressed pro-slavery sentiments, while the majority of Norwegians welcomed Lincoln, shared his opinion on the slavery issue, backed the Union in the Civil War, and supported Norwegian military participation on the Northern side.[10] The Republican platform of 1860, with its firm stand on the slavery question and its advanced program on land issues that led to the Homestead Act of 1862, had a strong appeal among Norwegians, Swedes, and many Germans.

Although we generally know more about Scandinavians in rural areas than in the cities, there has been little systematic research on their role in local politics. Merle Curti's meticulous study of frontier democracy in Trempeleau County, Wisconsin, however, contains interesting notions on Norwegian activity at the grass roots level. Norwegians arrived in Trempeleau at the same time as native Americans, but Yankees had a virtual monopoly on county offices during the area's first decades as an independent county. This was not a case of conscious discrimination but rather resulted from the natives' acquaintance and broader experience with American institutions. In 1868 the county records stated that Norwegians demonstrated 'a good sense of law and order by voting the Republican ticket'.[11]

Norwegians were gradually drawn towards the center of the county's political power field, first as longed-for voters, then as party functionaires. A landmark was achieved in 1877, when Norwegians nominated a candidate of their own to the prestigious position of

7 A.W. Andersen 1953, 26–29 and 1975, 59–64.
8 A.W. Andersen 1953, 26–29 and 1975, 59–64.
9 A.W. Andersen 1953, 67.
10 Th. Blegen 1940, 389–400.
11 M. Curti 1959, 104.

Secretary of State of the county. This was a highly conscious action and reflected a critique of the American office-holders. The election led to a partial Norwegian take-over in Trempeleau County.[12]

At the edge of the frontier, where new townships were set up and immigrants made up a substantial number or even outnumbered the native Americans, immigrants were relatively early drawn into community affairs. One should not forget, though, that many immigrants arriving on the frontier did not necessarily come directly from Europe but had spent some time in the country and therefore had first-hand experience of American institutions. The political activities of Nordic immigrants in states like Washington and California, which received many second-stage migrants, must be viewed in this perspective.[13] The role of the Irish settlers, who often arrived in the Midwest by way of other American places further east, must, *mutatis mutandis*, be viewed the same way when one looks at their confrontations with Scandinavians.

The same clear pattern is visible in Pepin and Burnett Counties in Wisconsin. Where there were many Scandinavians, they were elected to more positions of responsibility (three quarters) than their share of the counties' population (two thirds) would have justified.[14]

In Trempeleau County, Curti observed that in townships where Norwegians comprised a considerable portion of the population, they had a substantial influence upon the administration. Where they held a majority, they were able in time to sweep all offices and escaped the less influential role of minority voters. The strong tendency among Norwegians to settle close to their kin and countrymen and form ethnically homogeneous settlements was an advantage from a political point of view, but it also produced disadvantages. As an ethnic group they could more easily form voting blocks, but the other side of the coin was relative isolation.

The contents of politics could to some extent be influenced by the immigrants' experiences from the home country, e.g., concerning school and education, but the state laws regulated forms and rules on the local level. Nonetheless, within this American organization some leeway at the local level was also possible. One study reports a mixture of American and Swedish procedures in the Chisago Lake area during the latter part of the nineteenth century. Swedish forms of cooperation among farmers combined with American rules for

12 M. Curti 1959, 104.
13 Cf. J. Dahlie 1967, 124.
14 H. Norman 1974, 262–263.

meetings and the keeping of minutes.[15] To find competent people to fill political posts on the local level was a problem, and in this regard Merle Curti's study of Norwegians at township and county levels is of interest. 'The early Norwegian clerks, treasurers, and supervisors, were not immoral or grossly incompetent. They were generally more inexperienced than the Yankees'. He also concludes that Norwegians willingly accepted their share of duties and that they left their mark on American self-government.[16]

The political advancement of immigrants followed different stages, and their activities may be systematized as follows:

1. inclination to become American citizens,
2. inclination to register as voters,
3. participation as voters,
4. activity in party organizations,
5. seeking of nominations for political posts,
6. activity as elected officers in political posts.

Naturalization. The propensity of an ethnic group to become American citizens has been used as a measure of Americanization and assimilation, as signs of patriotism and loyalty to the new country, and as a criterion of willingness to participate in political life. But one cannot be sure that inclination to acquire American citizenship implies readiness to surrender one's identity with an ethnic group. Rather it could be highly compatible to become naturalized and to actively support the ambitions of one's own national group. This could be as simple as lauding both America and the homeland and carrying two nations' flags in a Fourth-of-July parade. Applying for American citizenship was an instrumental act when it had an economic objective, for example, when an immigrant took out first papers in order to qualify for a homestead.

Swedes in Chicago, with the supposed goal of naturalizing fellow citizens, formed political clubs in the 1890's, but the prime motivation seems to have been to create stronger voting blocks to support Swedish ethnic politicians. One of the men behind this movement was Edward C. Westman.[17]

Aggregate data put into perspective the tendency to naturalization of various immigrant groups. Table 9 contains information from

15 N. Hasselmo 1974, 287.
16 M. Curti 1959, 319.
17 G. Johnson 1940, 39–40.

the U.S. Census of 1910 and 1930 on naturalization by nationality groups in America. Although differences were small, Danes among the Nordic group showed the highest figure of naturalization, while Norwegians showed the lowest among the Scandinavian immigrants. The low number of naturalized citizens among Finns in America can be primarily explained by their later arrival.

Becoming American was for many an immigrant an emotional affair: Taking a new nationality further distanced the home country, a step which could be burdensome if one felt strong ties with the fatherland. This is evidenced in the Scandinavian immigrant literature, which does not contain examples of anyone who resists becoming a citizen of the country of immigration.[18] Some immigrants, however, never became American citizens. To illustrate, 10 percent of the Nordic immigrants living in Seattle and Ballard around the turn of the century with twenty years or more in the country had not acquired naturalization.[19]

Registration as voters. The inclination to become an American citizen has been used as an indication of political mobilization. In two steps Patsy Hegstad has quantified naturalization and voting registration data to measure the political activity of Nordic immigrants. She examined the five Nordic immigrant groups in Seattle and Ballard in 1892 and 1900. Her work is a sophisticated piece of quantitative history, based on a meticulous examination of official

Table 9. Naturalized and Alien Men over 21 Years of Age in the United States, 1910–1930. Percent of All Men.

Country	1910 Naturalized	First Paper	Aliens	Un-known	1930 Naturalized	First Paper	Aliens	Un-known
England	–	–	–	–	69.6	11.8	14.6	4.0
Norway	57.1	15.2	16.2	11.5	70.8	12.2	13.2	3.8
Sweden	62.8	11.5	14.9	10.8	72.1	12.1	12.8	3.0
Denmark	61.6	12.6	13.8	12.0	75.3	11.4	10.1	2.2
Germany	69.5	7.2	9.9	13.4	72.3	13.3	10.8	3.6
Finland	30.6	15.9	45.9	7.6	50.5	16.2	31.0	2.3
Italy	17.7	7.8	65.7	8.8	55.3	12.1	30.3	2.3
Poland	–	–	–	–	55.4	16.6	25.8	2.2
Russia	26.1	13.0	52.4	8.5	67.7	11.4	18.2	2.6
All Foreign Born	45.6	8.6	34.1	11.7	62.0	13.6	21.1	3.3

Source: S. Lindmark 1971, 45.

18 D. Burton Skårdal 1974, 159–160.
19 P. Hegstad 1982, 180–256.

records. It demonstrates that it is possible to distinguish the Nordic groups as to political activity on the basis of citizenship and voter registration sources. Her study sheds light on some more sweeping generalizations stemming from advocates of the ethnic groups themselves. Danes in the Seattle area, who displayed many signs of being structurally assimilated, frequently chose American citizenship and went to the polls, something which could, however, be explained by their longer history in the region.[20]

This data on Danes may be juxtaposed with Stephan H. Rye's study of Danish voting behavior, which identified five distinctly Danish townships in Iowa. Danes naturalized quickly, and eligible Danes displayed a high voting turnout in elections but refused to behave as a uniform voting-bloc.[21]

City Politics. An ethnic group's struggle to come of age in the political world of a medium-sized American city is illustrated by the Swedes of Jamestown, New York, a city located southwest of Buffalo. Swedes first arrived in 1849 and eventually became the city's largest foreign-born group. Most Swedes were industrial workers, but some of them advanced and became factory-owners. Swedish entrepreneurs became a significant force, especially in furniture production and the mechanical industry.

The Jamestown Swedes' quest for political power ended in full blossom, and one of the renowned city politicians of the day, Samuel Carlson, held the mayoralty with only short interruptions for a thirty-year period (1908–1938). Carlson was born in Jamestown of Swedish parents soon after their arrival in the United States. He made his career in the Republican party but became more and more independent. Some labeled his tenure as mayor socialistic, since he strongly advocated that public utilities should be administered by the municipal government.

Parallel to the situation in Trempeleau County, Yankee domination hindered political influence. Mobilization of Swedes in Jamestown came gradually, and the newspaper *Vårt land* (Our Country) urged the Swedes to participate in the Republican caucus for the 1876 election, arguing that the Swedes ought to have some of their own countrymen nominated. Yankee Republicans did not accept this idea, so the Swedes ran as independents and were elected to two minor offices. During the first phase of the Swedish advance-

20 P. Hegstad 1982.
21 J.H. Rye 1979.

220

ment into the city's political structure, the Swedish newspaper discussed 'Swedish interests' but did not link this with specific political issues. Swedishness per se was the important thing.

In 1876 the leading Swedish newspaper in Jamestown reflected a sense of inferiority, and the Swedes' ambition to advance seems to have had its base in the lack of self-confidence. By the turn of the century the political position of the Swedes was secure: They held important offices in the city and had also made a breakthrough on the county level. Between 1876 and 1900 a shift in ethnic identity occurred also. In 1876 they spoke of themselves as 'Swedes', but by 1900 they labeled themselves as 'Swedish-Americans'.[22]

In cities like Jamestown, where Nordic immigrants arrived early and had numerical strength, they could gain ground in politics by sticking together and displaying ethnic unity, a necessary strategy because Yankees did not voluntarily make room for newcomers. Especially hard to penetrate were the caucuses of the national political parties, the Democratic and the Republican.

Ethnic subdivisions in the party organizations offered one way to harness Scandinavian voting power and to gain influence. In Chicago a Swedish Republican club was organized in August 1860 and functioned in support of Lincoln's candidacy. A Scandinavian Democratic club followed in 1863. Thereafter Swedish, and sometimes Scandinavian, clubs and leagues organized electoral support among Chicago's immigrants and also, thereby, boosted candidates from their own ethnic groups in local elections. Supporting major Yankee candidates brought political rewards, such as positions as court clerks and other minor posts.[23]

In Chicago politics, Scandinavians faced an uphill battle even during years when they were still among the more numerous immigrant groups. In reviewing Swedish contributions to the city's politics Ulf Beijbom has stressed the passivity of the Swedes, and he even goes so far as to discuss Swedish political impotence, a judgment which may not be wholly fair. If Swedes in Chicago were unable to make a definite breakthrough before 1880 (the final year of Beijbom's investigation), this must be seen in the light of some basic facts: the absolute number of Swedes, their relative number compared to the city's population, and their formal capacity as residents and voters. The last factor is important, since newcomers

22 I. Holmberg 1985.
23 U. Beijbom 1971.

lacked the right of full participation in elections. Since the Swedish element in Chicago to a great extent consisted of transient migrants who were bound for areas further west, one cannot expect much of a commitment to the city's political life from this group. Figures alone say a lot about the potential strength of the Swedish electorate. According to the 1870 census only 350 male Chicagoans were naturalized.[24] Nonetheless, some successes were noted, for example, in 1874, when two Chicago Swedes won seats in the Illinois state legislature.[25]

Political Positions. One way to measure ethnic involvement and success in politics is simply to count the number of political positions held by immigrants. According to Martin Ulvestad as many as 2,221 Norwegians served in posts as county officials between the years 1847 and 1905, and 669 Norwegians were members of U.S. state legislatures during the same period.[26] These figures are difficult to evaluate because of the lack of comparative data. Some figures exist for Scandinavians in the Midwest. Jon Wefald has compared the numbers of Danes, Germans, Norwegians, and Swedes in the House of Representatives in Minnesota and the Dakotas.[27] His figures are as follows:

Persons of Foreign Birth or Parentage in Minnesota, 1910

	Norwegians	Germans	Swedes	Danes
Percentage	18.8	26.7	18.1	2.5
Number	279,606	396,859	268,018	37,524

Minnesota House of Representatives

Year	Number	Norwegians	Germans	Swedes	Danes
1893	115	12	4	8	0
1901	118	17	8	8	0
1917	130	21	10	10	2
1931	131	30	10	14	4

Persons of Foreign Birth or Parentage in South Dakota, 1910

	Norwegians	Germans	Swedes	Danes
Percentage	19.1	26.0	7.2	4.2
Number	60,746	82,793	23,292	14,963

24 U. Beijbom 1971, 135, 315–335.
25 U. Beijbom 1971, 315–316.
26 Figures cited from C. Chrislock 1976, 106.
27 J. Wefald 1971, 27–28.

South Dakota House of Representatives

Year	Number	Norwegians	Germans	Swedes	Danes
1917	103	22	3	4	1
1925	103	21	4	7	2

Persons of Foreign Birth or Parentage in North Dakota, 1910

	Norwegians	Germans	Swedes	Danes
Percentage	30.3	14.7	6.6	3.0
Number	123,284	59,767	26,800	12,203

North Dakota House of Representatives

Year	Number	Norwegians	Germans	Swedes	Danes
1907	103	30	4	0	1
1913	103	25	3	4	1
1919	103	26	4	3	1

The tendency is similar in all three states. The Norwegians outnumbered the Swedes and the Swedes and Norwegians together by far outnumbered the Germans, who in relation to their large population figures had weak representation. Wefald not only refers to Norwegian prominence over the other ethnic groups, but he also stresses their key role in politics.[28] Sten Carlsson has presented figures on the impact of different ethnic groups on state politics in Minnesota and on the national scene, but he puts more emphasis on joint Scandinavian prevalence over the Germans.[29]

Knute Nelson was the first Midwestern Scandinavian politician who made a breakthrough on the state and national levels. He was born in Voss, Norway, came to the United States in 1849 at the age of six, and made a career as a lawyer. His first election to the Minnesota senate in 1874 was, evidently, the result of systematic Scandinavian efforts.[30] The question of what role ethnic background and ethnic arguments played in politics arises. Nelson is an interesting example. He resided in Alexandria in western Minnesota's Douglas County, an area with a mixed population of Norwegians and Swedes. In the 1882 Congressional election Nelson sought the Republican nomination in the fifth, so-called bloody, Minnesota district. The Swedish newspaper *Svenska Folkets Tidning* exhorted its readers to show all native citizens in the whole U.S. that a

28 J. Wefald 1971.
29 S. Carlsson 1970, 1973, 1976, 1980.
30 C. Chrislock 1976, 107.

Norwegian could win over an economically privileged Yankee. Nelson won the nomination and took seat in the House with the help of Scandinavian votes. Until Scandinavians had established a firm foothold in Minnesota state politics, ethnic background could be used as political argument, as when Knute Nelson ran for governor in 1892, but later the electorate considered this kind of argumentation inappropriate, even immoral.[31]

Norwegians and Swedes had an upper hand in politics in Minnesota and the Dakotas, as shown in the figures above. They also had a strong position in Wisconsin. One could add, especially for Minnesota, that the representation of these two ethnic groups on the national scene has also been considerable. All Minnesota governors from 1896, when Knute Nelson was first elected, until the late 1970's have been of Norwegian or Swedish background, with the exception of one term. In the 1930's there was a saying that Minnesotans did not care who was governor as long as he was Scandinavian.[32]

In Minnesota politics Scandinavians advanced gradually. Until about 1880 Norwegians at first, but also Swedes, made inroads on the political stage at the municipal and county levels. From the late 1870's onwards Scandinavians won election to the state legislature. From the early 1890's they achieved the governorship, and from about the same time they successfully sought positions as representatives and senators of the U.S. Congress. It is characteristic that the Norwegians were one step ahead of the Swedes. In some cases it is evident that Scandinavians sought political posts in order to take the initiative from the Yankees. This ambition helped Norwegian candidates receive marginal votes from Swedes and vice versa. Hence one can speak of Scandinavian collaboration in politics, but this factor should not be overdramatized. In some cases it could, however, add support for Democratic candidates from voters who would normally have gone for the Republicans.[33]

The study of Scandinavian political clout in the United States has naturally focused primarily on Minnesota, the state where Scandinavians make up the largest segment of the population. Nordic immigrants also formed considerable voting blocks in Wisconsin, the Dakotas, and Washington. In Minnesota, though, the Scandinavian element is more discernible than elsewhere. Among politicians who

31 S. Carlsson 1973.
32 S. Carlsson 1973, 234.
33 S. Carlsson 1973.

won national recognition were Democrat John Albert Johnson, an influential governer and seen by many as a potential candidate for the presidency before he died in 1909. Charles Lindbergh Sr., born in Sweden and father of the aviator, was a progressive Republican in the House of Representaties 1907–1917 but protested his party's official line on the issues of finance and trusts. Third-party politics has had a good ground in Minnesota. A typical Minnesota phenomenon was the Farmer Labor Party, and the stronger the Scandinavian base was in the election districts, the more votes they cast for Farmer Labor Party candidates. Floyd Björnstjerne Olson was one of the state's most radical front-rank politicians and was elected governor three times in the 1930's on the Minnesota Farmer Labor Party's ticket.[34]

The Homeland Legacy and American Politics

Ethnicity has been an extremely important ingredient in shaping the character of American politics, but one must guard against looking for, say, specifically Norwegian and Swedish influences. Jon Wefald, in his study on Norwegian politicians in the Midwest, has taken up the question of homeland legacy in American politics. He describes Norwegian-Americans as 'one of the most consistently reform-minded ethnic groups' and 'unrelentingly progressive' and their politics as 'uniformly left of center'.[35] Wefald found Norwegians avantgardists and leading spirits in all protest, reform and progressive movements in the Midwest: in the Populist movement, in the Nonpartisan League, in the American Society of Equity (a farmers' alliance which aimed to keep farm products off the markets until the prices had been set), and the Farmer Labor Party of Minnesota. They were also progressives and left-of-center politicians in the Republican Party. In North Dakota, where Norwegian radicalism was strongly felt, they were in the vanguard of the Socialist Party. In Wisconsin they praised Robert M. LaFollette's program. Wefald underscores LaFollette's semi-Norwegian background: He was raised in a Norwegian neighborhood and spoke Norwegian.[36] Wefald finds a strong strain of egalitarian thinking in the Norwegian-American press, that was in line with the mainstream of Norwegian-American political thinking. The newspaper editors

34 B.L. Larson 1978; R.B. Lucas 1974.
35 J. Wefald 1971, quotations from pages 3 and 29.
36 J. Wefald 1971, 55–58.

were 'apostles of community spirit and social responsibility', striking qualities that were also found among some of the most successful Norwegian-American   businessmen.[37]

Wefald's main explanation for Norwegian-American reformism, radicalism and inclination to revolt, points to the impact of culture and values. Norwegian-American protest, according to Wefald, drew upon Old World spirit that Norwegian immigrants brought to the New World and to some extent originated in impulses from leftist politics in Norway. Norwegian American left-of-center politics is juxtaposed with certain Norwegian traits: folk heritage, social cohesion, compassion for the have-nots, and concern for the common good. Leaning on sociologist Peter Munch's research on rural-urban conflicts in Norway, Wefald stresses rural devices, such as the ethos of farm life and the concept of sharing, and also the tendency among the rural population in Norway to check the expanding urban liberal capitalistic culture. In other words, Wefald sees in the Norwegian political movement in America a rural protest against the growing industrial combines and the tendency of large financial firms and credit houses to control markets, hence the strong Norwegian opposition to American values.

There is every reason to dwell upon Wefald's conclusions since his theme, the cultural and political heritage of the homeland and its impact on behavior in America, is one of the main questions in our analysis of Nordic immigrant life. Wefald's main line of thought, that Norwegians were second to none among ethnic groups displaying political radicalism, cannot be wholly accepted, because it is not founded on any real comparisons with other groups. For one, the Finnish contribution to American politics was of an even more radical brand, even though Finns entered the political scene at a later stage and never reached the same heights in state and national politics.

As to the issue of whether Old World heritage or the American social and economic environment played the most active role in forming the character of Norwegian immigrant politics, one may regret the absence of a closer analysis. Wefald more or less takes for granted that a common spirit, based on homeland values, existed among Norwegians in America and that this affected their political make-up. First, one may question Wefald's portrait of the homeland community. The tradition of freedom in Norway was indeed strong,

---

37 J. Wefald 1971, 43–44.

and feudalism never had any grip on the country. The nobility never dominated the economy and had little impact on social life. Bureaucrats and politicians who favoured centralistic tendencies met strong opposition after 1814 in the rural population, but one must guard against reading back twentieth century welfare-state egalitarian ideology into the nineteenth century. Rather, the social order in the Norwegian rural sector ascribed strict roles: there existed an established hierarchy between freeholding farmers, lease-holders, and cottagers. In addition, population pressure and short-age of soil aggravated social tensions in the rural milieu during the hundred years before the peak of Atlantic immigration. It may be, though, that Norwegian-Americans, like most ethnic groups, had a distorted and idealized picture of the homeland, one which por-trayed Norway as the prototype of liberty, equality, and fraternal feelings.

Second, one could with Carl Chrislock, examine 'environmental factors'. Chrislock has found that the Norwegian political orien-tation in Minnesota deviated most pronouncedly from the tra-ditional Republicanism in the state's wheat belt, where farmers felt oppression, real or supposed, at the hands of economic powers that controlled the grain trade. One could go a step further: The radical tendency among Norwegians was evidently stronger in the Dakotas than in Minnesota, obviously for the same reason. These states fell more within the wheat belt than Minnesota, and one-crop farmers were more vulnerable to price fluctuations and the financial practices of combines and purchasers.[38]

The point is not to refute Wefald's thesis of the homeland impact but rather to argue that the issue is rather complex: Influences from Norway were not alone in shaping Norwegian radicalism.

38 C.H. Chrislock 1976.

16. Labor Union Activities of Nordic Immigrants

For a variety of reasons socialism has never become a viable force in American politics. Among the widely discussed reasons why organized political radicalism and labor unionism have not developed any considerable strength is the workers' conflict of loyalties *vis-à-vis* their ethnic group and economic class. This problem cannot be dealt with here in more general terms, but narrowing the scope to Nordic immigrants will also have some bearing on the broader class-versus-ethnicity issue. Several questions are posed here: What was the role of Nordic immigrants in American labor politics and trade unions? What were the relations between Scandinavia and America as far as political radicalism and labor unionism are concerned? To what extent did workers form unions along ethnic lines and to what extent were they willing to cooperate outside their own group?

The first part of this section will deal with Danes, Norwegians, and Swedes and the second with Finns, a separation primarily justified by the very special role that Finnish immigrants played as radicals in America.

Early Immigrant Labor Activists

Looking first at individuals, it is obvious that Danish and Swedish labor leaders and union activists left their countries for reasons that were clearly linked to their labor activism. Some were exiled by force, others left feeling that they were considered *personae non gratae* by their government or by local authorities or simply because they saw America as a better place for work and unionism.

The 'first Norwegian socialist', Marcus Thrane (1817–1890) ended up in America. Thrane founded an organization which later became the Norwegian Labor Party, and he was sentenced to prison because of the radicalism he expressed. Released after five years, he experienced new hardships because of his political activities and decided to emigrate to America in 1863, where he continued his mission as a protagonist of the workers' cause. Thrane had wide cultural interests and a literary vein. He started a couple of radical newspapers (*Marcus Thrane's Norske Amerikaner, Dagslyset*) and edited for some time *Den Nye Tid* (*The New Time*) in Chicago, a paper started by the Danish immigrant Louis Pio. Thrane's socialism did not meet any wide response among Norwegians in America, but, nonetheless, he was under strong attack from Norwegian churchmen in the immigrant country. In a pamphlet sent out from the Missouri Synod in 1866 his socialist ideas were branded.[1]

Another interesting case is the socialist Louis Pio who brought socialist ideas from Denmark to the United States. Like many early Scandinavian socialists and labor pioneers, he received an intellectual upbringing and obtained a degree in philosophy from the University of Copenhagen.

As one of the leaders of the Danish Social Democratic Party (founded in 1871) Pio took an active part in a bricklayers' strike in the Danish capital in April 1872. Together with other leading activists he was sentenced to prison (five years in Pio's case) but was released before that time span had elapsed. Having recommenced his union activism, he came on counter course with other leaders who preferred short-range goals as opposed to Pio's more long-term political plans. To this predicament were added the financial problems of a socialist paper he edited as well as private troubles.

Pio had propagated his ideas to found a Danish Socialist colony in America. But in the eyes of some of the rank and file whom Pio had promised to bring to Kansas, he had engaged in improper and underhand dealings with the Copenhagen police commissioner, who was willing to pay his and Poul Geleff's (his companion-in-arms) way out of the country. With a sum of 10,000 Danish crowns, drawn from Danish industrialists who were willing to get rid of him, Pio left Denmark. His 'betrayal' damaged the cause of socialism in Denmark, and in America he only half-heartedly tried to implement his semi-utopian ideas of a Socialist colony.

Like other Scandinavian, purely intellectual, socialist 'leaders' in the New World, Louis Pio encountered a series of frustrations mostly because of his inability to combine intellectual activities

1 I. Semmingsen 1950, 242–244; O. Lovoll 1983, 106; A.W. Andersen 1975, 90.

with permanent income-producing jobs. Pio's immigrant career took many turns and he experienced one disappointment after another. His background did not prepare him to become an apostle of socialism in the New World; instead his main role became that of editor for a half year of *Den Nye Tid* (*The New Time*) in Chicago. During seventeen years in this city he moved at least eleven times. His sundry jobs included those of professor, editor, translator, notary public, customs house clerk, county architect, and realtor.[2]

Even though Pio's story is conspicuous, it has some parallels. One is Atterdag Wermelin's, who played a prominent role in the early history of socialism in Sweden. Born in the province of Värmland in 1861 as a minister's son, he came into liberal circles at Uppsala University, where he expressed radical ideas in the so-called *sedlighetsfrågan* (the morality issue). Through contacts with socialists, Wermelin developed a strong interest in theoretical questions and also translated the writings of Karl Marx into Swedish. Hampered by poor economic circumstances and without the possibility of earning a decent living by writing, since he was totally unwilling to make any intellectual compromise, he saw no other way out than to head for America. He emigrated in 1887 (two years before the Swedish Social Democratic Party was formally founded), wandered between places of work in the New World, and suffered during recurrent periods of unemployment. With no possibility of carrying on his intellectual work, and with no place in the American or Swedish labor movement, Wermelin ended his life as uncompromisingly as he had lived it: After slashing a vein, he threw himself from the Brooklyn Bridge in 1905.[3]

In their critique of the existing order in the country, the Swedish labor movement, in some instances, pointed to emigration as a sign of social disorder and misery. For propagandistic reasons they gathered to hail some of its more prominent members who departed for the New World. Upon these occasions labor leaders addressed the authorities and employers, emphasizing that the working people's situation was unbearable and that reforms were necessary. Send-off ceremonies were also used to display loyalty with the workers' cause all over the world, and at such occasions the departing member promised to work for the venerable cause in America and to serve as a link between the struggling labor movement in the

2 G.R. Nielsen 1981, 184–188.
3 F. Nilsson 1970, 233–234.

230

two countries. Such a celebration accompanied the Swedish tailor and popular stump orator Gustaf Adolf Ahlenius, born in Småland in 1858, when he left Stockholm in 1888. It should be added that Swedish labor had few illusions about the United States at this time. The Swedish labor press was well-informed about the American labor market, and earlier immigrants passed on information about U.S. conditions. The labor movement, at least in Sweden, furnished its emigrating members with an image of America that included unemployment risks, harsh work conditions, and bossism. But even worse conditions in Sweden could justify emigration.[4]

While in Chicago, Ahlenius reported back to the Stockholm newspaper *Social-Demokraten* that he had tried to sow some socialistic seeds in his new environment by starting a discussion club, but there is no indication that he played any active role as unionist in the new country.[5] The opposite is the case with Erik Amandus Nordman, also born in Småland, in 1859, who spoke on behalf of unemployed workers in Stockholm in 1887. Feeling forced to leave the country, he played an influential role in the Scandinavian section of the Socialist Party in New York. Nordman is an early example of a labor leader whose career started in Scandinavia and continued overseas.[6] A few individuals brought experiences and impulses from America back to Scandinavia. For example, Marcus Thrane returned for a short time to Norway in 1883 and distributed a pamphlet with the title *Norge som Republik* (Norway as a Republic), which Norwegian authorities viewed with strong suspicion.[7] The campaign for the eight-hour day in Norway often referred to American examples.[8] The Swedish labor leader August Palm visited Swedish immigrant socialist clubs and other labor organizations on a grand tour in 1900 to leftist fellow countrymen in the New World.[9]

Ostracism of union leaders became more common in Scandinavia around the turn of the century when industrialization had progressed, the class consciousness of workers had developed, and when laborers and employers had created nation-wide organizations. Hence, disputes between labor and capital often took more militant forms than before. The major bone of contention was the right of

---

4 F. Nilsson 1970, 206–229; cf. L.-G. Tedebrand 1985, 547–580.
5 F. Nilsson 1970, 236–237.
6 F. Nilsson 1970.
7 A.W. Andersen 1975.
8 J.B. Danielson 1985, 191.
9 August Palm, *Ögonblicksbilder från en tripp till Amerika.* Stockholm 1901.

workers to organize and form unions. Thus animosity between industrial employers and organized workers reached its climax after the turn of the century. One indicator of this development is the number and the intensity of strikes on the Swedish labor market. (See table 10.)

The Swedish so-called Great Strike (actually a lock-out which originated from a limited strike) in 1909, an extremely bitter and protracted conflict, resulted in an extensive and severe blow to the Swedish Confederation of Trade Unions (*Landsorganisationen*, founded in 1898). This event had clear repercussions on the relations between laborers in Sweden and America, since both unemployment and 'obnoxious' union activities forced workers to venture to America. Earlier immigrants followed the news about their brethren at home and supported them with money collected in the union much like Danish workers in the United States had done during the Great Lockout in Denmark in 1899.[10]

Finally, emigrating strikers replenished the cadres of Scandinavian workers' clubs and associations in the United States.[11]

Scandinavian Immigrants in Trade Unions

With the exception of Finns, the role of Nordic immigrants in the American trade union and socialist movements is so far almost unresearched. The meagre data hardly permit even drawing its contours. One may, tentatively, group Scandinavian workers in four categories. First, a large majority of rank and file workers had relatively conservative values and cared little about the class strug-

Table 10. Strikes in Sweden, 1873–1909.

1873	11	1882	4	1891	64	1900	135
1874	7	1883	5	1892	26	1901	118
1875	3	1884	6	1893	53	1902	139
1876	1	1885	10	1894	44	1903	142
1877	3	1886	28	1895	65	1904	215
1878	1	1887	16	1896	102	1905	189
1879	7	1888	41	1897	114	1906	290
1880	3	1889	38	1898	163	1907	312
1881	10	1890	105	1899	105	1908	302
						1909	138

Source: L.-G. Tedebrand 1983, 200.

10 H. Bengston 1955, 26; G.E. Johnson 1940, 26; J.B. Danielsson 1985.
11 H. Bengston 1955, 82, 197.

232

gle, or only passively let themselves be organized in labor clubs, shops and associations. Second, there was a more active category who made up the backbone of the Scandinavian-American labor movement. They had an unrewarding task, trying to move and register the mass of members, collecting membership fees, and putting up with the animosity of employers. Third, a smaller group of labor leaders existed, to be counted only by the scores, ardent souls, some with considerable theoretical knowledge in socialism, who against all odds kept newspapers, small publishing companies, and nation-wide organizations alive.

This third category included the Danish newspaperman Dane Christian Botker, who for decades provided his reading public with socialist news and views, and Henry Bengston, who served as editor of the *Svenska Socialisten* (The Swedish Socialist) in Chicago.

The fourth category would include more pragmatic socialists who used their labor union and leftist convictions as a basis for political careers, mostly on the municipal level. Among these was the abovementioned mayor of Jamestown, Samuel Carlson, a man who resisted political labeling but felt that public utilities should be in the hands of the city government, a conviction he did his utmost to implement during three decades in the leading post of the city's administration.

Sucessful 'pragmatic' socialists also included another mayor of Swedish background, Herman Hallström. He was born in Östergötland, Sweden in 1888, emigrated at the age of 20, and started off as a bricklayer's hand in the Swedish-dominated city of Rockford, Illinois. After a quick career in the city's Swedish branch of the Socialist Party, including the editorship of an English-language socialist newspaper, he ran as the Socialist Party's candidate for mayor in 1921, won the race, and stayed in this post for six two-year terms. Both Carlson and Hallström served in cities with large cadres of industrial workers of Swedish descent. One might discuss to what extent the Swedish 'factor' explains their election victories.

Danish, Norwegian, and Swedish laborers organized in clubs which aimed at gathering 'Scandinavian' members, but nonetheless there was a strong tendency to organize along purely national lines. Nation-wide 'Scandinavian' organizations were affiliated with the Socialist Party of America. As long as workers really grouped together with immigrants from the neighbor countries in Scandinavia, this allowed a pan-Scandinavianism which was difficult to realize in other endeavors in America. In this case, however, it had a parallel in the home countries, where a Scandinavian Trade Union Congress was active in collaboration and exchange of ideas between the national leaderships.

A Scandinavian Socialist Workers Association (*Skandinaviska Socialistiska Arbetarförbundet*) was founded in the mid-1880's with headquarters in New York City and its strongest foothold in the East. Its membership reached 500 in the 1910's. The Scandinavian Socialist Federation (*Skandinaviska Socialistförbundet*) which adhered to the Socialist Party of America (founded in 1901) had its member-base in Chicago and the Middle West. Its membership, never impressive, reached a peak of 3,700 around 1915. Thereafter the Scandinavian Socialist organization gradually dissolved due to the impact of loyalist campaigns during the war, the internal struggles that followed the Russian Revolution, and the splits within the international labor movement.[12]

Finnish-American Labor Radicalism

The Finnish legacy in America is to a great extent linked to labor radicalism, and many observers and scholars have held the Finns as one of the most radical immigrant groups in the United States.[13] During a long period they were the largest ethnic group in the Socialist Party, but did not play leadership roles for the radical movement.[14] Only in recent years has a Finnish-American attained a position as head of a radical party, namely Gus Hall, who during the 1970's and the early 1980's ran as the presidential candidate of the Communist Party.

The factors underlying Finnish-American radicalism can be found both in the Old World and the New. Emigration from Finland reached its climax during a period when social tensions in the country reached a critical level, and many who were active in the labor movement in Finland left for America. Finland's relation to Russia stimulated radicalism among Finnish-American workers in many ways, and finally, Finland's situation during the First World War had repercussions on the political attitudes of the Finnish labor movement in America. One should add, however, that radicalism

---

12 Membership figures from P. Nordahl 1985.
13 E.g., A. Kostiainen 1978, 10.
14 Cf. P.G. Hummasti 1979, 63–64, who gives examples of weak Finnish leadership also on the local level.

was not embraced by all Finns in America, probably not even by a majority.

During the 1970's and 1980's Finnish historians and scholars of Finnish descent in the United States and Canada devoted their research to the study of Finnish labor radicalism in the New World.[15] They treated subjects that have long been taboo or at least regarded as unbecoming. Second and third generation Finnish immigrants have evinced how reminiscences and knowledge of the early decades of the Finnish-American labor movement have been repressed. To rephrase Michael Passi's words, a new generation of historians has rediscovered the history of Finnish-American radicalism and created a 'usable past'.[16]

One reason for the earlier generation's reluctance to deal with the history of Finnish-American labor may have been the strong trauma many individuals experienced and the disappointments that arose in collectives of Finnish immigrants. Finnish socialism and union activities in the U.S. made Americans hostile towards the Finnish immigrants. This, in turn, led conservative Finns to repudiate their radical fellow countrymen. A cleft resulted between conservative, primarily church-oriented, Finnish immigrants and labor Finns, many of whom developed a strong antireligious attitude in the new country.

The Finnish experience in American labor was also negative in another sense. Most of the militant activities which radical Finns participated in led to defeats. The organized walk-out in Mesabi in 1907, where Finns played a leading role, ended in a rout. The outcomes of other encounters with capitalist companies that could fall back on strike-breakers and paramilitary intervention were similar. Finnish-American labor history is one of intense frustration, perhaps best demonstrated in the re-emigration to the Soviet Union of thousands of Finnish-American radicals in the 1920's and the early 1930's as a result of their disappointment with their situation in the New World.

The combination of these and other factors led two generations of immigrants to neglect the fate of the Finnish labor struggle in America, a disregard that researchers who felt the atomosphere of the New Ethnicity in the 1960's have now made it their task to remedy.

15 E.g., P.G. Hummasti 1979; M. Karni, P. Kivisto 1985; A. Kostiainen 1979; E. Laine 1981.
16 M. Passi 1977, 21.

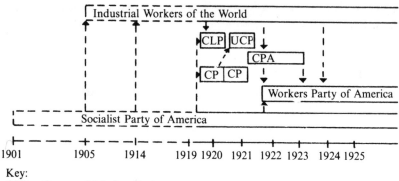

Key:
CLP = Communist Labor Party
UCP = United Communist Party
CPA = Communist Party of America
CP = Communist Party

Figure 32. Leftist Parties in the United States, 1901–1925.
Source: After A. Kostiainen 1978, 24.

The question of Finnish labor radicalism in America should also be linked to more general aspects of American labor history. Socialist ideas have not found fertile ground in the United States, and trade unions have been much weaker than in most comparable industrialized countries. Radical unions and parties have indeed existed but have not been noted for their success; for example, the Industrial Workers of the World (IWW), which had many Finnish members. IWW was founded in 1905 with the syndicalist-anarchist aim of replacing the state with an industrial syndicate. Unlike the American Federation of Labor (AFL), the IWW made strong efforts to organize immigrant workers. Torn by factionalism and made suspect during World War I, it soon lost its vigor and was dissolved in 1925.

Ethnic diversity, competition between ethnic groups on the shop floor, language problems, and divergent experience from the home countries have contributed to the weakness of the American labor movement. Our aim here is to view Finnish radicalism against this background.

The history of organized Finnish labor in America can be described in terms of gradual radicalization from the late 1890's to the mid-1920's, the determining factors for this development located in the international scene, in Finland proper, and in the experiences

236

Finns met on the American labor market. Finnish-Americans closely followed politics and labor disputes in Russia, and, especially
from 1917 onwards, Finnish-American radicalism mirrored developments overseas.

Finnish labor leaders in America in the 1890's have been viewed
as 'bourgeois socialists', since reformist thought had a strong impact
on the labor movement in Finland until the turn of the century.
Many of those who took the lead in the organization of Finnish
labor in the U.S. had a past as functionaries and leaders within the
labor unions in Finland. Around the turn of the century, when the
russification drive, conducted by the czarist authorities in Finland,
was most intense, many socialists were forced to leave the country.
This meant a considerable loss for the socialist movement in Finland, but at the same time redoubled Finnish radicalism overseas.
Among those arriving in America at this time who played important
roles in the new country were Vihtori Kosonen, Matti Kurikka,
Eetu Salin, Frans Josef Syrjälä, Taavi Tainio, and Alfred S. Tanner.
Kurikka's failure to establish a utopian colony in British Columbia
has been described above.[17] Tanner had been forced out of Finland
after having given so-called scientific lectures in which he criticized
the church. He came to America in 1899 and was instrumental
in founding the first Finnish-American socialist organization, the
Myrsky (storm) Society in Rockport, Massachusetts.[18] With the
exception of Kurikka the ambitions of these early leaders were to
gather all Finnish laborers in America in one organization.

A debate occurred among the Finns as to whether one should
aim at collaboration with other ethnic groups. One standpoint was
to subordinate ethnic interests to goals common to the entire working class, but most Finnish labor leaders recommended that ethnic
organizations be formed for practical reasons. The strongest argument for an ethnic strategy was the language question.

Numerous labor organizations of Finnish character were established during the first years of the new century; the Saima Society
in Fitchburg, Massachusetts, and Imatra League in New York City
were among the first and the most influential in the East. Early
Finnish socialism was linked to temperance lodges, and in many
places socialists took over existing fraternal organizations.

During the first years of the twentieth century Finnish labor was

17 See above, pp. 131–33.
18 A. Kostiainen 1978, 27.

organized all over the United States. In 1903 and 1904 leagues were established in Gardner, Massachusetts, and Duluth, Minnesota, whereby a national organization of Finnish labor clubs, societies and factions was created. At a meeting in Cleveland, Ohio, in October 1904, where most of the existing societies were represented, it was decided that all Finnish-American workers' associations were to join the Socialist Party of America (SPA). A step in this direction was the formation in 1906 in Hibbing, Minnesota, of the Finnish Socialist Federation (FSF, *Yhdysvaltain Suomalainen Sosialistijärjestö*). The FSF functioned as a link between Finnish labor and the Socialist Party of America. At the same time the Finnish-American working-class newspapers *Työmies* (*Worker*) and *Raivaaja* (*Pioneer*) were acknowledged as party organs.[19] The stronghold of Finnish labor in America was the upper Midwest, especially the mining areas in northern Minnesota and northern Michigan.

Finns as Strikers

Compared to other ethnic groups in the mining areas, Finns were inclined to strike. They played a leading role in the Mesabi Strike in 1907 and in the Copper Country Strike in 1913. Several factors ought to be considered when explaining the important Finnish role. The Finns were well-organized. Finnish chapters were found in almost every mining town. They had a strong leadership, since many front-rank members had emigrated from Finland in the late 1890's and during the first decade of the twentieth century. This cadre of leaders knew the theories of socialism and were willing to put them into practice. The Finns also had low social positions in the mines, and they were among the lowest paid and the worst housed, a factor which evidently made them more inclined to strike.

Naturally the harsh conditions in the mining fields affected all immigrant working groups. Accidents in the mines were frequent, and working opportunities were sporadic, since operations were closed now and then, especially during the winter season. The working force was ethnically mixed, a large part coming from Eastern and Southern Europe, but there were also many Swedes, French-Canadians, Irish, and Italians. Language problems were great, and suspicion between language groups was evident.

The inclination towards strike actions has been discussed with

19 A. Kostiainen 1978, 31.

reference to the background and labor union experience of the respective groups. Although most of the Finnish mine workers came from rural Finland, some originated in industrial areas in the southern part of the country and brought union experience to America. The political repercussions of the General Strike of 1905 in Finland and Russia animated Finnish-American labor as did the mutiny of the Russian garrison at Suomenlinna (Sveaborg) in Helsinki the following year. One should note, however, that the General Strike was aimed less at the employers and industrialists than at the Russian political authorities in the Grand Duchy.[20]

Among other ethnic groups in the mining areas of the Upper Midwest the Italians had some experience with labor conflicts, while most East European immigrants came from countries where strikes were either forbidden or strongly repressed. These groups were not so well-organized and sometimes borrowed Finnish halls for their meetings. In the Mesabi Strike of 1907, Finns, according to some estimations, made up as much as three quarters of the striking force, and many of the leaders were Finns. One of the top organizers was a Finnish immigrant named John Maki. Nineteen Finns were arrested and imprisoned for one month before they were tried and found not guilty, while many other Finnish laborers were fired and blacklisted. In contrast to several mining strikes in the Western United States the Mesabi Strike was relatively peaceful, partly because of the lame effort of employers to organize vigilante groups and partly because the Minnesota state administration, under the leadership of Governor John A. Johnson, took an impartial stand in the conflict.[21] Nonetheless the strike ended in a vexatious defeat for the laborers who after two months went back to work.

The Mesabi conflict of 1907 taught the Finns a lesson in American capitalism. For the first time Finns had joined other ethnic workers in practical action, and contacts between Finns and American labor organizations were also strengthened. Individual Finns reacted differently; some left the mines and tried a life as farmers, while some were radicalized and prepared themselves for further actions against their employers.

The Copper Country Strike in Northern Michigan in 1913 had similar effects. Technological development led to the introduction of new equipment, more capital-intensive labor processes, concen-

20 E. Juttikala 1965, 288.
21 N. Betten 1967.

tration on fewer enterprises, and changed conditions for the workers. In 1912 and 1913 conflict arose concerning wages, safety questions, the length of the workday, and the replacement of two-man drills with one-man drills (called 'man killers' and 'widow makers' by some workers). The dispute resulted in a strike at a time when the market for copper was depressed. After several months the workers capitulated without achieving much. Many Finns left the area; some moved to the Minnesota Iron Range, others gave up mining work and started farming operations on marginal lands, while still others in their bitterness became more radical. The *Työmies* paper was moved to Superior, Wisconsin. The center of Finnish labor activities shifted back to Minnesota, where Finns played a leading role in the 1916 Strike on the Mesabi, which resulted in a new defeat for organized labor. Heavy European demand for American ore during World War I caused U.S. Steel to use everything in its power to get laborers back to work. The workers' organizational resources were depleted, the IWW was indecisive in its policy, and the AFL only reluctantly endorsed the strike. The Finns, who were best organized, had taken the lead and inspired other ethnic groups to support the strike, and Finnish halls were centers for union activities.

Decline of Finnish-American Radicalism

Above all, the Mesabi Strike of 1916 demonstrated the weakness of the IWW, which by that time had passed its heyday. It was not long before Finnish labor, influenced by the revolutions in Russia, became further radicalized and finally left the IWW. As Auvo Kostiainen has pointed out, Finnish radicals in America saw the Russian Revolution in the light of developments in Finland.[22] The overthrow of the czarist government in 1917 stimulated discussions about revolutionary tactics and led the Finns to think of the future of America in terms of a nation-wide revolution.

Finns in America identified themselves with radicals who had fled from Finland to Russia during 1918 and who had established the Communist Party of Finland in Moscow. American Finns gradually joined the communist movement in America, but in contrast to other groups Finns were not very active in the early underground communistic circles. On the other hand Finns became active in the

22 A. Kostiainen 1978, 189.

legal Communist Party. Finns left the Socialist Party in large numbers, and in 1922 the Finnish Socialist Federation joined the Workers Party of America, becoming the largest foreign-language group in this party. Finns made up about 50 percent of its membership, but their role in the Party's leadership did not correspond to their membership.

Comintern (The Third International), founded in 1919, stressed the need for internationalization of the Communist movement. In an American context this meant that immigrants should 'Americanize' and join the American front against capitalism. This was a crucial question for Finnish-American labor, which had always been inclined to work within the framework of its own ethnic group. Various resolutions by Finnish-American labor organizations, for example the FSF in 1912, had stressed the necessity to cooperate with the English-language branches of the Socialist Party, but in practice Finns displayed a certain degree of ethnic exclusiveness. John I. Kolehmainen has gone as far as to say that Finnish workers expressed an ethnic consciousness within the framework of labor associations, one reason being that Finns had a stronger social, cultural, and educational orientation than other ethnic groups.[23]

Sometimes this phenomenon has been referred to as hall socialism: Finns were loyal to the ethnically organized socialist clubs and societies and their cultural ambitions but were weak in their contribution to the labor movement as such and were not politically conscious. It is against this background that one must see the reluctance of Finns to respond to the solidarity drives of the international communist movement during the 1920's as well as the weak Finnish participation in the leadership of the Workers Party of America. Despite external pressure Finns remained within their own ethnic group.

Migration to Soviet Karelia

There was another category of Finnish immigrants in the United States and Canada that became disappointed with the social and economic order in these countries, and who therefore sought the socialist heaven elsewhere. Some of them re-emigrated to Europe and joined the labor forces in Soviet Karelia, where they joined other categories of Finns: so-called 'red refugees' from the Civil

---

23 I. Kolehmainen, here cited from A. Kostiainen 1983.

War of 1918, Finns who had immigrated legally in the interwar years, and other fellow-countrymen who had left Finland unlawfully in the 1930's.[24]

According to the then current five-year plan, Soviet Karelia was expected to increase its production of timber and the authorities were in deep need of skilled labor. The idea of migrating to the 'worker's homeland' was not new among Finnish immigrants in North America but had arisen in the early 1920's. Around 6,000 Finns in North America responded to campaigns from Soviet recruiters.

A Karelian fever burst out in 1932 and 1933 during the deepest period of the Great Depression. A majority of those who went were skilled laborers, several of whom were lumber workers accustomed to technical equipment and machinery, a category much desired by the Soviet authorities because of the lack of technical expertise. Many of the re-emigrating Finns had strong communist leanings and arrived in Karelia with expectations of a better order in the Soviet Union. Many brought capital, equipment and tools.

For a majority the Karelian adventure ended in deep tragedy, one element being the strong Great Russia chauvinism which from 1933 was perpetrated against Finnish immigrants, another being the formation of *sovhozes* and *kolhozes* which made many Finns into second-class agricultural workers. Disillusioned Finns deserted the socialist haven; some went to Finland, others re-emigrated to North America, while others were caught in the Soviet Union because they had given up their former citizenship.[25] To some the Russian adventure became a trauma which tended to socially isolate them for the rest of their lives.

24 A. Kostiainen 1985b.
25 R. Kero 1983.

17. Immigrants and Languages

Language Maintenance in America

Only three immigrant languages in North America have survived and manifested themselves as languages of national importance: English in Canada and the United States, Spanish in Mexico and the United States, and French in Canada. Some groups have shown stronger language retention than others, for example, the Pennsylvania Germans (or Pennsylvania Dutch as they also are called), whose first settlement occurred in Germantown, Pennsylvania, in 1683. They developed their own standard of German, a 'hybrid' of several German dialects, mainly based upon south German dialects with some blend of Swiss variants. Pennsylvania Germans had two language norms, dialect in home and neighborhood, and high German in church and school. After 150 years the institutional forces in favor of English became too strong. When the parochial school, where instruction had been in German, gave way to the public school in the 1830's, a process commenced which undermined German usage, erasing the language within a few generations. Not even the strong influx of new German-speaking immigrants during the nineteenth century could prevent this process.

One or another small group, for example, the Hutterites who live in self-chosen isolation and reduce their contacts with the larger society, seems to belie the general tendency where English forms the all-embracing and dominant language in the United States. The Hutterites, who nowadays live mainly in South Dakota, Montana, and in the Canadian prairie provinces, are totally bilingual in English and German.

The Swedish-speaking population in the New Sweden colony along the Delaware River was too small and too weak to be able to retain the home language in the long run. The administrative language of the colony was Swedish, and since the colonization was an undertaking of the Swedish state, the colonists received assistance from the Swedish government in religious and other matters. This also meant support for the language. The Swedish Church sent pastors more than one hundred years after the colony had been conquered by the Dutch in 1655, but in 1786 the New Sweden colonists broke the bonds with the Swedish State Church. At that time the language proficiency of those who identified themselves as Swedes was very weak, and Swedish died out as a language before the mass immigration started from Sweden in the 1840's.

Nordic Languages in America

The life cycle of the Scandinavian languages (Danish, Icelandic, Norwegian, Swedish) and Finnish (which is a Finno-Ugrian language) in North America is roughly the same. The first generation adhered to the old language, but a large number used two languages, although their English remained incomplete and deficient. For the second generation, English formed the main language, and command of the immigrant language became, largely, only receptive. The overwhelming majority of the third generation did not develop any knowledge of the ancestral language. There were, of course, strong individual variations, not only within the generations, but also within the community and the smaller groups, even within circles of brothers and sisters. It is probably fair, however, to state that 'Nordic' America produced relatively few truly bilingual individuals, although there is reason to surmise that the share of those who possessed full oral and written command of two languages was considerably higher among the Icelandic immigrants than among the other Nordic groups.

The Scandinavian languages and Finnish have left minimal identifiable marks on American English, whether in pronunciation, vocabulary, or grammar, but the encounter of the immigrant languages and English led to mixtures where the main body was the immigrant language and influences from English were very strong. These mixed 'languages' (of which the Finnish variant often is called Finglish) never developed into stable language varieties and did not survive.

Although the pattern is uniform, there remain in the general picture of declining language retention among Nordic emigrants some subtle variations which make it worthwhile to include the linguistic question in a general history of the immigrants. One important aspect is the role of dialects; another consists of the attitudes of, and discussion among, the immigrants themselves, since many held language as the most important factor of their ethnicity.

Demography and Language

There is an interaction between language retention and group cohesion. Language communion strengthens the group and encourages concentration in settlement; population density, in turn, facilitates the retention of language, but a variety of institutional and attitudinal factors is active in this complex sociolinguistic process. Several important factors influence the pace and degree of language survival: the *demography of the language group* (total population, geographical distribution, population density, sex distribution, age composition, social mobility, and degree of urbanization); the group's *migration history* (group character, time span of the migration, and replenishment of new migrants from the sending country); the *character of the immigrant language* (similarity of the language of the minority and the host country, the number and character of dialects, language norms and diglossia); and finally, *institutional factors*, notably the character of the official language and the minority policy of the receiving country. Also, the role of the countries of origin should not be forgotten, since many countries have supported the language of their overseas populations. In the wake of nationalistic revival in Europe, the Scandinavian countries directed some attempts of this kind to America after the turn of the century.

Data from the U.S. and Canadian censuses, although inconsistent and not always reliable, provide information on languages by area and generation and shed light on the correlation between demographic factors and language retention.

Leaving Finns and Icelanders aside for a moment, one notes that the numbers of second generation Danes, Norwegians, and Swedes in the United States were at their peak in 1920. The nearly 3 million inhabitants who declared that they used Scandinavian languages certainly included many second generation immigrants who had only a receptive command of the ancestral language.

The figures from 1920 and 1940 show that Norwegians were more apt to retain their language than Danes and Swedes. The censuses give no figures for bilinguals, and therefore the conclusion should not be drawn that Norwegians necessarily spoke less English.

The language retention of the third generation Scandinavians is low in general, but even here Norwegian-speakers were much better off, and they were, in relative and nominal figures, more numerous than both Danes and Swedes. These data are supported by a 1960

245

survey by Joshua Fishman and his research group, who estimated that for all three Scandinavian groups, 63,000 retained the native language, with Norwegians accounting for roughly two-thirds of the total.[1]

The three groups had varying geographical strongholds. In 1940 the Danes had the highest rate of mother tongue retention for the second generation in Iowa (45.3 percent), the Danish state *par excellence*. Norwegians had the highest rate in North Dakota (66.7 percent), Minnesota (63.6 percent) and Wisconsin (62.0 percent), while Swedish was most frequently preserved in Minnesota (55.1 percent). The 'old' Scandinavian immigrant states in the Midwest provided a more fertile ground for language preservation than the 'younger' immigration states of Washington and California, which had also been the targets for second-stage Scandinavian migration. Scandinavians achieved higher levels of language preservation in rural areas than in urban areas.

In Canada the number who spoke Norwegian, Swedish, or Icelandic reached a peak in 1931, while the maximum figure for Danish-users was reported in 1951, a difference due to the large number of Danish immigrants to Canada during post-war years. The general impression from the Canadian censuses is that Scandinavians (Danes, Norwegians, Swedes) had much lower language retention than other groups. The Dutch and Germans formed a middle level, while much higher retention has been reported among the Italians and Ukrainians.[2] Generally, one must warn against comparison of groups in different phases of the immigration process in a certain country. The Icelanders, however, deviate from the total Scandinavian picture. Their frequent use of Icelandic is explained by a combination of factors: group migration at an early stage in the history of migration to the Canadian prairie provinces, concentrated settlement with southern Manitoba as a core area, and a balanced population among the first generation as far as age and sex are concerned. In addition, they transferred strong literary ambitions and kept close contacts with the home country. The experience of Icelanders in Canada definitely shows that large total immigration population *per se* is no prerequisite for language maintenance. Icelandic in Canada has some parallels in Swedish and Norwegian 'language islands' in the United States, of which more will be said later.

1 Figures on language retention are partially taken from N. Hasselmo 1977.
2 'The Cultural Contribution of the Other Ethnic Groups', *Report of the Royal Commission on Bilingualism and Biculturalism*, Book IV, Ottawa 1973, 121–134.

Inroads of English

The Scandinavian immigrants who arrived in America up to the 1850's found themselves in an unfamiliar language atmosphere. They felt forced to learn English, and one may ask how concerned they were about the future of their mother tongue. Rather they took measures to foster a rapid adjustment to the dominant language. One observer who visited Illinois in 1845 noted that most settlers understood English and attended American churches.[3] Some early Norwegian church leaders encouraged the immigrants to shift to English; so did the newspaper *Nordlyset* in 1847.[4] Early-arriving Swedish pastors also stressed the importance of assimilation to the new milieu and its institutions: One of the founding fathers of the Swedish Augustana Church, Erland Carlsson, introduced English as the language of instruction in church and Sunday school in Chicago in 1855.[5] But the outlook soon changed. The Norwegian Synod took an official stand in favor of Norwegian in 1859, and the churches became the institution in the new country which did most to keep the immigrant languages alive.

Nonetheless, English, unavoidably, made inroads. Expressed schematically, the churches went through three stages in the use of language: first, a monolingual phase using the immigrant language; second, a bilingual phase; and third, a monolingual phase, or almost so, in English. The second phase started with swelling cadres of the American-born generation after the turn of the century. The transition to English in the instruction of children and young people in the Norwegian Evangelical Lutheran Church started in the 1910's and was nearly complete by the mid-twenties. The number and share of divine services in Norwegian declined sharply during the First World War. This process was largely restrained during the 1920's but again accelerated during the 1930's. (See figure 33.) The switch to English was slower in the Midwest and Canada where the Lutheran churches had a largely rural base, as compared to the East, the Rockies, and the West where Norwegian churches were more often found in the cities. By the end of World War II only 5 percent of the services were held in Norwegian.

If we turn to other fields of activity, for example newspapers, journals, and books, the picture is similar; the output of printed

3 E. Haugen 1953, I, 240.
4 E. Haugen 1953, I, 240.
5 N. Hasselmo 1974, 44.

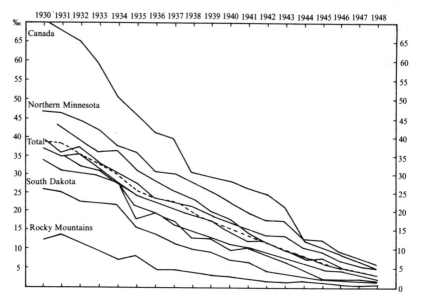

Figure 33. Norwegian Services in the Norwegian Lutheran Church (Evangelical Lutheran Church), 1930–1948. Percentage of Total Services in Each District. Source: E. Haugen 1953, I, 266.

material reached a peak around 1910–1915, but thereafter a regression set in. (See figure 34.) This development coincides with the apex of the foreign-born population in the United States; Danes, Norwegians, and Swedes reached their highest numbers in the 1910 Census.

The language question was debated everywhere: in the family, in the neighborhood, in the church, and in ethnic organizations. Many considered the language critical to the future of Swedish-American and Norwegian-American cultures. After the turn of the century associations were formed whose prime task was to safeguard and preserve the national heritage, and some of these also worked for the preservation and care of languages.

The political and social situation in the United States during World War I, with the drive for 100 percent Americanism during U.S. intervention in the war and consequent demands for loyalty of the immigrants to their new country, had prohibitive effects on the use of languages other than English. Restrictions on immigrants' use of their own idiom in official meetings, on the telephone, etc., it has been argued, hastened the language shift.[6] Many observers

6 F.C. Luebke 1980.

248

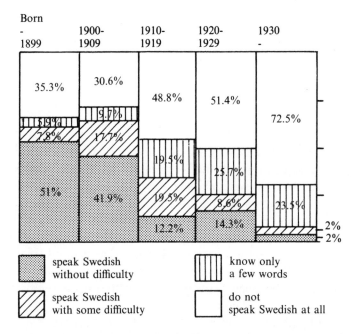

Born
-	1900-	1910-	1920-	1930
1899	1909	1919	1929	-

35.3%   30.6%   48.8%   51.4%   72.5%

51%   41.9%   19.5%   8.6%   23.5%

12.2%   14.3%   2%
2%

☐ speak Swedish
without difficulty

☐ know only
a few words

☐ speak Swedish
with some difficulty

☐ do not
speak Swedish at all

Figure 34. The Ability to Speak Swedish in Five Age Groups, Chisago County, Minnesota. Tests made in the 1960s among first, second, and third generation immigrants.
Source: Nils Hasselmo 1974, 174.

associated Lutheran churches with Germany, and hence suspicion and contempt for Germany spilled over to Scandinavians and probably made them cautious about the use of their language in public places.[7] Statistically, as already mentioned, one can point at a regression of Norwegian, Swedish, and evidently also Danish during the war years. But one can too easily overemphasize the effects of the wartime ban on languages. There were other strong forces that worked toward a language shift. As stated above, the number of first generation immigrants had already reached its peak. More important, perhaps, is the fact that many children of immigrants who arrived during the culmination period in the 1880's had already reached adulthood. Their first language was English since their education had been in English. During the 1910's they also made their way into Scandinavian-American organizations and became

7 S. Lindmark 1971.

functionairies in schools and churches. To borrow the words of Einar Haugen: 'The quarter of the century from 1890 to 1915 was a period when Norwegian activity was slowly dying at the root, but nevertheless shew higher and finer blossoms than at any earlier period in its history'.[8]

Competing Language Norms

Einar Haugen and Nils Hasselmo have meticulously described the contacts between English and Norwegian, and English and Swedish, respectively. These two scholars have shown that very consistent linguistic rules work in the direction of American variants of the two languages. Hasselmo accordingly entitles his magnum opus *Amerikasvenska* (*America Swedish*). Folke Hedblom has shown the patterns of interrelation between Swedish dialects and English. Despite some efforts there seem to be few corresponding studies on the encounter between Danish and Finnish, on the one hand, and English on the other hand.[9]

There is need for a more comparative approach to the study of interlanguage contact between the Nordic languages and English. One could, for example, ask what the norm systems within the various immigrant languages meant for their life-force in America. Were there factors in the languages that made them more or less adaptable or useful in the turbulent American society and in their encounter with English, which like the Scandinavian languages is also a Germanic language? Nils Hasselmo has noted different norms in the use of Swedish in America. The *codified norm* governed the so-called high language that the immigrants mostly met in written form (in the newspapers, in books, in official documents) and heard in church and schools. This norm differed from the the *de facto norm* which characterized the language many immigrants spoke and consisted of a large variety of dialects. Finally, *the perceived norms* were those perceived by outsiders to govern the verbal behavior of certain reference groups.[10]

The question of language adaptability is closely related to the development of the low language (in its many forms) and the high language. In Sweden a diglossia system existed: A high language was used in church and school and other more or less official

8 E. Haugen 1953, I, 247.
9 S. Sahlman-Karlsson 1976; R. Virtanen 1979; D. K. Watkins 1980.
10 N. Hasselmo 1980, 48.

contexts, while the low language was used elsewhere. In America, with the addition of English, a triglossia system emerged. Swedish and English interacted, and according to Hasselmo English influence widened the gulf between high and low Swedish. While a democratization of the high language occurred in Sweden, this had no parallel in America. Nonetheless, the low language gave way to the high language in parts of America where many dialects were spoken.[11] On the other hand, composite dialects of the Pennsylvania-German type never developed.[12]

The Swedish dialects brought to America were so numerous and so different from one another that in some cases speakers could not understand each other or failed to recognize each other as Swedes. In compact settlements with immigrants from Rättvik, or other places in upper Dalarna which had strong dialect deviations, this tended to isolate the group. In some locations in the Midwest – where Norwegians and Swedes arrived early, made up fairly homogenous communities with regional bases in the home country, had a low out-migration, and received replenishment by continued immigration – the vernacular was used daily in the third generation and could even be understood by individuals of the fourth generation. The Bishop Hill area in western Illinois, where Swedish dialects from Hälsingland were spoken, and the Chisago Lake area, which received a large part of its population from Småland in Sweden, are good examples of this pattern.[13] In Waupaca County, Wisconsin, Norwegians held their language tenaciously. They settled this area early, and continuously received new immigrants from Norway.[14]

In the new land the Nordic languages, through their contact with English, lost irrelevant words, acquired English ones and, in addition, were influenced by English grammar. According to Nils Hasselmo one cannot speak of Swedish-American language or Swedish-American dialect or dialects, but rather of a set of contact variants that appeared in bilingual situations. Under the influence of English there were tendencies towards development of a new language, but instead of this transformation a language shift occurred that could not be prevented.

The norm system of the Norwegian language was maybe even

11 N. Hasselmo 1980, 49.
12 F. Hedblom 1980, 43–44.
13 F. Hedblom 1978; N. Hasselmo 1974.
14 E. Haugen 1959, I, 237.

more complicated. The written high language in Norway was Dano-Norwegian, a result of centuries of Danish political domination and cultural influences. This led to increasing stratification of the written and the spoken languages in Norway. In addition to a spoken high Norwegian, there was a rich variety of dialects. During the second half of the 19th century an intensive language debate *(sprog-spørsmålet)* took place, inspired by Ivar Aasen, who on the bases of Norwegian dialects created a new Norwegian language, *landsmål* or *nynorsk* (New Norwegian), which along with *bokmål* today is one of the two official variants of Norwegian. The language debate in Norway also reached America but had nothing of the intensity there that it had in the homeland, because no strong personality fought for Aasen's ideas in America.

The norms for users of Norwegian in America were hence written Dano-Norwegian, spoken high Norwegian, and low Norwegian in the foms of dialects and English. One could also add the mixed language American-Norwegian, which evidently had English ingredients similar to the American-Swedish variants.

We have noticed that Norwegian had a stronger life-force in America, but the question remains whether the norm systems of the languages had any impact on the degree of resistance to English. Variation of dialects and strong differences between dialects could, hypothetically, lead to quicker acceptance of the high variant of the immigrant language or to a quicker switch to English.[15] The very status of the dialects is of importance. During the last one hundred years dialects have had higher status in Norway than in Sweden. If this status was brought over to America, and much suggests this, for example, in the revival of regionalism among Norwegian-Americans at the turn of the century, then the higher status of Norwegian dialects in America together with other social and demographic factors increased the resistance of Norwegian towards English.

15 Cf. F. Hedblom 1982, 178.

18. Immigrants and Literature

Immigrant Authors and Literary Systems

One way to understand the immigrant experience passes through the study of ethnic fiction, but this is a narrow and risky approach, and it requires the conscious use of methods only now being established. As a scholarly subdiscipline Comparative Ethnic Literature is still in its first stage of development. One of the few contributions which develops a comparative approach to Scandinavian literatures in America is Dorothy Burton Skårdal's book *The Divided Heart: Scandinavian Immigrant Experience through Literary Sources*, published in 1974. Skårdal treats an extensive amount of the fictional literature written by Danish, Norwegian, and Swedish immigrants in America, including the second and sometimes the third generations. Skårdal uses the literature as a corpus of historical documents. Her main principle is that this literature 'reflected the attitudes, ideas and emotions of thousands of people who turned to it for an enhanced understanding of their own lives'. Thus, with the justification that popular literature tends to focus on the normal and usual rather than the exceptional in the immigrant's life, Skårdal constructs ethnic history on the basis of immigrant fiction.[1]

The many pitfalls awaiting those who use a historical method of this kind cannot be discussed here.[2] Suffice it to say Skårdal's book is unique in its boldness and a rich well for anyone who seeks an avenue to various segments of Scandinavian life in America. The ambition here will be limited to the question of the relationship between the immigrant authors and immigrant literature in America and the literary worlds in the Nordic homelands. To what extent did ethnic literature serve as a carrier of traditions from the sending countries? What was the role of literature in shaping immigrant life?

---

1 D.B. Skårdal 1974.
2 For an animated discussion on the use of ethnic fiction as a source for immigrant history see *American Studies in Scandinavia* vol. 16 (1984), 65–101 with contributions by Dorothy Burton Skårdal, Kristian Hvidt, Reino Kero, and Fredrik Chr. Brøgger.

How did literature, through interaction with immigrant languages, influence the acculturative process? Since ethnic literature plays a social role and since the mere aesthetic aspects of immigrant literature are not the most important, there is good reason to consider literary production from a sociological point of view rather than from the more traditional viewpoints of historians of literature. Lars Furuland has discussed the role of the immigrant press and immigrant literature, taking as his point of departure the concept of literary systems. Much of his cogitation leads to the conclusion that immigrant newspaper editors and ethnic authors were active within literary spheres, for example the sphere of popular movements.[3] Swedish-American writers worked within a literary system defined by language and national background, so they did not have many inroads into the 'American' literary system.

Since reading requires literacy and literary production calls for people who can write, it is significant that Nordic immigrants had a high literacy rate, close to 100 percent. They had the habit of reading and the skill to write.[4]

Reading and writing have always been very strong elements in Icelandic culture, as is shown today in the large book production in Iceland: Icelanders produce far more books per capita than any other nation in the world. The Icelandic contribution to Old Norse literary tradition is threefold: rich oral tradition, documentation of this tradition, and rich literary creation. There are evidently strong links between the old saga traditions and the sharp interest in literature in modern Iceland. Also, the Icelandic immigrants in America had very strong ambitions to preserve their active culture, of which literary life was a central element. Once settled in Canada they immediately took steps to maintain the literary tradition of the homeland. This is reflected in the school programs and in the publication of newspapers in Manitoba during the late 1870's.[5] Among the early Icelandic immigrant authors was Stephan Stephansson who soon reached a prominent position in Canadian literature.

One can apply different perspectives when studying the immigrants' production and consumption of literature. Seen from the point of view of high literature the Nordic immigrants made meagre contributions to the literatures of the New World with only a few

3 L. Furuland 1986.
4 Th. Blegen 1931, 1940.
5 W. Kristjánsson 1965.

exceptions. Stephan Stephansson stands out as one of Canada's foremost poets, and the Norwegian-American author Ole Rølvaag is the only immigrant writer of the first generation who has received national recognition as a first-rate author in the United States.

Nordic immigrant authors who wrote in the homeland languages seldom took prominent positions in American literary history, a fate they shared with almost all immigrant writers. Also, their roles in the literary history of the home countries have been minimal. For example, while study of Swedish literature in Sweden has included Swedish-writing authors of Finland (like Johan Ludvig Runeberg and Edith Södergran), scholars of literature have left in oblivion overseas authors who wrote in Swedish. The chief criterion for selection has been aesthetic, as applied by the leading critics, and consequently scholars of literature and writers of literary overviews and handbooks have absorbed these values.[6] One conclusion must be that the Scandinavian literary worlds in America were more or less isolated from the literatures of the homelands. For example, Swedish writers in America had minimal contact with Sweden's foremost poets and novelists.

The relationship between consumption of Swedish literature produced in America and the state of Swedish-American literary life has not been elucidated. We know that Swedish authors had a market among Swedish immigrants in America and that this market was served by publishing offices run by immigrants. The immigrant periodical press was an important channel for literary material from the homeland. Books were imported or printed in America, often in the form of pirated editions.

From the perspective of literary consumption one should note that material transmitted from the old countries to a large extent dominated the literary market in the new country. Swedish-American calendars and magazines carried material that was taken over from Sweden and reprinted in various forms, sometimes touched up, sometimes blacked out. Closer studies would certainly reveal the procedures of those publishers who were instrumental in serving the Swedish-American readers with Swedish literature from the homeland. They also acted as gate-keepers and sometimes slowed down the literary transfer between writers in the homeland and their readers overseas, to the extent that they were at all aware of having readers on the other side of the Atlantic. We know little about the

6 Cf. L. Furuland 1986.

role of the immigrant publishing houses, and their history awaits writing.

It is evident that the new literature produced in Sweden during the heyday of emigration was often delayed in reaching the immigrant reading public in America. Also, some writers had a more long-lasting popularity in Swedish America than in Sweden. For example, Esaias Tegnér and Emilie Flygare-Carlén retained a following in America at a time when their popularity had slackened in Sweden, even while it took a long time for Verner von Heidenstam to reach a relatively wide circle of readers among the Swedish immigrants overseas. August Strindberg and Selma Lagerlöf were more broadly introduced to the Swedish-American public only after they had first appeared in English translations.[7]

None of the foremost of the Swedish Parnassus visited America for any longer period of time. There was an air of contempt when Swedish authors commented upon literary phenomena in Swedish America.[8] Relations were apparently stronger between Norway and Norwegian America in this respect, and this may stem from the fact that some of the leading Norwegian writers visited America, wrote about their experiences, made America the topic of debate in Norway, and kept contact with their fellow countrymen overseas. Both Knut Hamsun and Bjørnstjerne Bjørnson integrated American experience into their literary deeds.[9] Bjørnson gradually came to the conclusion that the Norwegian world should embrace all overseas immigrants.

Some attempts have been made to look at immigrant authors collectively. Thus, Göran Stockenström has examined Swedish-language writers as a group, counting 203 authors of fiction in America up to 1897. Only a handful of Swedish-American writers were women. Almost half of the researched authors had come to America during the high tide of emigration in the 1880's. The majority were between 25 and 30 years of age at the time of emigration, and the rate of those who returned to Sweden approximates the percentage of re-emigration in general. A few made repeated moves back and forth between the countries. Most of them had a middle-class background, and a high proportion had been brought up in cities. The group's formal education exceeded the average for Swedish immigrants even though many left school before graduation. The

---

7 Vilhelm Berger, *Svensk-amerikanska meditationer* (Rock Island, Ill., 1916).
8 P. Sedgwick 1973, 25.
9 Cf. S. Skard 1976.

reasons may have been economic or personal, but one gets the impression that many who became writers in America had known unfulfilled ambitions and that others had experienced failures which influenced their decisions to seek fortune in America.[10]

Less than a handful of Swedish immigrant authors were able to live off their craft, unless one counts those who combined free-lance authorship with jobs as newspaper editors. The rest, who could not earn their bread from writing books, combined writing with such positions as teacher, priest or journalist. According to Stockenström's study 132 (out of 203 authors) were newspaper editors or journalists, 62 ministers, and fourteen were educators or scholars.[11]

Literary Careers on Two Continents

Following the sociological line of investigation taken by Stockenström one could see the immigrant literatures as parts of literary systems working in the home country and the countries of immigration. The approach suggests several questions: What were the conditions of literary production as a whole? What constituted the market for literary products? Who were the readers? What kind of needs did the literary production fill for the writers and the readers, and what was the role of distributors? One may also ask what factors determined whether an author wrote in the immigrant language or in English. Full answers to these weighty questions would require an overview of all kinds of literature: religious literature in all its forms, schoolbooks, calendars, song and hymn books, the periodical press, newspapers, fiction in its various appearances, and so forth.

Here the objective has to be more moderate, namely, to sample the works of fiction writers from a certain perspective: What were their positions *vis-à-vis* the literary scenes in America and in the homeland, or rather, what was their relation to the literature of their homeland and to American mainstream literature, accepting that these concepts are somewhat blurred? This point of view posits three literary worlds, or 'literatures', between which one could move:

| The literature of the homeland | → | The immigrant (ethnic) literature | → | American literature |

10 G. Stockenström 1978.
11 G. Stockenström 1978, 259–260. Anna Williams, Uppsala, researches one of the most versatile and prolific authors, Jacob Bonggren.

Each of these literatures had its own boundaries, codes and rules. It was possible to be an immigrant writer in America and belong to the literary scene of the homeland, and it was feasible to move from the status of author of ethnic literature and become an acknowledged American author, but as noted above, few Nordic immigrants mastered these transitions.

For the purpose of illustration we will here group Nordic immigrant authors according to six categories to show their footing in different literary worlds. (Names of the authors discussed later on are given in parentheses.)

1. Authors who write both in the homeland language and publish in the homeland but have experience as immigrants in America (Henning Berger, Aksel Sandemose).

2. Authors writing in the homeland language, starting their careers as writers in the homeland but completing them as immigrants in America (Jacob Bonggren).

3. Authors writing in the homeland language but with their careers wholly in America (Leonard Strömberg, Stephan Stephansson).

4. Immigrant authors publishing in the homeland language *and* in English with their careers in America (Ole Rølvaag).

5. Authors writing almost wholly in English, aiming at a public even outside their own immigrant group and with a literary production that reflects their immigrant background (Hjalmar Hjort Boyesen, Sophus Keith Winther).

6. Immigrant authors writing in English who have adapted to American style and motives (Carl Sandburg).

Studying authors along a spectrum from the homeland to the American 'scene' enables one to see ethnic literature as information systems, as a defensive mechanism in the immigrant environment, and as a vehicle for adaptation to the American society. Some authors who doubtless 'belong' to the Danish, Norwegian etc. literature spent periods of their lives among their fellow countrymen in the U.S. and Canada, but cannot be included in the category of immigrant authors. Aksel Sandemose represents this category (1). Born in Nykøbing, Denmark in 1899, he made his literary debut in

1923 with *Fortællinger fra Labrador* (*Narratives from Labrador*), a collection of short stories. In 1928 he published *Ross Dane*, a novel which reflects his experiences as a settler on the prairies in Alberta. In 1930 he moved (from Denmark) to Norway, and he is held as one of the most prominent writers in twentieth century Norwegian literature.[12]

In the same category (1) one ought to place Henning Berger, many of whose stories and novels are enacted in the milieu of the American metropolis. Berger (1872–1924) was born in Stockholm, came to America in the early 1890's, and spent about ten years as an immigrant – during one period as streetcleaner and another as a clerk at the office of the White Star Shipping Line in Chicago. Feeling uncomfortable with his work, he returned to Sweden. His first book-length work, *Där ute* (*Out There*), was published in Stockholm in 1901. It reflects much of his experience abroad. Several of his later works also have American motifs, and Chicago is the setting of many of the plots.[13] Berger is not considered a first-rank author, though he has a place in Swedish literature and has lately received some recognition.[14] Berger, who thought endlessly about his social position, never achieved the social advancement he had hoped for. He was a restless wanderer and spent the last part of his life in Denmark.

Jacob Bonggren (1854–1940) was born in Dalsland, Sweden, and emigrated in 1882, the peak year of Swedish emigration. Bonggren belongs to category 2. In Sweden he published a couple of books before going to America, among them *Förstlingar* (*Firstlings*) 1882, a collection of poems. In America his literary production covered a broad spectrum: poems, occultist writings, newspaper articles, and translations. He was a prolific newspaperman and the editor of *Svenska Amerikanaren*. He is not mentioned in handbooks of Swedish literary history and he did not reach farther than the Swedish immigrant public in America. He belongs to the Swedish-American literature.

One of the few, or maybe the only one, who could make a fortune writing Swedish fiction in America was Leonard Strömberg, but even he combined his writing with duties as a pastor. Born in 1871, he graduated from the Swedish Methodist Theological School in Uppsala in 1894 and stayed active in the Methodist Church in America. His

12 R. Birn 1984, 1–19, 74–75.
13 L. Wendelius 1982, 13–16.
14 S. Lagerstedt 1963.

roughly forty novels and one hundred short stories have a strong moral tone, and Strömberg was the only Swedish writer in America who had a wide circle of readers in the homeland. His books were extremely popular, and although his works were never praised by literary critics, he had one of the largest public readerships in Sweden. In this respect he was definitely an exception.[15]

One of the Nordic immigrant authors who secured the finest reputation in America was Stephan Stephansson, an Icelander who at the age of twenty emigrated to Wisconsin, spent a period in the Dakota territory, and eventually settled in western Alberta. He has been called an Icelandic-Canadian poet of the Rockies, but he was actually a farmer who spent all his life on the prairie. His days were filled with all of the agriculturalist's responsibilities and he never identified himself as an intellectual, considering himself a laborer.

Stephansson's attitude to literary work was typically Icelandic and in exile he was the incarnation of Icelandic literary traditions. He believed in the written word, not least in poems, as a way for men to communicate. Stephansson espoused romanticism, which had a short period of prosperity in Iceland. Some of his poems reflected life on the farm in the shadow of the Rockies, while others reflected reminiscences from the home country.

Poetry made up all of Stephansson's literary production; his poems were written in an Icelandic language that bore in it much of centuries-long tradition. He constantly widened his vocabulary and elaborated his style, and his language even became somewhat archaic. He has also been said to have revitalized the Icelandic language.[16] For decades this prolific poet published his works in the Icelandic press in Canada, which did not afford him much revenue.

Stephansson is one of the few Nordic immigrant authors who achieved full recognition both in his new and his old country, although he never aspired to become acknowledged as a Canadian author. He even refused to accept the invitation in 1924 to join the Canadian Authors Association, since he did not feel he belonged in that company.

Ole Rølvaag (1876–1931), like most authors, is difficult to place in any single category, but he will best fit in category 4 above. He emigrated in 1896 and spent his first years on his uncle's farm. Rølvaag was determined to get an education, and he studied at the

15 G. Strombeck 1979.
16 J.W. MacCracken 1982.

Norwegian St. Olaf College in Northfield, Minnesota, spent a period in Norway after graduation, and finally received a position as professor in Norwegian literature at his *alma mater*. Through his life Rølvaag affiliated with the Norwegian cultural establishment in America: he was active in immigrant organizations and instrumental in founding the Norwegian-American Historical Association in 1925.

There is an ongoing discussion in Rølvaag's works about the immigrant's experience and his position between two worlds.[17] Rølvaag's main characters are Norwegian immigrants in the Midwest, but the author's sensitivity, broad outlook, and literary talents allowed him to express these newcomers' dilemma in a universal way. He reached the apex of his literary production with a series of books which were introduced in English with the volume *Giants in the Earth* (published in America in 1929, published in Norwegian as *I de dage* 1924, and *Riket grundlaegges* in 1925, followed by *Peder Seir* 1928 and *Den signede dag* 1931). These books convey the struggle of men and women of the first and second generation who seek to find their positions and their identities in the new society. Rølvaag's alter ego is Beret, the immigrant woman, who suffered and pined for her fatherland during long and lonesome days on the prairie in North Dakota, and who eventually mastered the situation and developed a strategy for survival. Beret's and Rølvaag's philosophy of life affirmed that the Norwegian immigrant would go astray if she lost touch with her roots and denied her cultural heritage. *Nemesis divina* fell upon Beret's son who revolted against his mother, denied his background, and married an Irish woman, but never became successful.

It is ironic but instructive for those studying cultural transformation and assimilation that Rølvaag's books appeared almost at the conclusion of the high point of Norwegian immigrant culture in America. When the last volume in the immigrant suite, *Den signede dag*, was published in 1931 (the same year Rølvaag died), Norwegian immigration came to a halt, the language shift from Norwegian to English was in full swing, Norwegian-American church life entered a phase of Americanization, and the heyday of Norwegian-American organizations had almost vanished. To rephrase Einar Haugen's words, Rølvaag was the full blossom of the tree which had already started to die at the roots.

17 See e.g., G.H. Gvåle 1962; O. Øverland 1981, and E. Haugen 1983.

Ole Rølvaag, if not unrealistic in the sense that he thought a Norwegian-American culture would last forever, believed that the most salubrious way to become American was to accept one's cultural background. The prairie and America were a challenge to the immigrant, but one that could not be taken up without a conscious mind.

As an author Rølvaag found acceptance in three worlds, the homeland, the Norwegian-American immigrant community, and the American reading public. In this respect he was an exception among Scandinavian authors in the New World.

One author, Hjalmar Hjort Boyesen, took strides early to become an *American* author. According to our classification he can be placed in category 5 as an author who wrote in English, and aimed at an American public while drawing on an immigrant background. But Boyesen's development as an author could also place him in category 6 among those whose literature takes them away from immigrant-related themes. Boyesen, born in Norway in 1848, emigrated at the age of twenty-one. He became professor in Germanic languages at Columbia University, New York and in his profession became an ardent promoter of Scandinavian literature to the American public. His ambition to become American is evident: He married an upper-class American woman and even tried to isolate himself from other Norwegians.

The title of Per Seyersted's book on Boyesen is indicative of the author's development: *From Norwegian Romantic to American Realist*.[18] Boyesen's first opus, which appeared in 1874, carried the title *Gunnar* and was written in English. It told an idyllic story about a Norwegian farmer's life. Boyesen depended greatly on Björnstjerne Björnson, from whom he received much inspiration, not only stylistically. By profession, he was, of course, extremely well-read in Norwegian literature, and his early production largely reflected the Norwegian literary legacy: His first books gained success because the author successfully exploited American interest in Norse motives. Gradually trying to shake off his romantic style, Boyesen turned a realist, but he never reached the position of an American realist in the way he had aspired. In some sense he was caught in the role of an immigrant author, but he found late in life that he had pulled up his roots. He was not Norwegian, he excluded

18 P. Seyersted 1984.

262

himself from other Norwegian immigrants, yet he did not become recognized as a full-fledged American.

Boyesen's position between three worlds (the homeland, the immigrant world and mainstream America) illustrates the dilemma in which many authors found themselves. They were chasing an identity, sometimes trying to combine elements from two or three worlds.

Another Nordic immigrant author, Sophus K. Winther, the son of Danish immigrants, represents the same category (5) as Boyesen since Winther wrote wholly in English. Winther reached an established position as a professor at a nonethnic institution, the University of Washington in Seattle, and had his books published at a non-immigrant, commercial press while aiming at an American public. There are few examples of writers besides Winther and Boyesen who reached out to an American public but who drew mostly on their experiences as newcomers or children of newcomers.

Winther published a trilogy in which the exodus, settlement, and the tension between Old World and New World values are described from the perspective of the young generation. His trilogy (*Take All to Nebraska*, 1936; *Mortgage Your Heart*, 1937; and *The Passion Never Dies*, 1938) in yet another way takes up the dilemma of many immigrants, namely by dealing with the tension between rural life and the attraction of the city. In this respect he wrote from an American perspective.[19]

Carl Sandburg (1878–1967), one of America's most praised poets and sometimes called the 'voice of the Midwest', had his roots in Swedish immigrant culture, but it would be misleading to say that he was a Swedish-American author. His poems and novels do not allude to the experiences of a son of Swedish immigrants.

Sandburg's cradle stood in Galesburg, Illinois, a frontier town founded in 1836 and remarkable because it housed three colleges at an early date. Swedish immigration to the place started in the late 1840's.[20] Carl's parents harbored many Old Swedish mores, but Carl himself followed his own genius. He volunteered for the Spanish-American War in 1898, started college at the age of 20, sought all types of employment, traveled widely and became familiar with the conditions of America's huddled masses of immigrants and sweatshop workers. His breakthrough as an author came with *Chi-*

19 C.L. Forsberg 1981, 41–42.
20 H. Nelson 1943, 168.

263

cago Poems (1915), which portrayed the city of broad shoulders and its inhabitants in expressive and colorful language. His six-volume biography on Lincoln, published in 1939–1940, made him a great American.

References to his Swedish background seldom emerge in Sandburg's works. His land was America, and his sympathy with the masses of Americans. He became the interpreter of the American city and rural landscape, especially the prairie. It may be, though, that his Swedish ancestry played some role in forming his personality. One learns from his autobiographical *Always the Young Strangers*, which he published at the age of seventy-five, that, although invisible in his art, many of Sandburg's memories from a Swedish immigrant community influenced him. This autobiographical work affirms the lovable personality of his mother and the consummate character of his father, even if these characteristics contain something of an old man's rationalizations.

On a couple of occasions Sandburg returned to his parents' homeland. As a special war correspondent for the Newspaper Enterprise Association he was sent to Europe in October 1918 and stationed in Stockholm. Among the Swedes he met was Per Albin Hansson, at the time left-wing social democrat and later on Swedish prime minister.[21] Sandburg kept a special attachment to Sweden, probably due to his early recognition by Swedish critics, who, however, did not overstress his Swedish background but saw him first and foremost as a great American author.[22] One may add that this recognition occurred just as American literature came into vogue in the late 1920's, some years before Sinclair Lewis's reception of the Nobel prize in 1930 marked a definite recognition in Europe of American literature.

The examples given here display the wide variety of Nordic immigrant literatures. Depending upon the perspective taken, one may reach different conclusions as to the role of fiction. Seen from potential writers' perspective, outstanding positions in the literary world were almost unachievable for first generation immigrants. Few immigrant authors in America were able to tackle the severe market conditions. The dispersion of readers impeded communication, and competition between languages and the role of English meant that the circle of readers was decreasing for authors who chose to publish in their native language.

21 N. Callahan 1970, 58.
22 H. Durnell 1963, 191.

We have here almost wholly overlooked the role of newspapers in the Nordic immigrant society. As to the role of literary institution, suffice it to say that newspapers and magazines in many respects were the best means by which an author could get published and reach a public.[23] The immenseness of the Nordic immigrant press is understood first and foremost by the sheer number of publications. However, most of the thousands of papers and magazines were of an experimental nature, both as journalistic and economic enterprises, and were not long-lasting.

Many tasks lie ahead for researchers who venture to use newspapers as their foremost source, one being to study the communication between newspaper editors and their readers. In this communication there is much to learn about the experiences and feelings of ordinary people, since many newspapers were open to the readers for the publication of poems, short stories, and letters to the editor. There are signs that the immigrants wrote poems to a much greater extent than the native population, perhaps because the circumstance of being an immigrant required special forms of emotional outlets.

23 Eric Johannesson, Uppsala University, will stress this in a forthcoming study of fiction in immigrant newspapers.

19. The Nordic Experience in North America: Some Conclusions

Seen from the sending countries the population transfer from the Nordic countries to countries overseas was of an immense magnitude. The total number of emigrants, around 2.5 million during the eighty year period following 1850, is equivalent to one third of the total population of the five countries in that year. An attempt to answer the question as to what would have happened in the sending countries in terms of population pressure, social constraint and political conflict had these numbers not found an abode overseas, would only lead to fruitless discussion. For example, the agricultural crisis in Scandinavia in the 1880's was both caused by and the reason for population transfer to the Midwest where immigrant farmers helped produce cereals at prices that, despite the long transportation, defied competition from European agriculture.

In contrast to southern Europe, migrants from the Nordic countries went almost exclusively to North America. The streams bound for South America and Australia were minimal. A comparison may be made with Italy, another area of high emigration, which sent her population surpluses to France, Argentina, Australia, the U.S. and Canada.

The Geography of Immigration. The area of early Nordic settlement in North America was the Midwest. Much immigrant traffic went through Chicago, which served as the gateway to the West. The large number of early immigrants coming from a rural background was striking, and the initial goal in America was the countryside rather than the city. Even those who settled in cities prior to the 1870's saw urban life as a springboard to the farm. However, from the 1870's onwards there was a marked shift to the cities. For a majority emigration from the Nordic area soon also meant a shift from rural to urban life. This urbanization was less marked among the Norwegians who even in the second generation, were strongly

266

inclined to stay on the farms. At an early stage secondary migration led to a wide geographical dissemination in America. When Nordic emigration still had a rural orientation these second-stage migrations were not always socially disruptive. In many core areas in the Midwest links were maintained with places of origin in the sending countries and with secondary settlements in the U.S. and Canada.

Women. The role of women is a neglected aspect in the historiography of Nordic immigration in America. This is all the more deplorable since women play the role of bearers of values and transmitters of culture between generations. Until 1880 most Nordic female immigrants came as members of families and as dependants. During the early stages of mass migration family-building for most female immigrants had started in the old country and continued overseas. As wives their social positions were relatively fixed in the new country. They contributed to the building of close-knit communities where the cultures of their respective homelands or home regions comprised the basis for spiritual life in all its forms.

After 1880 most immigrant women arrived alone. They came at a younger age, normally before they had started to make definite marriage plans. Like their male compatriots they arrived in America as job seekers, and as long as they settled in large cities they automatically had easy avenues to American ways of life. To the extent that they found employment as maids in American homes, a prevalent occupation of Scandinavian and Finnish women in cities such as Chicago, New York, and Toronto, they came into close contact with everyday American family life. Hence they could also serve as transmitters of American life-styles to their own ethnic group.

Nordic immigrants had left countries with considerable social constraint and economic problems, especially during the latter decades of the nineteenth century. Population growth had pushed large shares of the population into marginal economic situations. Proletarianization of the countryside had accelerated since the middle of the eighteenth century. Industrialization and capitalist development resulted in higher income and social advancement for some, while others envisioned minimal prospects for upward social mobility. In this situation emigration to America was an attractive alternative, and for many women the chances of realizing life-goals were much more positive overseas than in the old country. The limited means of support in Sweden, for instance, left many women unmarried around the turn of the century. Not only was the marriage rate low, the average age at marriage was also such that many women started family building at a relatively late age. This changed drastically in America, where young immigrant women had greater opportunities to marry, and to marry young, and did so.[1]

Pure demographic data help to explain the weakness of ethnicity among Nordic immigrants in certain areas and during specific periods. Where immigrant women were scarce in relation to men of the same ethnic group, the basis for ethnic family-building was weak, and with a weaker basis for endogamous marriages, ethnic communities were ephemeral and ethnic institutions fleeting. This partly explains why ethnicity was generally stronger among Scandinavian immigrants in the Midwest than in the American West and in Canada as a whole. Large-scale migration to Canada from the Nordic countries, for instance, occurred at a time when immigrants arrived as singles, the sex balance was uneven, and the labor market conditions forced immigrants to make many secondary moves, weakening the foundation for community building and ethnicity.

Factors of Tradition. There were strong factors of tradition in the overseas migration. First, Nordic parishes and communities which sent migrants overseas at an early stage tended to do so over a long period and to send many of them to the same places and regions that the pioneers had gone to. This stock effect led to the build-up of cultural strongholds in the New World where cultural links were maintained with the home parishes and home regions. The Midwest enticed early group migration during the 1830's, 1840's and 1850's and has since remained the heartland of Scandinavian America. Many places where Norwegians and Swedes settled at an early date gradually developed as outposts of Old World culture with excessively strong language retention and great awareness of homeland culture. During the post-war period, and not least after the ethnic revival in the 1960's, some of these areas obtained a higher dignity and became symbols of the earlier mass immigration. The Finns in America have developed Hancock, Michigan, while the Swedish descendants have made Bishop Hill, Illinois, a symbol of Swedish community building in the U.S. Both cases conceal the fact that these towns were highly controversial: Hancock was the battleground of church conservatives and labor radicals, and Bishop Hill was the result of a highly controversial splintering from the

1 S. Carlsson 1976. H. Norman 1976.

state church in Sweden and served as a red flag waved at the leaders of the Augustana Synod.

Ethnicity. For collectives and individuals the question of Americanization was all-pervasive once the first mass contingent of Nordic settlers had landed on the American shore and settled in the New World. The discussion of whether to adopt the manners, rules, and morals of the host society took place in the home and the neighborhood as well as in churches and associations. Individuals and groups developed shifting strategies when coping with these problems, and it is therefore essential to distinguish between individual and group behavior in this respect. The collective behavior differed according to time of arrival, conditions of settlement, and social composition; and the individual variations were always large, even within kin groups and families.

How can the extant material that reveals attitudes concerning Americanization versus preserving the homeland culture and ethnic traditions be measured and evaluated? Those immigrants who were indifferent to or who early decided to abandon their homeland heritage left relatively few sources for the historian of immigration and ethnicity.In interpreting an immigrant group's positions in relation to the homeland and the host society there is, therefore, a risk of placing too much stress upon evidence that points in the direction of cultural preservation. A sheer examination of numbers is enough to substantiate this. In urban areas, only a minority of the Nordic immigrants were members of churches linked to the homeland, and clubs, lodges, and associations, although they were counted in thousands, did not reach out to the majority of immigrants.

Nonetheless one can point to Nordic immigrants' mass behavior in terms of ethnic awareness and expression of pride for the homeland and its culture. One may refer to the mass meetings of Norwegian *bygdelags,* assemblies of thousands of Swedes in celebration of jubilees with relation to Swedish endeavors in past times, and manifestations of striking Finnish workers, organized along ethnic lines, during labor conflicts in mining areas.

One theme in our treatment of mass migration has been to illuminate what role the social, cultural, and political background from the homelands has played for the Nordic immigrants in America. The objective has been to link various expressions of immigrant behavior to the situation in the overseas countries, and one of the main questions has been to what extent their different backgrounds explain the shifting behavior of Nordic immigrants in America.

It would be misleading to speak of any *Scandinavian* or *Nordic* ethnicity in North America. Ethnicity was formed along national lines, but one can also, as shown above, speak of ethnicity formed along to subnational lines, when immigrants showed a strong tendency to form neigborhoods, networks, and organizations according to provincial and regional background. Immigrants who arrived in America in the middle of the 1800's had a much less developed sense for their home nations than those who arrived at the turn of this century.

Many immigrants arrived with much stronger feelings for their home region than for their home countries. Subgroups based on regional provenience were created in rural communities where geographical background in the home country to a large extent determined the settlement patterns. Much of the cultural characteristics of Norwegian *bygds* were preserved among Norwegian immigrants in the Midwest. One can also see the Icelandic community around Winnipeg as a transplant of regional culture. The regionalization of Nordic culture in certain areas of immigration probably helped to preserve dialects, cultural traits in song, instrumental music etc. for generations.

Towards the end of the nineteenth century the drive for nationalism in the Nordic countries was reflected overseas. In many cases, though, the immigrants' experience in America and frequent intercourse with fellow-countrymen in the New World created an understanding and an increased awareness of the homeland as nation and unity. This is most evident among the Norwegians and the Finns, while Icelanders already upon arrival in the new country were much more cognizant of their national culture. The nation-building process in Finland and Norway had reverberations among the overseas populations, and the increasing national consciousness of overseas Finns and Norwegians resembles what immigrants from Poland experienced in America when they found that they were also Poles and not only people with roots in a certain region.

Swedish-speaking Finns to some extent blur the picture. In national terms they were Finns. In no way can they be labeled as Swedes, unless from a historical perspective all Finns are labeled Swedes. The question is, though, whether one can look upon Swedish-speaking Finns as an ethnic group. They may be regarded as an ethnic subgroup (just as Finnish-speaking Finns). Swedish-speaking Finns immigrated to and settled in the same areas as their Finnish-speaking fellow countrymen, their choices of employment were simi-

270

lar, but they formed their own churches, clubs, and societies, often parallel to their Finnish-speaking brethren.

Seen against the backdrop of the relative similarity in terms of historical backgrounds and cultural traits in the communities, there was a striking 'nationalism' in the cultural activities of Nordic immigrants. Associations and cultural undertakings of a *Scandinavian* character were formed more for practical reasons during the early decades of mass immigration, when potential membership was meagre and external circumstances forced immigrants of various Nordic backgrounds to cooperate. The idea of Scandinavianism, which was *en vogue* in liberal, political circles in Denmark, Norway, and Sweden from the 1840's to the 1860's, had little impact on cooperation among immigrants in America. Danish-Norwegian combinations were the most common: Newspapers combined Danish and Norwegian material, and clubs and mutual-aid societies had members of both nationalities, a form of joint action which gradually disappeared.

Language was a barrier, although Danes, Norwegians, and Swedes could and still can understand each other without much effort. The role of idiom was most clearly displayed in the religious sphere: God's word should preferably be listened to in the mother tongue. Cooperation in religious matters failed after the initial period. For example, the Norwegians and Swedes split the Augustana Synod in 1870, with the result that there are, still today, two colleges of Augustana, a Swedish one in Rock Island, Illinois, and a Norwegian one in Sioux Falls, South Dakota.

Americanization. There were certain factors that were more or less constant, that worked in the direction of Americanization, and, in the long run, led immigrants into the mainstream of American culture. Public education was probably the strongest single factor. No Nordic group revolted against the pressure to send their children to public schools; and while the Sunday schools organized by the churches probably did not slow down the process of English-learning, they had some effect in delaying the transition from bilingualism to monolingualism. Another factor which had a strong Americanizing effect was the dynamics of the American economy which opened up opportunities for geographical and social mobility.

Ethnic groups had shifting qualifications, varied mental preparation and different aptitudes with which to avail themselves of these possibilities of social climbing. Some ethnic groups, such as the Chinese and other East Asians, were the victims of discrimination by

271

law; others, like the Irish, were the objects of more or less open nativisim; and still others, such as the Italians who experienced various forms of Italophobia, suffered the pressures of xenophobia from Yankees and others ethnics.[2]

Nordic immigrants in America, however, were little affected by discrimination as ethnic groups. They were usually welcomed as farmers and laborers, and official statements with an anti-Nordic slant were scarce. On the other hand, Finnish radicalism and the Finns' role as the avant-garde in mining strikes in the upper Midwest and in Canadian extraction industries rendered them a bad reputation in certain quarters. Within the Department of Immigration and Colonization in Ottawa actions were started that aimed at stopping Finnish immigration after World War I because Finns were assumed to spread IWW propaganda.

Cultural Transfer. Various aspects of Nordic culture were brought overseas: language, literary norms, political behavior, values, manners, ways of intercourse, knowledge in practical matters, and even material culture. Parts of this Nordic culture remained relatively intact for some time, while other parts were quickly assimilated into American life. In the economic sphere assimilation was quick. The ecology of agriculture and market conditions normally made farmers adapt to standards set by Yankees and other immigrants. Norwegian farmers soon produced corn and in Wisconsin even tobacco.

In one respect Nordic immigrants differed from most other immigrant groups, namely in their preoccupation with land. In their attitude to land itself they seem to have conserved an Old World outlook. Because mass migration from the Nordic countries had its roots in lack of land, immigrants initially arrived as homesteaders. Finland, Norway, and Sweden were among the least urbanized countries in Europe. The population increase resulted in a shortage of land and a desire for land among depressed groups in the rural sector. Finnish immigrants who settled in the mining regions in the United States bore an obsession for land which led them to seek and buy marginal stump lands and small farms. Norwegians had a tendency to stay on the farms even in the second generation to an extent unmatched by all other immigrant groups.

Although overseas migration included urbanization of the Nordic populations, these immigrant cultures as a whole had a strong rural

2 R. F. Harney 1984.

orientation, visible also in church and association life. The rural orientation of Norwegian immigrants also helps to explain the consistency in other aspects of culture. Language retention among second and third generations of immigrants was very strong among Norwegians. There is a correlation between rural-urban distribution and the tendency to keep up the homeland language.

Immigration led to a period of intense Nordic cultural life overseas. Immigrants built institutions which reflected the homeland cultures. Seen in retrospect these had their life cycles, and once they were founded they went through the phases of growth, maturation, decline, and eventually permutation into American phenomena or extinction. They reflected the homeland cultures but they were seldom mere replicas of institutions in the sending countries. Nordic immigrant churches in North America, indeed, mirrored religious conditions and ecclesiastical organization in the countries of origin but they also adapted to American conditions. Although the preservation of fatherland culture became important secondary goals in the programs of some of the larger immigrant churches, these became Americanized within two or three generations and lost most of their homeland essence. The last step was normally a merger with American synods.

Secular associations developed according to patterns from the respective countries, and for many the goal was to uphold traditions from the Old World. Some of these traditions were invented or reinvented overseas. Fatherland-based ideologies developed and took elements from the European cultures and adapted them to the immigrant situation. To borrow terminology from individual psychology, these institutions went through a process of separation (from the mother church and from their mother associations in the country of origin), but in the creation of their own individuality, they borrowed components from the mother organization and ideologies in the old country.

The cultural heritage from the Old World (the Viking tradition, Old Norse virtues, music, literature) was thus brought over, transplanted and given a partially new content. This process was linked to ethnic self-protection. The cultivation of the history of the old countries and of the ethnic group in the new country was also an important part of this process. To display a rich and eventful past had a legitimizing effect and was in the decades before the Great Depression instrumental in erecting a barrier towards new ethnic groups that arrived from southern Europe and Asia.

273

Long-Term Effects of Migration. In a way that is hard to measure
and difficult to express more precisely, the transatlantic population
movement helped to bring Scandinavia into closer contact with the
outside world. Despite some attempts, the Nordic countries, as
opposed to many West European countries, never developed as
colonial powers. Hence the geographically isolated Nordic populations were less global in their outlook. In this sense the mass migration widened the people's idea of the world. As Sten Carlsson
has noted: 'Both emigration and the more limited re-migration from
North America opened new perspectives for the masses who were
often more familiar with conditions in Chicago and Minnesota than
with the situation in their provincial capital.'

Seen in a long-term perspective, one of the greatest effects of the
overseas migration was the strong links that developed between the
sending and the receiving countries. Because of migration the Nordic
countries have stronger relations with the U.S. in many fields than
with other parts of the world, including Europe. To a large extent
the depth and intensity of contacts with America stem from mass
migration.

Migration resulted not only in chain migration but also in re-
migration, personal contacts over the ocean, flows of capital from
immigrants to family members in the old country, and an exchange
of information between individuals and groups in the two countries.
Thus mass emigration resulted in networks of personal contacts
over the ocean, and even if many of these networks were weak,
many were strong enough to hold families and kin together for long
periods of time. These were also exploitable for certain purposes on
a national level. When the U.S. during World War II launched a
campaign on a global scale to inform the world about her military
goals, the propaganda played on the fact that immigrants and their
ancestors from Scandinavia served as United States troops on the
battlefields. Films and radio interviews told audiences in Scandinavia about the descendants from Denmark, Norway and Sweden
who fought to make Europe safe for democracy. The aim was to
gain sympathy among Scandinavians for the U.S. war goals, and
evidently this propaganda was successful.

Of even greater importance, perhaps, than the network-building
among individuals were the contacts with the homelands that were
erected by ethnic institutions. The creation of colleges in the U.S.
has long included strong efforts to preserve ethnic culture and
relations with the homeland; this in sharp contrast to Canada,

where the ideals adopted from Great Britain led to stronger public institutions and weaker ethnic undertakings in the educational field. Like some other groups, Nordic immigrants have had their strongest and most long-lived cultural safeguards in their schools, academies and colleges, and for some of them the bonds with the old countries are still strong in the 1980's.

On point after point it has been shown that Danes both in the United States and Canada have shown a lower degree of visability than other Nordic immigrants. More efficiently than any other Nordic group they spread over the continent. Towns and cities with a distinctive Danish mark have been few. Danes were also more widely distributed within communities and cities. Danish participation in ethnic organizations seems to have been lower than that of their Nordic brothers and sisters. Statistics on language retention point in the same direction. Danes kept their mother tongue to a lesser degree than practically all other immigrant groups, and their tendency to seek marriage partners outside their own ethnic group was stronger than elsewhere. Also, Danes have not achieved a reputation as an ethnic group of voters. Taken together this is a portrait of an immigrant group with a low ethnic consciousness.

It is difficult to evaluate these observations and explain them. Many factors are interrelated: Low population concentration leads to a weak foundation for ethnic life. One may assume that Danes in areas with many Norwegians and Swedes were to a certain extent absorbed by these other Nordic groups. One should also note that Danish immigrants had a more urban background. Collectively, urban emigrants, especially if they came from the Scandinavian capitals, were evidently less ethnic-oriented than rural emigrants.

Another explanation for lower Danish visibility overseas may be that America as a whole played a minor role for Denmark in comparison with the other Nordic countries. Finland, Iceland, and Norway were in a vital nation-building process during the age of transatlantic mass migration. There was an interplay between the Norwegians in Norway and the country's overseas population. Norway's struggle for independence became an affair of the heart for Norwegian-Americans, who mobilized for this purpose. When the once deeply divided Norwegian churches reunited in America in 1917 this was a reflection of the nationalization process in Norway proper. The activities among Norwegians in America must also be viewed in combination with the fact that, with the exception of Ireland and maybe Iceland, Norway had, in relative terms, sent

275

more emigrants to America than any other European nation. To take another example, in 1917, the year of Finnish independence, many Finnish-Americans were preoccupied with the fate of their fatherland, even though Finnish politics comprised many components not found in Norway. The Norwegian and Finnish cases illustrate that homeland politics played a role in ethnic mobilization in North America.

The Nordic nations slowly but gradually understood the potential of their overseas populations. It was first in 1905 that Norway fully realized the importance of Norwegian-Americans for the nation's sake. Organizations founded in the old countries after the turn of the century tried to build a bridge between their populations divided by an ocean and to promote the use of the homeland language and culture among emigrants. This started parallel with anti-emigration propaganda and with fruitless attempts to promote re-immigration, activities that were also linked to rearmament and a new wave of nationalism in European politics.

The ethnic revival in America from the days of the Vietnam War did not significantly include the Nordic immigrant populations, but it did stimulate interest in the old countries among descendants of immigrants. The back to roots movement also led to revitalization of forgotten personal bonds. Many families learned of one another's existence, and meetings between third and forth cousins strengthened the feeling of togetherness among individuals in a way perhaps important also for the relations between nations.

In seeking new avenues to American import markets and in trying to 'sell' their countries and propagandize for their cultures, Nordic governments have also turned to the history of mass migration. Through their embassies and information agencies in the 1970's and 1980's they have underlined the early Nordic presence in North America. Vinland, Delaware, and Minnesota have been brought to life again.

Appendices

Research on Overseas Migration from the Nordic Countries: A Bibliographical Essay

By Hans Norman & Harald Runblom

The massive population movement from Europe to countries over-seas has been researched from many angles by scholars from many disciplines. The purpose of this essay is to sketch the historiography mainly from a Nordic viewpoint, give examples, and to guide the reader to further bibliographical sources.

For rich bibliographies on the Danish, Finnish, and Norwegian transatlantic migrations, see E.E. Riber Christensen & John Peder-sen, *Bibliografi over Dansk-amerikansk utvandrerhistorie: Den dans-ke udvandring til USA fra 1840 til 1920 og den dansk-amerikanske historie til 1983* (Aalborg: Aalborg Universitetsforlag 1986); Olavi Koivukangas & Simo Toivonen, *Suomen siirtolaisuuden ja maassa-muuton bibliografia: A Bibliography on Finnish Emigration and Inter-nal Migration* (Turku: Migration Institute, 1978); and Johanna Bar-stad, ed., *Litteratur om utvandringen fra Norge til Nord-Amerika: En bibliografi basert på katalogen over Norsk-amerikansk Samling* (Oslo: Universitetsbiblioteket i Oslo, 1975). There is no modern bibliography of the same kind covering Swedish migration. Still indispensable, however, is O. Fritjof Ander, *The Cultural Heritage of the Swedish Immigrant: Selected References* (Rock Island, Illinois: Augustana College Library, 1956). Concerning Iceland see Helge Skúli Kjartansson (1977, 1980). Odd S. Lovoll (1983) contains a rich bibliography on Norwegian emigration. A. William Hoglund's *Immigrants and Their Children in the United States: A Bibliography of Doctoral Dissertations, 1885–1982* (New York: Garland Publish-ing, 1986) is the best source to track published and unpublished U.S. doctoral dissertations dealing with Nordic immigrants.

For current bibliographies see *Emigranten* (published yearly in Aalborg by Dansk utvandrerhistorisk selskab); *Siirtolaisuus – Mi-*

gration (issued by the Migration Institute in Turku); *Norwegian-American Studies* (published every two years); and the *Swedish American Historical Quarterly*. It is rewarding, also as far as Nordic emigration is concerned, to consult the bibliographical documentation in *Studi Emigrazione*, regularly published by the Centro Studi Emigrazione Roma. A useful research tool is *Guide to Swedish-American Archival and Manuscript Sources in the United States* (Chicago: Swedish-American Historical Society, 1983).

Invaluable for scholarly investigations are source publications. The Norwegian-American Historical Association has collected and edited a great deal of material in the biennial publication *Norwegian-American Studies*. Theodore Blegen published Norwegian letters in *Land of Their Choice* (Minneapolis 1955). H. Arnold Barton edited *Letters from the Promised Land – Swedes in America 1840–1914* (Minneapolis: University of Minnesota Press, 1975; Swedish edition Stockholm: Askild & Kärnekull, 1979). Two Danish source publications are *Brev fra Amerika. Dansk udvandrerbreve 1874–1922* (Copenhagen: Gyldendal, 1981) and Frederich Hale, ed., *Danes in North America* (Seattle: University of Washington, 1984). Useful for the study of early Swedish mass emigration are passenger arrival lists from New York and other North American ports of entry, published by Nils William Olsson (1967, 1979), which also provide a lot of genealogical information.

Many of the intricate questions of evaluating statistics on early mass migration were taken up by Gösta Lext (1977), Kristian Hvidt (1971) and Lars-Göran Tedebrand (1972, 1976), while Ulf Beijbom (1971) and Hans Norman (1974) discussed in depth the use of American population censuses and sources of immigrant churches for the reconstruction of immigrant populations.

There are numerous essays summing up the development of migration research in the Nordic countries. Hans Norman edited *Demografisk-historisk forskning i Uppsala* (Uppsala: Historiska institutionen, 2nd ed., 1984), which contains articles dealing with Swedish migration and demographic research from various perspectives. For research overviews see also Ingrid Semmingsen, 'Emigration from Scandinavia', *Scandinavian Economic History Review* 1972, 45–60, and Kristian Hvidt, 'Nordiske studier over emigration 1965–75', *Historisk tidsskrift* (Copenhagen 1979). Lewis Hanke, *Guide to the Study of United States History outside the U.S., 1945–1980* (New York: Kraus, 1985), volumes 2 and 3, contain essays country by country on America-related historical research

(Inga Floto on Denmark, Reino Kero on Finland, Geir Lundestad on Norway, and Harald Runblom on Sweden) and guides to sources for the study of U.S. history in the Nordic countries; volumes 4 and 5 of the *Guide* contain annotations on scholarly books and articles published in Denmark, Finland, Norway, and Sweden during the years 1945–1980. Note also H. Arnold Barton (1978) on Clio's role as far as Swedish immigration to America is concerned! Several books have ample bibliographies and research overviews, e.g., Harald Runblom & Hans Norman (1976, 325–368), on Swedish migration; many research tendencies in recent historiography on Nordic immigration are noted in an overview by Jon Gjerde (1985, 295–305).

Early immigration studies evolved among immigrants themselves. The writing of chronicles, histories, and settlement stories was an important aspect of immigrant self-reflection. As a Swedish-American phenomenon this has been treated by Ulf Beijbom (1977). Reflections on the role of immigrant history are found in Odd S. Lovoll & Kenneth O. Bjork, *The Norwegian-American Historical Association 1925–1975* (Northfield, Minnesota: NAHA, 1975).

Through Theodore Blegen's (1931 & 1940) and George M. Stephenson's (1932) landmark studies, Norwegian and Swedish immigration research gained academic respectability in the United States. Another Nordic descendant, Marcus Lee Hansen, of mixed Danish-Norwegian background, whose most important books are *The Atlantic Migration, 1607–1860: A History of Continuing Settlement of the United States* and *The Immigrant in American History* (both edited by Arthur M. Schlesinger, Cambridge, Massachusetts: Harvard University Press, 1940) treated the Atlantic migration in a more general perspective and referred only in passing to aspects on Nordic immigration. As a scholarly phenomenon Finnish immigration research is of a later date; John I. Kolehmainen's books and articles pioneered in this area. Icelandic-centered research has had its strongest quarter at the University of Manitoba, Winnipeg. An important publication on Icelanders in North America is Th. Thorsteinsson & T. Oleson (5 vols. 1950–1953).

Fiction has meant a lot to the public image of early mass migration and the settlement history in rural surroundings. Jørund Mannsåker (1971) researched the attitudes to American migration in Norwegian poetry and novels. Ole Rølvaag's novels, published in the 1920's, were bestsellers both in the United States and Norway. Interpretations of Rølvaag's novels are legion, for example G.H.

Gvåle (1962) and Einar Haugen (1983). The Swedish author Vilhelm Moberg contributed to the interest in the story of pioneering with his four novels (1949, 1952, 1956, 1959) on group migration from Småland to Minnesota. Gunnar Eidevall (1974) examined Moberg's role as an emigrant author. The use of fiction as historical sources are thoroughly discussed by Dorothy Burton Skårdal (1974); her book also contains lists of novels and short stories written by Danish, Norwegian, and Swedish immigrant authors. Sigmund Skard (1976) had a lot to say about the role of literary contacts between Norway and America in a book which deals with the reception of American culture in Norway. Nils Runeby (1969) brought to light the contrasting Swedish views of the United States during the era before and after the inception of mass emigration. The study of Scandinavian immigrant literature is in a period of strong development. Indicative of this is Dorothy Burton Skårdal's project in Norwegian immigrant authors at the University of Oslo and research in Swedish literary systems in America under the leadership of Lars Furuland, Uppsala University.

Although migration from the Nordic countries culminated in the late 1800's, Nordic researchers were fairly late in turning their attention to these mass movements, but there were exceptions. The Swedish statistician Gustav Sundbärg turned a Swedish state investigation (1907–1913) into a landmark inquiry into the causes of Swedish transatlantic exodus; the Emigration Commission's main report (*Betänkande*) and its twenty accompanying volumes on various topics are a mine of statistics and other data on demography, economy, popular attitudes, and much more.

Groundbreaking in Nordic emigration research were historian Ingrid Semmingsen's two volumes on Norwegian migration (1941, 1950), and parallel with her, Einar Haugen (1953) worked in America on a thorough study of Norwegians in the United States, stressing the language component. Geographer Helge Nelson (1943), who as a young scholar had assisted the Swedish Royal Commission on emigration, prepared his monumental study on Swedish emigration and Swedish settlements in North America over two decades. Noteworthy also are several books by ethnologist Albin Widén (e.g., 1962) on Swedish immigrant life in America.

Within the so-called Stockholm School, which gathered economists from several countries, Gunnar Myrdal initiated fundamental investigations concerning the relationship between internal migration and economic and social changes. In this framework sociologist Dorothy Swaine Thomas researched *Social and Economic Aspects of Swedish Population Movements 1750–1933* (New York 1941). In Sweden, however, cultural geographers paved the way in migration research with studies of innovation processes of internal migration through the works of Edgar Kant (1946), Karl-Erik Bergsten (1951), and Torsten Hägerstrand (1953).

Hence, numerous theoretical and empirical studies had established a ready foundation when emigration research was taken up on a larger scale in the Nordic countries in the 1960's. From the European perspective Frank Thistlethwaite's challenging lecture to the XIth International Congress of Historians in Stockholm in 1960 marked the beginning of a new European trend in emigration research. He argued that Old World historians should not leave the writing of the history of transatlantic mass migration to scholars in the New World. Thistlethwaite stressed the importance of links that were established between Europe and America through the migrants and underlined that this history could never be understood without deep insights into the European background of the millions of migrants. A research agenda for Scandinavian emigration was an article by Birgitta Odén (1963), who stressed that emigration be studied in its relation to industrialization and urbanization, as opposed to earlier investigations which had taken their point of departure in the agricultural sector.

Thistlethwaite's admonitions marked the beginning of a new European trend in emigration research, reflected in Sweden by the start of a multimember project under the leadership of Sten Carlsson, Uppsala University: 'Sweden and America after 1860; Emigration, Re-migration, Social and Political Debate'. Clio had entered the era of quantitative research, and many of the project's investigations took the shape of history from the bottom up: aggregations of individual-level data proved indispensable to analysis of mass migration movements. The research was characterized by an openness to international theories and methods and led to a wide net of contacts with researchers in other Nordic countries and overseas. In this development Sune Åkerman played a leading role. Research groups of the same character, but not as large, began at other Nordic universities: in Turku under Vilho Niitemaa and Reino Kero, in Oslo under Ingrid Semmingsen, in Reykjavik under Thorhallur Vilmundarson. The Danish contribution to this phase in historiography was a *one-but-a-lion* one by Kristian Hvidt (1971). Later Erik Helmer Pedersen not only wrote fundamental overviews on Danish life and culture overseas (1985, 1986) but also introduced the topic to young researchers at Copenhagen University.

Many of the investigations from the 1960's onwards relate migration to demographic, economic, and social developments of society. Some of them sought inspiration in econometric and other heavily quantitative studies by social scientists, such as Torvald Moe's (1970) investigation of the relations between migratory behavior and wage levels in a sending and a receiving country. These studies on Nordic overseas migration deal with most phases and aspects of migration: the purely internal migration, the complex social and economic background of emigration, the social composition of groups on the move, and the course of overseas movements. Many of these studies profited from excellent sources in Nordic church and police registers, not least the parish registers in Finland and Sweden, and the archives of the Copenhagen police. Among Finnish studies heavily based on quantification and demographic sources are Reino Kero (1974) and Keijo Virtanen (1979); Swedish examples of the same kind are Fred Nilsson (1970), Björn Rondahl (1972), Lars-Göran Tedebrand (1972), and Margot Höjfors (1986); Kristian Hvidt (1971) is based on a mass of Danish aggregate data, while an in-depth demographic study on a Norwegian area is Andres Svalestuen (1972).

Nordic research into overseas migration in the 1960's and 1970's resulted in many specialized studies. Agnes Wirén (1975) and Kjell Söderberg (1981) made regional investigations of the pioneer period. Berit Brattne (1973) looked into the ramifications of the international transportation of emigrants, while Lars Ljungmark (1971) described the build-up of Minnesota's propaganda campaigns to stimulate immigration from Scandinavia. Around the turn of the century there was a reaction in most European countries to the heavy outflow of overseas migrants. In a Nordic setting this has been most throughly discussed by Ann-Sofie Kälvemark (1972).

Very few studies on Nordic emigration have isolated the aspect of women. One should note, though, Varpu Lindstrom-Best's articles (1981, 1986) on Finnish immigrant women in Ontario and Ann-Sofie Kälvemark's (1983) inquiry into the conditions of Swedish female emigrants.

While Scandinavian human geographers have not been inclined to work within the scholarly field of Atlantic migration, American geographers have made important contributions to the knowledge of Nordic immigrants' settlement behavior. For example, Arnold

284

Alanen (1975, 1981, 1982) has studied Finnish immigrants in various environments; Matti Kaups (1975, 1978, 1981) has treated many aspects of Nordic immigration in the upper Midwest; and further, John Rice (1973, 1978) and Robert C. Ostergren (1976, 1981) have shaped tools for investigations of the spacial behavior of Nordic settlers.

One aspect of international migration is its relation to other forms of mobility. Internal and inter-Nordic migration have often served as alternatives to emigration from a social point of view. Eric De Geer (1959, 1977) disclosed fundamental differences in the interplay between population flows to expanding cities and overseas migration targets during the era of mass emigration, while Holger Wester (1977) on the basis of Finnish microstudies made observations on the diffusion of migratory behavior in different social categories. Studies by Sune Jungar (1974) and Max Engman (1983) analyze Finnish migration patterns with special emphasis on the role of St. Petersburg. Richard Willerslev has created a portrait of Swedes in Denmark during the mass emigration period and Lars Olof Larsson (1978) has emphasized the heavy emigration from southern Sweden to Denmark and Germany during the early phase of mass emigration. Sune Åkerman (1971) contributed a principal study of the interrelationship between internal and external migration. This aspect is also discussed by Ulf Beijbom (1971) and Hans Norman (1974), two authors who linked studies on areas of emigration in the sending country with immigration areas in the receiving country.

This connection is explored even further in Robert C. Ostergren's dissertation (1976), which combines observations of a circumscribed population group in Sweden and the United States. Jon Gjerde's (1985) dissertation, which focuses on the migration from one area in Norway to various localities in the Midwest, has the same character.

Studies of Scandinavian contributions to American political life have mostly been made by American researchers, e.g., George Stephenson (1935) on the role of governor John Lind; Carl Chrislock (1981) on Norwegian responses to American nationalism during the First World War; Jon Wefald (1971) on Norwegian and Michael Karni (e.g., 1977) on Finnish radicalism; Bruce Larson (e.g., 1978) on Swedish politicians in the Midwest; and Peter Kivisto (1984) on Finnish radicalism in the United States. One could perhaps question if it is meaningful to distinguish between European and North American research, but it is noteworthy that Nordic scholars in recent years have also researched political aspects of

285

immigrant life. Sten Carlsson (1973, 1976, 1980) researched the role of ethnicity in Minnesota elections. Sture Lindmark (1971) focused on the relations between politics and ethnicity among Swedish-Americans during the pre-Depression era. Richard Lucas (1974) investigated the electoral support for Congressman Charles Lindbergh, Sr., and his role as a political insurgent. Auvo Kostiainen (1977, 1978, 1985) has produced several studies on Finnish labor radicalism in the U.S. and Canada, stressing the legacy from the homeland.

The study of immigrant languages has during recent years developed into a subdiscipline of linguistics, but Folke Hedblom (1973–1974), Nils Hasselmo (1974), and Einar Haugen (1953, 1980) have studied this topic in a wide context. Gunvor Flodell (1986) has described the contact between Spanish and Swedish among immigrants in an Argentinean area.

The 1970's witnessed strong cooperation among researchers in the Nordic countries. Emigration was one theme at the Nordic conference of historians in Copenhagen in 1971. Among Nordic enterprises within emigration research there was an atlas project to which Sune Åkerman, Kristian Hvidt, Reino Kero, Helgi Skúli Kjartansson, Ingrid Semmingsen, and Andres Svalestuen contributed. The atlas was later published by Hans Norman & Harald Runblom (1980). Bo Kronborg, Thomas Nilsson & Andres Svalestuen (1977) edited a series of local emigration studies, one from each Nordic country, shedding light on the origin, distribution, and extent of emigration.

One side of Nordic response to the new wave of interest in mass emigration led to the founding of documentation centers and separate migration research institutes. In Sweden the Emigrant Institute (*Emigrantinstitutet*), Växjö, documenting Swedish culture overseas, started its activities in 1966 in the heartland of Vilhelm Moberg country, while the Emigrant Register in Karlstad, founded in 1960, concentrates on the emigration from the province of Värmland. A Norwegian documentation center was founded in Stavanger, the earliest mass emigration port from Norway, while Aalborg was chosen as the place for the Danish Worldwide Archives. Because of concern about heavy Finnish emigration to Sweden in the post-war era, Finnish authorities founded The Migration Institute in Turku in 1974; however, it has used much of its energy to document and research the history of Finns on other continents.

During the 1970's scholars on both sides of the Atlantic also met at conferences specifically devoted to the population movements between selected countries and the United States. Conference reports which combine European and American perspectives on migration and immigrant life are Nils Hasselmo (ed. 1978), Michael G. Karni, Matti E. Kaups & Douglas Ollila Jr. (eds. 1975), and Harald S. Naess (ed. 1976). Another manifestation of Nordic unity in research is a volume edited by Ingrid Semmingsen and Per Seyersted (1980). Michael Karni (1981) edited two volumes on studies of Finnish immigration in three continents, resulting from a conference in Toronto. The transformation of Scandinavian culture overseas was the topic of a conference documented by Harald Runblom & Dag Blanck (1986). Three volumes edited by Dirk Hoerder (1983, 1985, 1986) have combined European and American perspectives on mass migration.

Australia's role as a target of Nordic emigration can be studied in books by Olavi Koivukangas (1974, 1983 ed., 1986), while Ulf Beijbom (1983) wrote the history of two centuries of Swedish emigration to the same continent. Many perspectives on migration to, from, and within Latin America are found in Magnus Mörner (1985). Reports from a conference in Köln in 1975 on mass migration from European countries are published in *Jahrbuch für Geschichte von Staat, Wirtschaft und Gesellschaft Latinamerikas* 13 (1976). For Swedish emigration to the continent see Karin Stenbeck (1973). Danish travel to all points of the compass are recorded by Erik Helmer Pedersen (1986).

Statistics

1. Registered Emigrants to North America from Denmark, Finland, Iceland, Norway, and Sweden, 1851–1930.
2. Total Number of Immigrants to the United States, 1820–1950, and Peak Years of Emigration from Respective Countries.
3. Immigrants from the Nordic Countries in the United States, 1910. Foreign-Born by State.
4. Immigrants to Canada with Ethnic Origin in the Nordic Countries, 1900–1955.
5. Nordic-born in Australia, 1871–1966. By State.

Table 1. Registered Emigrants to North America from Denmark, Finland, Iceland, Norway and Sweden, 1851–1930.

Year	Denmark[1]	Finland	Iceland	Norway[2]	Sweden
1851	14			2,640	932
52	3			4,030	3,031
53	32			6,050	2,619
54	691			5,950	3,980
55	528			1,600	586
56	173			3,200	969
57	1035			6,400	1,762
58	232			2,500	512
59	499			1,800	208
1860	542			1,900	266
61	234			8,900	758
62	1,658			5,250	947
63	1,492			1,100	1,216
64	712			1,300	2,593
65	1,149			4,000	3,906
66	1,862	52		15,455	4,466
67	1,436	82		12,829	5,893
68	2,019	54		13,211	21,472
69	4,282	31		18,070	32,050
1870	3,041	45	5	14,838	15,430
71	2,346	115	7	12,276	12,985
72	3,758	598	14	13,865	11,838
73	5,095	980	334	10,352	9,486
74	3,188	101	386	4,601	3,380
75	1,951	93	67	4,048	3,591
76	1,624	128	1,191	4,355	3,702
77	1,617	145	56	3,206	2,921
78	2,688	137	484	4,863	4,242
79	3,532	506	328	7,608	12,761
1880	8,778	1,881	94	20,212	36,263
81	8,951	2,914	140	25,976	40,620
82	12,769	3,734	253	28,804	44,359
83	9,747	2,735	1,216	22,167	25,678
84	7,633	1,775	103	14,776	17,664
85	5,870	1,077	138	13,981	18,222
86	6,634	3,324	510	15,158	27,917
87	9,305	7,857	1,978	20,741	46,264
88	8,756	4,862	1,089	21,452	45,567
89	5,504	5,204	710	12,642	28,543
1890	9,366	6,700	207	10,991	29,499

[1] 1851–1900 to the USA, 1901–1930 to the USA and Canada.
[2] Transoceanic emigration.

Table 1. Continued.

Year	Denmark	Finland	Iceland	Norway	Sweden
1891	10,659	7,800	223	13,341	36,165
92	10,593	8,000	283	17,049	41,103
93	8,779	9,117	706	18,778	37,382
94	5,581	1,380	103	5,642	9,559
95	4,244	4,020	7	6,207	15,002
96	3,167	5,185	9	6,679	14,911
97	2,085	1,916	51	4,669	10,148
98	1,946	3,467	75	4,859	8,569
99	2,690	12,075	128	6,699	11,875
1900	2,926	10,397	634	10,931	16,302
01	4,431	12,561	246	12,745	20,363
02	6,572	23,152	283	20,343	33,336
03	7,867	16,964	616	26,784	35,768
04	8,789	10,952	293	22,264	18,866
05	7,611	17,427	273	21,059	20,773
06	8,080	17,517	49	21,967	21,606
07	7,345	16,296	32	22,135	19,724
08	3,947	5,812	2	8,497	9,117
09	6,150	19,144	33	16,152	18,664
1910	8,232	19,007	78	18,912	24,184
11	7,553	9,372	52	12,477	16,240
12	6,926	10,724	57	9,105	14,507
13	7,744	20,057	97	9,876	17,021
14	5,683	6,474	75	8,522	9,900
15	3,163	4,041	2	4,572	4,577
16	4,183	5,325	9	5,212	7,421
17	1,614	2,773	2	2,518	2,538
18	793	1,900	4	1,226	1,473
19	3,087	1,085	18	2,432	3,889
1920	5,816	5,595	20	5,581	6,945
21	4,675	3,557	8	4,627	5,693
22	3,307	5,715	16	6,456	8,758
23	6,894	13,835	4	18,287	26,370
24	5,853	5,108	17	8,492	8,228
25	3,895	2,075	6	7,009	9,375
26	4,838	5,638	–	9,326	10,847
27	6,797	5,696	–	11,881	10,727
28	6,980	4,742	–	8,832	11,485
29	5,730	6,119	–	8,029	8,833
1930	2,902	3,657	–	3,673	3,474

Sources:
Denmark: Official Statistics of Denmark. Statistisk Tabellverk V, A.V. (1904). Statistiske Undersøgelser nr. 16 (1966).
Finland: 1866–69 och 1893–1930 Official Statistics of Finland. 1870–1889; R. Kero 1974, 26, 28, 36, 1890–1892; Swedish passenger lists.
Iceland: Sagnfræðistofnun's data set.
Norway: Official Statistics of Norway (Folkemengdens bevegelse 1821–1918, 1901–1943).
Sweden: Official Statistics of Sweden (BiSOS, A 1851–1900, Befolkningsrörelsen 1901–1930).

Table 2. Total Number of Immigrants to the United States, 1820–1950, and Peak Years of Emigration from Respective Countries.

Land of Emigration	Immigration 1820–1950	Peak Year
Germany	6,248,529	1882
Italy	4,776,884	1907
Ireland	4,617,485	1851
Great Britain	4,386,692	1888
Austria-Hungary	4,172,104	1907
Russia	3,343,895	1913
Canada	3,177,446	1924
Sweden	1,228,113	1882
Mexico	838,844	1924
Norway	814,995	1882
France	633,807	1851
West Indies	496,686	1824
Greece	439,581	1907
Poland	422,326	1921
China	398,882	1882
Finland (1866–1930)	390,807	1902
Turkey	362,034	1913
Denmark	340,418	1882
Switzerland	306,227	1883
Japan	279,146	1907
The Netherlands	268,619	1882
Portugal	263,467	1921
Spain	173,021	1921
Belgium	170,374	1913
Rumania	158,021	1921
South America	143,133	1924
Czechoslovakia	128,360	1921
Iceland (1870–1925)	13,811	1887

Source: Official immigration statistics of the USA. The tabular is from O. Handlin 1959, 16; Official statistics of Finland, R. Kero 1974, 17, 26, 28; Official statistics of Iceland.

Note: Border alterations make it difficult to put immigration figures together for long periods. Moreover the immigration statistics of the USA differ from the statistics of the delivering countries.

Table 3. Immigrants from the Nordic Countries in the United States, 1910. Foreign-Born by State.

	Born in Denmark	Finland	Norway	Sweden
Maine	929	831	580	2,203
New Hampshire	131	1,198	491	2,068
Vermont	172	293	102	1,331
Massachusetts	3,405	10,744	5,432	39,562
Rhode Island	328	297	578	7,405
Connecticut	2,724	776	1,265	18,208
New York	12,544	8,760	25,013	53,705
New Jersey	8,746	1,640	5,351	10,547
Pennsylvania	3,034	2,413	2,320	23,467
Ohio	1,837	3,988	1,110	5,522
Indiana	900	215	531	5,081
Illinois	17,369	2,390	32,913	115,424
Michigan	6,315	31,144	7,638	26,374
Wisconsin	16,454	5,705	57,000	25,739
Minnesota	16,137	26,637	105,303	122,428
Iowa	17,961	140	21,924	26,763
Missouri	1,729	120	660	5,654
North Dakota	5,355	1,186	45,937	12,160
South Dakota	6,294	1,381	20,918	9,998
Nebraska	13,674	79	2,750	23,219
Kansas	2,760	49	1,294	13,309
Delaware	52	9	38	332
Maryland	237	47	363	421
District of Columbia	176	21	149	359
Virginia	240	50	311	368
West Virginia	67	127	38	279
North Carolina	36	18	39	112

Table 3. Continued.

	Born in Denmark	Finland	Norway	Sweden
South Carolina	51	42	82	95
Georgia	112	49	145	289
Florida	295	89	304	729
Kentucky	78	18	53	190
Tennessee	163	21	89	363
Alabama	197	38	266	753
Mississippi	119	88	91	292
Arkansas	178	15	76	385
Louisiana	239	118	295	344
Oklahoma	550	18	351	1,028
Texas	1,289	160	1,785	4,706
Montana	1,943	4,111	7,170	6,412
Idaho	2,254	652	2,566	4,985
Wyoming	962	1,380	623	2,497
Colorado	2,756	1,239	1,787	12,446
New Mexico	116	26	151	365
Arizona	284	560	272	845
Utah	8,300	1,012	2,305	7,227
Nevada	616	174	255	708
Washington	7,804	8,719	28,368	32,199
Oregon	3,215	4,734	6,843	10,099
California	14,209	6,159	9,952	26,212
USA total	181,649	129,680	403,877	655,207

Source: 13th Census of the US 1910, Vol. 1. Population. Dept. of Commerce. Bureau of the Census. Washington D.C. 1913, table 33, 834–839. Data from Iceland is not available.

Table 4. Immigrants to Canada with Ethnic Origin in the Nordic Countries, 1900–1955.

	Danish	Finnish	Icelandic	Norwegian	Swedish
1900–01	88	682	912	265	485
1901–02	163	1,292	260	1,015	1,013
1902–03	308	1,734	917	1,746	2,477
1903–04	417	845	396	1,239	2,151
1904–05	461	1,323	413	1,397	1,847
1905–06	474	1,103	168	1,415	1,802
1906–07	297	1,049	46	876	1,077
1907–08	290	1,212	97	1,554	2,132
1908	146	453	33	654	1,015
1909	254	1,348	85	1,285	1,905
1910	476	2,262	244	2,019	3,065
1911	602	1,637	219	1,829	2,589
1912	848	2,135	215	1,798	2,330
1913	868	3,508	306	1,698	2,671
1914	419	637	150	967	1,086
1915	163	91	15	196	152
1916	165	276	10	359	360
1917	17	129	3	230	166
1918	38	15	10	71	96
1919	189	25	10	176	188
1920	478	1,198	50	412	645
1921	603	460	22	489	509
1922	297	654	33	448	666
1923	1,025		26	1,670	3.295
1924	2,066	6,123	48	3,216	2,550
1925	983	1,561	50	841	1,218
1926	1,467	4,721	31	2,607	2,324
1927	3,778	5,054	28	5,102	3,164
1928	3,732	3,674	26	2,241	3,424
1929	2,852	4,614	8	2,549	3,073
1930	1,184	2,749	25	1,049	1,022

Table 4. Continued.

	Danish	Finnish	Icelandic	Norwegian	Swedish
1931	65	100		66	62
1932	49	32	1	54	34
1933	46	45		29	13
1934	23	63		34	15
1935	22	38	7	27	26
1936	22	50		35	15
1937	1,348	73	3	22	44
1938	45	67		28	18
1939	78	63		38	14
1940	21	3		24	8
1941	7	1		8	2
1942	5		1	25	5
1943	6			6	3
1944	13	1	2	15	5
1945	21	6	2	69	21
1946	83	22	15	269	86
1947	195	43	8	178	63
1948	616	200	3	355	137
1949	863	236	14	355	172
1950	905	483	13	237	139
1951	4,613	4,130	18	896	798
1952	2,056	2,293	35	1,209	503
1953	1,562	1,232	53	939	435
1954	1,399	697	39	993	306
1955	1,393	632	19	709	271

Source: *Report of the Royal Commission on Bilingualism and Biculturalism. Book IV. The Cultural Contribution on the Other Ethnic Groups.* Ottawa 1973. Appendix II, Table A-1.

Table 5. Nordic-born in Australia, 1871–1966. By State.

Country of Birth	Census	New South Wales	Victoria	Queensland	South Australia	Western Australia	Tasmania	Australian Capital Territory	Northern Territory	Australia Males	Australia Females	Australia Total
Denmark and Dependencies	1871	a	1,014	554	a	a	15			a	a	a
	1881	1,069	1,039	2,223	264	11	136			3,617	1,125	4,742
	1891	1,488	1,394	3,071	270	43	137		6	4,824	1,585	6,409
	1901	1,368	1,020	3,158	262	320	155		3	4,753	1,533	6,206
	1911	1,300	912	2,644	274	418	121	1	3	4,276	1,397	5,673
	1921	1,577	1,035	2,553	308	393	123	3	10	4,479	1,523	6,002
	1933	1,252	752	1,828	235	324	76	9	8	3,348	1,136	4,484
	1947	844	517	968	145	225	45	6	11	2,032	727	2,759
	1966	1,991	1,094	1,113	580	382	111	81	49	3,472	1,929	5,401
Sweden	1871	a	845	253	a	a	28			a	a	a
	1881b	(1,755)	(1,375)	583	(765)	21	66			(4,594)	(454)	(5,048)
	1891b	(3,397)	(3,214)	(1,955)	(1,148)	(204)	(194)		(9)	(9,221)	(900)	(10,121)
	1901b	(3,190)	(2,207)	(2,142)	(931)	754	219		(7)	(8,888)	(982)	(9,870)
	1911	1,797	1,220	1,054	653	740	119		3	5,084	502	5,586
	1921	1,695	1,115	911	560	630	101	2	11	4,542	483	5,025
	1933	1,333	897	705	426	445	69	4	16	3,487	408	3,895
	1947	832	529	334	239	230	32		13	1,938	271	2,209
	1966	1,010	573	437	262	144	58	51	23	1,846	712	2,558
Norway	1871	a	395	118	a	a	16					
	1881	b	b	442	b	18	23			b	b	b
	1891	b	b	b	b	b	b			b	b	b
	1901	b	b	b	b	420	b			b	b	b
	1911	1,032	807	685	453	426	43	2	5	3,038	413	3,451
	1921	978	726	580	338	340	41	1	9	2,613	401	3,014
	1933	822	635	530	264	398	19	5	11	2,337	343	2,680
	1947	723	491	344	175	256	18		12	1,745	279	2,024
	1966	1,200	707	391	303	365	61	107	32	2,429	737	3,166

Country of Birth	Census	New South Wales	Victoria	Queensland	South Australia	Western Australia	Tasmania	Australian Capital Territory	Northern Territory	Australia		
										Males	Females	Total
Finland	1886	c	c	81	c	c	c			c	c	c
	1901	c	77	197	c	c	c			c	c	c
	1911	c	c	c	c	c	c			c	c	c
	1921	550	242	254	160	128	23		1	1,227	131	1,358
	1933	570	291	632	133	175	13	3	8	1,607	218	1,825
	1947	476	230	422	102	124	9	1	9	1,158	215	1,373
	1966	1,976	1,126	1,491	534	191	86	484	37	3,423	2,502	5,925
Total	(1871	a	2,254	925	a	a	59			a	a	a
	(1881	2,824	2,414	3,248	1,029	50	225			8,211	1,579	9,790
	(1891	4,885	4,608	5,026	1,418	247	331			14,045	2,485	16,530
Exl. Finland	(1901	4,538	3,227	5,300	1,193	1,494	374			13,641	2,515	16,156
	(1911	4,129	2,939	4,383	1,380	1,584	283	1	11	12,398	2,312	14,710
	1921	4,800	3,118	4,298	1,366	1,491	288	7	31	12,861	2,538	15,399
	1933	3,977	2,575	3,695	1,058	1,342	177	17	43	10,779	2,105	12,884
	1947	2,873	1,767	2,068	659	835	104	12	45	6,873	1,492	8,365
	1966	6,177	3,500	3,432	1,679	1,082	316	723	141	11,170	5,880	17,050

a = Not available
b( ) = Norway included in Sweden
c = Finland included in Russia
Source: Australian Censuses. Hereafter O. Koivukangas 1974, 287.

List of Tables

1. Total Population and Population Increase in Europe, Including European Russia, 1750–1950.
2. Transoceanic Emigration from the Nordic Countries and Some Other European Countries, 1851–1910. Mean Annual Emigration per Ten-year Periods. Promille of the Population.
3. Population Growth in the Nordic Countries, 1801–1900. Percent, 50-Years Periods.
4. Urban Population in the Nordic Countries, 1850–1920. Percent of the Total Population.
5. Overseas Emigration from the Nordic Countries According to Destination, 1871–1925, Finland 1901–1923. Distribution in Percent.
6. Emigration to North America from Denmark, Iceland, Norway and Sweden, 1880–1889 and from Finland, 1900–1909. The Average Yearly Emigration and the Emigration per Thousand Inhabitants from the Cities and the Rural Areas together with the Cities' Portion of the Total Emigration to North America.
7. Birth Dates and Emigration Patterns of the Family of Peter Peterson, Brickegården, Karlskoga Parish, Örebro County, Sweden.
8. Concentration of Nordic Minorities in the United States in 1910. Distribution by States with at Least 5 percent of Each Population Group Foreign-Born Persons.
9. Naturalized and Alien Men over 21 Years of Age in the United States, 1910–1930. Percent of All Men.
10. Strikes in Sweden, 1873–1909.

List of Figures

1. Changes of Political Borders in the Nordic Countries.
2. Emigration from Norway to the Netherlands in the Seventeenth and Eighteenth Centuries.
3. Some Important Seasonal Labor Migration Streams in the Nordic Countries.
4. In-migration to the USA during the Peak Years of Emigration from Europe 1854, 1882 and 1907. Total Number of Emigrants during the Respective Years.
5. Annual Emigration from the Nordic Countries to North America, 1851–1930. Total Number of Emigrants per Thousand Inhabitants.
6. Total Transoceanic Emigration from Europe and from the Nordic Countries (Denmark, Finland, Iceland, Norway and Sweden). Mean Annuals per Five-Year Periods.
7. Crude Birth and Death Rates in the Nordic Countries, 1750–1950.
8. The Proletarianization of the Rural Population in Norway during the First Half of the Nineteenth Century. The Main Occupational Categories.
9. Migration Overseas from the Nordic Countries a) 1865–69, b) 1885–89, c) 1900–04.
10. Emigrants to Australia from Denmark, Finland, Norway and Sweden, 1949–1971.
11. Distribution of Urban and Rural Emigration from the Nordic Countries during Peak Decades. For Denmark, Iceland, Norway and Sweden, 1880–1889; for Finland, 1900–1909.
12. Major Directions of the Migration from Gräsmark Parish (Värmland County) 1860–1979 and from Revsund Parish (Jämtland County) 1890–1894 to Destinations outside the Counties.
13. The Influence-fields on Migrants of Some Cities in Southern Finland during the Middle of the Nineteenth Century. Schematic Outline.

14. Migration to Russia, Sweden and America from Vaasa County, Finland, 1861–1892. A Schematic Diagram of the Total Migration to Destinations outside Finland.
15. Proportion of Men in Total Emigration from the Nordic Countries. Percent.
16. Emigration from Fredriksborg *Amt* 1869–1899 by Occupational and Social Groups. Number of Emigrants.
17. Population Movements in Toholampi 1870–1889.
18. Migration in Vopnafjördur, 1873–1893.
19. Emigration from East Agder, West Agder and All of Norway, 1850–1915.
20. Immigration to Sweden per Thousand of the Median Swedish Population, 1875–1913, and Trade and Business Cycles of the USA.
21. Emigration Routes from Europe to North America.
22. The Spread of Norwegian Settlements in Wisconsin and Minnesota, 1830–1880.
23. Immigrants from the Nordic Countries in the United States, 1910. Distribution by States.
24. Nordic Populations in Canada, 1931. Numbers of Persons Born in Respective Nordic Countries. Distribution by Provinces.
25. The Frontier Movement in the United States, 1810–1890.
26. Five Typical Cases of Migration among Långasjö Emigrants in North America.
27. Westward Movement of Immigrants from Östmark Parish, Sweden.
28. Settlements in the Upper Middle West Populated by Immigrants from Balestrand, Norway.
29. From Downtown to Suburbs. Swedish Movements in the Chicago Metropolitan Area.
30. The Gradual Movement of the Main Norwegian Neighborhood in New York City.
31. The Size of Culture Groups in Six Townships in Kandiyohi County, Minnesota, 1870–1910. Number of Households at Five-Year Intervals.
32. Leftist Parties in the United States, 1901–1925.
33. Norwegian Services in the Norwegian Lutheran Church (Evangelical Lutheran Church), 1930–1948. Percentage of Total Services in Each District.
34. The Ability to Speak Swedish in Five Age Groups in Chisago County, Minnesota.

Administrative areas. The figures are explained in the list on pp. 301–307.

List of Administrative Areas in the Nordic Countries

On the map the numbers are printed instead of the names of the areas.

Denmark: amt

1 København
2 Frederiksborg
3 Holbæk
4 Sorø
5 Præstø
6 Bornholm
7 Maribo
8 Svendborg
9 Odense
10 Vejle
11 Århus
12 Randers
13 Ålborg
14 Hjørring
15 Thisted
16 Viborg
17 Ringkøbing
18 Ribe

Norway: fogderier

19 Idd and Marker
20 Moss and Tune
21 Rakkestad
22 Aker and Follo

23 Nedre Romerike
24 Øvre Romerike
25 Vinger and Odal
26 Solør
27 Sør-Østerdal
28 Nord-Østerdal
29 Hedmark
30 Toten
31 Sør-Gudbrandsdal
32 Nord-Gudbrandsdal
33 Hadeland and Land
34 Valdres
35 Hallingdal
36 Numedal and Sandsvær
37 Ringerike
38 Buskerud
39 Jarlsberg
40 Larvik
41 Bamble
42 Nedre Telemark
42 Øvre Telemark
44 Nedenes
45 Setesdal
46 Mandal
47 Lista
48 Jæren and Dalane

301

49	Ryfylke	87	Luggude
50	Sunnhordland	88	Ingelstads
51	Hardanger and Voss	89	Järrestads
52	Nordhordland	90	Albo
53	Sogn	91	Gärds
54	Sunn- and Nordfjord	92	Villands
55	Sunnmøre	93	Östra Göinge
56	Romsdal	94	Västra Göinge
57	Nordmøre	95	Norra Åsbo
58	Orkdal	96	Södra Åsbo
59	Guldal	97	Bjäre
60	Strinda and Selbu	98	Listers
61	Fosen	99	Bräkne
62	Stjør- and Verdalen	100	Medelstads
63	Inderøy	101	Östra
64	Namdal	102	Höks
65	Sør-Helgeland	103	Tönnersjö
66	Nord-Helgeland	104	Halmstads
67	Salten	105	Årstads
68	Lofoten and Vesterålen	106	Faurås
69	Senja and Troms	107	Himle
70	Alta	108	Viske
71	Hammerfest	109	Fjäre
72	Tana	110	Sunnerbo
73	Vardø	111	Allbo
74	Varanger	112	Kinnevalds
		113	Norrvidinge

Sweden: härader
(or equivalent)

		114	Konga
		115	Uppvidinge
75	Skytts	116	Västbo
76	Vemmenhögs	117	Östbo
77	Ljunits	118	Västra
78	Herrestads	119	Östra
79	Oxie	120	Mo
80	Bara	121	Tveta
81	Torna	122	Södra Vedbo
82	Färs	123	Norra Vedbo
83	Frosta	124	Vista
84	Harjagers	125	Södra Möre
85	Onsjö	126	Norra Möre
86	Rönnebergs	127	Stranda

128	Handbörds	169	Åse
129	Aspelands	170	Kållands
130	Tunaläns	171	Kinnefjärdings
131	Sevede	172	Skånings
132	Södra Tjusts	173	Gudhems
133	Norra Tjusts	174	Kåkinds
134	Gräsgårds	175	Valle
135	Möckleby	176	Kinne
136	Algutsrums	177	Vadsbro
137	Runstens	178	Kinds
138	Slättbo	179	Marks
139	Åkerbo	180	Vättle
140	Gotlands Södra	181	Bollebygds
141	Gotlands Norra	182	Veden
142	Ydre	183	Ås
143	Kinda	184	Redvägs
144	Lysings	185	Gäsene
145	Göstrings	186	Kullings
146	Vifolka	187	Ale
147	Valkebo	186	Flundre
148	Hanekind	189	Bjärke
149	Bankekind	190	Väne
150	Skärkind	191	Sundals
151	Hammarkind	192	Valbo
152	Björkekind	193	Nordals
153	Östkind	194	Vedbo
154	Lösings	195	Tössbo
155	Memmings	196	Sävedals
156	Åkerbo	197	Askim
157	Gullbergs	198	Östra Hisings
158	Bobergs	199	Västra Hisings
159	Dals	200	Inlands Södre
160	Aska	201	Inlands Nordre
161	Finspånga läns	202	Inlands Fräkne
162	Bråbo	203	Inlands Torpe
163	Vartofta	204	Tjörns
164	Frökinds	205	Orust Västra
165	Vilske	206	Orust Östra
166	Laske	207	Lane
167	Varne	208	Stångenäs
168	Viste	209	Sotenäs

210 Tunge	251 Selebo
211 Kville	252 Åkers
212 Sörbygdens	253 Öster-Rekarne
213 Bullarens	254 Väster-Rekarne
214 Tanums	255 Åkerbo
215 Vette	256 Snevringe
216 Näs	257 Tuhundra
217 Nordmarks	258 Norrbo
218 Gillbergs	259 Siende
219 Grums	260 Ytter-Tjurbo
220 Karlstads	261 Simtuna
221 Väse	262 Torstuna
222 Ölme	263 Våla
223 Visnums	264 Över-Tjurbo
224 Färnebo	265 Vagnsbro
225 Nyeds	266 Gamla Norberg
226 Kils	267 Skinnskattebergs
227 Jösse	268 Bro
228 Fryksdals	269 Håbo
229 Älvdals	270 Trögds
230 Sundbo	271 Åsunda
231 Kumla	272 Lagunda
232 Sköllersta	273 Hagunda
233 Askers	274 Ulleråkers
234 Grimstens	275 Vaksala
235 Hardemo	276 Bälinge
236 Edsbergs	277 Norunda
237 Örebro	278 Rasbo
238 Glanshammars	279 Olands
239 Fellingsbro	280 Örbyhus
240 Karlskoga	281 Sotholms
241 Grythytte and Hällefors	282 Öknebo
242 Nora and Hjulsjö	283 Svartlösa
243 Lindes and Ramsbergs	284 Värmdö
244 Nya Kopparbergs	285 Färentuna
245 Jönåkers	286 Sollentuna
246 Rönö	287 Danderyds
247 Hölebo	288 Åkers
248 Oppunda	289 Vallentuna
249 Villåttinge	290 Ärlinghundra
250 Daga	291 Seminghundra

304

292	Långhundra	332	Lits
293	Sjuhundra	333	Brunflo
294	Frötuna and Länna	334	Sunne
295	Bro and Vätö	335	Rödöns
296	Lyhundra	336	Offerdals
297	Närdinghundra	337	Undersåkers
298	Väddö and Häverö	338	Hallens
299	Frösåkers	339	Ovikens
300	Falu Domsagas Norra	340	Hackås and Näs
301	Falu Domsagas Södra	341	Bergs
302	Stora Skedvi	342	Hede
303	Säters	343	Sveg
304	Husby	344	Torps
305	Hedemora and Garpen-	345	Tuna
	bergs	346	Njurunda
306	Folkare	347	Selångers
307	Gagnefs	349	Sköns
308	Leksands	349	Indals
309	Rättviks	350	Ljustorps
310	Mora	351	Säbrå
311	Orsa	352	Gudmundrå
312	Älvdals	353	Nora
313	Särna and Idre	354	Nordingrå
314	Malungs	355	Boteå
315	Nås	356	Sollefteå
316	Grangärde	357	Ramsele
317	Norrbärke	358	Resele
318	Söderbärke	359	Nätra
319	Ovansjö and Ockelbo	360	Själevads
320	Gästriklands Östra	361	Arnäs
321	Bollnäs	362	Nordmalings and Bjur-
322	Ala		holms
323	Arbrå and Järvsö	363	Umeå
324	Enångers	364	Degerfors
325	Forsa	365	Bygdeå
326	Ljusdals	366	Nysätra
327	Delsbo	367	Lövångers
328	Bergsjö	368	Burträsk
329	Revsunds	369	Skellefteå
330	Ragunda	370	Norsjö and Malå
331	Hammerdals	371	Lycksele lappmarks

372	Åsele lappmarks	408	Siikajoki
373	Piteå	409	Rantsila, Vihanti
374	Älvsbyns	410	Kestilä, Pulkkila
375	Arvidsjaurs lappmarks	411	Haapavesi, Ylivieska
376	Arjeplogs lappmarks	412	Pyhäjoki, Alavieska
377	Neder-Luleå	413	Kalajoki
378	Över-Luleå	414	Sievi
379	Jokkmokks lappmarks	415	Himanka, Kannus
380	Råneå	416	Toholampi, Karleby
381	Neder-Kalix	417	Perho, Karstula
382	Över-Kalix	418	Kaustinen, Veteli
383	Gällivare lappmarks	419	Kronoby, Pedersöre Ter-
384	Neder-Torneå and Karl		järv
	Gustavs	420	Munsala, Evijärvi
385	Över-Torneå	421	Lapua, Lappajärvi
386	Korpilombolo	422	Vörå, Korsholm
387	Pajala	423	Malax, Teuva
388	Jukkasjärvi lappmarks	424	Laihia, Isokyrö
389	Karesuando lappmarks	425	Seinäjoki, Ilmajoki
		426	Alavus

Finland: parishes or groups of parishes

427	Alajärvi
428	Lehtimäki
390	Enontekiö, Inari	429	Kivijärvi
391	Sodankylä	430	Pihtipudas, Viitasaari
392	Muonio	431	Petalax, Närpes-Sideby
393	Kolari	432	Kauhajoki, Peräseinäjoki
394	Salla	433	Virrat, Ähtäri
395	Kemijärvi	434	Saarijärvi
396	Rovaniemi	435	Haapajärvi, Pyhäjärvi
397	Turtola	436	Iisalmi landsförs., Piela-
398	Tornio, Kemi		vesi
399	Simo, Haukipudas	437	Kuopio län (except nr 436
400	Pudasjärvi, Taivalkoski		and 440)
401	Kuusamo	438	Merikarvia, Parkano
402	Suomussalmi, Hyrynsal-	439	Ruovesi, Keuruu
	mi Kuhmoniemi	440	Kiuruvesi
403	Puolanka	441	Pieksämäki, St. Michel's
404	Sotkamo		rural parish
405	Paltamo, Utajärvi	442	Tavastehus län (except
406	Oulujoki, Muhos		parts of nr 439) and Huit-
407	Liminka		tinen

443	Pomarkku, Ulvila	**Iceland: härader**

443 Pomarkku, Ulvila
444 Hämeenkyrö, Eura
445 Luvia, Uusikirkko
446 Laitila, Säkylä
447 Vehmaa, Kiikala, Kimito
448 Loimaa, Marttila
449 Maaria, Nagu
450 Lokalahti, Houtskär
451 The province of Åland
452 Nylands län (except Ruotsinpyhtää)
453 St. Michel's län (except nr 441)
454 Ruotsinpyhtää, Valkeala
455 Vehkalahti, Ruokolahti
456 Säkkijärvi, Viborg's rural parish
457 Karelian isthmus and the Ladoga area (except nr 458 and 459)
458 Jaakkima
459 Pyhäjärvi
460 Jyväskylä rural parish and Laukaa

Iceland: härader
461 Vesturskaftafellssýsla
462 Rangarvallasýsla
    Vestmannaeyjar
463 Árnessýsla
464 Gullbringusýsla and Kjosarsýsla
465 Borgarfjarðarsýsla
466 Mýrasýsla
467 Hnappaduls and Snæfellsnessýsla
468 Dalasýsla
469 Barðustrandarsýsla
470 Isafjardarsýsla
471 Strandasýsla
472 Húnavatnssýsla
473 Skagafjardarsýsla
474 Eyjafjardarsýsla
475 Suður-Þingeyjarsýsla
476 Norður-Þingeyjarsýsla
477 Norður-Múlasýsla
478 Suður-Múlasýsla
479 Austur-Skaftafellsýsla

Bibliography

Abbreviations
NAHA = Norwegian American Historial Association
SPHQ = Swedish Pioneer Historical Quarterly

Ahlstrom, Sydney E., *A Religious History of the American People*. New Haven: Yale Univ. Press, 1972.

Åkerman, Sune, 'Intern befolkningsomflyttning och emigration', in *Emigrationen fra Norden indtil 1. Verdenskrig: Rapporter til det Nordiske historikermøde i København 1971*, pp. 61–107. Copenhagen, 1971.

Åkerman, Sune, 'From Stockholm to San Francisco: The Development of the Historical Study of External Migrations', *Annales Academiae Regiae Scientiarum Upsaliensis* 19 (1975), 5–46.

Åkerman, Sune, 'Theories and Methods of Migration Research', in H. Runblom & Hans Norman, eds., *From Sweden to America: A History of the Migration*. Minneapolis & Uppsala: Acta Universitatis Upsaliensis & University of Minnesota Press, 1976.

Åkerman, Sune, 'Stability and Change in the Migration of a Medium-Sized City: The Case of Worcester, Massachusetts', in Ingrid Semmingsen & Per Seyersted, eds., *Scando-Americana: Papers on Scandinavian Emigration to the United States*, 65–94. Oslo: American Institute, 1980.

Åkerman, Sune & Norman, Hans, 'Political Mobilization of the Workers: The Case of the Worcester Swedes', in Dirk Hoerder, ed., *American Labor and Immigration History, 1877–1920s*. Urbana: University of Illinois Press, 1983.

Alanen, Arnold, 'The Development and Distribution of Finnish Consumers' Cooperatives in Michigan, Minnesota and Wisconsin, 1903–1973', in Michael G. Karni, Matti E. Kaups & Douglas J. Ollila Jr., eds., *The Finnish Experience in the Western Great Lakes Region: New Perspectives*, 103–129. Turku: Migration Institute, 1975.

Alanen, Arnold, 'Finns and the Corporate Mining Environment of the Lake Superior Region', in Michael G. Karni, ed., *Finnish Diaspora II*, 33–62. Toronto: 1981.

Alanen, Arnold, 'In Search of the Pioneer Finnish Homesteader in America', *Finnish Americana* 4 (1981), 72–92.

Alanen, Arnold, 'Kaivosmiehistä maanviljelijöihin: suomalaiset siirtolaiset pohjoisten Suurten järvien alueella Yhdysvalloissa', *Terra* 94 (1982), 189–206.

Allswang, John M., *A House for All Peoples: Ethnic Politics in Chicago, 1890–1936*. Lexington: Univ. Press of Kentucky, 1971.

Ander, Fritiof O., 'The Swedish-American Press and the American Protective Association', *Church History* 6 (1937), 165–179.

Andersen, C., *White Protestant Americans: From National Origins to Religious Group*. New Jersey: Prentice Hall, 1970.

Andersen, Arlow William, *The Immigrant Takes His Stand: The Norwegian-American Press and Public Affairs, 1847–1872*. Northfield: NAHA, 1953.

Andersen, Arlow William, *The Norwegian-Americans*. Boston: Twayne, 1975.

Appel, John J., *Immigrant Historical Societies in the United States, 1880–1950*. New York: Arno, 1980.

Archdeacon, Thomas J., *Becoming American: An Ethnic History*. New York: The Free Press, 1983.

Babcock, Kendrick Charles, *The Scandinavian Element in the United States*. Urbana: Univ. of Illinois, 1914.

Baltensprenger, Bradley H., 'Agricultural Change Among Nebraska Immigrants, 1880–1900', in Frederick C. Luebke, ed., *Ethnicity on the Great Plains*, 170–189. Lincoln: Nebraska Univ. Press, 1980.

Barton, H. Arnold, 'Clio and Swedish America: Historians, Organizations, Publications', in Nils Hasselmo, ed., *Perspectives on Swedish Immigration: Proceedings of the International Conference on the Swedish Heritage in the Upper Midwest, April 1–3, 1976, University of Minnesota, Duluth*, 3–24. Chicago: Swedish Pioneer Historical Society, 1978.

Barton, Josef J., *Peasants and Strangers: Italians, Rumanians, and Slovaks in an American City, 1890–1950*. Cambridge, Mass.: Harvard Univ. Press, 1975.

Beijbom, Ulf, *Swedes in Chicago: A Demographic and Social Study of the 1846–1880 Immigration*. Uppsala: Studia Historica Upsaliensia, 1971.

Beijbom, Ulf, 'Emigrantkyrkan som sociokulturell organisation: En typstudie av svenskarna i Chicago, 1846–1880', *Kyrkohistorisk årsskrift* (1972).

Beijbom, Ulf, 'Från slum till förort: Chicagos Swede Town', in Ann-Sofie Kälvemark, *Utvandring: Den svenska emigrationen till Amerika i historiskt perspektiv: En antologi*. 179–211. Stockholm: Wahlström & Widstrand, 1973.

Beijbom, Ulf, *Amerika, Amerika: En bok om utvandringen*. Stockholm: Natur & Kultur, 1977.

Beijbom, Ulf, *Guldfeber: En bok om guldruscherna till Kalifornien och Klondike*. Stockholm: Natur & Kultur, 1979.

Beijbom, Ulf, *Australienfararna: Vårt märkligaste utvandringsäventyr*. Stockholm: LT, 1983.

Beijbom, Ulf, 'Swedish-American Organizational Life', in Harald Runblom & Dag Blanck, eds., *Scandianvia Overseas: Patterns of Cultural Transformation in North American and Australia*. Uppsala: Center for Multiethnic Research, 1986.

Beijbom, Ulf, *Utvandrarna och Svensk-Amerika*. Stockholm: LT, 1986.

Bengston, Henry, *Skandinaver på vänsterflygeln i USA*. Stockholm: Kooperativa förbundet, 1955.

Bergendoff, Conrad, 'The Role of Augustana in the Transplanting of a Culture across the Atlantic', in J. Iverne Dowie & J. Thomas Treadway, eds., *The Immigration of Ideas: Studies in the North Atlantic Community*, 67–84. Rock Island: Augustana Historical Society, 1968.

Bergsten, Karl-Erik, *Sydsvenska födelseortsfält*. Lund: Lund Studies in Geography, Series B, 1981.

Betten, Neil, 'Strike on the Mesabi 1907', *Minnesota History* 40 (Fall 1967), 340–347.

Birn, Randi, *Aksel Sandemose: Exile in Search of a Home*. Westport, Conn.: Greenwood Press, 1984.

Bjork, Kenneth O., *Saga in Steel and Concrete: Norwegian Engineers in America*. Northfield: NAHA, 1947.

Bjork, Kenneth O., *West of the Great Divide: Norwegian Migration to the Pacific Coast, 1847–1893*. Northfield: NAHA, 1958.

Bjork, Kenneth O., 'Scandinavian Migration to the Canadian Prairie Provinces, 1893–1914', *Norwegian-American Studies* 26 (1974) 3–30.

Bjornson, V., 'Icelanders', in Thernstrom, Stephan, ed., *Harvard Encyclopedia of American Ethnic Groups*, 476–478. Cambridge: Belknap Press, 1980.

Blanck, Dag, 'An Invented Tradition: The Creation of Swedish-American Ethnic Consciousness at Augustana College, 1860–1900', in Harald Runblom & Dag

Blanck, *Scandinavia Overseas: Patterns of Cultural Transformation in North America and Australia.* Uppsala: Centre for Multiethnic Research, 1986.

Blegen, Theodore C., *Norwegian Migration to America, 1825–1860.* Northfield: NAHA, 1931.

Blegen, Theodore C., *Norwegian Migration: The American Transition.* Northfield: NAHA, 1940.

Bodnar, John, *The Transplanted: The History of Immigrants in Urban America.* Bloomington: Indiana Univ. Press, 1985.

Brattne, Berit, *Bröderna Larsson. En studie i svensk emigrantagentverksamhet under 1880-talet.* Uppsala: Studia Historica Upsaliensia, 1973.

Brattne, Berit & Åkerman, Sune, 'The Importance of the Transport Sector for Mass Emigration', in H. Runblom & Hans Norman, eds., *From Sweden to America: A History of the Migration,* 176–200. Minneapolis & Uppsala: Acta Universitatis Upsaliensis & University of Minnesota Press, 1976.

Braudel, F., *Vardagslivets strukturer: Det möjligas gränser. Civilisation och kapitalism 1400–1800.* Vol. 1. Stockholm: Gidlunds, 1982.

Briggs, John W., *An Italian Passage: Immigrants to Three American Cities, 1890–1930.* New Haven & London: Yale Univ. Press, 1978.

Broberg, Richard, 'Invandringar från Finland till Sverige före 1700-talet i verklighet och tradition', in *Migrationen mellan Sverige och Finland,* 91–112. Stockholm, 1970.

Bro-Jørgensen, J. O., 'Dansk Vestindien indtil 1755. Kolonisation og kompanistyre', in *Vore gamle tropekolonier,* bind 1, 1952.

Brozek, Andrzej, 'The National Consciousness of the Polish Ethnic Group in the United States, 1854–1939, Proposed Model', *Acta Poloniae Historica* 37 (Warzaw, 1978), 95–127.

Brozek, Andrzej, 'The Historical and Economic Determinants of Contemporary Migrations from Upper Silesia to Germany', *Polish Western Affairs* (1982:1), 51–65.

Brozek, Andrzej, *Polish Americans, 1854–1939.* Warsaw: Interpress, 1985.

Brye, David L., 'Wisconsin Scandinavians and Progressivism, 1900–1950', *Norwegian-American Studies* 27 (1977), 163–193.

Callahan, North, *Carl Sandburg: Lincoln of Our Literature.* New York: New York Univ. Press, 1970.

Capps, Finis Herbert, *From Isolationism to Involvement: The Swedish Immigrant Press in America, 1914–1943.* Chicago: Swedish Pioneer Historical Society, 1966.

Capps, Finis Herbert, 'The Views of the Swedish-American Press Toward United States – Japanese Relations 1914–1945', *SPHQ* 20:3 (1969), 133–146.

Carlsson, Sten, 'Norrmän i Sverige 1814–1905', in *Historielärarnas förenings årsskrift* (1963–64), 47–63.

Carlsson, Sten, 'Frikyrklighet och emigration: Ett bidrag', in *Kyrka, folk, stat: Festskrift till Sven Kjöllerström,* 118–131. Lund, 1967.

Carlsson, Sten, *Skandinaviska politiker i Minnesota 1882–1900: En studie i den etniska faktorns roll vid politiska val i en immigrantstat.* Uppsala: Acta Universitatis Upsaliensis, 1970.

Carlsson, Sten, 'Flyttningsintensiteten i det svenska agrarsamhället', *Turun Historiallinen Arkisto* 28 (1973). [S. Carlsson 1973a].

Carlsson, Sten, 'Skandinaviska politiker i Minnesota', in Ann-Sofie Kälvemark, *Utvandring: Den svenska emigrationen till Amerika i historiskt perspektiv: En antologi,* 211–243. Stockholm: Wahlström & Widstrand, 1973. [S. Carlsson 1973b].

Carlsson, Sten, 'Chronology and Composition of Swedish Emigration to America', in Harald Runblom & Hans Norman, eds., *From Sweden to America: A History of the Migration,* 114–148. Minneapolis & Uppsala: Acta Universitatis Upsaliensis & University of Minnesota Press, 1976.

Carlsson, Sten, 'Swedes in Politics', in Harald Runblom & Hans Norman, eds., *From Sweden to America: A History of the Migration*, 291–300. Minneapolis & Uppsala: Acta Universitatis Upsaliensis & University of Minnesota Press, 1976.

Carlsson, Sten, 'Scandinavian Politicians in the United States', in Ingrid Semmingsen & Per Seyersted, eds., *Scando-Americana: Papers on Scandinavian Emigration to the United States*, 153–166. Oslo: American Institute, 1980.

Carlsson, Sten, 'Tyska invandrare i Sverige', *Fataburen: Nordiska museets och Skansens årsbok* 1981, 9–31.

Chrislock, Carl H., *Ethnicity Challenged: The Upper Midwest Norwegian-American Experience in World War I*. Northfield: NAHA, 1981.

Chrislock, Carl H., *The Progressive Era in Minnesota, 1899–1918*. St. Paul: Minnesota Historical Society, 1971.

Chrislock, Carl H., 'The Norwegian-American Impact on Minnesota Politics: How Far "Left-of-Center"?' in Harald S. Naess, ed., *Norwegian Influence on the Upper Midwest*, 106–116. Duluth: Univ. of Minnesota, 1976.

Chrisman, Noel J., 'Ethnic Persistence in an Urban Setting', *Ethnicity* 8 (1981), 256–292.

Christensen, Thomas Peter, *A History of the Danes in Iowa*. Solvang: Dansk Folkesamfund, 1952.

Chudacoff, Howard P., *Mobile Americans: Residential and Social Mobility in Omaha, 1880–1920*. New York: Oxford Univ. Press, 1972.

Chudacoff, Howard P., 'A New Look at Ethnic Neighborhoods: Residential Dispersion and the Concept of Visibility in a Medium-Seized City', *Journal of American History*, 60:1 (1973), 76–93.

Cipolla, Carlo, *The Economic History of World Population*. Harmondsworth, Penguin Books 537, 1967.

Conzen, Kathleen Neils, *Immigrant Milwaukee: Accomodation and Community in a Frontier City*. Cambridge, Mass.: Harvard Univ. Press, 1976.

Conzen, Kathleen Neils, 'Historical Approaches to the Study of Rural Ethnic Communities', in Frederick C. Luebke, ed., *Ethnicity on the Great Plains*, 1–14. Lincoln: Nebraska Univ. Press, 1980.

Copeland, William, 'Early Finnish American Settlements in Florida', in Michael G. Karni, ed., *Finnish Diaspora* II, 127–142. Toronto, 1981.

Curti, Merle, *The Making of an American Community: A Case Study of Democracy in a Frontier County*. Stanford: Stanford Univ. Press, 1959.

Dahlie, Jorgen, *A Social History of Scandinavian Immigration: Washington State, 1850–1910*. New York: Arno Press, 1980.

Dahlgren, Stellan & Norman, Hans, 'Governor Johan Risingh and New Sweden: The Swedish Colonial Experience in the Light of the Risingh Journal'. (Manuscript 1986).

Danielsen, Jens Bjerre, 'Ethnic Identity, Nationalism and Scandinavianism in the Scandinavian Immigrant Socialist Press in the U.S.' in Christiane Harzig & Dirk Hoerder, *The Press of Labor Migrants in Europe and North America, 1880s to 1930s*, 181–204. Bremen: Labor Migration Project, 1985.

De Geer, Eric, 'Emigrationen i Västsverige under 1800-talet'. *Ymer* 3 (1959), 194–233.

De Geer, Eric, *Migration och influensfält: Studier av emigration och intern migration i Finland och Sverige 1816–1972*. Uppsala: Acta Universitatis Upsaliensis, 1977.

De Geer, Eric, 'Finlands emigration till Sverige 1808–1945', in Olavi Koivukangas, ed., *Utvandringen från Sverige till Finland genom tiderna*, 45–62. Turku, 1980.

De Geer, Eric & Wester, Holger, 'Utrikes resor, arbetsvandringar och flyttningar i Finland och Vasa län, 1861–1890', *Österbotten* Vasa: Skrifter utgivna av Svensk-Österbottniska Samfundet, 1975.

[The Dillingham Commission.] U.S. Senate, 61 Congress, 3rd Session, Doc. No. 747. Reports of the Immigration Commission, *Abstracts of Reports of the Immigration Commission*. Vol. I. Washington, D.C. 1911.

Douhan, Bernt, *Arbete, kapital och migration: Valloninvandringen till Sverige under 1600-talet.* Uppsala: Acta Universitatis Upsaliensis, 1985.

Durnell, Hazel, *The America of Carl Sandburg: An Analytical Study of his Works as an Expression of the National Mind.* Genève: Université de Genève, 1963.

Dyrvik, Ståle, 'Den lange fredstiden 1720–1784', in *Norges Historie* 8 (1978), 220ff.

Dyrvik, Ståle, 'Comment to the session 'The Decline of Mortality ca. 1740–1850', of the Fifth Scandinavian Demographic Symposium 13–16 June 1979 at Hurdalsjöen, Norway', *Scandinavian Population Studies* 5. Oslo, 1979.

Eidevall, Gunnar, *Amerika i svensk 1900-talslitteratur: Från Gustaf Hellström till Lars Gustafsson.* Stockholm: Almqvist & Wiksell, 1983.

Elovson, Harald, *Amerika i svensk litteratur: En studie i komparativ litteraturhistoria.* Lund, 1930.

Emigrationsutredningen. Betänkande och bilagor, 21 vols. Stockholm, 1908–1913.

Engman, Max, *St. Petersburg och Finland: Migration och influens, 1703–1917.* Helsinki, 1983.

En Smålandssocken emigrerar. En bok om emigrationen till Amerika från Långasjö socken i Kronobergs län. Växjö, 1967.

Eriksson, Ingrid & Rogers, John, *Rural Labor and Population Change: Social and Demographic Developments in East-Central Sweden during the Nineteenth Century.* Uppsala: Acta Universitatis Upsaliensis, 1978.

Essinger, 'La Emigración Danesa', in *La emigración europea a la América Latina: Fuentes y estado de investigación,* 85–99. Berlin: Colloquium Verlag, 1979.

Estay J. A., *Business Cycles: Their Nature, Cause, and Control.* 3rd. ed., New Jersey, 1956.

Fishman, Joshua A., *Language Loyalty in the United States: The Maintenance and Perpetuation of Non-English Mother Tongues by American Ethnic and Religious Groups.* The Hague: Mouton & Co., 1966.

Fjellström, Phebe, *Swedish-American Colonization in the San Joaquin Valley in California: A Study of Acculturation and Assimilation of an Immigrant Group.* Uppsala: Studia Ethnographica Upsaliensia, 1970.

Fladby, Rolf, 'Gjenreisning 1536–1648', in *Norges Historie,* vol. 6, 118ff. Oslo, 1977.

Flodell, Gunvor, *Misiones-Svenska: Språkbevarande och språkpåverkan i en sydamerikansk talgemenskap.* Uppsala: Institutionen för nordiska språk, 1986.

Flodell, Sven Arne, *Tierra Nueva. Svensk grupputvandring till Latinamerika. Integration och församlingsbildning.* Uppsala: Studia Missionalia Upsaliensia, 1974.

Forsberg, Karin, 'Bishop Hill'. Unpublished licentiate thesis, Stockholm University 1958. (Copy available at the Emigrant Institute, Växjö, Sweden).

For The Common Good: Finnish Immigrants and the Radical Response to Industrial America. Superior: Tyomies Society, 1977.

Fridholm, M., M. Isacson & L. Magnusson, *Industrialismens rötter. Om förutsättningarna för den industriella revolutionen i Sverige.* Lund 1976.

Friedman, Philip S., 'The Danish Community of Chicago', *The Bridge* (Journal of the Danish-American Heritage Society) 8:1 (1985), 3–95.

Friman, Axel, 'Svensk utvandring till Nordamerika 1820–1850', *Personhistorisk tidskrift* (Stockholm) 1974, 18–35.

Furuland, Lars, 'The Swedish-American Press as a Literary Institution of the Immigrants', in Harald Runblom & Dag Blanck, *Scandinavia Overseas Patterns of Cultural Transformation.* Uppsala: Centre for Multiethnic Research, 1986.

Gelberg, Birgit, *Auswanderung nach Übersee: Soziale Probleme der Auswandererbeförderung in Hamburg und Bremen von der Mitte des 14. Jahrhunderts bis zum ersten Weltkrieg.* (Beiträge zur Geschichte Hamburgs, Volume 10.) Hamburg: Christians, 1973.

Gerson, Louis L., *The Hyphenate in Recent American Politics and Diplomacy.* Lawrence: Univ. of Kansas Press, 1964.

Gjerde, Jon, *From Peasants to Farmers: The Migration from Balestrand, Norway, to the Upper Middle West.* Cambridge: Cambridge Univ. Press, 1985.

Glasrud, Clarence A., *Hjalmar Hjort Boyesen.* Northfield: NAHA, 1963.

Gordon, Milton M., *Assimilation in American Life: The Role of Race, Religion, and National Origins.* New York: Oxford Univ. Press, 1964.

Greene, Victor, 'Ethnic Confrontations with State Universites, 1860–1920', in Bernard J. Weiss, *American Education and the European Immigrant, 1840–1940.* Urbana: Univ. of Illinois Press, 1982.

Greene, Victor, 'Swedish-American Identity: A Dilemma Resolved', in Odd S. Lovoll, ed., *Scandinavians and Other Immigrants in Urban America: The Proceedings of a Research Conference, October 26–27, 1984,* 123–140. Northfield: Saint Olaf College Press, 1985.

Gunnlaugsson, Gísli Á., 'Millithinganefndin i fátaekramálum 1902–1905: Thróun framfaerslumála 1870–1907', *Saga* XVI, (1978).

Gunnlaugsson, Gísli Á., 'The Poor Laws and the Family in 19th Century Iceland'. Uppsala: History Dept., unpublished paper, 1984.

Gunnlaugsson, Gísli Á., Population Change and the Family in Iceland 1801–1930. Uppsala: History Dept., unpublished paper, 1985.

Gunnlaugsson, Gísli Á., 'Den isländska familjen 1801–1930', in *Mødeberetning: Rapporter til den XIX nordiske historikerkongress,* bind III (Familjen i forandring i 18- og 1900-tallet), 12–31. Odense, 1986.

Gvåle, Gudrun Hovde, *O. E. Rølvaag, nordmann og amerikanar.* Oslo: Universitetsforlaget, 1963.

Hägerstrand, Torsten, *Innovationsförloppet ur korologisk synpunt.* Lund, 1953.

Hamberg, Eva, 'En jämförande undersökning av jordbruk'. *Statistisk tidskrift* (1969:6), 456–477.

Handlin, Oscar, *The Uprooted: The Epic Story of the Great Migrations That Made the American People.* Boston: Little, Brown & Company, 1951.

Handlin, Oscar, *Immigration as a Factor in American History.* 1959.

Hansen, Marcus Lee, *The Immigrant in American History.* New York: Harper Torchbooks, 1964.

Hansen, Marcus Lee, *The Problem of the Third Generation Immigrant.* Rock Island: Augustana Historical Society, 1938.

Hansen, Svend Aage, *Økonomisk vækst i Danmark, bind 1, 1720–1914.* København, 1972.

Harney, Robert F., *Dalla Frontiera alle Little Italies: Gli Italiani in Canada 1800–1945.* Roma: Bonacci, 1984.

Harzig, Christiane & Hoerder, Dirk, *The Press of Labor Migrants in Europe and North America, 1880s to 1930s.* Bremen: Labor Migration Project, 1985.

Hasselmo, Nils, *Amerikasvenska: En bok om språkutvecklingen i Svensk-Amerika.* Lund: Esselte Studium, 1974.

Hasselmo, Nils, 'De nordiska språkens situation i Nordamerika', in Bengt Sigurd, ed., *De nordiska språkens framtid: Bidrag vid en konferens,* 103–131. Stockholm: Esselte Studium, 1977.

Hasselmo, Nils, 'The Language Question', in Nils Hasselmo, ed., *Perspectives on Swedish Immigration: Proceedings of the International Conference on the Swedish Heritage in the Upper Midwest, April 1–3, 1976, University of Minnesota, Duluth,* 225–243. Chicago: Swedish Pioneer Historical Society, 1978.

Hauge, Alfred, *Cleng Peerson.* Oslo, 1961.

Haugen, Einar, *The Norwegian Language in America.* 2 vols. Philadelphia: Univ. of Pennsylvania Press, 1953.

Haugen, Einar, *Riksspråk og folkemål: Norsk språkpolitikk i det 20. århundre.* Oslo: Universitetsforlaget, 1966.

Haugen, Einar, 'Svensker og nordmenn i Amerika: En studie i nordisk etnisitet', *Saga och Sed, Kungl. Gustav Adolfs Akademiens årsbok* 1976, 38–55.

313

Haugen, Einar, 'Immigrant Language as an Index of Social Integration', Ingrid Semmingsen & Per Seyersted, eds., *Scando-Americana: Papers on Scandinavian Emigration to the United States, 182–201*. Oslo: American Institute, 1980.

Haugen, Einar, *Ole Edvart Rølvaag*. Boston: Twayne, 1983.

Hedblom, Folke, 'Svenska dialekter i Amerika: Några erfarenheter och problem', *Annales Societatis Litterarum Humaniorum Regiae Upsaliensis, Årsbok 1973–1974*, 34–62.

Hedblom, Folke, *Svensk-Amerika berättar*. Stockholm: Gidlunds, 1982.

Hegstad, Patsy A., 'Citizenship, Voting, and Immigrants: A Comparative Study of the Naturalization Propensity and Voter Registration of Nordics in Seattle and Ballard, Washington, 1892–1900'. Seattle: Univ. of Washington, Ph.D. diss., 1982.

Higham, John, *Strangers in the Land: Patterns of American Nativism, 1860–1925*. New York: Atheneum, 1974.

Higham, John, ed., *Ethnic Leadership in America*. Baltimore: John Hopkins Univ. Press, 1978.

Hildebrand, Ingegerd, *Den svenska kolonin St. Barthélemy och Västindiska kompaniet*. Lund 1951.

Hodne, Fritz, *Norges ökonomiske historie 1815–1970*. Oslo, 1981.

Hodne, Kåre Oddleif, 'Fra Agder til Amsterdam. En studie av norsk emigrasjon til Nederland i tiden ca. 1625–1800'. Oslo: Oslo Univ., unpublished thesis, 1976.

Hoerder, Dirk, ed., *Labor Migration in the Atlantic Economies: The European and North American Working Classes During the Period of Industrialization*. Westport & London: Greenwood, 1985.

Hoerder, Dirk, *'Why Did You Come?' The Proletarian Mass Migration: Research Report 1980–1985*. Bremen: Labor Migration Project, 1986.

Hoerder, Dirk, ed., *'Struggle a Hard Battle': Essays on Working-Class Immigrants*. DeKalb, Ill.: Northern Illinois Univ. Press, 1986.

Hoglund, A. William, *Finnish Immigrants in America, 1880–1920*. Madison: Wisconsin Univ. Press, 1960.

Hoglund, A. William, 'No Land for Finns: Critics and Reformers View the Rural Exodus from Finland to America Between the 1800's and World War I', in Michael G. Karni, Matti E. Kaups & Douglas J. Ollila Jr., eds., *The Finnish Experience in the Western Great Lakes Region: New Perspectives*, 36–54. Turku: Migration Institute, 1975.

Hoglund, A. William, 'Breaking With the Religious Tradition: Finnish Immigrant Workers and the Church, 1890–1915', in *For The Common Good: Finnish Immigrants and the Radical Response to Industrial America*, 23–64. Superior: Tyomies Society, 1977.

Hoglund, A. William, 'Flight from Industry: Finns and Farming in America', *Finnish Americana* 1 (1978), 1–21.

Höjfors Hong, Margot, *Ölänningar över haven: Utvandring från Öland 1840–1930. Bakgrund, förlopp, effekter*. Uppsala: Acta Universitatis Upsaliensis, 1986.

Hokanson, Nels, *Swedish Immigrants in Lincoln's Time*. New York: Harper & Brothers, 1942.

Hollingsworth, Rogers J. & Ellen Jane Hollingsworth, *Dimensions in Urban History: Historical and Social Science Perspectives on Middle-Size American Cities*. Madison: Univ. of Wisconsin Press, 1979.

Holmberg, Inga, 'Svenskar i Jamestown, N.Y. Etnisk politisk mobilisering som denna kommer till uttryck i den lokala svenskspråkiga pressen'. Lund: Dept. of History, unpublished paper, 1985.

Hudson, John, 'Migration to an American Frontier', *Annals of the Association of American Geographers*, 66:2 (1976), 242–265.

Hummasti, Paul George, *Finnish Radicals in Astoria, Oregon, 1914–1940: A Study in Immigrant Socialism*. New York: Arno, 1979.

Hutchinson, E. P., *Immigrants and Their Children, 1850–1950.* New York: Wiley, 1956.

Hvidt, Kristian, *Flugten til Amerika eller Drivekræfter i masseutvandringen fra Danmark 1868–1914.* Odense, 1971.

Hvidt, Kristian, 'Informationsspredning og emigration med særligt henblik på det atlantiske transportsystem', in *Emigrationen fra Norden indtil 1. Verdenskrig: Rapporter til det Nordiske historikermøde i København 1971,* 129–158. Copenhagen, 1971.

Hvidt, Kristian, *Flight to America: The Social Background of 300,000 Danish Emigrants.* New York: Academic Press, 1975.

Hvidt, Kristian, *Danske veje vestpå. En bog om udvandringen til Amerika.* Copenhagen, 1976.

Hvidt, Kristian, 'Emigrant Agents: The Development of a Business and its Methods', *Scandinavian Journal of History* 3 (1978), 179–203.

Isaksson, Olov & Hallgren, Sören, *Bishop Hill: A Utopia on the Prairie.* Stockholm, 1969.

Jansson, Torkel, *Samhällsförändring och sammanslutningsformer: Det frivilliga föreningsväsendets uppkomst och spridning i Husby-Rekarne från omkring 1850 till 1930.* Uppsala: Acta Universitatis Upsaliensis, 1982.

Jerome, H., *Migration and Business Cycles.* New York: National Bureau of Economic Research, 1926.

Johannisson, Karin, 'Society in Numbers: Statistics in 18th Century England, Germany and Sweden', in T. Frängsmyr & J. Heilbron, eds., *The Quantifying Spirit in 18th Century Thought* (preliminary title, forthcoming).

Johansen, Hans Chr., *En samfundsorganisation i opbrud 1700–1870.* (Dansk social historie 4). Copenhagen, 1979.

Johansson, Anders, *Amerika: Dröm eller mardröm?* Stockholm: LT, 1985.

Johnson, Gustav E., 'The Swedes of Chicago'. Univ. of Chicago, Ph.D. dissertation, 1940.

Jonassen, Christen T., *Value Systems and Personality in a Western Civilization: Norwegians in Europe and America.* Columbus: Ohio State Univ. Press, 1983.

Jonassen, Christen T., 'Macro and Micro Ecological Factors in the Founding and Evolution of an Urban Norwegian Immigrant Community', in Odd S. Lovoll, ed., *Scandinavians and Other Immigrants in Urban America: The Proceedings of a Research Conference, October 26–27, 1984,* 75–90. Northfield: Saint Olaf College Press, 1985.

Jörberg, Lennart, 'The Industrial Revolution in the Nordic Countries: A Survey of Economic Developments' in Carlo H. Cipolla, *The Fontana Economic History of Europe,* vol. 4 (2), 375–485. Glasgow: Fontana/Collins, 1979.

Jungar, Sune, *Från Åbo till Ryssland. En studie i urban befolkningsrörlighet 1850–1890.* Turku: Acta Academiae Aboensis, A 47:3, 1974.

Jutikkala, Eino, *Bonden i Finland genom tiderna.* Stockholm, LT:s förlag, 1963.

Jutikkala, Eino, *Finlands historia.* Stockholm: Natur och kultur, 1965.

Jutikkala, Eino & Kauppinen, M., 'The Structure of Mortality During Catastrophic Years in a Pre-Industrial Society', *Population Studies* 25 (1971), 283–285.

Kälvemark, Ann-Sofie, *Reaktionen mot utvandringen: Emigrationsfrågan i svensk debatt och politik, 1901–1904.* Uppsala: Acta Universitatis Upsaliensis, 1972.

Kälvemark, Ann-Sofie, 'Swedish Emigration Policy in an International Perspective, 1840–1925', in Harald Runblom & Hans Norman, eds., *From Sweden to America: A History of the Migration,* 94–113. Minneapolis & Uppsala: Acta Universitatis Upsaliensis & University of Minnesota Press, 1976.

Kälvemark, Ann-Sofie, 'Fear of Military Service – A Cause of Emigration?' in Harald Runblom & Hans Norman, eds., *From Sweden to America: A History of the Migration,* 164–171. Minneapolis & Uppsala: Acta Universitatis Upsaliensis & University of Minnesota Press, 1976.

315

Kälvemark, Ann-Sofie, 'Utvandring och självständighet. Några synpunkter på den kvinnliga emigrationen från Sverige', *Historisk tidskrift* (Stockholm 1983:2), 140–174.

Kant, Edgar, 'Den inre omflyttningen i Estland', *Svensk Geografisk Årsbok*, 1946.

Karni, Michael G., 'The Founding of the Finnish Socialist Federation and the Minnesota Strike of 1907', in *For The Common Good: Finnish Immigrants and the Radical Response to Industrial America*, 65–86. Superior: Tyomies Society, 1977.

Karni, Michael G., ed., *Finnish Diaspora, 2 vols.; I: Canada, South America, Africa, Australia and Sweden; II: United States*. Toronto: Multicultural History Society of Ontario, 1981.

Karni, Michael G., 'Finnish Temperance and its Clash with Emerging Socialism in Minnesota', in Michael G. Karni, ed., *Finnish Diaspora II*, 163–174. Toronto, 1981.

Karni, Michael G., Matti E. Kaups & Douglas J. Ollila Jr., eds., *The Finnish Experience in the Western Great Lakes Region: New Perspectives*. Turku: Migration Institute, 1975.

Kaups, Matti E., 'The Finns in the Copper and Iron Ore Mines of the Western Great Lakes Region, 1864–1905: Some Preliminary Observations', in Michael G. Karni, Matti E. Kaups & Douglas J. Ollila Jr., eds., *The Finnish Experience in the Western Great Lakes Region: New Perspectives*, 55–88. Turku: Migration Institute, 1975.

Kaups, Matti, 'Swedish Immigrants in Duluth, 1856–1870', in Nils Hasselmo, ed., *Perspectives on Swedish Immigration: Proceedings of the International Conference on the Swedish Heritage in the Upper Midwest, April 1–3, 1976, University of Minnesota, Duluth*, 166–198. Chicago: Swedish Pioneer Historical Society, 1978.

Kaups, Matti, 'Finns in Urban America: A View from Duluth', in Michael G. Karni, ed., *Finnish Diaspora II*, 63–86. Toronto, 1981.

Keil, Hartmut & John B. Jentz, eds., *German Workers in Industrial Chicago, 1850–1910*. DeKalb: Northern Illinois Univ. Press, 1983.

Kero, Reino, *Migration from Finland to North America in the Years between the United States Civil War and the First World War*. Turku: Annales Universitatis Turkuensis, 1974.

Kero, Reino, 'Emigration of Finns from North America to Soviet Karelia in the Early 1930's', in Michael G. Karni, Matti E. Kaups & Douglas J. Ollila Jr., eds., *The Finnish Experience in the Western Great Lakes Region: New Perspectives*, 212–221. Turku: Migration Institute, 1975.

Kero, Reino, *Population Movements in Toholampi during the Years 1870–1889*. Turku, 1976.

Kero, Reino, *The Finns in North America: Destinations and Composition of Immigrant Societies in North America before World War I*. Turku: Annales Universitatis Turkuensis, 1980.

Kero, Reino, 'The Canadian Finns in Soviet Karelia in the 1930s', in Michael G. Karni, ed., *Finnish Diaspora I*, 203–214. Toronto, 1981.

Kero, Reino, *Neuvosto-Karjalaa Rakentamassa. Pohjois-Amerikan suomalaiset tekniikan tuojina 1930-luvun Neuvosto-Karjalassa*. Helsinki: Societas Historica Finlandiae, 1983.

Kivisto, Peter, *Immigrant Socialists in the United States: The Case of Finns and the Left*. London & Toronto: Associated University Presses, 1984.

Kjartansson, Helgi Skúli, 'The Onset of Emigration from Iceland', in Bo Kronborg, Thomas Nilsson & Andres Svalestuen, eds., *Nordic Population Mobility: Comparative Studies of Selected Parishes in the Nordic Countries, 1850–1900*, 87–94. Oslo: Universitetsforlaget, 1977.

Kjartansson, Helgi Skúli, 'Emigrant Fares and Emigration from Iceland to North America, 1874–1893', *The Scandinavian Economic History Review* (1980:1), 53–71.

Klehr, Harvey, 'Immigrant Leadership in the Communist Party of the United States of America', *Ethnicity* 6 (1979), 29–44.

Kolehmainen, John I., *The Finns in America: A Bibliographical Guide to Their History*. Hancock, Michigan, 1947.

Koht, Halvdan, *Amerika i Europa: Impulser från väster i teknik, politik, kultur*. Stockholm: Natur och kultur, 1950.

Koivukangas, Olavi, *Scandinavian Immigration and Settlement in Australia before World War II*. Turku: Migration Institute, 1974.

Koivukangas, Olavi, *Suomalainen siirtulaisuus. Australiaantoisen maailmansodan jälkeen*. Turku: Institute of Migration, 1975.

Koivukangas, Olavi, ed., *Scandinavian Emigration to Australia and New Zealand Project: Proceedings of a Symposium, February 17–19, 1982*. Turku: Institute of Migration, 1983.

Koivukangas, Olavi, *Sea, Gold & Sugarcane: Attraction Versus Distance: Finns in Australia, 1851–1947*. Turku: Institute of Migration, 1986.

Koivukangas, Olavi & John S. Martin, *The Scandinavians in Australia*. Melbourne: A. E. Press, 1986.

Koren, Elisabeth, 'Utvandringen fra Ullensaker 1867–1899'. Unprinted thesis. Oslo: Oslo University, 1976.

Kostiainen, Auvo, 'The Tragic Crisis: Finnish-American Workers and the Civil War in Finland', in *For the Common Good: Finnish Immigrants and the Radical Response to Industrial America*, 217–235. Superior: Tyomies Society, 1977.

Kostiainen, Auvo, *The Forging of Finnish-American Communism, 1917–1924: A Study of Ethnic Radicalism*. Turku: The Migration Institute, 1978.

Kostiainen, Auvo, 'For or Against Americanization? The Case of the Finnish Immigrant Radicals', in Dirk Hoerder, ed., *Labor Migration in the Atlantic Economies: The European and North American Working Classes During the Period of Industrialization*, 259–275. Westport & London: Greenwood, 1985.

Kostiainen, Auvo, *Dominating Finnish Minority? On the Background of the Nationality Problem in Soviet Karelia in the 1930's*. Oulu: Oulun Yliopisto, 1985.

Kristjánsson, Júníus H., *Emigration from Vöpnafjördur, 1873–93*. Reykjavik 1973.

Kristjánsson, Júníus H., *Vesturfaraskrá 1870–1914: A Record of Emigrants from Iceland to America 1870–1914*. Reykjavik, 1983.

Kristjanson, W., *The Icelandic People of Manitoba: A Manitoba Saga*. Winnipeg: Wallingford Press, 1965.

Kronborg, Bo & Thomas Nilsson, *Stadsflyttare. Industrialisering, migration och social mobilitet med utgångspunkt från Halmstad 1870–1910*. Uppsala: Acta Universitatis Upsaliensis, 1975.

Kronborg, Bo, Thomas Nilsson & Andres Svalestuen, eds., *Nordic Population Mobility: Comparative Studies of Selected Parishes in the Nordic Countries, 1850–1900*. Oslo: Universitetsforlaget, 1977.

Krontoft, Torben, 'Factors in Assimilation: A Comparative Study', *Norwegian-American Studies* 26, (1974), 184–205.

Lagerstedt, Sven, *Drömmaren från Norrtullsgatan. En studie i Henning Bergers liv och författarskap*. Stockholm, 1963.

Lähteenmäki, Olavi, 'Finnish Group Immigration to Latin America', in Michael G. Karni, ed., *Finnish Diaspora* I, 289–302. Toronto, 1981.

Laine, Edward W., 'Community in Crisis: The Finnish-Canadian Quest for Cultural Identity, 1900–1979' in Michael G. Karni, ed., *Finnish Diaspora* I, 1–10. Toronto, 1981.

Larsen, Emil, *Urovaekkeren Mogens Abraham Sommer*. Kirkehistoriske studier, 2, raekke, nr. 17, 1963.

Larsen, Ulla Margrethe, 'A Quantitative Study of Emigration from Denmark to the United States, 1870–1913', *Scandinavian Economic History Review* 30 (1982), 101–128.

Larson, Bruce L., 'Swedish-Americans and Farmer-Labor Politics in Minnesota', in Nils Hasselmo, ed., *Perspectives on Swedish Immigration: Proceedings of the International Conference on the Swedish Heritage in the Upper Midwest, April 1–3, 1976, University of Minnesota, Duluth,* 206–224. Chicago: Swedish Pioneer Historical Society, 1978.

Larsson, Lars Olof, *Kolonisation och befolkningsutveckling i det svenska agrarsamhället 1500–1640.* Lund: Bibliotheca Historica Lundensis, 1972.

Larsson, Lars-Olof, 'Utvandring från södra Småland fram till 1870', in Ulf Beijbom, ed., *Utvandring från Konoberg: En temabok. Kronobergsboken* (Växjö) 1978, 133–204.

Lext, Gösta, *Studier rörande svensk emigration till Nordamerika 1850–1880. Registrering, propaganda, agenter, transporter och resvägar.* Göteborg: Landsarkivet i Göteborg, 1977.

Lindén, Ingemar, *Biblicism, apokalyptik, utopi. Adventismens historiska utformning i USA samt dess svenska utveckling.* Uppsala: Acta Universitatis Upsaliensis, 1971.

Lindmark, Sture, *Swedish America, 1914–1932: Studies in Ethnicity with Emphasis on Illinois and Minnesota.* Uppsala: Studia Historica Upsaliensis, 1971.

Lindquist, Emory, *Bethany in Kansas: History of the College.* Lindsborg: Bethany College, 1975.

Lindstrom-Best, Varpu, 'Finns in Canada', *Polyphony* (Toronto) 3:2 (Fall 1981), 3–15.

Lindstrom-Best, Varpu, 'I Won't Be a Slave: Finnish Domestics in Canada, 1911–30', in Jean Burnet, ed., *Looking into My Sister's Eyes: An Exploration in Women's History.* Toronto: Multicultural History Society, 1986.

Ljungmark, Lars, *Den stora utvandringen: Svensk emigration till USA, 1840–1925.* Stockholm: Sveriges Radio, 1965.

Ljungmark, Lars, *For Sale Minnesota: Organized Promotion of Scandinavian Immigration, 1866–1973.* Göteborg: Studia Historica Gothoburgensia, 1971.

Ljungmark, Lars, *Swedish Exodus.* Chicago: Swedish Pioneer Historical Society, 1979.

Loukinen, Michael, 'Second Generation Finnish-American Migration from the Northwoods to Detroit, 1920–1950', in Michael G. Karni, ed., *Finnish Diaspora* II, 107–126. Toronto, 1981.

Lovoll, Odd S., *Det löfterike landet.* Oslo: Universitetsforlaget, 1983.

Lovoll, Odd S., *A Folk Epic: The Bygdelag in America.* Northfield, Minnesota: NAHA, 1975.

Lovoll, Odd S., ed. *Scandinavians and Other Immigrants in Urban America: The Proceedings of a Research Conference, October 26–27, 1984.* Northfield, Minnesota: Saint Olaf Press, 1985.

Lucas, Richard B., *Charles August Lindbergh, Sr.: A Case Study of Congressional Insurgency, 1906–1912.* Uppsala: Acta Universitatis Upsaliensis, 1974.

Luebke, Frederick C., *Immigrants and Politics: The Germans of Nebraska, 1880–1900.* Lincoln: Univ. of Nebraska Press, 1969.

Luebke, Frederick C., 'Legal Restrictions on Foreign Languages in the Great Plains States, 1917–1923', in Paul Schach, ed., *Languages in Conflict: Linguistic Acculturation on the Great Plains,* 1–19. Lincoln and London: Univ. of Nebraska Press, 1980.

Lundkvist, Sven, 'Rörlighet och social struktur i 1610-talets Sverige', *Historisk Tidskrift* (Stockholm, 1974), 192–258.

Lundkvist, Sven, *Folkrörelserna i det svenska samhället 1850–1920.* Uppsala: Acta Universitatis Upsaliensis, 1977.

MacCracken, Jane W., *Stephan G. Stephansson: A Poet of the Rocky Mountains.* Sine locu: Alberta Culture, Historical Resources Division, Occasional Papers, No. 9, 1982.

Mannsåker, Jørund, *Emigrasjon og dikting: Utvandringa till Nord-Amerika i norsk skjönnlitteratur.* Oslo, 1971.

Martinius, Sture, *Befolkningsrörlighet under industrialismens inledningsskede i Sverige.* Göteborg: Meddelanden från Ekonomisk-historiska institutionen, 1967.

Marzolf, Marion T., *The Danish-Language Press in America.* New York: Arno, 1979.

Matthiasson, John, 'The Icelandic Canadians: The Paradox of an Assimilated Ethnic Group', in Jean Leonard Elliott, ed., *Two Nations, Many Cultures: Ethnic Groups in Canada,* 195–205. Scarborough: Prentice-Hall of Canada, 1979.

Måwe, Carl-Erik, *Värmlänningar i Nordamerika: Sociologiska studier i en anpassningsproccess: Med särskild hänsyn till emigrationen från Östmark.* Säffle, Sweden, 1971.

McQuillan, D. Adian, 'Territory and Ethnic Identity: Some New Measures of an Old Theme in the Cultural Geography of the United States', in James R. Gibson, ed., *European Settlement and Development in North America: Essays on Geographical Change in Honour and Memory of Andrew Hill Clark,* 136–169. Toronto: Univ. of Toronto Press, 1978.

Moberg, Vilhelm, *Utvandrarna.* Stockholm: Bonniers, 1949.

Moberg, Vilhelm, *Invandrarna.* Stockholm: Bonniers, 1952.

Moberg, Wilhelm, *Nybyggarna.* Stockholm: Bonniers, 1956.

Moberg, Wilhelm, *Sista brevet till Sverige.* Stockholm: Bonniers, 1959.

Moe, Thorvald, 'Demographic Developments and Economic Growth in Norway, 1740–1940: An Econometric Study'. Stanford Univ.: Ph.D. dissertation, 1970.

Moltmann, Günther, 'Auswanderung als Revolutionsersatz', in Michael Salewski, ed., *Die Deutschen und die Revolution,* 272–279. Göttingen, 1984.

Moltmann, Günther, 'Transportation of Immigrants from Europe to the United States, 1850–1914: Social, Commercial and Legal Aspects'. (Paper presented at the Congress of Historical Sciences, Stuttgart, 1985).

Mörner, Magnus, *Adventurers and Proletarians: The Story of Migrants in Latin America.* Paris, 1985.

Mossberg, Christer Lennart, *Scandinavian Immigrant Literature.* Boise: Boise State Univ., 1981.

Mulder, William, *Homeward to Zion: The Mormon Migration from Scandinavia.* Minneapolis: Univ. of Minnesota Press, 1957.

Munch, Peter A., 'Segregation and Assimilation of Norwegian Settlements in Wisconsin', *Norwegian-American Studies* 18, (1954), 102–140.

Munch, Peter A., 'Norwegians', in Thernstrom, Stephan, ed., *Harvard Encyclopedia of American Ethnic Groups,* 750–761. Cambridge: Belknap Press, 1980.

Myhrman, Anders, *Finlandssvenskar i Amerika.* Helsingfors: Svenska Litteratursällskapet, 1972.

Mykland, Knut, 'Gjennom Nödsår og krig 1648–1720', in *Norges Historie* 7 (Oslo, 1977), 1–447.

Mykland, Knut ed., 'Historisk atlas', *Norges Historie* 15 (Oslo, 1979).

Naess, Harald S., ed., *Norwegian Influence in the Upper Midwest.* Duluth: Univ. of Minnesota, 1976.

Nelli, Humbert S., *From Immigrants to Ethnics: The Italian Americans.* Oxford: Oxford Univ. Press, 1983.

Nelson, Helge, *The Swedes and the Swedish Settlements in North America.* 2 vols., Lund, 1943.

Nelson, Helge, *Studier över svenskt näringsliv, säsongarbete och befolkningsrörelser under 1800- och 1900-talen.* Lund: Kungl. Humanistiska Vetenskapssamfundet, 1963.

Niemi, Einar, 'Trekk fra Nord-Norges historie til og med 2. Verdenskrig', in Einar Niemi et al., *Trekk fra Nord-Norges historie.* Oslo: Gyldendal, 1978.

Nielsen, George R., *The Danish Americans.* Boston: Twayne, 1981.

319

Nilsson, Fred, *Emigrationen från Stockholm till Nordamerika, 1880–1893: En studie i urban utvandring*. Uppsala: Studia Historica Upsaliensia, 1970.

Nilsson, Runo, *Rallareliv: Arbete, familjemönster och levnadsförhållanden för järnvägsarbetare på banbyggena i Jämtland – Härjedalen, 1921–1928*. Uppsala: Acta Universitatis Upsaliensis, 1982.

Nilsson, Sven A., 'Krig och folkbokföring under svenskt 1600-tal', *Scandia* (1982:1), 5–29.

Norberg, Anders, *Sågarnas ö. Alnö under industrialiseringen 1860–1910*. Uppsala: Acta Universitatis Upsaliensis, 1980.

Nordahl, Per, 'Svensk-amerikansk arbetarrörelse. En organisations- och pressstudie'. Unpublished paper, History Department, Umeå University, 1985.

Nordahl, Per, *De sålde sina penslar. Om några svenska målare som emigrerade till Amerika*. Stockholm: Tiden, 1987.

Nordstrom, Byron J., 'Ethnicity and Community in the Sixth Ward of Minneapolis in 1910', in Odd S. Lovoll, ed., *Scandinavians and Other Immigrants in Urban America: The Proceedings of a Research Conference, October 26–27, 1984*, 33–53. Northfield: Saint Olaf College Press, 1985.

Nordvik, Helge, 'Emigrants and Timber: Norwegian Shipping to Quebec, 1880–1875'. (Commentary paper presented on the session on Maritime Aspects of Migration at the Congress of Historical Sciences, Stuttgart, 1985).

Nordqvist, Kjell, 'När Karlskoga-borna fick Amerika-feber', *Emigranten* (1969:2, 3, 4).

Norman, Hans, *Från Bergslagen till Nordamerika: Studier i migrationsmönster, social rörlighet och demografisk struktur med utgångspunkt från Örebro län, 1851–1915*. Uppsala: Acta Universitatis Upsaliensis, 1974.

Norman, Hans, 'Causes of Emigration: An Attempt at Multivariate Analysis', in Harald Runblom & Hans Norman, ed., *From Sweden to America: A History of the Migration*, 149–163. Minneapolis & Uppsala: Acta Universitatis Upsaliensis & University of Minnesota Press, 1976.

Norman, Hans, 'Swedes in North America', in Harald Runblom & Hans Norman, eds., *From Sweden to America: A History of the Migration*, 228–290. Minneapolis & Uppsala: Acta Universitatis Upsaliensis & University of Minnesota Press, 1976.

Norman, Hans, 'Swedish Communities in Wisconsin', in Nils Hasselmo, ed., *Perspectives on Swedish Immigration: Proceedings of the International Conference on the Swedish Heritage in the Upper Midwest, April 1–3, 1976, University of Minnesota, Duluth*, 120–135. Chicago: Swedish Pioneer Historical Society, 1978.

Norman, Hans, 'Stor rörlighet – liten förändring. Livet i den agrara köpstaden Örebro årtiondena runt 1800', in Hans Norman, ed., *Den utsatta familjen. Liv, arbete och samlevnad i olika nordiska miljöer under de senaste två hundra åren*. Gävle: Cikada, 1983.

Norman, Hans, 'Svält och epedimier. Krisåren 1773 och 1808–1811 i Örebro, Stora Mellösa och Hällefors. Omfattning, dödsorsaker och demografiska följder', *Bebyggelsehistorisk tidskrift* (1983:5).

Norman, Hans & Harald Runblom, *Amerikaemigrationen i Källornas belysning*. Stockholm: LTs förlag, 1980.

Norman, Hans & Harald Runblom, eds., *Nordisk Emigrationsatlas*. 2 vols. Gävle: Cikada, 1980.

Norman, Hans & Harald Runblom, 'Migration Patterns in the Nordic Countries', in Dirk Hoerder, ed., *Labor Migration in the Atlantic Economies: The European and North American Working Classes During the Period of Industrialization*, 35–68. Westport & London: Greenwood, 1985.

Nörregaard, Georg, *Guldkysten. De gamle danske establissementer på guldkysten*. (Vore gamle tropekolonier, vol. 8). Copenhagen, 1953.

Novaky, György, 'Kompaniet och staten. Statens roll för handelskapitalet belyst genom Svenska Afrikanska Kompaniet'. (Uppsala: History Dept., manuscript, 1985).

Nyberg, Janet, 'Swedish Language Newspapers in Minnesota', in Nils Hasselmo, ed., *Perspectives on Swedish Immigration: Proceedings of the International Conference on the Swedish Heritage in the Upper Midwest, April 1–3, 1976, University of Minnesota, Duluth,* 244–255. Chicago: Swedish Pioneer Historical Society, 1978.

Odén, Birgitta, 'Emigrationen från Norden till Nordamerika under 1800-talet', *Historisk tidskrift* (Stockholm, 1963), 261–277.

Odén, Birgitta, 'Ekonomiska emigrationsmodeller och historisk forskning: Ett diskussionsinlägg', *Scandia* (1971:1), 1–70.

Öhngren, Bo, 'Urbaniseringen i Sverige 1840–1920', in Grete Authén Blom, ed., *Urbaniseringsprocessen i Norden. Del 3: Industrialiseringens förste fase,* 261–356. Trondheim: Det XVII nordiske historikermöde, 1977.

Ollila, Jr., Douglas J., 'The Work People's College: Immigrant Education for Adjustment and Solidarity', in *For the Common Good: Finnish Immigrants and the Radical Response to Industrial America,* 87–118. Superior: Tyomies Society, 1977.

Olsen, Gunnar, *Dansk Ostindien 1616–1732. Det Ostindiske kompagnis handel på Indien.* (Vore gamle tropekolonier, vol. 5). Copenhagen, 1953.

Olson, James Stuart, *The Ethnic Dimension in American History.* New York: St. Martin's, 1979.

Olsson, Karl A., *By One Spirit: A History of the Evangelical Convenant Church of America.* Chicago, 1962.

Olsson, Karl A., 'Kontinuitet och förvandling inom svenska immigrantsamfund i USA', *Kyrkohistorisk årsskrift* (1982), 11–25.

Olsson, Nils William, *Swedish Passenger Arrivals in New York, 1820–1850.* Stockholm: Norstedts, 1967.

Olsson, Nils William, *Swedish Passenger Arrivals in U.S. Ports 1820–1850 (except New York).* St. Paul, Minn.: North Central Publishing Co., 1979.

Ordahl, Sverre, 'Emigration from Agder to America, 1890–1915', *Norwegian-American Studies* 29, (1983), 313–338.

Östberg, K., *Finnskogene i Norge.* Grue, Norway, 1978.

Österberg, Eva, 'Bofasta och flyttare i äldre vasatidens bondesamhälle', in *Historia och samhälle. Studier tillägnade Jerker Rosén,* 68–94. Lund, 1975.

Ostergren, Robert C., 'Rättvik to Isanti: A Community Transplanted'. Ph.D. dissertation, University of Minnesota, 1976.

Ostergren, Robert C., 'Prairie Bound: Migration Patterns to a Swedish Settlement on the Dakota Frontier', in Frederick C. Luebke, ed., *Ethnicity on the Great Plains,* 73–91. Lincoln: Nebraska Univ. Press, 1980.

Ostergren, Robert C., 'Land and Family in Rural Immigrant Communities', *Annals of the Association of American Geographers* 71 (1981), 400–411.

Øverland, Orm, 'Ole Edvart Rølvaag and Giants in the Earth: A Writer between two Countries', *American Studies in Scandinavia* 13 (1981), 35–45.

Paasivirta, Juhani, *USA ser på Finland: En liten nations problem i internationell politik.* Ekenäs, 1966.

Palmer, Howard, *Land of the Second Chance: A History of Ethnic Groups in Southern Alberta.* Lethbridge: Lethbridge Herald, 1972.

Paloposki, Toivo J., 'Utvandringen från Finland till Sverige från Gustav Vasas tid fram till Finska kriget', in Olavi Koivukangas, ed., *Utvandringen från Finland till Sverige genom tiderna,* 27–44. Turku, 1980.

Palmqvist, Lena A:son, *Building Traditions among Swedish Settlers in Rural Minnesota: Material Culture Reflecting Persistence or Decline of Traditions.* Stockholm & Växjö: Nordiska museet and Emigrantinstitutet, 1983.

Pálsson, Hjörtur, *Alaskaför Jóns Ólafssonar 1874.* Reykjavik, 1975.

Passi, Michael M., 'Finnish Immigrants and the Radical Response to Industrial

America', in *For the Common Good: Finnish Immigrants and the Radical Response to Industrial America* 9–22. Superior: Tyomies Society, 1977.

Pearson, Daniel M., *The Americanization of Carl Aaron Swensson*. Rock Island: Augustana Historical Society, 1977.

Pedersen, Erik Helmer, 'Danish Farmers in The Middle West', *The Bridge* (Journal of the Danish American Heritage Society) 8, (1982), 51–68.

Pedersen, Erik Helmer, *Drömmen om Amerika*. Copenhagen: Politikens forlag, 1985.

Pedersen, Erik Helmer, *Pionererne*. Copenhagen: Politikens forlag, 1986.

Pettersson, Birgit, *Den farliga underklassen. Studier i fattigdom och brottslighet i 1800-talets Sverige*. Umeå: Acta Universitatis Umensis, 1983.

Pettersen, Lauritz, 'From Sail to Steam in Norwegian Emigration, 1870–1910'. (Commentary paper presented on the session on Maritime Aspects of Migration at the Congress of Historical Sciences, Stuttgart, 1985).

Pilli, Arja, *The Finnish-Language Press in Canada, 1901–1939: A Study in the History of Ethnic Journalism*. Turku: Institute of Migration, 1982.

Puotinen, Arthur E., 'Early Labor Organizations in the Copper Country', in *For the Common Good: Finnish Immigrants and the Radical Response to Industrial America*, 119–166. Superior: Tyomies Society, 1977.

Puskas, Juliana, *From Hungary to the United States, 1880–1914*. Budapest: Studia Historica Academiae Scientiarum Hungaricae, 1982.

Qualey, Carlton C., *Norwegian Settlement in the United States*. Northfield: NAHA, 1938.

Qualey, Carlton C. & Jon A. Gjerde, 'The Norwegians', in J. D. Holmquist, ed., *They Chose Minnesota: A Survey of the State's Ethnic Groups*, 220–247. St. Paul, Minnesota Historical Society Press.

Regan, Ann, 'The Danes', in J. D. Holmquist, ed., *They Chose Minnesota: A Survey of the State's Ethnic Groups*, 277–289. St. Paul, Minnesota Historical Society Press.

Rice, John G., *Patterns of Ethnicity in a Minnesota County, 1880–1905*. Umeå: (Geographical Reports), 1973.

Rice, John G., 'The Role of Culture and Community in Frontier Prairie Farming', *Journal of Historical Geography* 3:2 (1978), 155–175.

Rice, John G., 'The Swedes', in J. D. Holmquist, ed., *They Chose Minnesota: A Survey of the State's Ethnic Groups*, 248–276. St. Paul: Minnesota Historical Society Press.

Rice, John G., 'Marriage Behavior and the Persistence of Swedish Communities in Rural Minnesota', in Nils Hasselmo, ed., *Perspectives on Swedish Immigration: Proceedings of the International Conference on the Swedish Heritage in the Upper Midwest, April 1–3, 1976, University of Minnesota, Duluth*, 136–150. Chicago: Swedish Pioneer Historical Society, 1978.

Rolén, Mats, *Skogsbygd i omvandling: Studier kring befolkningsutveckling, omflyttning och social rörlighet i Revsunds tingslag, 1820–1977*. Uppsala: Acta Universitatis Upsaliensis, 1979.

Rosander, Göran, *Herrarbete. Dalfolkets säsongvisa arbetsvandringar i jämförande belysning*. Uppsala: Landsmåls- och folkminnesarkivet, 1967.

Rosenzweig, Roy, *Eight Hours for What We Will: Workers and Leisure in an Industrial City, 1870–1920*. Cambridge: Cambridge Univ. Press, 1983.

Ross, Carl, *The Finn Factor in American Labor, Culture and Society*. New York Mills, Minn.: Partha, 1977.

Ross, Carl, 'Finnish American Women in Transition, 1910–1920', in Michael G. Karni, ed., *Finnish Diaspora II*, 239–256. Toronto, 1981.

Runblom, Harald, 'Swedish Emigration to Latin America', in Harald Runblom & Hans Norman, eds., *From Sweden to America: A History of the Migration*, 301–310. Minneapolis & Uppsala: Acta Universitatis Upsaliensis & University of Minnesota Press, 1976.

Runblom, Harald, 'Svenskarna i Canada. En studie i låg etnisk medvetenhet', in Lars-Göran Tedebrand, ed., *Historieforskning på nya vägar. Studier tillägnade Sten Carlsson 17.12.1977*. Lund: Studentlitteratur, 1977.

Runblom, Harald, 'Emigranten och fosterlandet', in *Att vara svensk*. Stockholm: Kungl. Vitterhetsakademien, 1985.

Runblom, Harald, 'United States History in Swedish Research and Teaching', in Lewis Hanke, ed., *Guide to the United States History outside the U.S., 1945–1980*, vol. III, 390–421. New York: Kraus, 1985.

Runeby, Nils, *Den nya världen och den gamla: Amerikabild och emigrationsuppfattning i Sverige, 1820–1860*. Uppsala: Studia Historica Upsaliensia, 1969.

Runeby, Nils, 'Americanism, Taylorism and Social Integration: Action Programmes for Swedish Industry at the Beginning of the Twentieth Century', in Ingrid Semmingsen & Per Seyersted, eds., *Scando-Americana: Papers on Scandinavian Emigration to the United States*, 110–141. Oslo: American Institute, 1980.

Rye, Stephen H., 'Danish American Political Behavior: The Case of Iowa, 1877–1936', *The Bridge* (Journal of the Danish American Heritage Society) 2 (1979), 31–44.

Saarinen, Oiva, 'Geographical Perspectives on Finnish Canadian Immigration and Settlement', *Polyphony* (Toronto) 3:2 (Fall 1981), 16–22.

Sahlman-Karlsson, Siiri, *Specimens of American Finnish: A Field Study of Linguistic Behavior*. Umeå: Almqvist and Wiksell, 1976.

Salisbury, Robert S., 'Swedish-American Historiography and the Question of Americanization', *SPHQ* 24, (1978:2), 117–136.

Schach, Paul, ed., *Languages in Conflict: Linguistic Acculturation on the Great Plains*. Lincoln and London: Univ. of Nebraska Press, 1980.

Scott, Franklin D., 'Literature in Periodicals of Protest of Swedish-America', *SPHQ* (1965:4), 193–215.

Sedgwick, Peter, 'Svensk-amerikansk litteratur. Dess sociala förankring och litterära stagnation'. (Unpublished M. A. thesis 1973. Copy at the Emigrant Institute, Växjö, Sweden).

Seip, Jens Arup, *Utsikt over Norges historie: bind 2: Tidsrommet ca. 1850–1884*. Oslo: Gyldendal, 1981.

Sejersted, Francis, 'Den vansklige frihet 1814–1850', in K. Mykland, ed., *Norges historie, bind 10*. Oslo 1978.

Seljas, Helge, 'Polygamy among the Norwegian Mormons', *Norwegian-American Studies* 27, (1977), 151–162.

Semmingsen, Ingrid, *Veien mot Vest: Utvandringen fra Norge til Amerika, 1825–1865*. Oslo, 1941.

Semmingsen, Ingrid, *Veien mot Vest: Utvandringen fra Norge til Amerika, 1865–1915*. Oslo, 1950.

Semmingsen, Ingrid, [Opening speech to plenum on 'Emigrationen fra Norden indtil første verdenskrig'], in *Beretning fra Det nordiske historiermöde in Köbenhavn 1971*, 37–51. Copenhagen, s.a.

Semmingsen, Ingrid, *Dröm og dåd. Utvandringen til Amerika*. Oslo: Aschehoug, 1975.

Semmingsen, Ingrid, 'Nordisk utvandringsforskning', *Historisk tidsskrift* (Oslo, 1977:2), 141–171. [I. Semmingsen 1977 a].

Semmingsen, Ingrid, 'Origin of Nordic Emigration', Bo Kronborg, Thomas Nilsson & Andres Svalestuen, eds., *Nordic Population Mobility: Comparative Studies of Selected Parishes in the Nordic Countries, 1850–1900*, 9–16. Oslo: Universitetsforlaget. [I. Semmingsen 1977 a.]

Semmingsen, Ingrid & Per Seyersted, eds., *Scando-Americana: Papers on Scandinavian Emigration to the United States*. Oslo: American Institute, 1980.

Seyersted, Per, *From Norwegian Romantic to American Realist: Studies in the Life and Writings of Hjalmar Hjorth Boyesen*. Oslo: Solum, 1984.

Skard, Sigmund, *USA i Norsk historie, 1000–1776–1976*. Oslo: Det Norske Samlaget, 1976.

Skårdal, Dorothy Burton, *The Divided Heart: Scandinavian Immigrant Experience through Literary Sources*. Oslo: Universitetsforlaget, 1974.

Skårdal, Dorothy Burton, 'Scandinavian-American Literature', in Robert J. Di Pietro & Edward Ifkovic, eds., *Ethnic Perspectives in American Literature: Selected Essays on the European Contribution*, 232–365. New York: Modern Language Association of America, 1983.

Skarstedt, Ernst, *Pennfäktare. Svensk-amerikanska författare och tidningsmän*. Stockholm, 1930.

Smith, Gibbs M., *Joe Hill*. Stockholm: Almqvist & Wiksell, 1971.

Smith, Timothy L., 'Religion and Ethnicity in America', *American Historical Review*, 83:5, (Dec. 1978), 1155–1185.

Söderberg, Johan, *Agrar fattigdom i Sydsverige under 1800-talet*. Stockholm, 1978.

Söderberg, Kjell, *Den första massutvandringen: En studie av befolkningsrörlighet och emigration utgående från Alfta socken i Hälsingland 1846–1895*. Umeå: Acta Universitatis Umensis, 1981.

Söderlund, Ernst, *Hantverkarna*, vol. 2. (Den svenska arbetarklassens historia). Stockholm, 1949.

Söderström, Hugo, *Confession and Cooperation: The Policy of the Augustana Synod in Confessional Matters and the Synod's Relations with other Churches up to the Beginning of the Twentieth Century*. Lund: Gleerups, 1973.

Stang, Gudmund, 'La emigración escandinava a la America Latina, 1800–1940', *Jahrbuch für Geschichte von Staat, Wirtschaft und Gesellschaft Lateinamerikas* 13, (1976), 293–330.

Stecher, Marianne T., 'Danish Settlement in Fresno County, California: An Example of Acculturation to a Foreign Environment, 1880–1920', *The Bridge* (Journal of the Danish American Heritage Society) 6, (1981), 8–21.

Stenbeck, Karin, 'Utvandringen från Sverige till Brasilien 1868–1891'. Unpublished licentiate thesis. Uppsala Univ.: History Dept., 1973.

Stephenson, George, *The Religious Aspects of Swedish Immigration: A Study of Immigrant Churches*. Minneapolis: Univ. of Minnesota Press, 1932.

Stephenson, George, *John Lind of Minnesota*. Minneapolis, 1935.

Stilling, Nils Peter, 'Udvandringen fra Fredriksborg amt 1869–1899', *Erhvervshistorisk årbog* (Aarhus 1978), 95–148.

Stockenström, Göran, 'Sociological Aspects of Swedish-American Literature', in Nils Hasselmo, ed., *Perspectives on Swedish Immigration: Proceedings of the International Conference on the Swedish Heritage in the Upper Midwest, April 1–3, 1976, University of Minnesota, Duluth*, 256–278. Chicago: Swedish Pioneer Historical Society, 1978.

Stokvig, Pieter, 'Mid-Nineteenth Century Emigration in a European Perspective', in H. Ganzevoort & H. Booekelman, eds., *Dutch Immigration to North America*, 35–55. Toronto: Multicultural History Society of Ontario.

Strombeck, Rita, *Leonard Stromberg: A Swedish-American Writer*. New York: Arno, 1979.

Svalestuen, Andres A., 'Nordisk emigrasjon – en komparativ oversikt', in *Emigrationen fra Norden indtil 1. Verdenskrig: Rapporter til det Nordiske historikermøde i København 1971*, 9–60. Copenhagen, 1971.

Svalestuen, Andres A., *Tinns emigrasions historie 1837–1907*. Oslo: Universitetsforlaget, 1972.

Svalestuen, Andres A., 'Professor Ingrid Semmingsen – emigrasjonshistorikeren', in Sivert Langholm & Francis Sejersted, eds., *Vandringer: Festskrift til Ingrid Semmingsen*, 9–42. Oslo: Aschehoug, 1980.

Swanson, Alan, 'Där ute: Moberg's Predecessors', in Nils Hasselmo, ed., *Perspectives* on *Swedish Immigration: Proceedings of the International Conference on the Swedish Heritage in the Upper Midwest, April 1–3, 1976, University of Minnesota, Duluth,* 279–290. Chicago: Swedish Pioneer Historical Society, 1978.

Swedish-American Historical Quarterly 35:3 (1984), 'An Ancient Folk in a New Land: Essays in Honor of Nils William Olsson'.

Taylor, Philip, *The Distant Magnet: European Emigration to the U.S.A.* London, 1971.

Tedebrand, Lars-Göran, *Västernorrland och Nordamerika, 1875–1913: Utvandring och återinvandring.* Uppsala: Studia Historica Upsaliensia, 1972.

Tedebrand, Lars-Göran, 'Remigration from America to Sweden', in Harald Runblom & Hans Norman, eds., *From Sweden to America: A History of the Migration,* 201–227. Minneapolis & Uppsala: Acta Universitatis Upsaliensis & University of Minnesota Press, 1976.

Tedebrand, Lars-Göran, 'Sources for the History of Swedish Emigration' in Harald Runblom & Hans Norman, eds., *From Sweden to America: A History of the Migration,* 76–93. Minneapolis & Uppsala: Acta Universitatis Upsaliensis & University of Minnesota Press, 1976.

Tedebrand, Lars-Göran, 'Strikes and Political Radicalism in Sweden and Emigration to the United States', *SPHQ* (1983:3), 194–210.

Tedebrand, Lars-Göran, 'The Image of America among Swedish Labor Migrants in Europe and North America, in Christiane Harzig & Dirk Hoerder, *The Press of Labor Migrants in Europe and North America 1880s to 1930s,* 547–560. Bremen: Labor Migration Project, 1985.

Thomas, Brinley, *Migration and Economic Growth: A Study of Great Britain and the Atlantic Economy.* Cambridge: Cambridge Univ. Press, 1954.

Thomas, Dorothy Swaine, *Social and Economic Aspects of Swedish Population Movements, 1750–1933.* New York, 1941.

Thomsen, Thomas, *Farvel til Danmark. De danske skillingsvisers syn på Amerika og på udvandringen dertil 1830–1914.* Aarhus, 1980.

Thorsteinsson, Thorsteinn & Tryggvi Oleson, *Saga Islendinga i Vesturheimi.* 5 vols. Winnipeg & Reykjavik, 1940–1953.

Thörnberg, E. H., *Sverige i Amerika, Amerika i Sverige: Folkvandring och folkväckelse.* Stockholm: Bonniers, 1938.

Tilly, Charles, 'Migration in Modern European History', in W. H. McNeill & R. S. Adams, *Human Migration: Patterns and Policies,* 43–52. Bloomington: Indiana Univ. Press, 1978.

Try, Hans, 'To kulturer, en stat 1850–1884', in K. Mykland, ed., *Norges historie, bind 11.* Oslo, 1979.

Try, Hans, *Assosiasjonsånd og foreningsvekst i Norge: Forskningsoversyn og perspektiv.* Övre Ervik: Alvheim & Eide, 1985.

Tveite, Stein, 'Overbefolkning, befolkningspress og vandring', in S. Langholm & Francis Sejersted, eds., *Vandringer. Festskrift til Ingrid Semmingsen på 70-årsdagen 29. mars 1980,* 43–52. Oslo, 1980.

Vecoli, Rudolph J., 'Contadini in Chicago: A Critique of The Uprooted', *The Journal of American History* (1964), 404–417.

Vecoli, Rudolph J., 'European Immigrants: From Immigrants to Ethnics', *International Migration Review* (1972:6), 403–434.

Weiss, Bernard J., ed., *American Education and the European Immigrant: 1840–1940.* Urbana: Univ. of Illinois Press, 1982.

Vig, Peter Sörensen, *Danske i Amerika,* 1908.

Virtanen, Keijo, *Settlement or Return: Finnish Emigrants (1860–1930) in the International Overseas Return Migration Movement.* Turku: The Migration Institute, 1979.

Wåhlin, Vagn, 'Omkring studiet af de folkelige bevaegelser', *Historisk tidskrift* (Stockholm, 1979:2), 113–151.

Walan, Bror, *Invandrarna och kyrkan.* Stockholm: Gummeson, 1963.
Ward, David, *Cities and Immigrants.* New York: Oxford Univ. Press, 1971.
Warner, W. Lloyd, *Democracy in Jonesville: A Study in Quality and Inequality.* New York: Harper & Row, 1949.
Weaver, Dale, *Evangelical Covenant Church of America: Some Sociological Aspects of a Swedish Emigrant Denomination, 1885–1984.* Lund: Lund University, 1985.
Wefald, Jon, *A Voice of Protest: Norwegians in American Politics, 1890–1917.* Northfield: NAHA, 1971.
Wendelius, Lars, *Bilden av Amerika i svensk prosafiktion, 1890–1914.* Uppsala: Litteraturvetenskapliga institutionen, 1982.
Wester, Holger, *Innovationer i befolkningsrörligheten: En studie av spridningsförlopp i befolkningsrörligheten utgående från Petalax socken i Österbotten.* Uppsala: Acta Universitatis Upsaliensis, 1977.
Westin, Gunnar, *Protestantismens historia i Amerikas förenta stater.* Stockholm 1931.
Widén, Albin, *Vår sista folkvandring.* Stockholm, 1962.
Widén, Albin, *Amandus Johnson, svenskamerikan: En levnadsteckning.* Stockholm: Norstedt, 1970.
Willerslev, Richard, *Den glemte indvandring: Den svenske indvandring til Danmark, 1850–1914.* Copenhagen, 1982.
Williams, Allen, Jr., Johnson, David R. & Carranza, Miguel A., 'Ethnic Assimilation and Pluralism in Nebraska', in Frederick C. Luebke, ed., *Ethnicity on the Great Plains,* 210–229. Lincoln: Nebraska Univ. Press, 1980.
Wilson, J. Donald, 'Never Believe What You Have Never Doubted: Matti Kurikka's Dream for a New World Utopia', in Michael G. Karni, ed., *Finnish Diaspora I,* 131–154. Toronto, 1981.
Wilson J. Donald, Matti Kurrikka: Finnish-Canadian Intellectual', *B. C. Studies,* no. 20 (winter 1973–74), 1974, 50–65.
Winberg, Christer, *Folkökning och proletarisering: Kring den sociala strukturomvandlingen på Sveriges landsbygd under den agrara revolutionen.* Göteborg: Meddelanden från Historiska institutionen, 1975.
Wirén, Agnes, *Uppbrott från Örtagård: Utvandring från Blekinge under begynnelseskedet till och med år 1870.* Lund: Bibliotheca Historica Lundensis, 1975.
Wonders, William C., 'Mot Kanadas Nordväst: Pioneer Settlement by Scandinavians in Central Alberta', *Geografiska Annaler,* 65 B, (1983), 129–152.
Wood, David, 'Scandinavian Settlers in Canada Revisited', *Geografiska Annaler,* 49 B, (1967), 1–9.
Wright, Robert L., *Swedish Emigrant Ballads,* University of Nebraska Press, 1965.

Index

Aalborg 21, 128
Aasen, Ivar 252
Abrahamson, Carl 163
Africa 25, 27
Aftonbladet (newspaper) 47
Agder 68, 101, 102
Ahlenius, Gustaf Adolf 231
Aiko (newspaper) 132
Alabama 61
Åland Islands 68
Alaska 130, 131, 164
Alberta, 71, 155, 259, 260
Alexandria, Minn. 223
Allan Line (Allanlinjen) 59
Alta 64
America, attitudes towards 51, 106; de-
pression in 107; images of 44
America-ballads 47
America-letters 46, 114, 121
American Federation of Labor (AFL)
236, 240
American Society of Equity 225
American Sons and Daughters of Swe-
den 209
Amsterdam 13
Andersen, H.C. 47
Anderson, Rasmus B. 207
anti-emigration movement 121-125,
276
Arboga, 18
Arendal 102
Argentina 30, 71, 72, 176, 177, 178, 179
Asia 27
Asiatic Russia 27
assisted passage 73, 122
Atlantic economy 114
Atlantic Ocean 26, 47, 54, 56, 60, 68,
80, 103, 108, 115, 121, 128
Augustana College 147, 199
Augustana Lutheran Church 56, 147,
196-200, 209
Augustdotter, Alma Linnéa 164
Australia 27, 45, 49, 50, 70, 71, 72, 109,
131, 175, 177

Balestrand 166
Ballard, Wash., 219
Baltic area 11, 15, 18, 25
Baltic provinces, Swedish 15
Baptists 47, 195, 197, 198
Barstad, Johanna 279
Belgium 15
Bengston, Henry 233
Bergen 13, 53, 79, 116
Berger, Henning 258, 259
Berger, Vilhelm 206
Bergslagen 14, 56
Bishop Hill, Ill. 56, 146, 150, 151, 170,
195, 251
Biskopskulla 55
Bjørnson, Bjørnstjerne 215, 256, 262
Björnsson, Páll 130
Bjurtjärn 50
Blackmun, Harry 211
Blacks 170
Blegen, Thodore 142, 212, 280, 281
Blekinge 5, 16
Bohuslän 5
bokmål 252
Bonggren, Jacob 258, 259
Boston 128, 208
Bothnia, Gulf of 20, 60
Botker, Dane Christian 233
Brazil 30, 59, 71, 72, 104, 106, 176, 177,
178, 179, 180, 181, 182
Bremen 115, 118
Bremer, Fredrika 46
British Columbia 71, 132, 133, 156
British Isles 26, 29, 53
Brittany 19
Brooklyn, N.Y. 133, 172
Brown Co., Wis. 57
Buenos Aires 71
Buffalo, Minn. 164
Buffalo, N.Y. 220
Bull, Ole 149
Burnett Co., Wis. 161, 217
bygdelags 174, 203-205, 269

Cabo Corso 25
Calcutta 129
California 50, 60, 72, 145, 164, 166, 177, 217, 246
Canada 26, 59, 69, 70, 130, 142, 154, 155, 156, 177, 188, 235, 243, 246, 247, 258
Canadian Prairie Provinces 243
capital flows, and migration 114
Carlson, Samuel 220, 233
Carlsson, Erland 247
Cassel, Peter 55
Catharina, Brazil 179
Charles XII 208
Chicago, 55, 127, 147, 151, 164, 168, 169, 170, 171, 173, 184, 197, 205, 206, 207, 208, 215, 218, 221, 229, 234, 247
Chile 176
Chisago lake 183, 217
Christensen Fugl, Hans 177, 182
Christensen, Christian Ludvig 57
Christianborg 25
Christiania (Oslo) 16, 21, 76, 79, 80, 88, 116
church life 191-201
circular migration 11
Clarks Grove 185
Clausen, C.L. 57, 147, 197
Clay Co., S.D. 162
Cleveland, Ohio 238
climatic conditions 41, 98
Columbus, Christofer 204, 207
Comintern 241
communists, in Finland 240, in the U.S. 234-242
conscription, impact on emigration 44, 124
Conventicle Act (konventikelplakatet, Sweden) 62
Coolidge, Calvin 209, 210
Copenhagen 11-13, 17, 21, 41, 72, 75, 80, 116, 119, 124, 128, 194, 229
Covenants 195, 197, 200
Crimean War 50
Cuba 30, 180

Dagens Nyheter (newspaper) 106
Dakotas 61, 166, 187, 222, 224, 227, 260
Dalarna 14, 19, 21, 56, 162, 186, 187, 205, 251
Dalsland, Sweden 6, 21, 259
Damm, Johan 178
Dane Co., Wis. 147

Danish Guinea 25
Danish Worldwide Archives 286
Danube 29
Danzig 13
Decorah, Iowa 169
Decorah-Posten (newspaper) 169
De Geer, Louis 15
Delaware 207, 209, 276
Delaware River 14, 25, 143, 243,
Delblanc, Sven 183
demographic transition 36
Den Nye Tid (newspaper) 229
dialects, 250-252
Dickens, Charles 46
Dietridson, C.W.C. 46
Dillingham Commission 31, 34
Dominican Republic 180
Dona Francisca, Brazil 179 ᐧ
Douglas Co. 223
Duluth, Minn. 208, 238
Dutch 15, 25, 62, 144, 246
Dyngjyfjöll 98

Eau Claire, Wis. 147
economic cycles, and international migration 49, 64, 112, in America 114
economic freedom, laws on 38
effective migration 11
egnahemsrörelsen 125
Eliasson, Johan Albert 163
Emigrant Institute, Växjö 286
emigrant letters, see America-letters
Emigrant Register, Karlstad 286
Emigranten (newspaper) 216, 279
emigration agents 119, 127
emigration, by stages 83, 85; causes of 35-41; composition of 85-86; from cities 78, 95; from Germany 29,53; from Holland 62; from southern and eastern Europe 31; intensity of 94; local variations 80; motives for 122; phases of 30, 107, 112; propaganda against 121-125; reaction to 121; regulation of 26; religious separatism and 61, 62; sex composition of 104
Enander, Johan 207, 209
enclosure movement, 39
England 12, 25, 30, 36, 53, 58, 114, 115, 122, 123
English language 106, 243-252
Englishmen 149
Enlarged Homestead Act of 1912 151
Episcopals 55, 196
Ericson, John 208

Erik Janssonites 56, 62, 150-151
Eriksson, Leif 207, 208
Esbjörn, Lars Paul 56, 196, 197
Estonia 15
ethnicity 141-144, 269-271
Europe, Eastern 29
Europe, Northwestern 53
Europe, Western 29, 34
Evanston, Ill. 195

Fäderneslandet (newspaper) 106
Falster 16
family emigration 85, 94, 100
famine, Scandinavian 1868-69 72
Farsund 102
female servants, in America 91, 104, in
    Stockholm 104
fertility, 18, 35-37
Finland-Swedes 125, 270, 271
Finn towns 149
Finnish Socialist Federation (FSF, in
    U.S.) 238, 241
Finnmark 75
Finnmarken 60
Finnmarkerna 14
Fitchburg, Mass. 97, 237
Fleischner, Knud 216
Flekkefjord 102
Flygare-Carlén, Emilie 256
fögderi 64
forest settlements, Finnish 14
Fort Christina 25
Fort Dansborg 25
forty-niners 50
Fox River, Ill. 54, 127
France 15, 19, 25, 26, 29
Franconia, Minn. 163
Fredriksborg 92, 94
Fredrikshamn (Hamina) 5
Free (religious group) 197
Freeman, Orville 211
Frémont, John C. 216
French-Canadians 238

Gävle 56
Gagnef 187, 188
Galesburg, Ill. 146, 215, 263
Gardner, Mass. 238
Gaspé, Quebec 155
Geleff, Poul 229
German areas 13, 20, 26, 29, 115, 123
German Order States 24
Germans 15, 23, 170, 215, 216, 222,
    223, 246

Germantown, Penn. 243
Germany 13, 16, 21, 30, 131, 214, 249
Germany 29
Gold Coast 25
gold rush, in California 50, 56, 57; in
    Australia 50
gold-seekers 60
Goodhue Co., Minn. 128
Gothenburg 21, 116, 121
Gräsmark 80
Grant, Ulysses S., 131
Great Britain 29, 44, 59
Great Lakes 103
Grimstad 101, 102
Grisslehamn 55
group emigrations 56, 62, 84
Grundtvigians 192
Gudbrandsdal 64
guilds 10, 19, 38, 76
Gustaf Adolf 209
Gustav(us) Vasa 7

Haderslev 127
Hälsingland 55, 56, 188, 251
Halland 5, 15, 64
Hallingdal 64
Hallström, Herman 233
Halmstad 79
Hamburg 21, 115, 118, 176
Hamburg Shipping Company 118
Hamina 5
Hamsun, Knut 256
Hancock, Mich. 149
Hanko (Hangö) 116
Hansson, Per Albin 264
Hardanger 185, 204
Hartland, Wis. 57
harvest failures 36
Hauge, Hans Nielsen 53
Haugians 53, 62
Hawaii 207
Hedberg, F.G. 56
Hedbergians 56
Hedström, Olof 195
Heidenstam, Verner von 256
Helsingør 93
Helsinki (Helsingfors) 20, 72, 80, 83,
    214,
Hemlandet (newspaper) 128, 215
Henschen, Vilhelm 195
Hepburn, 159
Herad 103
Hibbing, Minn. 238
Hjørring 64

Hjort Boyesen, Hjalmar 258, 262, 263
Holland 21
Holstein 16
Homestead Act in 1862 53, 63, 151, 216
Hornsherred 93, 95
Hovland, Gjert 54
Hudson, John C. 161
Humphrey, Hubert H. 211
Hungary 29
Hutterites 243
Hyskentraede 128

Iberian states 26
Icelanders, in Canada 59
Icelandic National League 209
Idaho 164
Illinois 128, 146, 147, 151, 159, 162, 169, 222, 247, 251
Imatra League 237
immigration propaganda, Brazilian 72; U.S. 114
India 25
Indians 25
Industrial Workers of the World 236, 240
industrialization, and population development 26, 41
information, acceptance of 113
Inner Mission 192
internal migration 5, 9, 17, 38, 52, 73, 75
international migration, long-term effects of 274-275
Iowa 57, 130, 145, 147, 159, 162, 220, 246
Ireland 27, 30, 31, 44
Isanti Co., Minn. 56, 186, 187
Italians 149, 170, 172, 173, 238, 239, 246
Italy 19, 34, 111, 266

Jämtland 80, 81
Jamestown, N.Y. 168, 220, 221, 233
Jansson, Erik 55, 150
Japan 214
Jefferson Co., 147
Jews 172, 194
Jews, emigration of 29
Jochomsson, Mattias 49
Johansson, Simon Petrus 163
John Ericson Monuments 208, 209
John Morton Building 210
Johnson, Amandus 163

Johnson, Eyvind 180
Johnson, John A. 239
Jutland 15, 21, 64, 75

Kåfjord 60, 75
Kalevala 133
Kalmar 14
Kandiyohi Co., Minn, 187
Kansas 145, 184, 229
Karelia 241, 242
Karelians 159
Karlskoga 50, 56, 62
Karlskrona 14
Karlsson, Karl Edvin 163
Kendall colony 54
Kendall Settlement 149
Kendall township 127
Kenora, Ontario 155
Keweenaw Peninsula 148
Kiel 6
Kilgubbin (area in Chicago) 170
Kiruna 72, 178, 179
Kisa 55
Kitson Co., Minn 129
Knights of Kalevala 133
Know Nothing Movement 215
Kodiak, Alaska 130
Königsberg 18
Kokkola (Gamla Karleby) 60, 72, 96
Kosonen, Vithori 237
Kristiansand 102
Kristiansandsposten (newspaper) 46
Kronoberg 16, 162
Kubakke, Stephen Olsen 54
Kurrikka, Matti 131, 133, 237

labor migration, 5, 10, 11, 71, 73 (see also seasonal migration)
labor movement, and attitude to emigration 106
labor movement, in Finland 131; Finnish in U.S. 133
La Crosse, Wis. 147
Laestadians 148
LaFollette, Robert M. 225
Lagerlöf, Selma 256
Lake Superior and Mississippi Railways 129
Lake Winnebago, Wis. 58
land agents 129
land grant system 118, 129
landless proletariat, growth of 49
landsmål 252
Långasjö 110, 163

Langeland 57
Lapland 178
La Salle Co., Ill. 127
Latin America 71
Le Havre 115
Leif Eriksson Day 208
Lewis, Sinclar 264
liberalism 45
Lincoln, Abraham 216, 221
Liverpool 115, 116, 119
Liverpool Conference 118
Lolland 16, 57, 178
London 13
Lübeck 13
lumber industry 81
Luther College 169
Luther, Martin 201
Lutherans, in America 199, 247 (see
    also Augustana)

Madras 25
Mälaren Valley 21, 81
Maki, John 239
Malcolm Island, B.C. 132
Malmö 176, 178
Malthus, Robert 43
Manitoba 71, 131, 145, 155, 156, 183,
    246, 254
Maribo 64
Marx, Karl 230
Massachusetts 97, 205
Mattson, Hans 128
McCarthy, 211
Mediterranean areas 30
Meeker Co., Minn. 164
melting pot ideology 142
Mendoza, Argentina 71
Mennonites 184
Mercantilism 42
Mesabi Range 148, 235
Mesabi Strike, in 1907 238, 239; in 1916
    240
Methodists 195-199, 259
Mexico 176, 243
Miami, Fla. 164
Michigan 34, 60, 75, 97, 145, 148, 149,
    189, 238, 239
Migration Institute, Turku 286
migration, and urbanization 18; be-
    tween Nordic countries 75; migration,
    tradition of 73, 162-168, 268
military service 44, 125
military service, and emigration 44
Milwaukee 130

Mining Immigrant Association 148
Minneapolis 129, 169, 203, 205, 209
Minnesota 34, 47, 56, 97, 128, 129, 142-
    148, 151, 161, 183-189, 203, 210-213,
    222-224, 227, 238, 239, 246
Minnesota Board of Immgiration 129
Misiones, Argentina 72, 179, 180
Mississippi River Valley 26
Mississippi Valley, Upper 56, 116
Missouri 127
Missouri Synod 192, 200, 216, 229
Moberg, Vilhelm 163, 183, 282, 286
Mockfjärd 187
Møn 178
Moline, Ill. 128, 169
Mondale, Walter 211
Montana 243
Mormons 58, 62, 192, 196
mortality 19
Muskego, Wis. 57

Närke 14
Närpes Festivals 205
Nanaimo, B.C. 132
National Society against Emigration,
    Swedish 125
naturalization 218-219
Nebraska 58, 130, 145, 159
Nelson, Knute 223, 224
Netherlands 12, 15, 25
Netherlands Reformed Church 62
New Denmark, Wis. 57, 58
New Elfsborg, N.J. 25
New England 169, 187, 189
New Iceland, Canada 59, 131
New Sweden Colony 25, 143, 243
New Sweden, Iowa 55
New Sweden, Del. 14,25,
New Uppsala 55
New York 115, 121, 127, 128, 133, 149,
    150, 168, 172, 174, 189, 195
New York City 169, 171, 173, 234, 237,
    267
New Zealand 70, 175
Newspapers, Swedish, and emigration
    106; Scandinavian in the U.S.
Niels, Marston 130
Nilsson Hasselquist, Tuve 197, 209
Nilsson, Fredrik O. 195
Nonpartisan League 225
Norður-Þingeyjarsýsla 64
Norður-Múlasýsla 64
Nordlyset (newspaper) 247
Nordman, Erik Amandus 231

Norleius, Erik 56, 129
Norrbottenskuriren (newspaper) 179
Norrköping 18
Norrland 23, 68, 75, 80, 81
Norrskensflamman (newspaper) 179
North (newspaper) 129
North Africa 29
North Dakota 161, 183, 223, 225, 246
North Sea 11, 13, 20, 21, 116
Northern Illinois Synod 98
Northfield, Minn. 261
Norwegian Evangelical Lutheran
  Church 247
Norwegian Lutheran Church in Ameri-
  ca 201
Norwegian Lutheran Synod 129
Norwegian-American Historical Asso-
  ciation 210, 261, 280
Nyhavn 128
Nykøbing, Denmark 258
Nyköping, Sweden 18
nynorsk (New Norwegian) 252

Oberá, Argentina 180
Öland 64, 205
Önnestad 128
Örebro 56
Österbotten, see Ostrobothnia
Östergötland 55, 206, 233, 115
Östmark 164
Olafsson, Olafur 130
Olafsson, Jóns 130, 131
Oleana, Penn. 149
Oleson, T. 281
Olson, Floyd B. 211
Ontario 71, 130, 145, 155, 156, 157
Ordahl, Sverre 92
Orleans Co. 127
Orsa 56
Oskar II 122
Oslo, see Christiania
Ostrobothnia 34, 60, 64, 68, 73, 74, 95,
  96, 125
overpopulation 42

Pacific Northwest 167
Palm, August 231
Palmqvist, Gustaf 56, 196
Panic of 1893, 68, 108
Paraguay 180
Paxton, Ill. 147
Peerson, Cleng 53, 54, 126, 127
Pehrson, Gerda 180
Penkere, Conn. 133

Pennsylvania 149
Pennsylvania Dutch 243
Pennsylvania Germans 243
People of Kalevala Colonization Com-
  pany 132
Pepin 161, 217
Petrograd 214
Pettersson, Anders 50
Pettersson, Erik 50
Pettersson, Erik 56
Pettersson, Jakob 50
Pettersson, Peter 50
Philadelphia 25, 210
Philippines 207
pietitistic movement 56, 62
Pine Lake 55, 57, 63, 150
Pio, Louis 229
pioneer emigrants 30, 51, 52, 63
Poland 13, 20, 29, 30
Poles 170
Poor Law, Swedish of 1847 44
population increase, and emigration
  36, 49, 95
population policy 26
population registers 43
Populist Movement 225
ports of departure 15
Portugal 26, 30
Præstø 64
proletaranization, rural, in Scandinavia
  39
propaganda, see immigration propa-
  ganda and emigration, propaganda
  against
Providence, R.I. 169, 206
Prussia 13, 29, 44, 61
Puerto Ricans 172
push and pull factors 113, 121

Quakers 53, 62, 26, 192
Quebec, Canada 115, 155, 171
Quincy Mining Company 60
quota legislation 126

radicals, Finnish 131
Rättvik 186, 187, 251
Raivaaja (newspaper) 238
re-emigration 68, 107-111, 241-242, 276
Red Wing, Minn. 128, 129
Reformation 194
Reiersen, Johan Rienert 46
Restauration (Norwegian emigrant
  ship) 54
Reuterdahl, Henrik 199

revolution in 1848 42
Revsund 80, 81
Rhineland 20
Rhode Island 169, 207
Rio de Janeiro 177
Rio Grande 175
Rio Grande do Sul 179
Rochester, N.Y. 149
Rock Co., Wis. 147
Rock Island, Ill. 147, 169,
Rockford, Ill. 168, 205, 233
Rockport, Mass. 237
Rølvaag, Ole 183, 186, 255, 258, 260,
  261, 281
Rogaland 126
Roosevelt, Theodore 144
Roskilde fjord 93
Rotterdam 115
Royal Investigating Commission on
  Emigration, Swedish 125
Runeberg, Johan Ludvig 255
Russia 6, 19, 29, 130, 214, 234, 239,
  240,
Russians 149, 170
Russification, in Finland 61, 72
Rynning, Ole 46

Saevik 103
Saima Society 237
Saint Barthélemy 25
Saint Croix 25
Saint John 25
Saint Thomas 25
Salin, Eetu 237
Sampon Takojat (Smiths of Sampo)
  133
San Francisco 50
San Francisco Bay 130
Sandburg, Carl 258, 263, 264
Sandemose, Aksel 258
Sands (part of Chicago) 170
Santa Catharina, Brazil 177
Sao Paolo 176, 178
Saskatchewan 71, 145, 155, 156
Savolax 14
sawmill industry, Swedish 49, 83
Saxony 13
Scandinavian Trade Union Congress
  234
Schéele, Henning von 199
Schneidau, Polycarpus von 55
Scotland 15, 36, 59, 116
Scott, George 195
seasonal migration 19

Seattle 164, 168, 205, 208, 219, 263
Seceders, Dutch 62
Seine 19
shipping companies 114, 115, British
  115, 118
Sicilians 204
Sifton, Clifford 155
Silesia 30
Sitka Region, Alaska 131
Sjödahl, Carl 61
Skandinaviska socialistiska arbeta-
  reförbundet, in the U.S 234
Skåne 5, 15, 21, 128, 188
Slogvig, Knud 54
sloopers 127, 149, 208
Småland 13, 21, 64, 110, 188, 195, 196,
  231, 251
social stratification 49
Social-Demokraten (newspaper) 106,
  231
Socialist Party, U.S. 231, 233, 234, 238,
  241
Söderblom, Nathan 199
Södergran, Edith 255
Sönderjylland 61
Sørensen, Rasmus 57
Sörlandet 68
Sogn 64
Sogn Fylke 166
Soitula, B.C. 132
Sommer, Mogens 57
Sommer, Mogens Abraham 127, 128
South Africa 70
South America 70, 176-182
South Dakota 161, 222, 243
Soviet Union 235, 242
Spain 25, 26, 30
Spind 102, 103
Spokane Wash. 164
St. Ansgar, Iowa 57
St. Ansgarius Church, Chicago 170,
  197
St. Olaf College 261
St. Paul, Minn. 169, 208
St. Petersburg (Leningrad) 20, 80-83,
  96-98, 214
statare 18, 39, 90
state church, Swedish 197-199
steamers 115
steamships 49
Steffens, Lincoln 169
Stege 178
Stephansson, Stephan 254, 258, 260
Stephenson, George 142, 209, 212

333

stock effect 63
Stockholm 11, 14, 17-21, 72, 79-81, 92, 103, 105, 164, 178, 231, 259
Stockholm, Wis. 50, 57
Stockraising Act of 1916 151
Stokkemarke 57
strikes 72, 179, 212, 232, 234, 238, 239
Strindberg, August 256
Strömberg, Leonard 258, 259
Sudbury, Ontario 156
Sundbärg, Gustav 49, 125, 282,
Sundsvall 72, 81, 178, 182
Suomenlinna, *see* Sveaborg
Suomi College 149
Suomi Synod 149
Superior, Wis. 240
Sveaborg (Suomenlinna) Helsinki 239
Svenska Amerikanaren (newspaper) 259
Svenska Folkets Tidning (newspaper) 223
Svenska Socialisten (newspaper) 33
Swedish Africa Company (Svenska Afrikakompaniet) 25
Swedish Historical Society, in the U.S. 209
Swedish South Company (Söderkompaniet) 25
Switzerland 122
Symra Society 169
Syrjälä, Frans Josef 237

Tainio, Taavi 237
Tandil, Argentina 177-181, 182
Tanner, Alfred S. 237
Tegnér, Esaias 256
Telemark 54, 64
tenancy 39
Texas 127
Thrane movement 42
Thrane, Marcus 228, 231
Thunder Bay, Ontario 156
ticket price 121
Tinn 54
Tisza Rivers 29
Toholampi 95-97
Tornedalen (Torne Valley) 23, 60
Toronto 156, 173, 267
trading companies 25
traditions, of migration 63, 80, 92, 94, 268-269
Tranquebar 25
trans-Atlantic labor market 34, 111
transportation, conditions of trans-Atlantic 123
Trempeleau, Wis. 159, 161, 216, 217, 220
Trondheim 6, 21, 116, 177
Troy, Idaho 164
Turlock, Cal. 166
Turner's thesis 186, 189
Tuscany 19
Työmies, Tyomies (newspaper) 238
Tysvaer 26

U.S. Steel 240
Ukrainians 246
unauthorized emigration 43
United Methodist Church 199
Unonius, Gustaf 46, 55, 63, 150, 196, 197
Uppland 15, 55
Uppsala, Sweden 55, 195
urban influence fields 80
urbanization 17, 18, 19, 38, 41, 76, 90, 125
Utah 58, 62, 196
Uusimaa 60

Vaasa (Vasa) 60, 72, 78, 83, 95, 116, 128
Värmland 14, 16, 21, 23, 64, 80, 81, 164, 185, 205, 230
Västerås 18
Västergötland 13, 21
Västernorrland 111
Västmanland 14
Vaino, Esa 92
Valdres 55, 64, 203
Vancouver 132, 133, 205
Vancouver Island 132
Vermillion, S.D. 162
vessels 115
Victoria, B.C., Canada 50, 73
Viipuri (Viborg) 20, 83, 96
Viking expeditions 24
Vinland 276
Virgin Islands 25
Vopnafjördur 98
Voss, Norway 233

Wallonia 15
Wallons 15
Wargelin, John 212
Washington, D.C. 209
Washington, state of 189, 217, 224, 246
Waterville, Quebec 155
Waupaca C., Wis. 251

Wergeland, Henrik 46
Wermelin, Atterdag 230
West Indies 25
Westman, Edward C.
Wiberg, Anders 47
Wilmington, Del. 143
Winnipeg 59, 148
Winther, Sophus Keith 258, 263
Wisconsin 54-59, 97, 130, 145, 147, 151, 166, 168, 187, 189, 203, 213, 217, 225, 246, 260
women 79, 88, 267-268
Worcester, Mass. 168, 169, 197
Workers Party of America 241

Yankees 45, 119, 120, 121, 138, 187-188, 215-224